*Seeds of Destruction*

# Seeds of Destruction

NATIONALIST CHINA IN WAR AND
REVOLUTION 1937-1949

*Lloyd E. Eastman*

STANFORD UNIVERSITY PRESS 1984
STANFORD, CALIFORNIA

Stanford University Press
Stanford, California
© 1984 by the Board of Trustees of the
Leland Stanford Junior University
Printed in the United States of America
ISBN 0-8047-1191-7
LC 82-42861

*For* MEYA

# Acknowledgments

"When a Chinese acts, he normally anticipates a response or return. Favors done for others are often considered what may be termed 'social investments,' for which handsome returns are expected." So writes Lien-sheng Yang in "The Concept of *Pao* as a Basis for Social Relations in China." It is my earnest hope that I will not be held to the traditional Chinese standards of *pao*, or reciprocity, because the favors that have been granted me in the preparation of this work have been enormous, and my capacity to reciprocate has been slight. Perhaps, however, I can in some small measure repay the "social investments" of those who helped me by acknowledging their contributions here.

Much of the research for this work was conducted in Taiwan. Authorities and scholars there knew that I viewed the history of the Kuomintang and the National Government rather more negatively than they did, and yet their assistance was gracious and unstinting. Mr. Ch'in Hsiao-yi and his staff in the Tang-shih-hui, including my friends Professor Li Yün-han and Mr. Lü Fang-shang, tremendously facilitated my work by opening the archives to me, through extended conversations, and by arranging interviews and meetings with other specialists. Mr. Fong Lung-hai was most helpful during the extended periods when I explored the rich materials in the archives of the Bureau of Investigation. The Institute of Modern History of the Academia Sinica is now for me virtually a second home; I worked there extensively while researching this book, and my many friends in the Institute made my work both pleasant and fruitful.

Lyman P. Van Slyke and Jerome B. Grieder both read a draft of the manuscript in its entirety; their insightful comments were highly useful in preparing the final version for the press. Others who in one way or another contributed to my work on this project are Dianne Bradford, Richard I-feng Chang, John K. Fairbank, John Israel, Thomas A. Krueger, Steven I. Levine, John P. McKay, Ramon H. Myers, Peter Schran, James E. Sheridan, Ronald P. Toby, and Sheh Wong. I am also deeply indebted to J. G. Bell, Editor of the Stanford University Press, for perspicacious comments that led to an improvement of the Introduction and Conclusion; and to Peter J. Kahn for meticulous and creative editing of the manuscript and for guiding it through to publication. Mr. Wei Qiwen, Lecturer in the Department of History at Peking University, was for a year a valued research assistant and dear friend; that his premature death interrupted our work together is a matter for me of profoundest regret.

Throughout the writing of these pages, I have constantly felt as though Professor Thomas G. Rawski of the University of Toronto were peering over my shoulder. Tom is a critic par excellence. Over the course of several years, he has commented extensively on my various manuscripts and publications and has shown me that nothing can be taken for granted in assembling evidence in support of an argument, that "anecdotal evidence" (as he delights in saying) does not constitute proof, and that my arguments must be made to withstand the critical examination of readers who do not share my prejudices and premises. He has also cautioned me against careless rhetorical flourishes in writing. What, for example, is the precise economic significance of "exploitative" rents or "extortionate" interest rates? I am certain that I have not always measured up to Tom's high scholarly standards, but this would have been a less rigorous study without his influence.

Mrs. Teresa Sih kindly gave permission to reprint the essay that appears here as Chapter One; it was originally published in *Nationalist China During the Sino-Japanese War*, edited by her late husband Paul K. T. Sih. Thanks also to Professor Brian Hook for permission to reprint a revised version of "Who Lost China? Chiang Kai-shek Testifies," first published in *The China Quarterly*, No. 88. I also wish to express gratitude to the following institutions that provided me research grants: The National Endowment for the Humanities (1974–75); the Fulbright-Hays Research Abroad Fellowship program (1977–78); and the Center for Advanced Study of the University of Illinois (1981–82).

Finally, this book is affectionately dedicated to my wife, Margaret M. Y. "Meya" Eastman, who would infinitely have preferred that I return to my early studies of the Ch'ing Dynasty rather than pursue research in the politically sensitive history of the Nationalist period.

L.E.

# Contents

# Seeds of Destruction

*A state sows the seeds of its own destruction*
*before others finally destroy it.*

MENCIUS

# Introduction

THE NANKING DECADE began on April 18, 1927, when the Nationalists led by Chiang Kai-shek established the National Government in the city of Nanking. Despite Chiang's recent bloody purge of the Communists at Shanghai, the new government acceded to power on a wave of popular enthusiasm. To a nation exhausted by the conflicts of warlords and humiliated by the arrogance of foreign powers, Nationalist rule seemed to augur a new era of peace, prosperity, and national pride.

Revolutionaries invariably discover, however, that the administration of governmental power is more challenging than the seizure of that power. Sun Yat-sen's revolutionary programs of democracy, national independence, and improved economic welfare consequently proved to be elusive goals. The years of the Nanking Decade were, moreover, particularly uncongenial to the government's efforts to solve the nation's political, economic, and social difficulties. The economic depression, Japanese aggression, and Communist insurrection all weakened the Nationalists' reformist resolve and depleted the material resources of the new government. Repeated revolts by provincial military commanders, singly and in coalition, occupied the first four years of Nationalist rule, with the result that the government had only about six years of relative tranquillity during which to implement its reform programs before the Japanese attacked in July 1937.

Still, the last year or two of the Nanking Decade displayed signs of promise. The economy was on the upswing, the provinces seemed to be falling in step with the central government, and the people generally were possessed of a new mood of optimism and good feeling toward the government. Especially after

2   *Introduction*

the peaceful resolution of a revolt by the warlords of Kwangtung and Kwangsi in September 1936, and then the release of Chiang Kai-shek by his kidnappers at Sian three months later, the government's popularity increased greatly. To many observers, foreigners and Chinese alike, the Nationalist regime seemed on the point of fulfilling its original promise.*

These signs were deceiving, however, for beneath the surface the regime remained weak and unstable. It had never developed a governmental administration capable of implementing the Kuomintang's policies and programs, or political institutions firmly rooted in Chinese society. Its existence depended almost wholly on the army. It was, in fact, a political and military structure without a social base, inherently one of the least stable of all political systems.

This is not to contend that the regime was wholly isolated from society. Groups and individuals—for example, some capitalists, some landlords, and some student and patriotic groups—did on occasion mount sufficient pressure to influence the formation or implementation of specific policies. There existed, however, no regular and institutionalized means by which to bring these pressures to bear upon the government. In such cases, Samuel P. Huntington has observed, "Each group employs means which reflect its peculiar nature and capabilities. The wealthy bribe; students riot; workers strike; mobs demonstrate; and the military coup."[1] The Nationalist regime was not immune to such outside influences, but neither could those influences impose accountability upon it.

Immediately following the outbreak of the war with Japan, however, the inherent weaknesses of the regime were forgotten by a people fired by anti-Japanese patriotism. Although the Nationalist armies retreated along a broad front in East and North

*People commonly use the term "regime" to refer to governments they dislike: thus they speak of the "Soviet regime" or the "Castro regime," but not of the "American regime" or the "British regime." I use the term for a different reason, namely to reflect the uncertain locus of power in the Nationalist political order, which lay somewhere within the triad of the Kuomintang, the formal institutions of the National Government, and the army. No pejorative connotation is intended here.

China, Chiang Kai-shek was now viewed by all as the country's indispensable leader. During the period prior to October 1938, when Chiang's headquarters were in Wuhan, people spoke of the "Wuhan Spirit" to refer to the high morale and dedication that infused all political groups there, including the Communists, in their common fight under Nationalist leadership.

Less than a dozen years later, the scene was completely changed. The Nationalists had lost the support of virtually every stratum of society. The army had lost all will to fight. Intellectuals—students, teachers, and members of the professional classes—had for the most part long since become disillusioned with the regime. Peasants, urban workers, and even the business classes (who, as members of the capitalist class, presumably had most to fear from the Communists) had likewise abandoned hope in the Nationalists. The Communists, meanwhile, had advanced from strength to greater strength. Their army by mid-1948 outnumbered that of the Nationalists. It was, moreover, an incomparably more effective fighting force, for it possessed an élan that was wholly lacking on the Nationalist side. The Heavenly Mandate, as it were, was shifting quickly and decisively to the Communists. On January 21, 1949, Chiang Kai-shek retired from the presidency and flew off to a melancholic exile, first in his home village of Hsi-k'ou in Chekiang, and ultimately on the island of Taiwan. Eight months later, from atop the Gate of Heavenly Peace in Peking, Mao Tse-tung announced the formation of the Chinese People's Republic.

What were the reasons for this abrupt reversal of political fortunes between 1937 and 1949? Was it the strains of the anti-Japanese war that had made the Nationalist regime susceptible to revolutionary overthrow? Or was it, as Kuomintang partisans have long contended, that the United States Government betrayed the Nationalists by withholding support and material aid at critical junctures of the civil war with the Communists? Or did the flaws that were evident in the Nationalist regime before 1937 somehow render it vulnerable to Communist insurgency in the late 1940's?

In searching for answers to these questions, I have adopted a

research strategy roughly analogous to that of a geologist studying an earth formation. Rather than merely describing the surface features, and rather than undertaking the impossible task
of excavating the whole formation layer by layer, the geologist
takes a series of core samples of the subterranean strata. These
provide sufficient data to form a hypothesis regarding the composition and development of the whole formation, not just of
the locations where the core samples were taken.

In this study, the core samples are selected topics in the history of the Nationalist regime from 1937 to 1949. By researching
these topics in detail, it has been possible to discern at least
some of the forces underlying the political events at the surface
and to gauge thereby the historical dynamics that made Nationalist China what it was, and that led it ultimately to succumb
to the Communist assault.

The success of this approach depends to a large extent on the
topics chosen for analysis. The criteria used in selecting the topics in this work were typicality and researchability. The criterion
of typicality required that the topic be representative of some
significant aspect of Nationalist rule, so that a detailed examination would illuminate general characteristics and processes of
Nationalist rule. The criterion of researchability required that
the source materials pertaining to a topic be sufficiently rich that
they would be productive of meaningful insights. (Several times
I began research on topics not included here, only to abandon
the effort because the necessary source materials could not be
obtained.) Because the research for this study has been selec-
tive, the insights and conclusions are by definition limited and
tentative. I believe, however, that they enhance our understanding of both the Nationalist regime and of the revolutionary process in China prior to 1949. Perhaps, too, they will be of use as
other students of modern China advance in the study of this
momentous and fascinating period of history.

The first of the topics examined in the following work, in
Chapter 1, is the relationship between the central government in
the wartime capital of Chungking and the provincial regime
headed by Lung Yün in Kunming. Writing in 1966, James E.

Sheridan coined the term "residual warlordism" to describe the perpetuation of provincial regimes headed by semiautonomous militarists during the period after 1928, when the Nationalists had ostensibly unified the nation.[2] Few have realized, however, how deeply imbedded those residues of warlordism remained even in the late 1940's. Indeed, the outbreak of the war with Japan exacerbated the centrifugal political tendencies within the Nationalist regime, for the units of the Nationalist army most loyal to Chiang Kai-shek were decimated during the initial fighting. The power of the central-government forces consequently declined relative to that of the provincial militarists. The political consequences of this shift were profound, and the leadership and authority of Chiang's government were thereafter under constant challenge. Several times during the war against Japan, overt conflict between the central-government and Yunnanese forces almost erupted. The hostility and distrust that persisted in the postwar years also contributed palpably to the Nationalist defeat in the war with the Communists.

The lack of unity between the central government and the provinces was a fundamental flaw in the Nationalists' political structure. But what were the sources of that disunity? Could the problem of disunity have been resolved if the central government had adopted alternative approaches to the provincial militarists? These are some of the questions for which we will have to find answers in the course of this study.

The Chinese Communist revolution is generally regarded as the classic example of a modern "peasant revolution." Existing studies of the revolution have consequently devoted considerable attention to the peasants in the areas under Communist control and to Communist policy toward them. Peasants on the Nationalist side have, however, been completely neglected. Chapters 2 and 3 attempt to rectify this oversight by examining the relationship between the National Government and *its* peasants. The Nationalists drew most of their supply of men, money, and grain for the war effort from the peasantry, and the well-being of the peasants was consequently much affected by the government's policies and actions. The government in 1941, for example, introduced a major innovation in the tax system whereby it began collecting the land tax in grains rather than in cash. Other taxes were simultaneously imposed on the peasants by official agencies at every level of administration. An examination of these various taxes and their impact on the peasants provides insights into the rampant corruption of the regime's underlings. More important, it provides insights into the government's relations with the taxpaying peasants and with the local elites that dominated political life in the villages. Here again, as in Chapter 1, we discover a serious flaw in the Nationalist structure, for never was the central government able to extend its authority effectively down to the local level. It had to compromise with local elites, conceding to them the final say in who was taxed and how much. The poor and powerless strata of rural society were consequently forced to bear an unjust share of the tax burden. The peasants' reactions to these and other inequities, such as those incurred in military conscription, significantly diminished the vitality of the Nationalist government and army during the war and postwar periods.

The third probe essayed in this study is into the intraparty politics of the regime. This has always been one of the murkier areas of the Nationalist system, for the actual operation of and relationships within the regime have customarily been hidden behind propaganda and ritualistic proclamations. Quite by accident, however, I discovered two topics providing access to this problem: the Three People's Principles Youth Corps and the Ko-hsin Movement, both of which enable us to sense the depth of factional enmities and to view the Kuomintang and the National Government unadorned, through the eyes of the Nationalist participants themselves.

I had not originally planned to study the Youth Corps as part of the research for this book, for I had thought of it as nothing more than an organization to control and to indoctrinate students. Nothing there, I thought, that would illuminate the general character of the regime. As my research progressed, however, I began to catch hints of conflict between the Youth Corps and the Kuomintang, and, without actually starting research on the subject, I decided to keep an eye open for more information on the subject. Authorities in Taiwan did nothing to encourage my curiosity. Once, for example, I interviewed the head of the Legislative Yüan, who had formerly been a high-level cadre in the Youth Corps. In response to a question about relations between the Youth Corps and the Kuomintang, he assured me with a straight face that there had been absolutely no friction between the two organizations, that they had been totally united in their common revolutionary endeavor.

The truth was dramatically different. Youth Corps leaders regarded the Kuomintang as superannuated and completely ineffectual, and they therefore sought to displace the Kuomintang as the dominant political organ of the regime. A furious struggle for power ensued, during which Youth Corps adherents issued damning indictments of their rivals.

Just as fortuitously, I discovered the Ko-hsin (or Renovationist) Movement, a Kuomintang reform movement in 1944–47. In the early stages of my research, I had never heard of this movement. One autumn day in the archives of the Commission on Kuomintang History in Taipei (the Tang-shih-hui), however, I was thumbing through a journal called the *Ko-hsin chou-k'an* (*Renovation Weekly*) and in it found articles by well-known Kuomintang figures, whose criticisms of the party and the government were at least as sharp as those expressed by the Communists. Puzzled, I inaugurated a search that uncovered other Ko-hsin Movement publications in the several archives and libraries in Taipei. The result is a picture no less revealing of the internal politics of the regime than that given us by the Youth Corps.

As a result of these studies of the Youth Corps and the Ko-hsin Movement, we discern a regime that was bitterly divided within itself and whose members generally lacked a commitment to goals other than personal and factional gratification. These Youth Corps and Ko-hsin Movement critics reveal that the demoralization of the Nationalist regime was greater than outsiders even suspected.

The central pillar of the Nationalist political structure was the army. The army had brought the regime to power, and the regime was thereafter largely dependent for its continued existence upon military strength. As Chapters 6 and 7 show, however, the Nationalist army was terribly weakened during the eight-year war against the Japanese. It incurred large and irreplaceable losses during the first year of fighting, and thereafter its quality was abysmally low. Chapter 6 examines the evidences of deterioration, as revealed particularly in the quality of the officer corps, the functioning of the conscription system, and the condition of the army medical service. It also shows that a large part of the Nationalist army was incapable during the last stage of the war of engaging in serious combat.

The quality of the army did not improve during the civil war with the Communists, as Chapter 7 shows. Based in substantial part upon an official Nationalist army assessment of the anti-Communist campaigns prepared in 1950, this chapter shows that the Nationalists were utterly outfought by the Communist army. The Nationalist generals who prepared that assessment not only admitted the serious demoralization and poor fighting qualities of their army, but also expressed lavish praise for the leadership, dedication, and combat capabilities of their adversary. This chapter should thoroughly dispel the notion that it was a shortage of weapons, resulting from a betrayal by the United States Government, that led to the Nationalists' defeat. But what, then, were the true causes of the military debacle?

In Chapter 8, our geologic probe is into the political and economic soil at the time of the gold yüan currency reform in August–October of 1948. Inflation during that summer was raging out of control. To forestall the impending economic collapse, which would surely have been followed by a political collapse as well, the National Government instituted a currency reform in which the old money (*fa-pi*) was replaced by the new "gold yüan currency" (*chin-yüan ch'üan*) at an exchange rate of 3,000,000:1. The government simultaneously declared a freeze on all prices and wages. Political decrees, it thought, could halt the inflation.

Chiefly responsible for implementing this reform in the Shanghai area was Chiang Kai-shek's eldest son, Chiang Ching-kuo.

Young Chiang, in contrast to most other Nationalist officials, was (so far as we know) completely incorruptible and absolutely dedicated to making the currency reform a success. Yet in just seventy days the reform was judged a failure.

This study of the gold yüan reform reveals in microcosm many of the economic and political woes of the Nationalist regime during the postwar years. It shows the difficulties of restraining the inflation, the terrible toll that the inflation took on the livelihood of the people, and, finally, the political costs of the economic collapse. The character and idiosyncratic ideology of Chiang Ching-kuo, future president of the National Government, likewise become evident in this study of what some scholars have asserted was the episode that sealed the Nationalists' fate.

The final chapter examines Chiang Kai-shek's assessment of his army and the civilian branches of his regime during the final phase of the struggle on the mainland. Here we see that Chiang clearly perceived most of the defects of his regime, and his "testimony" conflicts sharply with what his epigoni have contended were the reasons for the Nationalist defeat by the Communists. Indeed, so searing were his criticisms of his subordinates that they would not be credible if written by anyone else.

But why, if Chiang clearly perceived the defects in his regime, did he not provide remedies for them? If in the following pages we can answer this and the other questions posed in this Introduction, we will perhaps better understand the Chinese revolution in the 1940's.

# Regional Politics and the Central Government: Yunnan and Chungking

"THE GENERALISSIMO, far from being a dictator," remarked General Albert C. Wedemeyer, "was in fact only the head of a loose coalition, and at times experienced great difficulty in securing obedience to his commands." [1] The assertion that Chiang Kai-shek was not a dictator was only partially correct, for his arbitrary exercise of power, within the realms of Chinese life to which his power extended, was at times the very essence of dictatorship and tyranny. He could, for instance, summarily order the execution of a corrupt official or a defeated general. But Wedemeyer was assuredly correct that the power of Chiang Kai-shek and the National Government suffered numerous and severe limitations.

Even in the provinces most obviously subject to Nationalist authority, the lower levels of administration were customarily dominated by local elites over whom the central government had little control. Nearly half of the army was officered by generals who could not be trusted to obey the orders of the central authorities. Many of the provinces during the entire decade of the 1940's were ruled by "chairmen" who felt little loyalty to Chiang and who had autonomous sources of political and military power. Nationalist China was not, therefore, a modern nation-state in the sense that contemporary European states were. This fact influenced Nationalist China's conduct of the war with Japan and significantly contributed to its collapse in 1949.

During the decade before the war with Japan, the National Government had devoted most of its efforts and resources to expanding its territorial control. And by 1937 its power was more or less dominant in perhaps half the provinces of China proper. Following the Japanese invasion in 1937, however, even that degree of political control was sharply diminished. The Japanese quickly occupied the heavily populated and relatively advanced provinces that had provided the political and economic bases of the National Government. By late 1938, Chiang Kai-shek and his administration had retreated into the vast hinterland of West China where Nationalist power had always been weakest, and where the local satraps viewed the central government with suspicion, resentment, and foreboding.

In Szechwan, for example, large-scale fighting between provincial troops and the central government's army had been averted in the spring of 1937 only after sensitive negotiations smoothed over ruffled relations between Chungking and Nanking. But tensions persisted. In January of 1938, after the provincial chairman, Liu Hsiang, died (presumably of stomach cancer) in a hospital in Nanking, Liu's wife and other Szechwanese partisans loudly charged that agents of the central government had murdered him in order to eliminate an obstacle to Nanking's control of the province. The Szechwanese powers then rejected Nanking's appointment of Chang Ch'ün to replace Liu Hsiang as provincial chairman. Throughout the war, too, the provincial "warlords" in the province, especially P'an Wen-hua, Liu Wen-hui, and Teng Hsi-hou, continued to obstruct central-government control of the capital province of wartime China.[2]

Yen Hsi-shan's relations with Chungking during the war further exemplify how fragile was the political coalition that constituted Nationalist China. When the war began, Yen was named commander of the Second War Zone and was vice-chairman under Chiang Kai-shek of the Military Affairs Commission. Not once during the war, however, did Yen make an appearance in Chungking or even meet with Chiang. He reigned over that corner of his province of Shansi which was still left to him—most being in the hands of either the Japanese or the Communists—almost as though it were an independent kingdom. He maintained his own political party (the Democratic Revolutionary

Comrades' Association; *Min-chu ko-ming t'ung-chih hui*), did not tolerate the presence of central-government troops within his war zone, expunged from an oath of allegiance the references to the central government and Chiang Kai-shek, and, particularly in 1942 and thereafter, enjoyed close and amiable relations with the Japanese—even maintaining a liaison office in Japanese-occupied Taiyuan.

From Yen Hsi-shan's point of view, the Japanese during the latter part of the war were a lesser threat than the central government. According to a general in Yen's army, the term "enemy" in the many wall slogans in Yen's war zone referred primarily to the Communists. Ranking second as an enemy of Yen, because it constantly threatened to interfere in local affairs, was the National Government. Next on Yen's list of enemies were the Chinese puppets serving under the Japanese. Finally, lowest on the list, were the Japanese themselves.[3]

Each of the provinces differed in its relations with the center. Some, such as Kweichow and Chekiang, were highly loyal to the Chungking authorities. Others, such as Kwangtung, had a military commander (Yü Han-mou) whose loyalties were ambivalent counterbalanced by a provincial chairman (Li Han-hun) who was trusted by the central government. Yunnan cannot, therefore, be regarded as typifying the relations between all the provinces and the central government. Yet, by examining this one province in some detail, it is possible to discern some of the dynamics affecting Chiang Kai-shek's fragile political coalition.

Yunnan had seldom enjoyed prominence in the national politics of China until the war with Japan. Sequestered deep in the southwest, it was indisputably part of the Chinese polity, but culturally and ethnically it stood apart. It lay closer to Calcutta than to Shanghai; Burma and French Indochina were its neighbors; and over half of its sparse and—even by Chinese standards—impoverished population were ethnically non-Chinese. The French-owned Kunming-Hanoi railroad provided the province's primary access to the outside world, and over it came French cigarettes, guns, and cultural and economic influences. Kunming, capital of the province, even had something of a

French flavor, for numerous French-built offices and homes stood among the crowded, noisy Chinese shops and streets. Indeed, until 1940, the American consulate in Kunming kept its financial records in French piasters rather than in the Yunnanese provincial currency.[4] But Yunnanese remained suspicious of all outside influences, French or Chinese. They were marked by a deep isolationism, and formidable emotional walls consequently obstructed the inflow of central-government influences throughout the war.

Warlord of Yunnan in the 1930's and 1940's was Lung Yün (1888–1962). Lung Yün was a Lolo (the Lolos were one of the largest minority tribes in the province), and he had had little experience outside his native Yunnan. As a youth, he had participated in the semiclandestine secret societies that were active in the province. In 1910, at the age of 22, he met T'ang Chi-yao, an instructor at the Yunnan Provincial Military Academy. T'ang arranged Lung's appointment as a cadet, and from then until 1927 their stars were to rise together. After the revolution against the Manchus, T'ang became a major political force in Southwest China—and under him Lung Yün took lessons in the rough-and-tumble of warlord and Kuomintang politics. An apt student, Lung led a coup against his mentor and replaced him as chairman of Yunnan in 1927. From then until he was ousted from office by Chiang Kai-shek in 1945, Lung was the dominant personality in Yunnanese politics.[5]

Assessments of Lung Yün vary widely. To some, particularly to partisans of the central government, he was an unregenerate warlord and opium addict, indifferent to all but his personal and provincial interests, and whose administration was backward and corrupt. In fact, however, he appears to have been, by the standards of his day, a relatively dedicated, progressive, and incorrupt provincial militarist. He never succeeded in bringing prosperity to the province, but he eliminated much of the banditry that had long bedeviled it. Although he was himself hopelessly addicted to opium, he undertook with considerable success after November 1934 to suppress cultivation and trade of the drug. Indeed, during 1936 and 1937 Lung transformed the financial base of his government by making mining and industry, rather than opium, the major source of its revenue. Aside from modern industry, Lung took an active interest in civic improvements and public health projects, and he gained a reputation for acting upon, as well as talking about, these interests. The shocking forms of warlord exploitation that beset neighboring Szechwan were not in evidence in Yunnan, and Lung seems to have attained genuine popularity with most of his fellow provincials.[6]

Although his province was the largest in China proper (and nearly twice the size of France), Lung Yün never became a major political force during the 1930's.[7] His army before the war numbered only 30,000–40,000 men, and the economic base of the province was small. He therefore moved with circumspection through the shoals of warlord politics. With the exception of occasional but fleeting leers at neighboring Kweichow, he was not tempted to become involved in affairs outside his own domain. Caution, restraint, and good sense marked his relations with the other provinces, and their leaders respected him as a result.

To all the provincial militarists in the 1930's the central government was, of course, the most formidable challenge. Eventually it was to be Lung Yün's undoing, but for 18 years he resisted its centralizing pressures with consummate skill. Among regional leaders in the 1930's, Lung stood out as one of the most supportive of the Nationalist government. When a warlord coalition attempted in 1930 to establish a separatist government in Peking, for example, Yunnanese troops moved against rebellious Kwangsi forces led by Li Tsung-jen and Pai Ch'ung-hsi. During the revolt of Kwangtung and Kwangsi in 1936, Lung again resisted the entreaties of the rebel leaders and declared his loyalty to the Nanking government. When Chiang Kai-shek was kidnapped at Sian, Lung offered to lead a punitive expedition against the kidnappers, and he was vituperative in his denunciation of Chang Hsüeh-liang. A local newspaper that reflected Lung's views called Chang "not only childish but also disloyal and unfilial. He is certainly most stupid and breaks wind."[8]

During the early 1930's, the National Government was a re-

mote influence that made little difference in the lives of the Yunnanese. The Kuomintang had branches in the province, but
without financial and other support from the provincial government it was virtually moribund. In 1934, the New Life Movement was instituted in government offices, the army, and the
schools, but except on special occasions, such as Chiang Kai-
shek's visit to the province in May 1935, it was seldom mentioned thereafter and was of no consequence. Occasionally, too,
an official delegation from Nanking, concerned with geologic
surveys or health conditions, would arrive and depart, causing
little stir in the affairs of the province.

By 1935, however, the central government was beginning to
make inroads in the province, largely as a result of the Communists' presence in the Southwest during their celebrated Long
March. Some 50,000 national troops entered the province; they
spent large sums of national currency, leading to the rumor that
the Central Bank of China would soon open a branch in Yunnan. In September 1935 a branch of the Central Military Academy opened in Kunming. Yunnanese army officers attended
central-government military schools in Nanking, Hangchow,
and Szechwan for advanced technical and, one presumes, political training. Roads were being planned and built, often with
subsidies from Nanking.[9]

On the eve of the war with Japan, therefore, the existence of
the central government had become a reality for the Yunnanese.
Throughout this process, Lung Yün had moved deftly. As quickly
as possible he arranged to have Nanking's anti-Communist
troops withdrawn from the province; and he quickly retired the
national currency from circulation, thereby preserving the province's monetary autonomy. Even while maximizing the semi-
independence of his province, however, he won at least the
grudging favor of Chiang Kai-shek. When a group of cadets in
the local branch of the Central Military Academy requested that
Lung be dismissed from the provincial chairmanship, Chiang
supported Lung and imprisoned the cadet agitators.[10] Lung was
also rewarded by Chiang in 1935 and 1936 with such prestigious posts as commander-in-chief of the Second Route Bandit-

Suppression Army, Pacification Commissioner of Yunnan and Kweichow, and membership in the Central Supervisory Committee of the Kuomintang.

Despite this considerable evidence that Lung Yün had become a faithful supporter of the Nationalist government, it may be doubted that he ever felt an emotional or moral commitment to national unity or to the doctrines of the Kuomintang. It appears rather that he pragmatically accepted the fact that the future of China lay with the central government and not with the provincial militarists. It was therefore to his advantage to offer at least limited cooperation to the central authorities. As a U.S. State Department official observed, his policy toward the central government was marked throughout by "cautious and well-balanced opportunism."[11]

With the outbreak of the war and the Nationalist government's subsequent retreat to the interior, the quality of the relationship between Yunnan and the central government changed fundamentally. Hitherto, Yunnan had been peripheral to the major concerns of the central government, and Nanking had had no need to ensure that the Yunnanese provincial government responded obediently and quickly to its will. Now all that was changed. Yunnan now became, second only to Szechwan, the most important province in wartime Nationalist China. Now it became a critical source of men, money, and matériel for the central government. It therefore became a matter of importance to the central government how Yunnan was ruled and how its rulers responded to its wishes.

During the initial months of the war, for example, Chiang Kai-shek was uncertain whether Lung Yün would support the war effort or would revolt against the central government. Chiang therefore felt it insufficient simply to order Lung to dispatch troops to resist the Japanese; he felt it necessary to send an emissary to entreat Lung to do so. In fact, Lung in early 1938 sent three divisions to the war zone, seemingly without hesitation.[12] Yet the fact is that Chiang Kai-shek doubted Lung's professions of loyalty. The widespread rumor that Chiang had attempted to oust Lung from the provincial chairmanship in January 1938 may well have been grounded in fact.[13]

When the Japanese invasion began, much of the Yunnanese population enthusiastically supported the cause of resistance. But the war soon imposed strains upon Yunnanese devotion to the Nationalist cause. Changes came flooding into the province, transforming Yunnan more in three years, perhaps, than in the preceding 30. Central-government influence accompanied these changes, and the Yunnanese authorities—some more than others—attempted to prevent the erosion of local power. By mid-1939, relations with the central government came very close to the breaking point.

The sources of change were everywhere. Not long after the war began, for example, Yunnan became Nationalist China's chief doorway to the outside world. In October 1938, both Wuhan and Canton fell to the Japanese; fortuitously, the Burma Road, with its terminus in Kunming, had just opened and therefore kept open a route to external sources of supply. Soon, two all-weather highways connected Yunnan with Szechwan. And Kunming's airport during the war was the busiest in China, servicing flights to Chungking, Hong Kong (until its fall in December of 1941), and India (Kunming was the destination for the famed flights over "the Hump" of the U.S. Air Force).

Suddenly, too, Yunnan was becoming integrated into the cultural and economic life of the nation. By 1938, some 60,000 refugees had moved into the province—not a large number in absolute terms, but a lot for Kunming (whose prewar population was less than 143,000),[14] where they concentrated. Moreover, many were middle- and upper-class sophisticates whose influence was disproportionate to their numbers. Kunming now became an educational center. Prior to the war, the only university in the province had been the undistinguished Yunnan Provincial University. In 1938, however, three of China's leading institutions of higher learning (Peking National University, Tsinghua University, and Nankai University, combined now as Southwest Associated University), together with several lesser universities, were relocated in or near Kunming. Kunming was thus immediately transformed from a cultural backwater into a center of intellectual, cultural, and political ferment.

Yunnan had experienced a modest development of industry

since 1935, but with the war a number of new factories were relocated or established in and near Kunming. The National Resources Commission of the central government, whose responsibility it was to develop the nation's defense and heavy industries, particularly sensed the advantages offered by Kunming's access to the Burma Road and its remoteness from the battlefront. It thus established there, for example, the Central Machine Works, which in early 1940 began producing motors, generators, and machine tools, and the Electrical Manufacturing Works, which in July 1939 began producing copper and steel wire, light bulbs, batteries, and telephones. The Bank of China established a cotton mill in Kunming, and the Ministry of War opened an optical instruments factory. By August 1939, a total of 49 factories had been moved from the east into the province.[15]

The Yunnanese had not obstructed these economic and educational incursions upon their placid insularity. The influx of industry created unprecedented prosperity in the province, and the Kunming authorities therefore encouraged further investments that contributed to industrial development and agricultural reconstruction. But the roads, industries, and schools also brought in their train the interests and influences of the central government, and during 1938 and 1939 strains in the relationship appeared.

The points of contention during the first several years of the war were, surprisingly, not political or military. In these areas, Chiang Kai-shek moved with a keen awareness of Yunnanese sensitivities. Friction developed instead in such areas as banking, finance, and foreign trade, as Yunnan was drawn inexorably but reluctantly into the economic orbit of the Nationalist government.

One of the pillars of Yunnan's semiautonomous position, for example, was the provincial government's virtual monopoly of banking and the issuance of currency. Despite the central government's currency reforms of November 1935, which had stipulated that the *fa-pi* (the currency of the Nationalist government) was to become the sole legal tender throughout China, Yunnan had continued to use primarily the currency issued by its own government-owned New Futien Bank. In December 1937, a branch of the Central Bank of China was established in Kunming,[16] but it initially restricted its activities to handling the receipts from the customs and from the sales of war bonds. These transactions did not interfere with the New Futien Bank's dominance of the provincial economy, and the Yunnanese authorities consequently sensed little threat from the new bank. In 1938, however, the Central Bank began to issue fa-pi through its Kunming branch. This did threaten the Yunnanese position, and the New Futien Bank attempted to stanch the inflow of fa-pi by manipulating the exchange rates of its notes for fa-pi. For several days in May of 1939, it even refused to accept fa-pi at all.[17] It was, however, a losing battle, because fa-pi were now pouring into the province from other sources. The growing numbers of central-government employees, such as workers in the new enterprises of the National Resources Commission and the Central Air Academy (which moved to Yunnan in 1938), were all paid in fa-pi. Refugees and the growing numbers of travelers through Yunnan also brought fa-pi in their baggage. By mid-1939, therefore, provincial currency was being accepted only at a discount, and by 1942 the fa-pi reigned supreme.[18]

Meanwhile, other national banks sought a foothold in the province. The powerful Bank of China, headed by T. V. Soong, attempted in November of 1938 to begin banking and investment operations. The Kunming authorities placed so many obstructions in its way, however, that in December it briefly abandoned the effort and withdrew its personnel to Hong Kong. The withdrawal of the Bank of China, according to an American official in Kunming, was "interpreted here as a recognition of the failure of the possibility of cooperation and also as a kind of declaration of war against the Provincial [New Futien] Bank."[19]

Once again, however, the Yunnanese were unable to hold off the incursions of the central authorities, and by early 1939 all four national banks, including the Bank of China, had opened branches in Kunming and even in other cities of the province. The Yunnanese economy was now booming, and the New Futien Bank was simply unable to accommodate the growing demands for capital, banking facilities, and foreign-currency exchange. The ascendancy of the central-government banks inevitably reduced Yunnanese control over the provincial economy. But these banks were sufficiently lavish with loans for agricultural reconstruction and with capital for the promotion of specifically Yunnanese industrial undertakings that most opposition was soon mollified.[20]

This tendency of the central government to placate opposition to its encroachments upon Yunnanese independence by remunerating the Yunnanese financially was evident also in a dispute over taxes. Early in the war, for example, the central government proposed that it take over the administration and control the receipts of all "national" taxes in the province, such as the salt tax. The authorities in Kunming initially protested. Finally they acquiesced, but only after the central government agreed to pay a "subsidy" to the Yunnan provincial government equivalent to the net revenue from the salt tax. Doubtless this loss of administrative control did not bode well for the long-term autonomy of the province. It was, however, an admirable device for giving face to all parties concerned.[21]

Just when the quarrel with the Bank of China was at its height in December 1938, the defection of Wang Ching-wei heightened the mistrust that permeated relations between Kunming and Chungking.[22] On his self-appointed mission of ending the war through negotiations with the Japanese, Wang's first stop after leaving Chungking on December 18, 1938, was Kunming. Lung Yün was an avowed admirer of Wang,[23] and Wang now hoped to persuade Lung and several of the other militarists in the Southwest, such as Chang Fa-k'uei, to support his peace movement.

What took place in the meeting between Wang and Lung Yün, which lasted into the small hours of December 19, is not known. Lung subsequently claimed that he told Wang that his plan was utterly unrealistic. But Chungking was on tenterhooks, for Lung's conduct during the ensuing months gave ample basis for the fear that he might join in Wang's scheme. On January 10, 1939, for example, Lung was conspicuously absent from a meeting of provincial leaders in Chungking. And wealthy residents of Hong Kong, supporters of Wang, transmitted three million *yüan* to Kunming, ostensibly to support the provincial program of financial reform, but probably as a bribe to win Lung Yün's support for Wang.[24]

On February 10, Lung finally issued a statement to the press. It was, however, ambiguous. He denied that he was associated with Wang Ching-wei's peace movement, and he asserted that he supported the central government's policy of continued resistance to the Japanese. At the same time, he added that he was not opposed to a peace movement as such if Japan would agree to treat with China on a basis of national equality. Meanwhile, Lung remained in contact with Wang, who was now in Hanoi. He did not issue a formal denunciation of Wang until May 2, a week after Wang had left Hanoi en route to the Japanese-occupied area of China.[25] The incident of Wang Ching-wei's defection thus passed, but it almost surely left a residue of bitterness that exacerbated the next and most serious confrontation between the provincial and national governments.

At issue in this newest dispute was control of Yunnan's extensive foreign trade. Increasingly after the fall of Hankow and Canton, the foreign trade of Nationalist China was channeled through Yunnan. The Yunnanese government, over the vigorous objections of the central government, levied a likin-type transit tax, euphemistically called the Special Consumption Tax, that was the province's largest single source of revenue.[26] Yunnan itself exported substantial quantities of such goods as tea, raw silk, tung oil, animal skins, and pig bristles. Tin, however, was the province's chief export commodity—one that was a lucrative source of tax income for the provincial government and from which the New Futien Bank derived most of its revenue.[27] So sensitive was the Yunnanese government about tin, in fact, that as early as October 1938 it instituted a monopoly over the export of tin, presumably as a means of forestalling central-government control over the metal.

The encroachments of the central government began during early 1939. In February the National Foreign Trade Commission established an office in Kunming, and the Ministry of Communications informed the provincial government that henceforward it would administer the examination and shipping of all Yunnan's export commodities—except tin. In April, Chungking also banned the local government from imposing the Special Consumption Tax on commodities passing through Yunnan from other provinces.[28]

This was a devastating blow to the provincial government's economic structure, and Lung Yün must have protested with unusual vehemence. In June, the U.S. State Department reported that "the Chungking authorities, having lost faith in Chairman Lung's professions of cooperation, are preparing arrangements for a full control of the province." At the same time, the central government was massing troops along the provincial border.[29]

Pushing its advantage, Chungking in July decreed that it was assuming control of all foreign trade throughout the country. This meant not only that the central government would tax all export-import items—now for the first time including also those that originated within Yunnan—but also that it would establish monopoly control of the trade of all major export commodities, including tin.

Kunming's response was immediate. It banned the export of any Yunnanese product that did not bear an exchange certificate from the New Futien Bank. Because that bank refused to issue any certificates, the flow of Yunnanese exports halted completely. In Chungking, a series of long and hard negotiations began, in which the Kunming representatives endeavored to settle not only the disputes over foreign trade and tin, but the whole range of provincial–central government problems. Relations became taut. In August, the attempt by one group of Yunnanese negotiators to reach a settlement was a total failure and they returned home. Chungking watched Yunnanese troop movements with unusually rapt attention. And for four months no tin or other Yunnanese goods moved out of the province.[30]

A second group of Yunnanese negotiators went to Chungking, however, and on October 12, 1939, an agreement was reached. Significantly, the central-government authorities once again avoided running roughshod over provincial interests, and the settlement was a compromise. The entire export trade of the province was henceforward to be controlled by a branch of the National Foreign Trade Commission, but this branch would be constituted jointly of Yunnanese and central-government representatives. The export of tin, tung oil, tea, and pig bristles now became a central-government monopoly, but the central government as compensation agreed to pay the provincial government an annual subsidy of £1,600,000. This sum probably more than repaid Yunnan for relinquishing control of its export trade.[31]

With this agreement in mid-October 1939, peace seemed to have been restored to Nationalist-Yunnanese relations. Lung Yün took the occasion to reaffirm his allegiance to the central government and to announce his determination to kill the traitor Wang Ching-wei.[32] "Politically," reported an American official on October 19, "Yunnan would appear to be now safe for the Nationalist Government."[33] This assessment was much too sanguine, however, for Yunnan's relationship with the Chungking government was even then entering a new and more critical phase.

Thus far during the war, the points of friction between the Yunnan and Nationalist governments had been chiefly economic. The reasons for this are clear enough. The Nationalists had had to create a wartime economic base in the interior. Yunnan, by dint of its seeming safety from Japanese attack, its vaunted though exaggerated stores of natural resources, and its proximity to Szechwan, the capital province, was an obvious place to establish strategic enterprises. Moreover, Yunnan's transportation outlets to Hanoi and Burma suddenly transformed Kunming into the nation's leading entrepôt for foreign trade—with obvious ramifications in the spheres of banking and taxation.

The process through which the Yunnanese learned to accommodate these economic changes was a painful one, for the foundations of Yunnan's economic autonomy were being eroded. Yet the Nationalist authorities attained their goal of integrating Yunnan into the wartime economic system by reimbursing the province financially: virtually every potential conflict was cushioned by grants of subsidies, by promises of loans for provincial reconstruction, or by capital investments in Yunnanese-owned enterprises. By October 1939, the basic economic differences had been ironed out.

But now political differences rushed to the fore. In September 1939, the central government resolved to tighten its grip on the provinces. To this end, the chairman of Szechwan, Wang Tsuanhsü, was transferred to a military command outside the province, Chiang Kai-shek temporarily assuming his office. In October, the central government directed Yunnan to dispatch two Yunnanese armies to the front in Hunan; it simultaneously ordered central-government forces to take up positions within Yunnan.[34]

These orders directly challenged Lung Yün's control of the province. Despite personal visits to Kunming by General Ch'en Ch'eng (head of the Political Department in the Military Affairs Commission) and by Chiang Kai-shek himself, Lung flatly refused to comply with Chungking's wishes. In November, when central-government forces moved toward the Yunnanese border, Lung Yün mobilized his army to resist what he regarded as an invasion by an unfriendly force. Later, however, Lung relented, and the first central-government divisions gained admission to the province in early 1940. Chiang Kai-shek partially appeased Lung by naming him commander of the Generalissimo's Field Headquarters in Yunnan and Kweichow (Chün-shih-weiyüan-hui-chang Tien-Ch'ien hsing-ying)—a position with indefinite military responsibilities but with a Y100,000 monthly stipend, ostensibly for the operation of the new headquarters.[35]

The Chungking government now had its foot in the door, but its demands to station more central-government troops in the province were insistent. The continuing parade of Nationalist officials traveling to Kunming, including Army Chief of Staff Ho Ying-ch'in and Ch'en Li-fu (director of the Kuomintang's Department of Social Affairs), suggests that Lung Yün was being obstructive. In August 1940, Lung reportedly rejected Ho Ying-ch'in's request that additional central-government troops be ad-

mitted to the province, arguing that the growing numbers of soldiers in the province were placing intolerable strains on food
supplies.[36] It is probable, too, that he argued for transferring
Yunnanese troops garrisoned elsewhere back to the province
rather than strengthening the contingent of central-government
troops. By the latter part of 1941, however, central-government
troops virtually had the run of the province, and in March 1943
they outnumbered local troops by a ratio of 4 to 1.[37]

The central government's efforts to introduce instruments of
political control into the province constituted another source
of friction. During 1939, the mood of political accommodation
resulting from the formation of the united front had begun to
dissipate. And the several secret police agencies of the central
government—most notably the bureaus of Statistics and Investigation of the party and the army—and the Three People's Principles Youth Corps were progressively employed to enforce an
ideological and political uniformity in the Nationalist areas. But
Lung Yün, like several of the other provincial militarists, sensed
a political advantage in giving refuge to political dissidents—
perhaps because these dissidents' criticisms embarrassed the
central authority or because, by harboring critics of the "downriver" government, he enhanced his popularity with the highly
ethnocentric Yunnanese.

To the intense perturbation of the central authorities, therefore, Kunming became a haven for Chinese liberals, particularly
after 1941, when Hong Kong could no longer provide a refuge.
Lo Lung-chi, for example, a professor at Southwest Associated
University and a member of the People's Political Council, had
criticized the National Government so vehemently that Chungking in 1941 ordered his dismissal from both positions. Lung
Yün then befriended him. And in 1944, when the Nationalist
government insisted that Lo be expelled from the province,
Lung refused and merely replied that he would keep Lo under
surveillance.[38]

Lo Lung-chi became a leader of the Federation of Democratic
Parties when it was formed in 1941. Despite—or because of—
the fact that the Federation's doctrinal cornerstone was opposi-

tion to the Nationalist's monopoly of government, Lung Yün became its friend and patron. Lung denied that he gave financial
aid to the organization, but in fact he employed several of the
Federation's leaders, including P'an Kuang-tan (Quentin Pan)
and P'an Ta-kuei as well as Lo Lung-chi, in the capacity of "advisers." And he assisted Federation members in financial straits
to publish their writings. Half of his huge home in Kunming
was also reportedly used as a dormitory for faculty of the Southwest Associated University, and quite possibly liberals among
the professors, rather than partisans of the central government,
received preference in obtaining accommodations there.[39]

Lung Yün was accordingly no friend of the central government's enforcers of political orthodoxy. A preparatory office of
the Youth Corps had been established in Yunnan in September
1939,[40] but early the next year Lung denied it permission to establish a branch in Chung-shan University. Lung even ordered
several of the leading cadres arrested, and they were released
only after Chungking interceded. Indeed, relations between
Lung and the Youth Corps were so bad that in April 1940 a
Youth Corps extremist incited one of Lung's cooks to poison his
food.[41] Although the Youth Corps throughout the war maintained a presence in Yunnan, it was never as vigorous or repres-
sive there as it was in areas more thoroughly subject to Nationalist controls.

It was impossible for Lung Yün to exclude the central government's secret police from the province, for almost all central-government enterprises, military units, and Kuomintang
branches contained sections concerned with "statistics and investigation." They conducted espionage in the province, and
even propagandized within the Yunnanese army—though not
to a large extent, perhaps because, as was reported in 1944,
Lung had extracted from the Chungking authorities a promise
to curtail secret-service activities in the province.[42]

A reflection of the greater political freedom in the province
was the relative outspokenness of the local press. The students
and faculty of Southwest Associated University published small
periodicals (for example the *Hsüeh-sheng pao* [*Student Press*] and

*Min-chu chou-k'an* [*Democratic Weekly*]) that would not have lasted a week in Chungking or Sian, though by any objective criteria they were restrained in their political comments. And the official organ of the provincial government, the *Yün-nan jih-pao* (*Yunnan Daily*), was sometimes vitriolic in its criticisms of central-government policies.[43]

No one who knew Lung Yün believed that his liberalism was more than superficial, a facade maintained for reasons of political advantage. Criticism of Lung himself, for example, probably would not have been tolerated in Yunnan. Nevertheless, Kunming throughout the war enjoyed greater political freedom than any major city in Nationalist China with the possible exception of Kweilin. One of the principal complaints of the Nationalist authorities against Lung was that he "harbored leftist elements, causing Kunming to become a hotbed of Communism."[44]

During the years 1939–42, Yunnan's relations with the Nationalist government were frequently tense, but only from 1943 on did the strains of the long war begin to have a telling effect. Inflation, which had been relatively moderate until 1942, was by 1943 corroding the economic and social foundations of the Nationalist government. Corruption was rampant throughout the bureaucracy; the industrial economy, beginning about September 1943, turned sharply downward; the army was passive and dispirited. Criticism of the situation, from both inside and outside the government, became widespread.

Conscious of its deterioration and increasing political vulnerability, the Nationalist regime was becoming even more authoritarian—or, as its critics phrased it, dictatorial—as the war dragged on. Chiang Kai-shek was less tolerant of criticism, more remote from even high-level officials, and concentrating even more power in his own hands. Clarence Gauss, the U.S. ambassador, observed in December 1943 that "Chiang . . . seems more and more to require that matters of all kinds and degrees be referred to him."[45]

Corresponding to Chiang's attitude was the growth of political repression throughout the Nationalist areas and the mounting influence of reactionary elements within the Kuomintang.

The secret services became more active; control over education was tightened; progressives, such as the liberal journalist Sa K'ung-liao, were thrown into political prisons. Censorship, too, now became more oppressive. The CC Clique, one of the least liberal of the several factions within the regime, was also in the ascendant, replacing less ideological and more pragmatic elements in the central councils of the Kuomintang (though not of the government).[46]

Provincial militarists like Lung Yün partook of the political malaise of this period. They were fearful, because Chiang Kai-shek's heightened authoritarianism implied a determination to repress the regionalists as well as the liberals and Communists. They were resentful, because they were convinced that Chiang had used the war to wear down their provincial armies by sending them into battle against the Japanese while he held his own divisions in reserve. And they were jealous, because Chiang's forces had received the lion's share of American Lend-Lease equipment whereas their provincial armies had to make do with inferior weapons, clothing, food, and training. As a result, Everett F. Drumright reported in April of 1943, there was a "bitterness and antagonism that seethes beneath the surface between authorities of the National Government on the one hand and the disappointed yet ever hopeful provincial militarists."[47]

Sensing their individual vulnerability to Chungking's centralizing tactics, provincial leaders at least as early as the spring of 1943 began to sound each other out on the possibility of concerting their opposition to the central government. The Federation of Democratic Parties, similarly discontented with the Nationalist government, though for different reasons, also began to participate in the conspiracy.

This conspiracy was still in its formative stages when, in April of 1944, the Japanese launched their Ichigo Offensive. This was Japan's most formidable military operation of the war in China, intended primarily to destroy the Chinese-American air bases in South and East China. It progressed with such ease—except for six weeks when General Hsüeh Yüeh's land forces and Claire Chennault's Fourteenth Air Force staged a heroic resistance in front of Hengyang—that the Japanese were able to establish a direct, albeit tenuous, link from North China to Indochina. During December 1944, when Operation Ichigo attained its furthest extent, a Japanese attack on Yunnan and Szechwan seemed a certainty.[48]

The political effects of the Ichigo Offensive were as devastating to the Nationalist government as the military effects, for the Japanese successes revealed as never before the corruption, ineptitude, and demoralization of the central government. It showed more starkly than ever that Chiang Kai-shek was willing to throw the provincial armies into decimating combat while his own armies conserved their American-supplied equipment. Moreover, Operation Ichigo caused even the people to lose confidence in Chiang. Prior to this, he had continued to be regarded as a dedicated, indispensable leader. Now, however, it burst upon at least part of the public consciousness that all of the corruption, factionalism, inefficiency, and political repression resulted not just from the shortcomings of Chiang's lieutenants, but from flaws in Chiang himself. Now, it was reported, even liberals who a year earlier had staunchly supported him saw "no hope for China under Chiang's leadership."[49]

The anti-Chiang movement in the provinces inevitably picked up momentum in the wake of the Ichigo Offensive. To the provincial militarists, it demonstrated—as Li Chi-shen put it—"a deliberate plan on the part of the central government to sabotage and destroy the armies of those southern leaders whose loyalty to the ruling clique is considered questionable."[50] Moreover, Operation Ichigo provided the provincial conspirators with unprecedented opportunities to act, for the Chungking government was now both militarily threatened and politically weakened.

There were two vortices of the anti-Chiang movement in the provinces, and Lung Yün was drawn into both of them. One was in Kwangsi, and was headed by that perennial political malcontent Li Chi-shen.[51] With the support of various military commanders in South China—reportedly including Lung Yün, Chang Fa-k'uei, and Yü Han-mou[52]—Li was forming an autonomous, democratic regime in east-central Kwangsi, near the border of Kwangtung. He believed that this regime, which was formally established in early November 1944 as the People's Mobilization Commission, would provide the nucleus of a new national government when Chiang's government disintegrated.[53]

The second center of the anti-Chiang conspiracy was in Kunming, where the prime movers, or at least the most articulate members, were radicals of the Federation of Democratic Parties, most notably Lo Lung-chi.[54] The Kunming movement was broader and more ambitious in its goals than its counterpart in Kwangsi. By mid-1944, the Federation had established contacts with a broad range of prominent political figures, including the Szechwanese militarists (P'an Wen-hua, Liu Wen-hui, and Teng Hsi-hou), Feng Yü-hsiang and Yen Hsi-shan, a group of Manchurian nationalists supporting Chang Hsüeh-liang, military commanders such as Yü Han-mou, and a group of Shensi generals such as Sun Wei-ju. Li Chi-shen was, of course, actively involved. Pai Ch'ung-hsi was virtually the only prominent provincial militarist that was not in some way associated with the movement. The Communists, who had hitherto remained aloof, had by about May 1944 expressed general approval for the policies of the movement, although they did not commit themselves to participate in it.[55]

This was an extraordinarily disparate group. As the American consul at Kunming aptly remarked, "It would indeed be difficult to imagine a more heterogeneous group of feudal barons and radicals, idealists and practical politicians."[56] Some of the Federation leaders, like Lo Lung-chi, seem to have held deeply rooted liberal convictions. The militarists and former warlords, however, were probably motivated primarily by the desire to preserve their regional power. Federation members understood that Lung Yün, for example, supported them less from any sense of ideological conviction than from a recognition that his only chance of survival after the war lay in the success of a "democratic" movement that would preserve a federal political structure.[57] In allying with the regional militarists, the Federation leaders displayed more than a little wishful thinking. They convinced themselves, for example, that they could cooperate with these "feudal barons" because China had now progressed to a stage where a return to the anarchy of warlordism was inconceivable. In explaining how the democratic protestations of someone like Lung Yün could be relied on, they lamely—and in complete disregard of decades of warlord betrayals—explained that Lung was "enough of a traditionalist" that he would not renege on his promises.[58]

The strategy of this Federation-led movement was formulated on the assumption that the Chungking government was on the verge of collapse. Federation leaders thus thought it possible to avoid violence and concentrated instead on preparing to fill the void that would be created by the approaching fall of the Nationalist government. They actively established contacts with the anti-Chiang elements, and attempted to design a political program that would be acceptable to all as a basis for the projected successor regime. The new government was to be a democratic coalition that would guarantee the basic political freedoms of the people. Social revolution was explicitly ruled out. As a sop to the provincial leaders, the new regime would avoid the excessive centralization of the Chungking government and would encourage greater regional autonomy.[59]

To formalize this political program, a people's congress—consisting of representatives 40 percent of whom were Kuomintang, 20 percent Communist Party, 20 percent Federation of Democratic Parties, and 20 percent other groups—was scheduled to be held in Chengtu on October 10, 1944. The congress would also lay the groundwork for a Government of National Defense (*Kuo-fang cheng-fu*) to serve as an interim government between the fall of Chiang Kai-shek and the creation of a permanent government after the defeat of Japan. Although the leaders of the movement anticipated the imminent collapse of the Nationalist government, the congress would precipitate that event by petitioning for Chiang Kai-shek's resignation.[60]

Virtually nothing resulted from all this conspiring and planning. It was naive in the extreme to believe that such a heterogeneous collection of dissidents could work concertedly in the creation of a viable national government. Perhaps because of the mixed character of the participants in the movement, they had not even agreed who would serve as the leader of the new Government of National Defense. Men mentioned as possible leaders included Li Chi-shen, Yen Hsi-shan, and Chang Hsüeh-liang. Mao Tse-tung was also suggested as a possibility, though he was dismissed as lacking sufficient stature to attract broad popular support. If a great deal of naiveté and wishful thinking suffused this movement, the fact that it existed and that such a broad spectrum of political elements in the nation associated with it reveals the extent of opposition to the Chungking government that had developed by 1944.

Certainly during the autumn of 1944 Lung Yün's relations with Chungking had gone from bad to worse. Yunnanese troops in late September had discovered and arrested a messenger who was carrying letters between Chiang Kai-shek and puppet officials in the Japanese-occupied area. Shortly after his arrest, however, military police of the central government seized the messenger. Thereupon Lung Yün sent his troops to surround the headquarters of the military police, and a major clash was avoided only when the agent was returned to the Yunnanese. Subsequently Lung Yün allowed the embattled messenger to proceed to Chungking. Then, however, Lung placed the commander of the central government's military police under arrest.[61]

Shortly after this prickly confrontation, a group of the central government's secret-service agents attempted to break up a mass meeting of several thousand people that was sponsored by the Federation of Democratic Parties—now, after October 10, 1944, known as the Democratic League. Rather than condoning the secret-police action, Lung Yün's military police arrested the central-government agents and imprisoned them for several hours.[62]

These incidents were but ripples on the surface. The basic cause of Lung Yün's discontent now was that, despite what was felt to be an imminent attack on the province by the Japanese, Chiang Kai-shek was still rationing out American military supplies only to his own central-government troops. Lung, and

other provincial militarists too, were thus faced with the worrisome prospect of having to defend their provinces with armies
that they knew were no match for the Japanese. Even if they did
successfully resist the Japanese, which they regarded as doubtful, they would be so weakened that they would be powerless to
prevent further centralization by the Nationalist authorities.

Lung Yün had appealed to Chungking for American weapons. Indeed, by October 1944 his sense of peril and frustration
caused him to speak out in a mass demonstration, demanding that the central government provide American arms for
the defense of the province. His newspaper, the *Yün-nan jih-
pao*, took up the refrain, its editorials bitterly castigating central-
government policies.[63]

Rebuffed by Chungking and with the Japanese armies moving
southward and westward, a group of provincial militarists—reportedly consisting of Lung Yün, P'an Wen-hua, Liu Wen-hui,
Teng Hsi-hou, Yü Han-mou, and a number of Manchurian generals formerly under the command of the now incarcerated Yang
Hu-ch'eng (whose crime had been to kidnap Chiang Kai-shek at
Sian)—decided after prolonged negotiations that they would
put up no resistance if the Japanese invaded their provinces. Instead, at the critical moment, and without forewarning Chungking, they would withdraw their armies into the security of the
mountains. There they would watch as the Japanese destroyed
Chiang Kai-shek's armies. After the war had been won by the
Allies, they would resume their accustomed positions of provincial leadership. If Chiang were not completely defeated by the
Japanese, at least his armies would be so weakened that the provincial armies could then easily complete the task.[64]

The conspiring provincial militarists did, however, leave themselves an alternative. Certain that Chiang Kai-shek would not
agree to provide them Lend-Lease arms, they appealed directly
to the American authorities. If the United States wished them to
continue the resistance against the Japanese, they said, then it
must immediately supply their armies with modern weapons.
Moreover, they expressed the hope that U.S. officers would assume full command of their troops. If this were done, they

thought, they could both resist the Japanese and emerge from the war in a strengthened position, at least the military equals of Chiang Kai-shek.[65]

This plan to let Chiang Kai-shek suddenly bear the brunt of the Japanese attack was as neat a bit of treachery as any that had been conceived in 30 years of warlord struggles and betrayals. Chiang Kai-shek, however, learned of the plot and moved to counteract it. To Lung Yün, who was planning to withdraw his Yunnanese forces to his native area near Chao-tung in the northern panhandle of the province, Chiang sent two of his most trusted emissaries. These were Liu Chien-ch'ün and Ho Ying-ch'in, natives of neighboring Kweichow, who were respected by Lung but whose loyalty to the central government was unquestioned. Liu Chien-ch'ün warned Lung, for example, that Japan was doomed to be defeated, and that, if Lung went through with the militarists' scheme, he would be on the losing side and would be branded a traitor. Far wiser, Liu told him, would be to resist the Japanese; for even if Lung's armies were defeated, he would be regarded as a national hero and his control of Yunnan would be correspondingly strengthened. This, Liu Chien-ch'ün said, was a strategy whereby "if you win you will be victorious, and if you are defeated you will also be victorious."[66]

The effect of this argument on Lung is unclear. It is known, however, that Lung, probably during January 1945, negotiated an agreement with the central government. Chungking promised, for example, to allocate sufficient American Lend-Lease materials to fully equip three of Lung's provincial divisions. Lung, for his part, would allow Chiang's secret police greater freedom in the province, would restrict the activities of the Democratic League, and would dismiss the editorialists on the *Yün-nan jih-pao* who had been so sharply critical of the Chungking government. Lung also, it may be inferred, promised to abandon his plan of retiring into the mountains in the event of a Japanese invasion.[67]

This compromise did not resolve the contradictions between Chungking and Kunming. Chiang Kai-shek now in the spring of 1945 was looking forward to the postwar situation. From the vantage point of Chungking, it appeared probable that a mortal struggle with the Communists was in the offing. If this were true, then Lung Yün's continued rule of Yunnan would be both inconvenient and dangerous. As Chiang Kai-shek put it, "The path of national reconstruction will be hard and long. We must therefore strengthen the central government and reorganize the local governments. For only if we unify will we be strong; then will victory be sure." [68] Lung Yün was an obstacle to that goal of unity, and he therefore had to be eliminated.

Chiang Kai-shek had decided to remove Lung from Yunnan at least as early as April of 1945. [69] His first move, so far as is known, was to summon General Tu Yü-ming (often referred to in English sources as Tu Li-ming) to Chungking. Tu was commander of the Kunming Defense Headquarters and one of Chiang's most trusted generals. In their meeting, arranged with the utmost secrecy, Chiang informed Tu of his plan to transfer Lung Yün from Yunnan and to appoint him to the post of chairman of the Military Advisory Council. (The council was an honorific graveyard for Chiang's former rivals; the chairmanship was prestigious but carried with it no substantive responsibilities or power.) Chiang Kai-shek feared, however, that Lung Yün would not submit passively to his political demise. He therefore instructed Tu to consolidate control over all key military installations in and around Kunming in the anticipation that Lung would forcibly resist his transfer. [70]

If the Japanese had not suddenly surrendered, Chiang Kai-shek's coup against Lung would have occurred in mid-August 1945. For in mid-July he had called in Li Tsung-huang, a Yunnanese but a staunch member of the CC Clique, and ordered him to make preparations to assume the chairmanship of Yunnan. On August 9, Tu Yü-ming was again called to Chungking for a meeting with Chiang, probably with last-minute orders regarding the approaching coup. Just then, however, Chiang learned of Japan's decision to surrender. This postponed the coup for about six weeks. [71]

During this period, the highly efficient Chinese grapevine carried rumors that Chiang was planning to dismiss Lung from his provincial chairmanship. Indeed, in August Lung even re-marked to an American that if Chungking wished to dismiss him, it had merely to issue an order; there was no need for con-spiracy because he lacked the power to resist.[72] Perhaps because of this fatalistic attitude, Lung fell in with a scheme concocted by Chiang to strip him of effective military support. For although he had received numerous hints of Chiang's attitude toward him, he acquiesced in an order from Chungking to send four di-visions of his provincial troops, commanded by his long-time in-timate associate General Lu Han, into Indochina, there to accept the surrender of Japanese forces. After the departure of those troops in mid-September, Lung was virtually devoid of military power. Only 9,000 regular troops and a collection of nondescript hsien militia remained to protect him.[73]

The denouement came in early October. At dusk in the eve-ning of October 2, Li Tsung-huang and a select group of other officials flew into Kunming with Chiang Kai-shek's written orders to be delivered to Lung by General Tu Yü-ming, dismiss-ing Lung from all his party and military posts in Yunnan and naming him chairman of the Military Advisory Council.[74] Tu, rather than delivering the order to Lung, set his troops into ac-tion. At about four or five o'clock on the morning of October 3, Lung Yün was shocked out of his sleep by the sound of shoot-ing. Dressing quickly, he discovered that a sizable force of the central government's Fifth Army had assembled outside his resi-dence. Lung and two aides, assuming the worst, disguised them-selves as civilians, stole from the grounds by means of a small back door, and made their way to the fortresslike and heavily defended provincial headquarters about a half-mile away. Mean-while, the conflict between the central-government forces and Lung's troops erupted into a miniwar. Throughout that morning and until the early afternoon, the sound of mortar, bazooka, machine-gun, and rifle fire echoed through the streets.

Not until noon, some seven or eight hours after the fighting began, did Tu Yü-ming present the order transferring Lung Yün to Chungking. Lung subsequently claimed that, immediately upon being informed of his transfer, he issued a cease-fire order to all his troops. The fighting continued, however, and it is probable that he was personally responsible for it, since he was now infuriated by Tu's peremptory resort to force. Perhaps too, because of Tu's use of force, Lung was concerned for the safety of himself and his family.[75]

Tu Yü-ming's decision to deploy his army against Lung before determining what Lung's response to his dismissal would be was bitterly criticized at the time, and even now one wonders whether the bloodshed might not have been avoided if more diplomatic methods had been employed. Both before and after the episode, Lung remarked that he had always been an obedient subordinate of the Generalissimo, and that if Chiang wished him to go to Chungking, he needed only to issue the order.[76]

Lung's protestations of loyalty to Chiang were something less than candid, but Chiang Kai-shek himself seemed to support the accusation that Tu had acted improperly when on October 16 he removed Tu from command of the Kunming Defense Headquarters. In punishing Tu, however, Chiang was merely offering a scapegoat to the Yunnanese, who had been infuriated by the central government's use of *force majeure*. In fact, in calling out his army Tu had acted in full accord with Chiang Kai-shek's wishes. For Chiang feared that Lung would resist being removed from Yunnan and had discussed those fears with Tu before the coup. Moreover, on October 2 Chiang had sent written instructions to Tu to seize control of all air bases in Yunnan "in order to prevent any treacherous disturbances"—clear evidence that Chiang anticipated that Lung Yün might resist his dismissal.[77] The punishment of Tu Yü-ming was therefore only nominal, and he was immediately thereafter rewarded with a new appointment as top commander of Nationalist forces in Manchuria.[78]

If Lung Yün would indeed have complied with an order from Chiang Kai-shek, then it was a tragic miscalculation to use force. For the resulting fighting fits none of the stereotypes of warlord battles. No love was lost between the Yunnanese and the central-government troops, and they killed each other with a vengeance that might better have been saved for the Japanese. Hundreds may have died. Prisoners were reportedly shot on the spot. The bodies of Yunnanese soldiers were found to have been bayoneted repeatedly after death. Yunnanese, possibly civilians, served as snipers against the detested central-government forces; when caught, they were "given a fair trial and shot." [79]

After the first day of fighting, however, Lung was badly outnumbered, and his only hope was to obtain reinforcements from outside the city. He wired magistrates in nearby hsien to dispatch militia to Kunming. Lung's son, commanding a brigade, was called back from Chao-tung, some 200 miles away. Until this help could arrive, Lung parlayed for time. He told his attackers that he would willingly go to Chungking, but that he wished to wait until General Lu Han could arrive from Hanoi to replace him as provincial chairman. But Lung's stalling merely angered Chiang Kai-shek, who feared what impression a protracted resistance might make upon other provincial leaders. Chiang therefore fixed October 5 as the deadline for Lung's departure for Chungking. [80]

Meanwhile, Lung's expected reinforcements did not arrive. The militia did not come because Tu Yü-ming's forces had cut the telegraph lines. And the relief column headed by Lung's son was badly mauled by the central-government troops while still some 40 miles from Kunming. [81] Learning of this, and after further negotiations with T. V. Soong and Ho Ying-ch'in (who came to Kunming to warn him that Chiang Kai-shek's patience was wearing thin), Lung Yün finally surrendered. On the afternoon of the next day, October 6, he flew to Chungking. [82] This was a notable victory for Chiang Kai-shek and the central government. It was, according to a Chungking newspaper, "equivalent to the recovery of enemy-occupied territory." [83]

Lung Yün, in Chungking, at first lived in trepidation. Chiang Kai-shek did not deign to see him or even go through the formalities of explaining why he had been removed from office in Yunnan. Tai Li's secret police kept him under close surveillance; former friends avoided him; and he was in fear for his life. [84] For the next three years he lived in Chungking and Nanking as a virtual prisoner—although his imprisonment was comfortable and he retained the title of chairman of the Military Advisory Council.

Reverberations from the October coup against Lung Yün were felt even years after the event. In a marginal way, they contributed to the final overthrow of the Nationalist government in 1949. The immediate effect of the coup was to free central-government agents to suppress Kunming's dissident intellectuals. Thus during November of 1945, when it became apparent that negotiations between the Communists and the Nationalists were breaking down, students and faculty in Kunming began protesting the resumption of civil war. Desperately anxious for peace and stability after the long war, and intimately familiar with the Nationalists' jealousy with regard to power, these intellectuals were less critical of the Communists than of the Chungking government. To avoid civil war, they argued, the Nationalists must abandon their "one-man monopoly" of government. Instead, a democratic coalition government must be created to restore efficiency and morality to government and to protect the freedoms of the common people. The students were also vehemently critical of the United States, which they contended was fostering the trend toward civil war by supporting the Chungking government.[85]

Central-government agents responded to these protests and accompanying demonstrations in their usual heavy-handed fashion. In the famous December First (1945) Incident, secret police murdered four students with hand grenades, bayoneted another, and beat up numerous others. Seven months later, in June of 1946, Li Kung-p'u and Wen I-to, leaders of the Democratic League, were assassinated.[86]

The consequences of these events are difficult to ascertain. Surely the fundamental sources of the students' and intellectuals' discontent, which contributed in significant degree to the overthrow of the National Government, lay deep in the political and economic maladies afflicting the nation. Yet these instances of brutal suppression in Kunming helped ignite the student movement. Demonstrations of sympathy for the martyrs in the

December First Incident had immediately been organized in Canton, Nanking, Shanghai, and other cities of the nation, and the murders of Li Kung-p'u and Wen I-to profoundly shocked the nation's political and moral sensibilities. Progressively thereafter the loyalties of the nation's intellectuals slipped from the Nationalists' grasp.

The repercussions of the overthrow of Lung Yün were also felt, somewhat later, in Manchuria. For the Yunnanese provincial troops that had been sent to Indochina in August 1945 realized that they had been deceived by the central government and sent from the province only to clear the way for the elimination of Lung. Moreover, in the eyes of the central government there was no room in Yunnan for 50,000 or more disaffected soldiers professing loyalty to a commander who was now under virtual arrest in Chungking. After completing their assignment in Indochina, therefore, they were transferred not back to their homes in Yunnan but to the Northeast to fight the Communists. There the Communists played on the discontents of the Yunnanese troops, stressing in their propaganda that Chiang Kai-shek had used them treacherously, that Yunnan under central-government control had deteriorated so badly that their families "cannot bear to live," and that the counterrevolutionaries in Nanking were laughing up their sleeves at seeing Yunnanese and Communists, both enemies of Chiang Kai-shek, killing each other in Manchuria.[87]

This was effective propaganda, and in March of 1946 the entire 184th Division of the Yunnanese 60th Army defected to the Communists. Thereafter Nationalist commanders treated the remainder of the 60th Army with suspicion, employing secret agents in its ranks and dispersing its divisions among troops more loyal to the central government. In October of 1948, however, during the battle for Changchun, this army too surrendered en masse to the Communists. In announcing his defection, the commander, General Tseng Tse-sheng, proclaimed: "After the victory in the War of Resistance, Chiang Kai-shek employed his deceitful schemes, sending our entire army to Hanoi on the pretext of accepting the surrender even while he plotted the Kunming Affair, sacrificing the people of Yunnan in order to eliminate his political rivals."[88] Thus, even three years later and in distant Manchuria, echoes of the coup against Lung Yün were still to be heard.[89]

Finally, as the Nationalists' house of cards collapsed, the principal leaders of Yunnan during the war opted for Communist rather than Nationalist rule. In December 1948, after over three years of honorific captivity, Lung Yün, in a dramatic and meticulously planned escape, fled from Nanking to Hong Kong. Subsequently, in 1950, he went to Peking, where—until he was charged with being a rightist in 1958—he served as vice-chairman of the National Defense Council.[90]

Lu Han served as provincial chairman of Yunnan and commander of the provincial garrison forces from December of 1945 to 1949, seemingly a relatively complaisant servant of the Nationalist authorities. When Chiang Kai-shek in late 1949 attempted to establish a final anti-Communist bastion in the southwest, however, Lu Han refused to cooperate. As a result, Chiang had to abandon this last foothold on the mainland and retreated instead to Taiwan. Lu Han remained in China after the Communist victory, and was presented with, among other honors, the Order of Liberation, First Class, in recognition of his contributions in 1949 to the Communist cause.[91]

The National Government never gained firm control over the territory, the people, or the resources that it ostensibly governed. It is a signal fact, for example, that in 1944 the National Government was able to marshal only about 3 percent (certainly less than 5 percent) of the nation's gross national product—as contrasted with about 47 percent in the United States—for support of all functions of government.[92] Nor did the government clearly prevail even in areas where its control was relatively firm. Local elites retained a tenacious hold on the levers of power at the lower levels of administration. The historian Wang Yu-chuan wrote that "Orders might come to a hsien from the government, but no order was carried out by the magistrates without the approval of the gentry. It was the gentry, and not the magistrates, who controlled local politics."[93] This quotation referred specifically to Shantung province early in the war, but it might have been written about virtually any rural area in Nationalist China, even down to 1949.[94] With much of the population either indifferent or antagonistic to its administrative agencies and army, the Nationalist regime lacked a broad base of popular support.[95]

The Yunnan connection with the central government reveals one of the deepest fissures in the Nationalist political structure: the existence of largely autonomous regional power centers, whose leaders did not share all the central government's policy goals and on occasion directly threatened the government's very existence. The regime was in fact extraordinarily weak, with a limited and slippery grasp on the nation's sources of power. In this context, Chiang Kai-shek's political strategy was what has been called a balance of weakness. That is, he worked to maintain himself and his government in a position of authority by keeping all other political forces weak. He denied arms to the provincial armies; he repressed intellectuals whose ideas seemed to him dangerous; he kept even his supporters weak by balancing them one against the other. For a time this strategy succeeded in the sense that it kept Chiang in power. In a fundamental sense, however, it failed, for by keeping all these elements weak, Chiang prevented the nation from becoming strong. China was therefore the loser, but so also in the long run was Chiang.

Was there an alternative? If we grant that a politician will usually seek to perpetuate his power as long as possible, then were there courses of action that might have enabled Chiang both to retain power and to strengthen the Chinese state? Might Chiang, for example, have strengthened the nation by sharing power and weapons with the provincial militarists? This is doubtful, for men like Lung Yün, Liu Wen-hui, and Li Chi-shen were not notably enlightened, modern-minded men. They seem to have been, taken as a group, as hungry to grasp power as Chiang Kai-shek was jealous of retaining it. And they were little if any more enlightened than he regarding how to wield that power for the welfare of the nation. Concessions by Chiang Kai-shek to the provincial militarists would probably, therefore, have resulted sooner or later in his own overthrow, and the rule of the provincial militarists would not have meant greater progress for China.

Or might Chiang better have formed a coalition government containing representatives of all political groups including the Communists? In the short run this might have been the wise course. But the Communists and the Nationalists could no more mix than could oil and water. Chiang correctly perceived, I think, that the Communists were too well organized, too disciplined, and too committed to suprapersonal goals to fail to dominate any coalition government in which they were included. If one accepted the premise (as Chiang did) that Communist rule would be bad for China, then rejection of this alternative was both logical and necessary.

The only viable and fundamental alternative for Chiang Kaishek, if he were both to perpetuate his own power and to strengthen China, was to broaden his base of political support. To do this, it would have been necessary to build a mass base among at least the non-Communist elements in the nation. This would have required, however, that he formulate an entirely different political strategy from that which he had pursued since coming to power. It would have required that he provide his potential supporters—such as the nation's intellectuals, or peasants, or bourgeoisie—access to the political process. To grant these groups a meaningful role in political affairs would have required, however, that he change the social and economic policies of the regime so as to retain their support.

Chiang Kai-shek, however, did not understand this form of modern pluralistic politics. Nothing in his experience had prepared him for a nonauthoritarian political process, and he felt uncomfortable with the openness and uncertainties of such a process. This was clearly evidenced in his reactions to the People's Political Council, a consultative group broadly representative of diverse interests and points of view that was formed early in the war to enhance national unity. As long as the Council supported Chiang's policies, he had no dispute with it. In 1942, however, after non-Kuomintang elements in the Council became sharply critical of the Nationalists' conduct of government, the Council was reorganized. Non-Kuomintang participation was markedly reduced, and the Council was thereafter an empty showcase of democracy in China, wielding no power that could in a meaningful way alter the policies and practices of the reigning elite.[96] Thus having rejected alternatives that might significantly have broadened his political base, Chiang was doomed to political weakness and to the debilitating competition of the provincial militarists.

Some might argue that Chiang committed his original mistake vis-à-vis the provincial militarists back in the late 1920's and the 1930's when he first admitted them into the regime without displacing them from their bases of power. The rationale at the time was that the military phase of the revolution would be shortened by enlisting those militarists and their troops into the Nationalist army. Indeed, it seems probable that the Northern Expedition in 1926–28 could not have succeeded if the Nationalists had pushed those militarists into opposition by refusing to compromise with them.

But had the Nationalists committed a mistake by establishing a *modus vivendi* with the provincial militarists? The subsequent experience of the Chinese Communists suggests that they had not, because after 1945 the Communists developed a formidable military force in large part by coming to terms with and using miscellaneous armies that were not Communist in origin. Units defecting from the Nationalist army were the best known of these. Less well known, but critical for the outcome in Manchuria, were the 300,000 or so troops of the Japanese puppet regime that, rejected by the Nationalists, joined the Communists.[97]

We still lack a study of the Communists' methods of handling these miscellaneous troops. It appears, however, that by means of political indoctrination, humane treatment of the soldiers, and social and economic achievements in society at large, the Communists were able to persuade both officers and men to fight fiercely and loyally. It seems obvious, then, that the Nationalists' problems had originated not in accepting the provincial militarists into the Nationalist army, but in not adopting political, social, and economic policies sufficiently attractive that the troops in the miscellaneous forces willingly transferred their loyalties from their warlord commanders to the central government.

## CHAPTER 2

# Peasants, Taxes, and Nationalist Rule: The War Years

PEASANTS DURING the war against Japan, it has long been assumed, fared relatively well economically. In economists' terms,
the "real income" of the farmers fell much less sharply than did
that of most other income groups. (See Table 1.) Because farmers generally do better during inflationary situations than workers on salaries, the assumption about the Chinese peasants' livelihood appeared commonsensical. Yet judgments about living
standards that are based upon calculations of "real income" may
be badly misleading. Government officials, for example, may indeed have seen their salaries fall in 1943 to 10 percent of the 1937
levels, but their total remuneration usually included rations of
rice, housing, and other perquisites that are not reflected in
Table 1. (Officials were not so well paid in 1937 that they could
otherwise have sustained a 90 percent cut in pay and still survived!) Similarly, calculations of the real income of the farmers
totally ignore political and social realities in the Nationalist area,
and thus reveal little about the actual conditions of life in the
villages.

In fact, the war exacted a heavy toll of the peasants, too. And,
as a result of a complex set of factors—including reduced production, unfavorable price relationships, and increased taxes
and rents—the condition of life in the villages during the latter
half of the war deteriorated seriously.

## Economic Trends Affecting the Peasants

During the first years of the war, nature smiled on the farmers
in Nationalist China: food production in 1938 and 1939 was bet-

TABLE 1

*Indexes of Real Income in Nationalist China, 1937–45*

(1937 = 100)

| Year | (1)<br>Farmers | (2)<br>Gov't<br>officials<br>(Chung-<br>king) | (3)<br>Professors<br>(Cheng-<br>tu) | (4)<br>Soldiers<br>(Cheng-<br>tu) | (5)<br>Laborers | (6)<br>Ind'l<br>workers<br>(Chung-<br>king) | (7)<br>Rural<br>workers<br>(8 hsien in<br>Szechwan) |
|------|------|------|------|------|------|------|------|
| 1938 | 87  | 77 | 95 | 95 | 143 | 124 | 110 |
| 1939 | 85  | 49 | 64 | 64 | 181 | 95  | 126 |
| 1940 | 96  | 21 | 25 | 29 | 147 | 76  | 66  |
| 1941 | 115 | 16 | 15 | 22 | 91  | 78  | 82  |
| 1942 | 106 | 11 | 12 | 10 | 83  | 75  | 78  |
| 1943 | 100 | 10 | 12 | 6  | 74  | 69  | 60  |
| 1944 | 81  |    | 11 |    | 65<br>(April) | 41<br>(April) | 89  |
| 1945 | 87  |    | 12 |    |     |     |     |

SOURCES: For column (1), Chou Shun-hsin, p. 243. For columns (2), (5), and (6), through 1943, Chang Kia-ngau, p. 63; for the 1944 figures in columns (5) and (6), *ibid.*, p. 64. For column (3), through 1943, Wang Yin-yüan, "Ssu-ch'uan chan-shih wu-chia yü ko-chi jen-min chih kou-mai-li," p. 263; for 1944 and 1945, the June ratios (salary/cost of living) in *Economic Facts*, no. 34 (July 1944), p. 479, and no. 46 (July 1945), p. 701. For column (4), Wang Yin-yüan, "Ssu-ch'uan chan-shih wu-chia yü ko-chi jen-min chih kou-mai-li," p. 263. For column (7), Wang Yin-yüan, "Ssu-ch'uan chan-shih nung-kung wen-t'i," p. 107.

ter than 8 percent above the average for the prewar years. From 1940 through 1943, however, food production fell below the prewar averages. And, most serious, the main food crop in the Nationalist area, rice, remained markedly below normal throughout the years 1940–45. (See Table 2.)

During the first two years of the war, however, virtually all farmers—and especially the poorer segments of the farm population—enjoyed relative prosperity. The sizable harvests offset the effects of a decline of farm prices. The greater availability of money, caused by the still relatively moderate inflationary trend, eased the traditional paucity of currency in the rural areas and thereby benefited those in debt, both borrowers and purchasers of land. The burden of taxes also declined significantly, because the tax-collecting agencies generally failed to increase the tax rates to compensate for inflation. If any part of the farm population was hurt by these economic trends, it was those who pre-

TABLE 2

Food Crop Production in 15 Provinces of Nationalist China, 1938–45

(million shih-tan)

| Year | Rice | | Wheat | | Total food crop | |
|---|---|---|---|---|---|---|
| | Quantity | Index | Quantity | Index | Quantity | Index |
| 1931–37 | | | | | | |
| average | 726.3 | 100 | 169.2 | 100 | 1,576.5 | 100 |
| 1938 | 747.6 | 102.9 | 202.9 | 120.0 | 1,766.9 | 112.1 |
| 1939 | 763.6 | 105.1 | 198.2 | 117.2 | 1,702.0 | 108.0 |
| 1940 | 618.9 | 85.2 | 201.1 | 118.9 | 1,545.6 | 98.0 |
| 1941 | 643.5 | 88.6 | 165.1 | 97.6 | 1,516.4 | 96.2 |
| 1942 | 635.3 | 87.5 | 209.7 | 124.0 | 1,512.2 | 95.9 |
| 1943 | 609.5 | 83.9 | 199.2 | 117.7 | 1,530.2 | 97.1 |
| 1944 | 674.7 | 89.2 | 248.3 | 146.8 | 1,768.8 | 112.2 |
| 1945 | 586.0 | 80.7 | 215.9 | 127.7 | 1,594.9 | 101.2 |

SOURCES: For 1931–37 average, *China Handbook, 1937–1945*, p. 433; for 1938–45, Yang Chia-lo, ed., vol. 4, p. 1279. Data should be considered approximations, since the National Government lacked the administrative resources and political control to collect full and accurate information on farm production. Chou Shun-hsin, pp. 92–93, gives a different series of index numbers, and Prof. Thomas Rawski of the University of Toronto is skeptical about the large increase in wheat production shown for 1944.

NOTE: 1 *shih-tan* = 1 hectoliter = 2.84 U.S. bushels.

sumably could most easily sustain modest losses, the creditors and rentiers.[1]

Beginning in 1940, however, trends changed, and the traditional gap in the villages between rich and poor widened. The class of large landlords now tended to prosper, whereas most other farmers, including small landowners, felt growing economic privation. This economic polarization of the farm population resulted, paradoxically, from a sharp upward spurt in farm prices. Rice prices in Chungking, for example, increased 500 percent between May and December 1940.[2] The poor rice harvest that year—19 percent below the preceding year—partially accounted for the price increase. That alone, however, does not explain the ensuing course of events. More important, perhaps, was that the government was making huge purchases of rice on the open market to feed its burgeoning army, and that in June 1940, the city of I-ch'ang, transshipment point to Szechwan from the rice-producing provinces of Hunan and Hupeh, fell to the

Japanese. These events generated fears that the reduced rice supply was more than a temporary phenomenon, and this resulted in a rash of hoarding and speculating. Individual consumers bought up large stores of rice in expectation of shortages and higher prices, whereas landlords and merchants held their stock of rice off the market in the hope of rising prices. A process by which shortages stimulated further shortages thus hurt civilian morale and began making it difficult for the government to obtain needed supplies. Panic spread and several rice riots erupted.[3] In response, Chiang Kai-shek in November 1940 declared, "We must punish the selfish rich. . . . No matter how these rich rice owners scatter their hoardings and how cunningly they hide them, I shall get to know about them. . . . If they do not give up their stocks, they . . . deserve severe punishment."[4] In fulfillment of this promise, the mayor of Chengtu was arrested for hoarding and in December was executed. Government legal action and even a program of price controls did not, however, impede hoarding or the escalation of the rice price.[5]

Large landlords profited greatly from the rising price levels. Most farmers, however, whether small landowners or tenants, did not share in the boom because they had little rice to sell on the market. In the fertile Chengtu Plain, for instance, less than 20 percent of the farmers possessed any surplus at all to sell on the market.[6] Of some minor significance in this regard was the fact that small farmers who did possess a marketable surplus of rice derived scant benefit from the rising prices, because they usually had to sell shortly after the harvest, when prices were relatively low.[7] Large landowners, by contrast, with sufficient financial reserves to tide their families over for a few months, held their rice off the market until dwindling stocks pushed prices upward.

Tenants, moreover, bore increasingly heavy burdens. Especially after 1941, landlords used the pretext of rising grain prices and increased taxes to renegotiate their tenants' land contracts. On the one hand, they increased the absolute amounts of the rents. On the other, those who had been collecting rents in cash now also began insisting on payment in grains, which were more valuable and secure than the depreciating currency.[8] Other common complaints at the time were that landlords had begun demanding that tenants pay part of the rising land tax, or that they were increasing the amount of rent deposit (*ya-chin*, a sum paid by a renter when a contract was signed, usually but not always returned when the tenant departed). When tenants objected to the increased rents, deposits, and taxes, landlords replaced them with farmers willing to pay the higher exactions.[9]

As a result of these various economic trends, by 1942 and 1943 landlord-tenant conflicts had reached epidemic proportions.[10] Some tenants were expelled from their land. Those who remained, agreeing to pay higher rents, felt their economic positions eroded—middle peasants frequently sinking to poor-peasant status, and poor peasants falling to the status of hired laborers.[11] Paradoxically, large farmers complained about the shortage of hired farm labor, for the countryside was being denuded of employable men as a result of military conscription, the flight of young men from the villages to evade the draft, and the attraction of jobs in the cities.[12] Farm wages therefore rose. In the Chengtu Plain, for example, labor costs, which in 1937 had accounted for only 12 percent of farm expenditures, had risen in 1941 to 26 percent.[13] As a consequence, many landlords who in the past had not labored on their land were reportedly now returning to the villages and themselves engaging in farming.[14]

## The Land Taxes

Reduced production, unfavorable price relationships, and increased rents clearly damaged the economic position of the majority of peasants. But government exactions—in the form of taxes, contributions, compulsory loans and purchases, the military draft, and labor conscription—also exacted a heavy toll of the farmers and deeply affected peasant attitudes toward government authority. These exactions were therefore an important factor in the complex political dynamics that resulted in the revolutionary dénouement of 1949.

Of the government's exactions, the land tax was second in importance only to military conscription (discussed in Chapter 6). Since 1928, the tax and the related surtaxes had been administered by the provincial and local governments. In July 1941, however, the central government nationalized the land tax and began collecting it in kind—that is, in grains and in other farm produce—rather than in cash. This was a major fiscal innovation, which profoundly affected the farmers and even the government itself.

The wartime tax-in-kind originated in Shansi province. Since the beginning of the war, large units of the army had been stationed there, and feeding them had become a major problem, particularly because the heavy demand on the market had pushed prices to unprecedented heights. In late 1939, the Shansi authorities hit upon the solution of collecting the land tax in wheat, thus assuring ample supplies of grain and obviating large government expenditures on the open market.[15]

Central-government authorities, facing increasing fiscal deficits as a result of having to buy grain for the army and civilian employees at ever higher prices, quickly realized the potential of collecting the land tax in kind. They were given pause, however, by the fact that the land tax was still a provincial and not a central-government levy. They further realized that collecting it in kind would be immeasurably more complex than collecting it in cash. Chungking therefore moved cautiously. In July 1940, it simply approved the Shansi initiative and ordered that other local authorities "consider" following Shansi's example. Fukien, Chekiang, and Shensi were the first provinces to respond to this suggestion by converting to the tax-in-kind.[16]

By late 1940 and early 1941, circumstances forced the Nationalist government to take a new look at the land tax. It now desperately needed new sources of tax revenue. Since retreating to the interior, its annual income had fallen to only 37 percent of prewar levels even as expenditures had risen about 33 percent.[17] The crisis in the rice market, moreover, demanded immediate resolution. The government's large purchases for the army were straining the national budget and pushing rice prices skyward. Hoarding exacerbated the difficulty of obtaining the needed

grains. The public was panicking as a result of the market's uncertainties. In the spring of 1941, therefore, the Chungking government decided to nationalize the land tax and to collect it in
kind. After extensive discussions in the Kuomintang's Central
Executive Committee in April and in the Third National Finance
Conference in June, the Executive Yüan ordered that the new
policy go into effect on July 1, 1941.[18]

Two agencies were charged with administering the new national tax. The Ministry of Finance would assess (*cheng*) the
properties to be taxed, and the newly created Ministry of Food
would collect (*shou*), transport, store, and disburse the tax grains.
This division of labor was designed to minimize corruption.
From the beginning, however, inefficiency bedeviled the system. In 1942, therefore, the Ministry of Finance collected as well
as assessed the tax, and the Ministry of Food transported,
stored, and distributed the tax grains. The next year the tax administration at the provincial and lower levels was fully unified.
At the central-government level, however, the ministries of Finance and Food retained a dual control over the system.[19]

The rate of the new tax was fixed in accordance with the principle that the total in-kind levy on a *mou* of land (one *mou* equals
about one-sixth of an acre) should be equivalent to the prewar
value of the regular land tax and all related surtaxes. Accordingly, the standard conversion rate in 1941 was set at two *shih-
tou* (standard pecks) of unhusked rice for each *yüan* (Chinese
dollar) of assessed tax.* (This standard conversion rate was
doubled, to four shih-tou, in 1942.)[20] Whenever possible, the
government would collect the tax in rice, because soldiers and
government employees expected to be supplied with rice, and
storing and shipping just this one kind of grain was relatively

---

*Chinese grain measures are confusing, even to specialists. The customary
measures of volume of grain were the *tan* (bushel), *tou* (peck), and *sheng* (pint).
Although the values of these measures varied greatly in different areas of China,
the National Government employed a standardized or "market" system of mea-
suring volume. These "market" units of volume were the *shih-tan, shih-tou,* and
*shih-sheng.* The equivalencies of these units are:

1 *shih-tan* = 10 *shih-tou* = 100 *shih-sheng*
1 *shih-tan* = 1 hectoliter = 2.84 U.S. bushels (*cont'd overleaf*)

simple. In only six provinces, however, was rice the sole grain collected (Yunnan, Kwangsi, Kwangtung, Hunan, Kiangsi, and Chekiang). In the areas that did not produce rice, other grains might be substituted (1.4 shih-tou of wheat, for instance, might be delivered for each yüan of assessed tax).[21] Because of the complexities of storing various kinds of grain and the difficulties of establishing fair conversion rates to their rice equivalent, such substitutions were not encouraged. Nevertheless, fully 11 of the provinces collected the tax-in-kind in four kinds of grain. And, in the extreme case of Kansu, payment of the land tax was made in nine different crops, including several varieties of beans, maize, and millet. Not until 1943, however, were the cotton-growing districts of Shensi, Honan, and Hunan permitted to pay the land tax in cotton. For two years, therefore, cotton growers had to bear the double burden of the tax per se and the expense of purchasing the required grains on the open market at inflated prices.[22] Finally, in some areas—most notably those near or behind enemy lines and those in which transportation was unusually difficult—the land tax continued to be collected in fa-pi.[23]

To the land tax itself, several levies were added that were collected along with it. There was, for instance, the hsien-

---

1 *shih-tou* = 1 dekaliter = 1.14 U.S. pecks
1 *shih-sheng* = 1 liter = 1.80 U.S. pints (0.908 U.S. quarts)

Traditionally, the character *tan*, which represents a unit of volume, was pronounced *Shih*. By the 1930's, however, it had become thoroughly confused with the character *Tan*[1], which was a unit of weight. During the period of this study, therefore, both the unit of volume and of weight were often pronounced *tan*, although the *tan* (or *Shih*) for volume and the *Tan*[1] for weight were not interchangeable; both, moreover, were often written with the same character (*Tan*[2]), and occasionally both were rendered into English as "picul." To compound the confusion, units of volume were in practice often assigned a fixed weight. Thus, a *tan* (unit of volume) of unhulled rice weighed about 128 pounds (whereas a *Tan*[1]—unit of weight—equaled 50 kilograms, or about 110 pounds).

A detailed discussion of *shih* and *tan* is in Han-sheng Chuan and Richard A. Kraus, *Mid-Ch'ing Rice Markets and Trade: An Essay in Price History*, pp. 79–98. Other sources for this note are *Tz'u-hai* (Shanghai: Chung-hua shu-chü, 1937), pp. 695, 1416; Young, *Wartime Inflation*, p. 356, note a; *China Handbook, 1937–1945*, p. 196; *Webster's Seventh New Collegiate Dictionary* (1971), p. 534.

level public grain levy (*hsien-chi kung-liang*), which customarily equaled 30 percent of the land tax proper. Following the nationalization of the land tax, local governments had created various miscellaneous levies (*t'an-p'ai*) to obtain needed grains. To mollify the public's dissatisfaction with these new exactions, the hsien-level public grain levy was instituted in 1942.[24] A further levy, the "grain-for-storage" (*chi-ku*) assessment, amounting to about 13 percent of the land tax proper, was also collected in most provinces. The purpose of this levy was to fill public granaries designated for relief purposes and to help stabilize grain prices.[25] In at least some provinces (e.g. Szechwan), a wastage fee of 10 percent was added to the basic land tax, too.[26]

The largest exactions accompanying the land tax, however, were those collected under the systems of compulsory purchase (*cheng-kou*) and compulsory borrowing (*cheng-chieh*) of grain. The provincial quotas for these exactions were approximately the same as those for the land tax. The exaction differed from the land tax, however, because the taxpayers were theoretically to be compensated for the grains borrowed or purchased from them.[27] In 1941, approximately 30 percent of the sale price of the compulsorily purchased grain was to be paid in cash, and the remainder was to be paid in some form of promissory notes (Food Treasury Notes, National Currency Savings Certificates, or U.S. Gold Dollar Savings Certificates).[28] The price that the government paid for the grain, however, was customarily well below the prevailing market price. Thus, if (as was standard practice in 1942) grain was purchased at half the market price, a taxpayer could hope to receive no more than 15 percent of the market value of the grain in cash. And because of corruption, he might not receive even that.[29]

By 1943, the Chungking government was feeling the strain of paying cash for even 15 percent of the market price of compulsorily purchased grain. It therefore instituted the system of "borrowing," rather than purchasing, the grains. In 1943 this system was implemented in nine provinces: Fukien, Kwangsi, Kansu, Szechwan, Kwangtung, Sikang, Chekiang, Shensi, and Yunnan. The next year it was extended throughout the Nationalist area.[30] Under this system, farmers received receipts for the "borrowed" grain; five years later, the government was to repay the farmers with an equal amount of grain. In fact, few if any of these receipts for the compulsorily borrowed grain, or of the promissory notes given for the compulsorily purchased grain, were ever honored by the National Government.[31] The systems of compulsory purchase and borrowing actually constituted, therefore, an additional tax on land approximately equivalent to the regular land tax.

Finally, the farmers were required to transport these in-kind taxes and levies to the government's collection stations. Typically, a Szechwanese farmer might have to pay about 500 pounds of unhusked rice in taxes. By government regulation, the collection stations were to be no more than a day's journey from any given farmer, but in practice they were often considerably farther away.[32] Thus, the time and labor required to convey the taxes to the government could be considerable. Farmers in Anhwei in 1946—and this was generally true of the wartime period as well—sometimes had to travel for five days to reach a collection station. Once there, they would have to wait from four days to two weeks to complete the process of paying the taxes.[33] The farmer, of course, had to bear the cost of transporting the grain, and of the board and room for himself and his helpers. As a high-level official complained in 1947, these expenses "in every instance exceed the value of the grain delivered. Thus the government receives one *tan* of grain, but the people's burden is two or three *tan*."[34] If, as sometimes happened, the taxpayer had to make more than one trip to the collection station—because the tax collectors had found fault with the quality or quantity of the grain being delivered or because of sheer harassment—the expenses would be even more onerous.[35]

## T'an-p'ai, Military Grain, and Other Exactions

Before the war, peasants in Nationalist China had been subject to a large array of taxes, levies, and services other than those explicitly assessed on the land. During the war, however, the variety and burden of these increased spectacularly. Some of these taxes were levied by the central government: the salt tax, for example, had by 1944 become Chungking's most important single source of cash revenue.[36] Much the greater number of these other taxes were generated, however, by the various local governments. An important reason for this was that by nationalizing the land tax, the central government had appropriated what had been the financial foundation of the provincial governments. As compensation, the central government in 1941 paid a stipend to the provincial and hsien governments equivalent to one-half their former income from the land tax. The next year, rather than a direct stipend, the central government allocated to these local governments a fixed percentage of revenue derived from various taxes—for example, 15 percent of the land tax, 30 percent of the business tax, and 25 percent of the inheritance tax.[37]

The stipends and allocations were, however, wholly inadequate to meet the expenditures of the local governments, which were consequently forced to search out alternative sources of revenue. Hsien governments, for instance, now placed a new emphasis upon the slaughter tax, a tax added to the price of pork, beef, and mutton. Prior to the war, in 1936, this tax had accounted for less than 4 percent of hsien-government revenues; beginning in 1942, it became a major source of provincial-government funding.[38] In addition, the local governments initiated a large variety of t'an-p'ai.

T'an-p'ai, miscellaneous and ad hoc forms of exaction, were sometimes collected yearly, sometimes monthly, sometimes only once or irregularly, and were used to meet a special need or fill a sudden deficit. Most t'an-p'ai were, strictly speaking, illegal. Nonetheless, most were also collected with the tacit approval of the higher authorities, and they were found everywhere in the Nationalist area. The system varied from place to place, but a detailed 1942 investigation of t'an-p'ai in 18 hsien in Szechwan may be taken as representative of the t'an-p'ai exactions elsewhere. In Szechwan, the only legal t'an-p'ai in 1942 were the *pao-chia* contribution and the education tax.[39] In the 18 hsien surveyed that year, however, 240 different types of t'an-p'ai were collected.[40] One hsien listed only 11 t'an-p'ai; one had as many as 67.

The variety was mind-boggling. There were, for example, a "contribute-straw-sandals-to-recruits" tax, a "comfort-recruits'-families" tax, a "train-antiaircraft-cadres" tax, and a "provide-fuel-for-garrisoned-troops" tax. Then there were taxes for national-salvation bonds, electric poles, road repairs, teachers' rice stipends, school equipment, food and fuel for *pao*-head conferences, administrative supplements for *pao* heads, and burial expenses for relatives of conscripted soldiers.[41] Some of these were fairly large; some were minuscule. A quarter were instituted by the central and provincial governments, a little less than that by local gentry and religious organizations, and more than half by village and pao-chia heads. Of all these, however, those collected to finance or provision the army were the most burdensome. As Wu Ting-ch'ang, governor of Kweichow and a leading Kuomintang worthy, complained, high-level authorities frequently ordered hsien to provide money for the army and other defense needs without regard to how the money was to be raised.[42] And army garrisons constantly needed pigs, chickens, firewood, fodder, tools, construction materials, and so on. In each case, the solution was to order a new t'an-p'ai exaction.[43]

A special form of t'an-p'ai—though I think it was never actually termed t'an-p'ai—was the military grain levy (*chün-liang*). In areas where the supply of tax grains was inadequate, or where problems of transportation impeded the supply of rice to the troops, high-ranking army commanders might requisition the needed rice from the local governments. The civilian authorities, in turn, would assign quotas to the local residents, supervise collection of the grain, and conscript laborers to transport it to the designated collection centers. According to a 1946 source, it was customary for 30 percent of the military grain quota to be assigned to merchants and 70 percent to farmers. Like the system of compulsory purchase, the allotted payment for military grain was invariably at prices well below market value. Moreover, because the money passed through the hands of many officials, who frequently skimmed off a part for themselves, there usually remained little for the individual farmer or merchant. From the vantage point of the ordinary citizen, therefore, military grain purchases were not easily distinguishable from a regular tax, except that the exaction might come at any time and in any amount.[44]

The total quantity of military grain collected from 1940 to 1944 appears, from crude calculations, to have been approximately 10 percent of the grain collected through the land taxes for that same period.[45] But the burden of the levy weighed unevenly upon different parts of the country. Some provinces, such as Hupeh, Honan, Shensi, and Szechwan, which had large concentrations of troops, paid an inordinate share of the levy. Szechwan, for example, provided one-fourth to one-half of all military grains.[46] In Hupeh, where troops of both the Fifth and Sixth War Zones were stationed, the military grain levy in 1942 equaled fully 77 percent of the combined land tax and compulsorily purchased grains.[47] The burden in the northwestern provinces such as Shensi was doubtless also large, because General Hu Tsung-nan's so-called crack troops only received a full supply of grain in one year, 1941. In all other years, as Hu's sympathetic biographer conceded, the troops had to "seek means on the spot."[48] Whether or not Hu's forces paid for all or even a part of the grains thus requisitioned is not stated.

Just as the peasants provided a disproportionate part of the money and grain for the war effort, so they also provided most of the manpower, both as soldiers and as coolies. The government's use of conscript labor was not new in Nationalist China, but the demands of war made the practice enormously more burdensome. Men, women, and children, most of whom were peasants, were conscripted to build fortifications, trenches, roads, and airports. On construction of the Burma Road, 160,000 workers were employed.[49] Half a million were conscripted to build the nine airfields designed to accommodate the Americans' B-29 bombers and accompanying pursuit planes.[50] Another half-million carried earth to prepare the bed of the Hunan-Kiangsi railroad. In Honan in 1943–44, unknown numbers were recruited to dig an antitank trench 15 feet deep, 20 feet wide, and over 300 miles in length, which subsequently proved to be completely useless.[51] Millions more were impressed to transport tax grains and military grain from the collection centers to the points of distribution. Boats, carts, and barrows were sometimes used, but in Hupeh, for example, fully half of the carts were unusable, and so human shoulders had to serve.[52] General Li P'in-hsien reported that in Anhwei, where he was provincial governor, long lines of people resembling uninterrupted streams of ants bore the grain to the provincial warehouses after each harvest.[53]

The conditions under which these conscripts worked were invariably harsh, although the severity of treatment varied from project to project. Workers received little or no remuneration; wages intended for the workers were often "squeezed" away by authorities at the various levels of the bureaucracy; shelter and sanitary conditions were primitive. On the Szechwan airfield projects, the workers toted baskets of rocks over such long distances that at best they could make only half a trip a day; tens of thousands of them died, deserted, or were severely injured.[54] Seven thousand reportedly died during the construction of the Burma Road.[55] A former supervisor of conscript laborers reported that the men came from 60 to 100 miles away, served for ten to 15 days each, ate coarse foods, and lived in crude straw huts. But, he recalled, they didn't mind.[56] In fact, the contrary must have been true. Hsü K'an, the former Minister of Food, admitted that, with regard to the transport of grain, "everyone was unhappy [at having] to engage in the work."[57] A native of Honan, who reached young adulthood during the war, contends that the peasants there feared these periods of conscript labor, and suffered more from them, than they did from either military conscription or government taxation.[58]

The government contended that, because China was an underdeveloped country fighting a modern war, the use of such primitive methods as mass conscription of labor was necessary.[59] Attempts were therefore made not to abolish, but to regulate, the system. In December 1943, Chungking promulgated a Compulsory Labor Law requiring that men between the ages of 18 and 50 annually perform ten days of labor with compensation.[60]

The Hupeh provincial government the same year drafted regulations stipulating that wages or specific amounts of grain, oil, and salt should be paid to the workers, and that the work should be limited to the farmers' slack season.[61] Like most Nationalist laws at the time, these regulations served largely as statements of future goals rather than as prescriptions for current practice.

## The Peasants' Tax Burden

That the peasants' tax burden increased during the war is not seriously disputed. Nor can the National Government be faulted for increasing the tax burden per se; this was war, and the citizens' burdens understandably became more onerous. What is disputed, however, is whether the increased tax burdens had seriously deleterious effects upon the peasants' economic livelihood and their political outlook.[62]

In strictly mathematical terms, the farmers' land taxes from 1942 on were nearly five times higher than the prewar rate.[63] Even when the collections were *at their peak* in 1942 and 1943, however, the tax-in-kind and the compulsory purchase and compulsory borrowing assessments still accounted for only about 8 percent of the total rice and wheat output. (See Table 3.) This percentage figure did not include the lesser assessments accompanying the tax-in-kind (such as the hsien-level public grain levy), and thus the total government tax exactions in those years were somewhat higher than 8 percent. Still, even a tax rate at that level—though sharply higher than before the war—probably was not, by itself, sufficiently high to damage seriously the average landowner's standard of living.

The actual tax burden of the peasants was determined less by formal tax schedules, however, than by the jagged realities of Chinese political life, and the incidence of the several taxes consequently varied from province to province, from village to village, and from individual to individual. There was, for example, a wide discrepancy among the several provinces in the conversion rates of the land tax as expressed in currency to it as expressed in quantities of grain. The "standard" conversion rate in 1943 of four shih-tou per yüan, therefore, was collected only in

Hunan and Shensi.[64] A rate of three shih-tou per yüan was more common. Yet Yunnan paid only 1.2 shih-tou per yüan. Sze-chwan, however, was assessed at the rate of seven shih-tou per yüan. Ostensibly, the major reason for the different conversion rates was that the pre-1941 yüan assessment had been heavier in some provinces than others. The relative abundance or dearth of grain in the various provinces was cited as another considera-tion.[65] In fact, because the quota assigned to each province was subject to negotiation between the central government and pro-

TABLE 3

Collection of the Land Tax-in-Kind, 1941–48

(million shih-tan)

| Year[a] | (1) Total rice and wheat production | (2) Tax collected | (3) National tax quota | (2)/(3) (percent) | (2)/(1) (percent) |
|---|---|---|---|---|---|
| 1941 | 808.6 | 24.1 | 22.9 | 105% [97.8][c] | 2.98% |
| 1942 | 845.0 | 67.7 | 65.0 | 104 [101.6][c] | 8.01 |
| 1943 | 808.7 | 65.2 | 64.2 | 102 [93.3][c] | 8.06 |
| 1944 | 923.0 | 57.9 | 64.6 | 90 | 6.27 |
| 1945 | 807.6 | 30.1 | 35.3 | 85 | 3.73 |
| 1946 | 1,357.5 | 42.5 | 54.4 | 78 [43][d] | 3.13 |
| 1947 | 1,402.8 | 38.3 | 58.8 | 65 [48][d] | 2.73 |
| 1948 | 1,356.0 | 20–25[b] | | | |

SOURCES: For column (1), Yang Chia-lo, ed., vol. 4, p. 1279. For columns (2) and (3), China Handbook, 1950, pp. 563–64. The figures in column (2) include compulsory purchase and compulsory borrowing.
NOTE: 1 shih-tan = 1 hectoliter = 2.84 U.S. bushels.
[a]Figures for 1941–45 are for 15 provinces; figures for 1946–48 are for 22 provinces.
[b]This figure, representing "requisitioned grains" as of November 1948, was provided by Minister of Food Kuan Chi-yü. The government, he said, actually needed 75 million shih-tan. See North China Daily News, Nov. 3, 1948, p. 1:2; New York Times, Nov. 3, 1948, p. 24:5.
[c]The alternative figures in brackets are from Ch'en Yu-san and Ch'en Ssu-te, tables, pp. 82–85.
[d]See the explanation for the bracketed figures on p. 86 below.

vincial authorities, the extent of the National Government's political control of a province may well have been the determining factor. Yunnan's low conversion rate, for example, was attributed to the fact that it was a grain-poor province. The relative autonomy of the province and its strained relations with Chungking, however, were doubtless the decisive considerations in the negotiations over the provincial quota. (See Chapter 1.)

Substantial variation in the farmers' tax burden was thus built into the national tax structure. What ultimately determined an individual landowner's tax payments, however, was the manner in which the taxes were administered, regardless of the nominal tax rates. The land records, for example, which provided the basis for the land-tax assessments, were both antiquated and corrupt. Some had been left unchanged for centuries, thus ignoring such possibly critical changes as the size and productivity of landholdings.[66] More important, over a third—perhaps a half—of the tilled land was not even recorded on the tax registers. This was strikingly revealed by a series of postwar land surveys in 108 hsien in six provinces, which increased the taxable acreage by 56 percent. In Anhwei, for instance, 54 percent of the taxable land had not hitherto been taxed; in Honan, 37 percent; in Chekiang, 27 percent; and in Hunan, 17 percent. Indeed, the land survey in one hsien in Anhwei revealed that less than 5 percent of the taxable land had been registered—resulting in an increase of over two million *mou* on the tax books.[67] That most of the unregistered land belonged to the more wealthy landowners is probable, though this remains a problem to be explored.

The tremendous diversity of China, too, complicated the whole system and created vast opportunities for corruption. For example, the seemingly simple regulation that landowners pay a specific number of tou of rice for each yüan of assessed tax became an administrative nightmare, because not all farms produced rice and because the units and utensils of measurement were not standardized in the rural areas. Although many hsien and villages did indeed use the tou as the usual measure of volume for grain, variations in the size of the tou were virtually infinite. In nearly half of the provinces, moreover, the custom was to measure grain by weight rather than by volume. In such places, the tax collectors had to convert not only the money assessment into grain, but the weight measure of that grain into shih-tou.[68] In some parts of the provinces, too, the tax assessment had customarily been made in silver (the *liang*, or tael), not in the national currency (fa-pi). Or, in Yunnan, the provincial currency (*tien-pi*) was initially the basis of the assessments.[69] Finally, farmers in non-rice-producing areas were permitted to pay their taxes in other crops, most notably wheat, but also millet, beans, potatoes, corn, cotton, etc., which had to be converted to their rice equivalents.

Conversion of these various measures, moneys, and grains to the official standards resulted in staggering confusion and gross inequities. Some of the inequities were doubtless inadvertent, as could easily occur when converting the market value of a tou of millet to that of a tou of rice. The tax collectors' opportunities to cheat the taxpaying farmers amid this confusion were, however, large and irresistible. The system therefore quickly became a quagmire of corruption. Besides bilking the farmers when converting prices and weights, the tax collectors frequently enriched themselves by arbitrarily increasing the tax quota, adding illegal charges to the regular assessment, or using measures larger than the legal shih-tou. Sometimes they demanded bribes so that the farmers could avoid a wait of several days to complete the complicated taxpaying procedures. Or they assessed fines, the money for which went no farther than their own pockets.[70]

With the collection of the grains, the officials' opportunities for peculation had but begun, for the grain had to be transported, stored, and cleaned. Millers, for example, falsely reported wastage from polishing and cleaning; granary employees regularly pilfered so-called "spillage"; and transporters reported that their boats had capsized or that bandits had seized their cargoes.[71] A favorite form of squeeze was to adulterate the grain, adding water, pebbles, or weeds to replace the grain filched to sell on the market. Later, other workers did the same. By the time the rice reached the cooking pots of the soldiers or officials, it was often barely edible.[72] With dark humor, this officially supplied rice was termed *pa-pao-fan*, "eight-treasures rice"—a reference to a popular rice dessert prepared by adding cherries, dates, and other rich sweets (rather than pebbles and chaff).[73]

Corruption in the handling of the tax grain was too extensive to be ignored. Minister of Food Hsü K'an confessed to the People's Political Council in September of 1944 that "not one of the four stages [of handling tax-in-kind]—collection, storage, transportation, and distribution—is without corruption. The rice that the common people harvest and pay [to the tax collectors] is invariably plenteous and of good quality. But in the end, when it is time for everyone to consume it, it is both scarce and poor in quality. When I speak of this situation, it pains the heart."[74] Hsü also complained of the difficulty of hiring capable and honest people to work in the ministry, and declared that those wanting jobs as supervisors of the granaries especially "are ill-intentioned and definitely not good people."[75] Thus, the pervasive corruption in the Food Ministry was an admitted fact. Indeed, the *Ta-kung-pao* estimated that, as a result of the peculation of officials and local elites, over 10 percent of the collected grains had been lost by the time they were polished. Another 30 percent was lost during storage. Further losses occurred during shipping of the grains.[76] Even if this estimate exaggerates the losses resulting from corruption, it shows clearly that the losses were very large and would have added significantly, directly or indirectly, to the farmers' tax burden.

The peasants, moreover, were not just passive objects of the taxation process. They, too, attempted to cheat by adulterating the grains delivered to the tax stations. The incidence of tax evasion, too, increased steadily after 1942. (See Table 3.) But the fact that the tax-in-kind system became less efficient in mobilizing the nation's grain output did not signify that the average farmer's tax burden was becoming lighter. In fact, when collections of the tax-in-kind fell, government exactions by means of irregular levies, such as of military grain and t'an-p'ai, rose. And since the government was less able to monitor these irregular exactions than it was the handling of the tax-in-kind, the corruption and inequities inflicted upon the peasants became greatly magnified.[77]

As a rule of thumb, the burden of t'an-p'ai during the latter part of the war was double that of the combined land taxes.[78] But the collection of these miscellaneous levies was more burdensome and variable than that of the land taxes. The 1942 survey of t'an-p'ai in Szechwan, for example, concluded that in only one of the 18 hsien investigated could the people easily bear the burdens of t'an-p'ai. In four hsien, the people could bear them with some effort. But in 13 hsien—that is, in the vast majority of cases—most of the people felt the burdens of t'an-p'ai were extremely heavy.[79] Such an observation was obviously impressionistic, yet it was probably an accurate representation of the range of reactions to the t'an-p'ai exactions. The survey also found that the t'an-p'ai burden weighed disproportionately on the poorer strata of rural society: the smaller landlords, landowning peasants who worked their own fields, and even tenants. The most wealthy villagers, large landowners with political or secret-society connections, could persuade the pao-chia heads and other t'an-p'ai collectors to overlook them or to force their tenants to pay the tax.[80]

Large landlords and rich members of the village elite, in fact, perennially refused to cooperate with the government's tax collectors. Most of them, Chiang Kai-shek asserted in 1942, were so selfish and so avoided their just share of the tax burden that they had forfeited their right to be considered citizens of China. And in 1947 he complained that they still "commonly" refused to pay the land taxes.[81] The anthropologist Fei Hsiao-t'ung, too, observed that the village elites were "not affected by the laws [and were] exempt from taxation and conscription." [82]

Commander Chu, a former army officer and public official in Yunnan, for instance, paid no taxes of any kind throughout the entire war with Japan. When a local official mentioned this fact in a meeting, he was warned by colleagues that "Commander Chu would make things difficult for him." Commander Chu's son explained that "My father has served the government for so many years that he should not be asked to pay any taxes." [83] When wealthy and influential people like Commander Chu paid no taxes, the pao-chia heads and other tax collectors had to increase the exactions on other villagers proportionately in order to fill their quotas for the district.

Pao-chia heads, who administered over 80 percent of the t'an-p'ai, were notorious for their corruption. They frequently collected several of the levies simultaneously, so that the peasants had no way of knowing what taxes they were paying or how much for each. Furthermore, they seldom issued receipts, so that restrictions on their squeeze were few and ineffective. As a consequence, the actual burden of the t'an-p'ai increased significantly. The Szechwan survey speculated that pao-chia heads pocketed about one-third of the money they collected for t'an-p'ai.[84] An official publication in 1947, too, stated that peculation frequently doubled the farmers' actual t'an-p'ai burden.[85] The corruption surrounding these miscellaneous taxes, bemoaned the Ministry of Finance, "dissipates the people's spirit and shakes the nation to its roots."[86]

What then, in the final analysis, was the total burden of the government's legal and illegal exactions upon the small and middle-sized landowners, who bore the brunt of the tax-collectors' persistent demands? According to the *Ta-kung-pao* in early 1945, small farmers were paying five times the taxes prescribed by the government because large landowners were sloughing the bulk of the tax load onto them.[87] This figure is compatible with contemporary estimates that the tax burden of many peasants was 30 percent, 50 percent, and even more of their harvest.[88] These figures, if understood as applying to the politically uninfluential poor and smaller landowners rather than to the landholding class generally, appear credible. We must acknowledge, however, that they are no more than estimates. In any case, as James C. Scott has shown, the welfare of the peasants was determined less by the percentage of the harvest that the government collected in taxes than by how much produce the peasants retained after the taxes had been collected.[89] On this, however, we completely lack hard data. Perhaps the most compelling nonquantitative assessment of the tax burden was rendered by a reputable observer in 1945: "Many already feel they cannot stand it."[90] Or, as the Kuomintang officially acknowledged in May of the same year, "During the war, the farmers have made the greatest contribution in the forms of money and service. But their livelihood is the most difficult."[91]

## Economic Effects and Political Reactions

By the latter part of the war, particularly from 1943 on, the ravages of taxation, corruption, decreased production, and inflation were markedly evident in the villages. A small minority of the farmers, especially the larger landlords, were thriving—a fact recognized by the central government in 1945 when, financially pressed to improve conditions in the army, it instituted a special "grain-contribution movement" directed specifically at the large and wealthy farmers.[92]

But was landlordism so profitable that it was leading to large increases in the concentration of landholdings? Certainly assertions that land concentration was becoming a major problem gained a virtually unchallenged currency during the war and continued afterward. The Communists, who of course delighted in exposing the darker sides of Nationalist society, asserted that government officials in particular were buying up land around Chungking, Chengtu, and Kunming, as well as in virtually all the provinces under Nationalist rule.[93] Even official Nationalist sources, including the Kuomintang newspaper *Chung-yang jih-pao* (*Central Daily News*) and Sun Fo, head of the Legislative Yüan, sometimes echoed these charges.[94] But reliable data demonstrating that land concentration was increasing significantly are notably lacking. A Communist historian has even cited as evidence a Nationalist government survey showing that, from 1937 to 1941, the landlords' share of the land in Szechwan increased from 69 to 70 percent, and in Sikang from 67 to 72 percent.[95] To build major conclusions about increasing landlordism upon such minuscule percentages is, of course, untenable. In all probability, therefore, the accusations were rooted more in political bias than in economic reality.[96] The fact is that investors found commodity speculation and purchases of United States securities to be far and away more profitable than landholding.[97] Profits from commodity speculation and U.S. securities, moreover, were seldom taxed, whereas investors in land had at least to be prepared to deal with the army of leeches that preyed upon rural properties.

Even though growing landlordism was not a serious problem, it remains true that large landlords generally prospered while the standard of living of the vast majority of farmers deteriorated. It is probable, too, that the socioeconomic gap in the villages widened during the latter part of the war more than at any previous time in the twentieth century. In P'eng-hsien near Chengtu, John Lossing Buck and Chong-chan Yien in early 1943 found that two-thirds of the farmers ate less meat, 59 percent purchased less clothing, and 83 percent spent less on entertainment than before the war. Indebtedness also increased from 19 to 38 percent.[98] A similar study the same year near Kunming in Yunnan revealed that 61 percent of the farm families had experienced a deteriorating standard of living during the war, only 24 percent (mostly big landowners) had improved their economic position, and 15 percent (mostly middle-sized landowners) remained generally unchanged.[99] In Kweichow at the same time, Governor Wu Ting-ch'ang noted the same tendencies. Only an "extremely small minority," he recorded, were living at a higher level of consumption than previously, whereas consumption on the part of the common people had been reduced to a point where it could not be reduced further.[100]

No single reason for the growing deprivation in the villages can be isolated. The inflation, which resulted in higher rents and reduced purchasing power, may have had some effect, but was not in itself devastating. Reduced production in many parts of the interior also took a real, but still relatively minor, toll. Together, these and other losses would have been sufficient to create at least some distress for the many peasants who ordinarily lived close to the subsistence level. But when, in addition, they had to bear a sharply increased tax burden and suffer immeasurable corruption, the distress was often widespread and severe.

The Honan famine in 1942–43 starkly demonstrated the critical difference that government exactions could make in the well-being of the peasants. There, drought, frost, hail, and locusts had reduced the spring and summer harvests of 1942 to about 25 percent of normal. As a result, the population faced certain privation during the coming winter. What transformed privation into a terrifyingly severe famine, in which several million persons starved to death, was the government's relentless exactions of taxes and the military grain levy. Close to a million troops were garrisoned in the province, and they had to be fed. Transportation facilities there had been devastated by the war, and food for the soldiers therefore had to be provided locally. The choice—either starve the troops or starve the peasants— may have been a difficult one for the authorities, but in wartime the army received priority. Whatever the justification, the results were grisly. Farmers were taxed of their last grains of wheat, whereupon there began an exodus of several million seeking refuge in Shansi and other neighboring provinces. Farmers, desperate for food, sold once-valuable farmland for a mere peck or so of wheat; many also reportedly sold sons and daughters. The government finally took cognizance of the crisis by remitting a fourth of the land tax, but the local officials' and the army's demands for grain were, by all reports, unrelenting. Leaves, bark, peanut husks, and even, it was said, human flesh kept many alive.[101] A sizable percentage of the famine victims expired in the spring of 1943, after the new crop of wheat had sprouted kernels. The desperate peasants had ground up the unripened wheat and, having eaten this paste, became so bloated that they died (*ch'ung-ssu-le*).[102] In March of 1943, Theodore White estimated that about five million human beings were "dead or dying" as a result of what some were calling a "man-made famine."[103]

The tragedy in Honan was an exceptionally grievous instance of how government exactions exacerbated the farmers' privation. Yet many of the same forces were at work elsewhere, explaining at least partially why, beginning in 1942, peasants throughout the Nationalist area were rising in increasingly intense protest and rebellion. In Kansu in early 1942, for example, 60,000 people stormed through 20 hsien of the province proclaiming the slogans, "Kansu people should rule Kansu! Oppose military conscription and the grain taxes! Kill all southern barbarians (*nan-man-tzu*)!" For over a year, the rebels defeated all local forces sent against them. Finally, after a 40-day campaign during June and July of 1943, some of General Hu Tsung-nan's best troops crushed the rebellion, reportedly killing over 14,000 and capturing another 18,000.[104] In 1944, some hundred men bearing slogans protesting the government's grain levies and the corvée killed officials and burned all the government administrative offices in three townships (*hsiang*) in northern Hupeh. Dispersed in June, the men rose again even more fiercely a month later.[105] Much more serious was the rebellion of over 10,000 people the same year in southern Hupeh. According to the provincial-government report, Communists allied with a local secret society, the Yellow Spears Society (*Huang-ch'iang-hui*), together had "utilized the dissatisfaction of the farmers toward grain levies and labor services" to attack government officials, army headquarters, and granaries.[106]

Similar uprisings were reported in virtually every province under Nationalist rule—many in the capital province of Szechwan and some as far away as Fukien. The sources of the people's grievances were customarily conscription, taxation, and compulsory labor service. The targets of the rebels' attacks, therefore, were government offices and officials. There was, too, a logical and thoroughly understandable sequel to the Honan famine. During 1944, as Nationalist troops retreated before Japan's Ichigo Offensive, Honanese peasants attacked the army that had caused them so much grief. Wielding farm tools, guns, and knives, they disarmed some 50,000 of the troops, killing some and at times even burying them alive.

Banditry—the traditional refuge of China's rural malcontents —now also underwent, in the words of an American missionary in Kansu, "a remarkable upsurge." Armed men, former peasants, draft evaders, and army deserters, often in bands of 200 to 4,000, preyed on the countryside, terrifying inhabitants and making travel on the highways risky and sometimes impossible. Even army convoys were vulnerable to their attacks.[107]

Rebels and bandits presumably made up only a small part of the total farm population, and peasants for the most part continued to till their lands and to obey the authorities. Yet grievances against the government were clearly reverberating through the nation's villages. Wong Wen-hao, chairman of the National Resources Commission, admitted in 1943 that corruption involving the land tax was causing peasants to revolt.[108] Wu Ting-ch'ang, governor of Kweichow, complained that people did not understand the government's need for manpower and money. Because of a "gap between officials and the people, and extortion and harassment that are not adequately investigated," he said, "bad people" played on their grievances to make trouble.[109] An American official in Fukien, John C. Caldwell, reported in early 1944 that "The feeling and temper of the people is near the boiling point." "The people," he warned, "are seething with unrest."[110] In less colorful language, a State Department official in mid-1943 similarly observed that, among the common people in the rural areas, the "prestige and influence [of the Kuomintang] have perhaps reached their lowest ebb."[111]

## CHAPTER 3

# Peasants, Taxes, and Revolution: The Postwar Years

POLITICALLY, THE WAR had been costly for the Nationalists in the rural areas; taxation, conscription, and corruption had seriously depleted the peasants' reservoir of good will toward the government. Yet the losses were not irreversible. A few years of good harvests, the return of peace, effective and incorrupt administration—these could quickly have dissipated the resentments that suffused the villages after about 1942. But it was not to be. Barely had the eight-year war with the Japanese ended when civil conflict with the Communists erupted. As before, the farmers had to provide the basic resources of war—men, money, and grain. The old resentments consequently did not subside, and the peasants became an important ingredient in the volatile revolutionary mix of the period leading up to 1949. Yet the true role of the peasants in these years belies facile generalizations that this was a peasant revolution.

## The Immediate Postwar Situation

Following the war, hunger and death stalked the provinces of China, especially in the central and southern sections of the country. Thirty-three million people were undernourished, according to an estimate of the United Nations Relief and Rehabilitation Administration (UNRRA) in the spring of 1946, of whom seven million faced imminent starvation.[1] In Hunan 10,000 actually died of hunger in the first eight months of 1946. Approximately 7 percent of the population were refugees.[2] Farmers who had fled the Ichigo fighting in 1944 returned in 1945 too late to seed the summer crops, or else they returned to find their seed-grains consumed, their draft animals, pigs, and chickens slaughtered, their tools stripped for their metal, and their houses and whole villages burned to the ground.[3] Large areas in 1945 had thus been left untilled; indeed some 30–40 percent of the farmland of Honan, Hunan, and Kwangtung was reportedly still untilled in early 1946.[4] Moreover, the fields in cultivation were farmed at less than peak efficiency as a result of the paucity of human and animal power, fertilizer shortages, and general neglect throughout the war. In Hunan, for example, farm production in 1945 stood at only about half the normal levels—and only a quarter in the southern part of the province.[5]

Conditions in the famine areas, reflected in the files of UNRRA, were grim. A famine-survey team in Hunan in the spring of 1946, for example, made the following report.

> Groups ranging from 20 to 50 persons were seen at ferry crossings and at small villages along the highway between Hengyang and Lingling begging for food. In their efforts to secure attention and food they obstructed the movement of vehicles by standing in crowds across the road, climbing on and in the vehicles. . . . In every instance it was necessary to physically "pull children loose" from the vehicles as they clutched tenaciously to the car, constantly crying and wailing. A mob spirit pervaded the groups and any attempts to disperse them resulted in a near riot.
>
> Practically every one in these groups were [*sic*] only partially clothed in filthy rags that hung on them in shreds, while many of the children were naked, their bodies encrusted with sores and infections.[6]

Throughout the famine areas, people subsisted on weeds, roots, grass, wheat husks, and rice polishings.[7] A survey in 11 Kwangsi villages stated that the average daily nutritional intake was 419 calories and 16 grams of protein.[8] Disease was pandemic. Malaria was encountered most frequently. In Ch'üan Hsien, Kwangsi, for instance, 80 percent of the population suffered from malaria, 21 percent of them in an acute form.[9] Epidemics of smallpox, cholera, diphtheria, dysentery, typhoid, typhus, and similar communicable diseases were common.[10] Medical treatment and medicines were virtually nonexistent, and death rates consequently soared. Children were especially vulnerable to the ravages of hunger and illness, and in many villages in the famine areas were seen but rarely, especially under the age of one year.[11] This famine in China during late 1945 and early 1946—affecting as it did some 33 million people—was probably the most severe and extensive crisis of its kind anywhere in the world during the immediate postwar period.

Peasant suffering in China at this time was not restricted to provinces that had lain in the path of the Ichigo Offensive. Everywhere economic dislocations were accompanied by the exactions of the National Government, which frequently transformed the peasants' hardships into calamity, and their hunger into starvation. The government had not intended this, and indeed, thinking to alleviate the suffering of those who had spent the war under Japanese occupation, had on September 3, 1945, proclaimed a policy of remitting the land tax. For one year, 1945–46, no land taxes (including compulsory borrowing and the hsien-level public grain levy) would be collected in the 24 provinces that had been occupied by the Japanese. The following year, the remaining provinces would be exempted from paying the land taxes.[12]

The policy of tax remission, on its face, appeared politically astute, for it would help win the support of the landowning classes in the forthcoming struggle with the Communists. Financially, however, it proved to be a catastrophic miscalculation. Collections of the tax-in-kind in the year following the end of the war with Japan fell to about a half of what they had been the preceding year. Yet the demands of the army and the government, rather than declining accordingly, actually increased as the regime moved into the former Japanese-occupied areas. The shipment of large quantities of grain to those areas from West China, moreover, was impracticable. As a consequence, the army and the various local governments were forced to satisfy their grain needs by resorting to arbitrary and illegal exactions from local sources, which stirred up widespread dissatisfaction. For villagers in the recovered areas, therefore, the bright promise of Nationalist rule quickly faded.[13]

The effects of the Nationalists' procurement policies in the former Japanese-held provinces were revealed in an unusually candid administrative report by the Kiangsu provincial government in 1946.[14] During the war, most Kiangsu government offices had moved to unoccupied territory in neighboring Anhwei. Late in the war, however, the central government anticipated an American landing on the coast, and it therefore ordered the Kiangsu authorities to return to their province. There they were secretly to restore the provincial administration and prepare to take control of the transportation network and other facilities before the Communists could do so. The Allies never undertook the anticipated amphibious landing in East China, but the cadres had taken up their posts inside Kiangsu, still nominally under Japanese control, by the end of May 1945.

Despite having returned to their native Kiangsu, these authorities possessed no legitimate sources of revenue. They therefore "borrowed." During the three to four months prior to the end of the war they borrowed only Y690,000. During the last four months of 1945, however, because of the remission of the land tax, they had to borrow an additional Y681,000,000. In January of 1946 the central government explicitly proscribed this policy of borrowing and finally began providing funds to the provincial government in the form of loans and subsidies as a substitute for the land-tax revenues. The sums thus received, however, were worth but a fraction of the value of the province's prewar revenues, and thus (according to the provincial report) "the finances of the hsien and municipalities fell into an impossible condition." [15] The provincial authorities therefore continued the policy of forced loans, collecting a total of Y1.4 billion in 1946.[16] During this same period, every hsien and municipality in the province had instituted various t'an-p'ai. These were still illegal. They were also onerous. "Nothing," admitted the Kiangsu authorities, "distresses the merchants and oppresses the people as much as these." [17]

The people of Kiangsu also had to support a large and growing military contingent. Nationalist troops poured into the province to disarm the Japanese and to counter the growing Communist threat. By May of 1946 there were nearly 700,000 soldiers stationed in just the northern part of the province.[18] Initially these forces had purchased supplies directly from local inhabitants. In December of 1945, however, the system had been rationalized by the creation of Military-Grain-Procurement Commissions in each hsien, staffed by civilian authorities. With funds provided by the central government, they administered the purchase and collection of grain for the army.[19] Initially, according to the official report, cooperation exceeded all expectations; the people even transported the grain voluntarily. The market price of rice soon shot up, however, and the government, as was commonly the case, paid but a fraction of the market value. The Kiangsu report does not disclose precisely what price the Procurement Commissions were paying the peasants, but many provinces paid only 20–30 percent of the market rate.[20] The official rationale for paying such a low price for the military grain was that this discouraged speculation and hoarding. Minister Hsü K'an admitted, however, that under these circumstances "the people were naturally unwilling to sell rice to the government."[21]

Government exactions soon threatened to take everything the people of Kiangsu had, and popular opposition to the regime became widespread. In June 1946, representative assemblies at the provincial and hsien levels appealed to the central government to stop the procurement of military grain. Their request was granted. At this time, however, fighting with Communist forces in northern Kiangsu intensified, with the result that the need for military grain became more urgent. In July, therefore, the provincial assembly contrived to obtain 300,000 shih-tan of rice by collecting the 1946–47 land tax in advance. This new demand brought the situation close to the breaking point. "The people are destitute," representatives in the hsien assemblies recognized, "and their strength is not yet restored." They also realized, however, that "the allotment of military grain will tolerate no delay," and they therefore approved the plan to collect the land tax in advance. In fact, less than 60 percent of the quota was collected during July, August, and September. "The reason," observed the official report, "was that the availability of grain, just before the new harvest, was extremely small. This was indeed a fact."[22]

If by mid-1946 Kiangsu was struggling to provide rice to the army, governmental exactions in several other provinces were equally oppressive. Honan, for example, had suffered unspeakably during the war. Repeated flooding of the Yellow River, the nightmarish famine in 1942–43, the occupation by the Japanese in 1944 of 109 of the province's 111 hsien, and the grisly devastation in the western part of the province during the Ichigo fighting—each had contributed to the prostrate condition of the province after the war. By a conservative estimate, at least two million people were in "desperate" need of food relief (by which UNRRA meant they would die within two to three months if aid were not provided).[23] Yet nearly a million regular troops, an unknown number of militia, guerrillas, and irregular troops, approximately 80,000 Japanese prisoners of war, and 50,000–60,000 army horses were deployed in the province and had to be provisioned.[24] With the transportation system in a shambles, all the food, fuel, and fodder had to be procured locally. The government attempted to distribute the burden fairly, requisitioning supplies for the most part from the relatively well-fed hsien in the eastern part of the province rather than from the areas that had been scourged by Ichigo and the Yellow River floods. Yet military necessity seldom permitted nice distinctions. According to the official history of UNRRA, government food levies for the army were "drawn not infrequently from deficit areas into which CNRRA [Chinese National Relief and Rehabilitation Administration] and UNRRA were sending food for relief. . . . Repeated efforts by CNRRA and UNRRA, through the Executive Yüan, to stop withdrawals from areas of food shortage were unavailing."[25] In some cases, UNRRA-supplied relief grain was appropriated by the army.[26] The accusation made in the People's Political Council in March 1946 that the government's military grain exactions were a cause of famine was therefore probably more than mere political rhetoric.[27]

## The Civil War Period

During the ensuing three years, from late 1946 until the Communist victory in 1949, conditions in the rural areas apparently deteriorated even further, producing not only economic decline but social and political turmoil. China is, however, a nation of contrasts, and to what extent the numerous local reports of desolation, suffering, and instability were characteristic of rural conditions generally may be disputed.

On the bright side, as a result of favorable weather and the astonishing resilience of the Chinese peasant, the autumn harvest of 1946 was surprisingly good, although Hunan, Hupeh, and Honan suffered relatively poor crops.[28] If Nationalist data are reliable, agricultural production during 1947 and 1948 showed further, if modest, increases. (See Table 4.) Farm production still fell short of the nation's total requirements, however, and vital food supplements, especially for the cities, were obtained through imports.[29] Still, the threat of famine on the scale of the winter of 1945–46 no longer existed.

A variety of economic and political factors, however, prevented the villages from enjoying a vernal renewal. The inflation, now rising uncontrollably, worked to the farmers' disadvantage. Despite urban protests against skyrocketing food prices, the prices of rice and wheat were, in fact, lower in real terms than before the war.[30] Food prices throughout 1946 and 1947 rose more slowly than the prices of other major items on the commodities price index, in large part because of substantial imports of food from abroad.[31] Moreover, the transportation system, badly damaged by the war, was constantly disrupted by Communist sabotage, and the army claimed priority over whatever trains and trucks were operating. As a result, the shipping of grain added inordinately to the consumers' price and prevented farmers from receiving the full benefit of the operation of market forces. This is starkly revealed in the geographical disparities in food prices. In May of 1947, for example, rice in Shanghai cost over Y300,000 per shih-tan, in Hankow only Y170,000, and in Chungking a mere Y72,000.[32] At the same time, the cost of cloth, tools, seeds, fertilizers, and other goods needed by the farmers had risen sharply.[33] Farm labor, in particular, was expensive as a result of the shortage of working-age males, who had left the villages to serve in the army, evade the draft, or seek

TABLE 4

*Food Crop Production in 22 Provinces of Nationalist China, 1946–49*

(million shih-tan)

| Year | Rice | | Wheat | | Total food crop | |
|---|---|---|---|---|---|---|
| | Quantity | Index | Quantity | Index | Quantity | Index |
| 1931–37 | | | | | | |
| average | 911.9 | 100 | 434.9 | 100 | 2,783.8 | 100 |
| 1946 | 861.3 | 94.4 | 454.7 | 105.0 | 2,785.5 | 100.1 |
| 1947 | 873.7 | 95.8 | 472.9 | 108.8 | 2,773.1 | 99.6 |
| 1948*a* | [876.4] | 96.1 | [479.6] | 110.3 | | |
| 1949*a* | [810.7] | 88.9 | [450.1] | 103.5 | | |

SOURCES: For 1931–37 average, *China Handbook, 1937–1945*, p. 433; for 1946 and 1947, *China Handbook, 1950*, pp. 538–39, 543, 545; for 1948 and 1949, Chou Shun-hsin, p. 93.

NOTE: 1 *shih-tan* = 1 hectoliter = 2.84 U.S. bushels.

*a*The bracketed figures for rice and wheat in these years are extrapolations from the index numbers provided by Chou.

better lives in the cities.[34] Rising costs of production, therefore, eroded the farmers' profit margins.[35]

Markets for nonfood crops had also dipped sharply from prewar days. The use of plastic reduced foreign demand for pig bristles; nylon in women's stockings now largely replaced silk, which had long been one of China's major export products. During the war, too, India and Ceylon had displaced China as major suppliers of the world's tea. The production and export of these commodities therefore dropped dramatically from prewar levels. Raw silk exports in 1946 were but one-eighth of the 1936 figure; tea, one-ninth; pig bristles, one-half; and tung oil, one-fourth.[36]

There was, by contrast, an unquenchable demand for raw cotton on the part of China's own textile mills. But the harvest of raw cotton during 1946–48 never rose to more than 66 percent of prewar levels, largely because the chief cotton-producing areas in Hupeh, Hopei, Shantung, and northern Kiangsu were the areas most disrupted by civil war. Dislocation of the transport system in North China was a further complication. As a consequence, the important textile industry had to rely on large infusions of raw cotton from the United States, India, and Egypt rather than on native production.[37]

Although these several economic factors caused considerable hardship in the villages, the exactions of the government, the corruption among lower-level officials, and military conscription continued to be the sources of the peasants' most bitter grievances. A special commissioner of the Control Yüan in Yunnan and Kweichow remarked in 1947 that "the impoverishment of the rural areas has now become extreme . . . and nothing creates greater suffering than does the land tax."[38] Participants in the Land and Grain Conference, held in July 1947, likewise expressed concern about the problem. The participants in this conference, high-level officials from both central and local governments, concluded that the whole system of land taxes was onerous and inequitable not because the quotas were unduly heavy, but because of defects in the administration of the system. Chiang Kai-shek set the tone for this criticism in his opening remarks to the conference, asserting that, "Now, rich families (*ta-hu*) in all the provinces usually do not pay the grain levies."[39] Several members of the Control Yüan elaborated on this complaint, telling the conference, "most of those who pay just a little [of the land tax] are the large landlords of the rich and grand families, whereas most of those who pay large amounts are usually the lower and middle strata of small landlords, landowners who cultivate their own fields, and part-owners–part-tenants."[40] Commenting on the conference, the official *Chung-yang jih-pao* added that the wealthy landlords, acting in concert with local officials, "pass on the burden of the levies to the suffering and inarticulate masses. Most of the common people do not understand the law; how can they resist the extortions of the lesser officials (*hsü-li*)?"[41]

The conference participants recognized that the land taxes per se constituted but a part of the farmers' burden. Military supplies and the expenses of hsien government, they observed, were largely supplied through t'an-p'ai. Because these were customarily administered by pao heads, who were seldom publicly accountable for their actions, "the evils are endless."[42] Transporting the tax grains, according to the conferees, also added greatly to the taxpayers' burdens.[43] Underlying the conference discussions was a concern that the peasants were on the verge of revolt. The participants therefore warned against a government proposal to perpetuate the system of compulsory borrowing of grain. Only four months earlier, government authorities had announced cessation of that policy; if that decision were now reversed, it might provoke widespread peasant opposition. "I am afraid," declared one participant, "that this will exceed the furthest limits of what they can bear." [44]

The government in 1947, however, could not lighten the farmers' burden. According to Premier Chang Ch'ün, the army and the government were suffering serious grain shortages. The compulsory borrowing of grain could not, therefore, be discontinued. [45] Not only did the government restore the system of compulsory borrowing, but its need for grain became more pressing as the war with the Communists continued. For 1948, Nanking consequently boosted the rate of the land tax. [46] By this time, however, the regime's ability to extract resources from the countryside had sharply diminished. The spread of Communist influence constricted the areas subject to Nationalist authority; even in villages nominally under the government's sway, effective political control had substantially declined and, in all probability, administrative efficiency had reached a nadir. The actual amount of grain that the government collected in 1948, therefore, reached the lowest level since 1941. (See Table 3 in Chapter 2.) Although precise figures are lacking, the tax share of national production was probably also at the lowest point since the introduction of the tax-in-kind.

The government's inability to enforce compliance with the land tax was but one manifestation of the general decline in peasant respect for constituted authority. Tenants, too, held back their rents, and several reports told of landlords organizing land-rent collection offices, which used force to collect their due (often in cooperation with government authorities). In at least some instances, tenants numbering several thousands rioted in opposition to these coercive tactics. [47]

No form of government activity created more distress for the peasants, however, than military conscription. The system, whose operation depended upon conscription officers suffering from the inflation and upon pao-chia heads defending their private interests, was frighteningly corrupt, inequitable, and cruel. So fearful of military service were the peasants that they fled their homes at the reported approach of conscription teams. By 1948, therefore, these teams usually conducted their work at night, descending upon villages while the men and boys were in their beds. Those who had the money for bribes would be set free; the others would be dragged off to "fight" the Communists.[48] The purchase of substitutes also continued to be a major source of bodies, or at least of numbers, for the army.[49] The entire conscription system sapped the morale and undercut the livelihood of the peasants. It also produced recruits who not only lacked a commitment to fight the Communists but felt a bitter resentment against the government in whose army they served.[50]

By late 1947 and 1948, the very fabric of rural society seemed to be unraveling. Banditry, the traditional sign of feeble political control and deteriorating economic conditions, was pervasive.[51] The inflated currency inspired so little confidence that exchange payments—such as land sales, bride prices, purchases of oxen or furniture, workers' wages, and loans—were being conducted by barter.[52] Villagers who did hold money, moreover, like their counterparts in the cities, spent it quickly, more often than previously on drinking, whoring, and especially gambling.[53] In reaction to the growing social and political turmoil and diminished physical security in the villages, landlords fled the countryside for the relative security of walled towns and the larger cities—often leaving behind, to be sure, local toughs to protect their properties and to extract rents from the tenants.[54] Ordinary peasants, too, abandoned the farms, becoming recruits to the growing ranks of the hungry and destitute, many of whom died in the streets and alleyways of the cities. (According to the government, 10 million people were threatened with starvation in 1948; 48 million—about one out of every ten Chinese—were refugees.[55]) The most desperate reportedly sold their wives and daughters—in 1946, the price of 15- and 16-year-old girls in

Chekiang was said to be Y4,ooo, about the cost of just 2–3 pounds of rice. Others reportedly took poison or threw themselves and their families into wells.[56] These tales of pathos may have been exaggerated or fabricated. There is no reason to doubt, however, that much of rural China lay in frightening desolation during these postwar years.

## Land-Reform Proposals

It is ironic—nay, sad and even tragic—that only as late as 1948, on the eve of the final collapse, did the gravity and consequences of the rural situation suddenly become apparent to leading figures in the Nationalist area. Like a dying man suddenly perceiving the errors of a misspent life, they now realized the mistake of having neglected the problems of the farmers. At the eleventh hour, therefore, they heatedly discussed how to end landlord exploitation and to change the tenancy system as a means of defusing the Communist insurrection.

This development must be seen in historical perspective, however, because Kuomintang leaders had advocated agrarian reform for close to five decades. "Equalization of Land Holdings" and "Land to the Tiller" had been cornerstones of Sun Yat-sen's revolutionary program. In 1930 the recently established National Government promulgated a Land Law sufficiently progressive and practical for the Communists to adopt it substantially unchanged during the New Democracy period. It also provided the model for the land-reform program in Taiwan in the early 1950's. Yet during most of its tenure on the mainland, the National Government had rarely acted on its commitments to the farmers. As Chiang Kai-shek admitted in 1946, land reform had not been carried out, because there had been "insufficient administrative push."[57] Although he did not say so, an important reason for that lack of push was that he himself had consistently placed a low priority on the rural problem.

Still, there had always been some within the Kuomintang who had attempted to implement the party's program of land reform.[58] In May of 1945, for example, at the Sixth Kuomintang Party Congress, a coterie of youngish "radicals" in the party suc-

cessfully agitated for a party resolution calling for the distribution of all farm land to the tillers and for the end of landlordism.
Immediately after the war, too, the government again ordered
that all rents be reduced by 25 percent. All these assertions of
good intention came to naught. As a result of opposition by con-
servatives associated with the CC Clique, the Central Executive
Committee in March 1947 abandoned the party plank of immediate land redistribution and adopted instead a program of more
moderate reform.[59] Opposition to land reform was even more
bitter at the local level. In Hunan, for example, one would-be re-
former was assassinated. And everywhere landlords frustrated
attempts to reduce rents or otherwise encroach on their preroga-
tives.[60] Two years after the end of the war, therefore, as a result
of inertia and obstructionism, the Nationalists had not perceptibly advanced toward their stated goal of agricultural reform.

By 1948, however, the Communist "insurrection" had moved
onto the offensive. A sense of desperation now filled the air, and
many in the Nationalist camp suddenly realized that the livelihood of ignorant and unwashed peasants was in some fundamental way related to the debility of their own government and
to the dynamism of the Communists. Rural reform therefore
acquired a new and uncommon urgency. Journals, newspapers,
and public meetings provided forums for specialists, all of whom
proffered solutions for the rural crisis. The Legislative Yüan, beginning in July, undertook a major discussion of the agrarian
problem. In September of 1948, 86 members of the Yüan finally
presented a bill that would abolish the system of tenancy and
make every farmer an owner of his land. Proponents of this bill
explained that the land problem was so serious that it was "the
source of all disasters and the key to the nation's survival." By
eliminating landlordism, they declared, "the treacherous bandits will be unable to create disorder, and the cause of rebellion
can be quashed."[61]

Within the administrative organs of the government, too, a
concern for land reform born of political panic led to the procla-
mation of a series of measures designed to win the affection of the
peasants. First, in the pacification areas—that is, areas recov-

ered from the Communists or close to Communist-held bases—
the central government ordered that rents be reduced by one-
third. It also formulated plans to buy up landlord holdings and
distribute the land to the cultivators.[62] Next, the government
ordered the National Land Administration to draw up plans to
nationalize all land in the country. Landlordism would thus finally be eliminated. "The Government," reported the army's official *Ho-p'ing jih-pao* in September 1948, "is fully determined
to carry out these measures."[63] In addition, several provincial
governments—from Manchuria to Kwangtung—in rapid succession during mid-1948 also proclaimed rent-reduction and
other agrarian-reform measures.[64]

These plans and proposals for attacking the landlord system
inevitably provoked a heated debate. Some opponents passion-
ately charged that proponents of reform had fallen into a trap set
by the Communists. Others argued sophistically that although
Sun Yat-sen had indeed advocated "Land to the Tiller," he had
not intended that nontillers could not own land.[65] More responsible critics like Tung Shih-chin, director of the China Peasant
Union, argued that the root of China's rural crisis was not landlordism at all, but the general process of rural impoverishment
that had resulted from primitive methods of production, political insecurity, exploitative taxes, natural calamities, and excess
population.[66]

As the whole Nationalist regime began caving in during late
1948, the Legislative Yüan continued fruitlessly and endlessly to
debate the problem. The reforms of the various government
administrations were similarly largely stillborn, for even if the
will to reform were real, the hour was late and the revolutionary
tide was irresistible.[67] The one lasting fruit of the Nationalist
agrarian reformers was the creation in 1948 of the Sino-American Joint Commission on Rural Reconstruction, which subsequently played a leading role in the agricultural renascence of
Taiwan.[68]

## The Peasants' Role in the Revolution

In the French and Russian revolutions, the peasantry rose in
vast storms of violence, attacking the power, property, and priv-

ileges of the landlord classes. In both revolutions, these were acts of spontaneous rebellion, unguided and even feared by antigovernment conspirators in the cities. In both revolutions, too, the peasant uprisings contributed critically to the social radicalization of political protest. Without them, the nascent revolutions might have faltered at the stage of political, constitutional reform.[69]

Although the Chinese revolution of 1949 is widely regarded as the classic example of a modern peasant revolution, the role of the peasants was markedly different from what it was in France and Russia. In China, peasant discontent was manifestly deep and was indeed vented in riots, pandemic banditry, and flight from the villages. But peasant revolts in China never in themselves threatened to overturn the socioeconomic order in the countryside as they did in the European revolutions. Indeed, Chinese peasants rarely attacked the existing socioeconomic institutions until the Communists' military or political presence assured them of protection from the retribution of the former elites, and until the Communists offered them the prospect, through either propaganda or achieved reforms, of a more attractive way of life than they had known under the old order. Communist leadership, organization, agitation, and protection, in other words, usually preceded the peasants' direct attacks on the social and economic institutions of rural China.

Yet even in the Nationalist areas the peasants' contribution to the revolutionary outcome in 1949 was real, perhaps even decisive. But it was indirect. Their contribution lay, first and foremost, in depriving the National Government of grain, money, and men. In 1947, for example, when nominally the Nationalists' territorial control reached its greatest extent during the postwar period, the central government collected only 38 million shih-tan of grain by means of the combined land taxes. This was 57 percent of the amount collected in 1942, when Nationalist control was confined largely to the western interior provinces, and far short of the government's projected needs.

Government grain collections likewise fell short of the assigned quotas. Official data reveal that the government collected only 78 percent of the quota for the combined land taxes in 1946, and only 65 percent in 1947—by contrast with 104 percent in 1942. (See Table 3 in Chapter 2.) Even these official figures, however, exaggerate the rate of collection, because the quotas had originally been set much higher. In 1946, for example, the original quota had been 99 million shih-tan (72.6 shih-tan for the land tax and 26.4 million shih-tan for compulsory borrowing); subsequently the quota was revised downward to 54 million shih-tan. In 1947, too, the quota was reduced from 80 million to 59 million shih-tan. Measured against the original, rather than the revised, quotas, the rates of collection during 1946 and 1947 were only 43 percent and 48 percent, respectively.[70] Figures on the collection of the land taxes in 1948 and 1949 are, unfortunately, unavailable. However, the amounts of grain collected were presumably much reduced as a result of, among other things, shrinking territorial control and progressively more unsettled political and economic conditions.

The deterioration of the government's capacity to mobilize the grain resources of the country was symptomatic of its political enfeeblement and contributed importantly to its fiscal bankruptcy, a factor that may ultimately have been the critical cause of its demise. As Harry Eckstein, one of the more insightful students of the revolutionary process, has noted, revolutions have customarily been preceded by functional failures, especially in financial administration, "perhaps because finance impinges on the ability of governments to perform all their functions."[71]

Surely this "functional failure" to mobilize the grain and other resources of the country had devastating consequences for the National Government, especially because the rural sector had served during the war and civil war as the central pillar of its revenue structure.[72] By 1948, only 21 percent of the National Government's expenditures were met through taxation; another 11 percent were met through such measures as sales of public properties, profits on government enterprises, and sales of bonds; the remaining 68 percent had to be met by issuing new, unbacked currency. This substantially contributed to the fatally soaring inflation.[73]

The fiscal failure also directly affected the fighting ability of the army. Without adequate grain supplies, troops were having to go hungry, or subsist on poor-quality rations, or forage locally. An official investigative team in North China concluded in the fall of 1947 that these factors contributed to the low fighting spirit of the troops and to the poor relations between the army and the civilian population.[74] Troop morale was damaged also by the growing discontent in the villages. As the *Chien-sien jih-pao*, a Shanghai paper with Kuomintang connections, concluded in late 1948, the spirit of the troops was "fundamentally a problem of the morale of the civilian population, and if the morale of the civilian population is low, it will affect that of the troops."[75] Communist propagandists were keenly aware of this link between deteriorating conditions in the villages and the diminishing willingness of the Nationalist troops to fight. They therefore plied the opposing side with pamphlets telling how government exactions were stripping farmers of all their grain and how the people were therefore rising in hungry protest.[76] Although the link between troop morale and village conditions is difficult to document—for example, it is unclear how word of conditions back home was communicated to troops at the front, because letter-writing to soldiers was seemingly rare—it is significant that military authorities in 1947 returned from the front lines asserting that effective mobilization would be impossible until the government's farm policies were improved.[77] Indeed, it is plausible that the soldiers, learning of hunger and dissatisfaction in their home villages, would have questioned whether they were fighting in a cause worth risking their lives for.

Finally, the Nationalist failure in the countryside—the regime's inability to assure land, security, and food to the peasants—sharply diminished the respect the peasants held for the government. The government, that is, was losing legitimacy. The heavy and frequently inequitable exactions, the corruption, and the bias that most officials showed for the landlord class against the tenants,[78] all undercut the authority of the government and the social value traditionally attached to licit behavior. As a result, peasants evaded the tax collectors and fled the conscription officers, presumably with little or no disapprobation from fellow villagers. In extreme cases they became bandits, thereby heightening the insecurity in the countryside, reducing production, and imposing further burdens upon the vitiated Nationalist administration.

In the Nationalist area during the civil war, therefore, the peasants did not rise, as the French peasants did in 1789, in a broadscale attack on the old order. In important, indirect ways, however, they withheld their support. In the Communist areas, by contrast, although most peasants probably remained essentially apolitical, they tended to cooperate with the insurgent regime. Some, particularly the youth, actively supported the Communists. The result was, in effect, to create a pressure differential: little pressure (or support) on the Nationalist side; some pressure (support) on the Communist side. A partial political vacuum favoring the Communists was thereby created.

In view of the factors explored in this and the previous chapter, it seems manifest that the inability of the National Government to generate support and cooperation among the mass of the rural population seriously affected its viability and contributed importantly to the political and military dénouement in 1949. That there were alternatives to the prevailing policy toward the villages was shown in 1948, when responsible Nationalist authorities began taking a serious interest in land reform. By then, of course, it was too late. If the Nationalists had undertaken those reforms shortly after their accession to power, however, the history of modern China would today tell a very different story. Nor is this view only the result of hindsight, for there were in 1928–29 many Kuomintang members who advocated precisely the kind of policies that might have generated peasant support and cooperation. As the Conclusion of this study will show, however, Chiang Kai-shek suppressed those "leftist" members of the Kuomintang. The legacy of that suppression was, in substantial measure, the Communist victory two decades later.

CHAPTER 4

# Politics Within the Regime:
# The Youth Corps

At the beginning of the Sino-Japanese War, Nationalist China was stronger and more unified than at any time in the ten years of its existence. Still, large problems persisted, and Chiang Kai-shek was convinced that China could effectively wage war and build the subsequent peace only if he could increase the moral and political unity of the nation. China must have, he said, "one faith, one party, and one will."[1]

To attain this goal, Chiang endeavored to unite all the various Chinese political parties into a single party shortly after the fighting erupted. He even offered to change the organization and name of the Kuomintang if that would facilitate the creation of a single and unified political body. The Young China Party accepted Chiang's plan, and the National Socialist Party of Carsun Chang expressed itself ready to negotiate the question. Chiang's plan to achieve "one faith, one party, and one will" foundered, however, when the Communists, although expressing a willingness to cooperate, rejected the proposal to merge with the Kuomintang.[2] The People's Political Council, a consultative body representing diverse political groups instituted in 1938, was the closest Chiang came to uniting the several non-Kuomintang groups under his leadership.[3]

Chiang's second political concern during the early months of the war—and it troubled him deeply—was that the Kuomintang itself was decrepit and ineffectual. "Our party," he declared to the opening session of the Extraordinary Congress of the Kuomintang on March 29, 1938, "has already become virtually an empty shell, without any real substance; the form of the party persists, but the spirit of the party has almost completely died out."[4] To utter such words, Chiang said, pained him profoundly, but the Nationalist revolution was on the brink of extinction, and unless the Kuomintang revived itself now, it would not be given a second chance.

Chiang Kai-shek's evaluation of the Kuomintang in the early period of the war is of paramount significance, because it reveals that the Kuomintang's organizational enervation, which would become painfully evident late in the war, was already pervasive when the war began. "The most obvious defects of our party," Chiang told the Extraordinary Congress, "are that organization is so lax and discipline so loose that the spirit of the party is feeble and dissipated, and the foundation of the party is wholly lacking in substance. There are no deeply rooted or real achievements in organization, training, or propaganda; the work of party headquarters at all levels tends to be formalistic, and the offices are all bureaucratized."[5] As for the party members themselves, Chiang found that most of them "appear dejected, their living is soft, they lack enthusiasm, and their work is slothful. Furthermore, just like ordinary commoners, they seek ease and pleasure, even struggling for power and fighting for their selfish interests. . . . How can they be revolutionary party members?"[6]

On another occasion, just before the Extraordinary Congress, Chiang had also complained of party members that

(1) They serve as officials, but do not work;

(2) They have selfish interests, but do not have public interests; they identify only with themselves, but not with anything beyond themselves;

(3) They place great value upon power and position, but place no value upon responsibility;

(4) They heed the superstructure, but ignore the foundation; they are concerned about party members, but not about the masses; they are arrogant, extravagant, wasteful, and lazy; they regard themselves as great and powerful, but they are ignorant of the people's sufferings and are isolated from the people;

(5) They have an organization, but no training; a party charter, but no discipline; policies, but no implementation.[7]

Because of the decrepitude of the party, Chiang declared, Kuomintang members who were capable and dedicated left, and talented persons outside were not attracted to it. The result, he complained, was that "the party within is hollow, weak, and rotten. . . . With party work so lax, how can it promote revolutionary affairs?"[8] "Party members," he added, "have almost become a special class, and the party is in fact unable to help the people; naturally it cannot guide the people. The people do not feel that the existence of the party is of any benefit to them; they are not only indifferent toward the party, they even develop animus toward it."[9]

## Formation and Shifting Goals of the Corps

It was within this context of Chiang Kai-shek's search for unity and his disillusionment with the Kuomintang that the Three People's Principles Youth Corps was born. Planning for such an organization had actually begun before the war, in May of 1937, but it was not until the Extraordinary Congress met in Wuchang that a proposal to create the corps was officially adopted. Thereafter, organization proceeded slowly; the first year of the Youth Corps' formal existence was devoted primarily to planning and preparation. Although General Ch'en Ch'eng formally held the post of secretary-general, his many other duties prevented him from assuming full-time leadership of the corps; Chu Chia-hua consequently served as acting secretary-general. In 1940, General Chang Chih-chung took over as secretary-general. Effective leadership of the corps, however, probably fell to lesser cadres. K'ang Tse seems to have been the dominant personality in the corps until about 1944; thereafter, at least according to some reports, Chiang Kai-shek's son, Chiang Ching-kuo, took a leading role.[10]

In creating the Youth Corps, Chiang Kai-shek hoped to provide a framework within which all true supporters of the revolution and the war of resistance could set aside their differences and work together in a common effort. He envisioned the corps as including all the competing factions within the Kuomintang —and to this end the Extraordinary Congress ordered the abolition of all "small organizations," which meant factions such as the Fu-hsing-she (Blue Shirts) and the Ch'ing-pai-she (CC Clique).[11] He also hoped to attract those leaders in society—such as the Szechwanese entrepreneur Lu Tso-fu and the economist Franklin Ho (Ho Lien)—who because of their distaste for the Kuomintang had not affiliated with the Nationalist movement.[12] Through these efforts Chiang expected to attract the nation's youth, who largely felt a revulsion for the Kuomintang. Consequently, the Extraordinary Congress abolished the system of probationary membership in the Kuomintang, so that youth could henceforth enroll not in the Kuomintang but directly in the corps.

In sum, Chiang's purpose in forming the Youth Corps was to form a new revolutionary organization that, by eliminating the divisive quarrels of the past and by attracting the nation's youth, would take up the revolutionary tasks the Kuomintang had forsaken. His expectations for the new organization were lofty. He declared in 1938, for instance, that "I regard the life or death, the survival or destruction, of our nation and the people as hinging entirely upon the formation of this corps." "The youth," he continued, "are the revolutionary vanguard and the new life of the nation. There is no social progress or political reform that does not depend upon the stimulus of youth as its primary force."[13]

Youth, he asserted, had provided the principal force in the revolution against the Manchus and again in the Northern Expedition against the warlords. Now, at this crucial stage of the nation's history, he was looking to the youth once again to "serve as the vanguard in creating a new China." They were, declared Chiang, "to establish in the very near future (*tsui-chin chiang-lai*) the cadre foundation of the nation's social reconstruction." And the mandate of the corps was "to gather the nation's youth to carry out the Outline of National Resistance and Reconstruction, and to unite with superior revolutionary elements in order to strengthen the force of the revolution."[14]

By creating the Youth Corps, Chiang Kai-shek hoped to resolve the political crisis then confronting the nation. In doing so, however, he disregarded or minimized the problem of what the relationship of the new organization would be to the old Kuomintang. A political ambiguity was thus created that never was resolved. In calling for the formation of the corps, the Extraordinary Congress had stated: "To strengthen the party's [i.e., the

Kuomintang's] organization and to firm up the party's foundation . . . [we resolve to] establish the Youth Corps which, under a united organization, shall train the nation's youth and cause everyone to believe in the Three People's Principles."[15] This resolution seemed clearly to indicate that the Kuomintang held primacy over the corps, and that the corps was to act in the service of the Kuomintang.

Yet, in initial statements to the Youth Corps itself, Chiang Kai-shek and Secretary-General Ch'en Ch'eng were notably silent about the relationship between the Kuomintang and the corps; moreover, in their comments they appeared to be investing the corps with the leading role in the revolutionary tasks then confronting the nation. Chiang on June 16, 1938, for instance, declared that the youth "should cause this organization [the corps] to become *the only organization (wei-i te tsu-chih)* to gather together the nation's superior, ardent youth *and revolutionary elements*."[16] This extraordinary statement—that the Youth Corps was to be the sole organization not only for youth but for other "revolutionary elements" as well—would seemingly leave no revolutionary role for the Kuomintang.

The interpretation that the Youth Corps was intended, at least by some of its leaders, to assume the leading revolutionary role in China is supported also by the fact that the corps' charter initially stipulated that members were to be between the ages of 18 and 38 *sui*. (Corps cadres, and members with special permission, were exempt from even these age limitations.)[17] The corps was thus spreading a broad net, and—potentially at least—leaving Kuomintang membership only to the nonrevolutionary middle-aged and those in their dotage. This impression was conveyed also by Ch'en Ch'eng, who declared, "the Three People's Principles Youth Corps has an unconventional definition of the limits of 'youth.' The corps' leader [Chiang Kai-shek] instructed us that who is a youth in the Youth Corps is something not necessarily determined by age. In our view, anyone who has revolutionary enthusiasm and possesses a youthful and forward-looking spirit, even though he is overage, is still a revolutionary youth."[18]

In this same speech, Ch'en Ch'eng did state that "the birth of this corps can also be said to be the birth of this party's [i.e., the Kuomintang's] new revolutionary life."[19] Ch'en Ch'eng therefore envisioned the Kuomintang as remaining in existence, and there are even indications that he saw it as having a leading role over the corps.[20] At the very least, however, Chiang Kai-shek and Ch'en Ch'eng held ambitious expectations for the newly established Youth Corps, and they bestowed upon it such a broad mandate that its relationship with the Kuomintang was inevitably ambiguous.

From the beginning there had been opposition to the formation of the Youth Corps. Some, even those who had acquiesced in its creation, argued that it should be simply a social club for youth.[21] Official histories of the Youth Corps, however, state that Chiang Kai-shek disregarded such objections and insisted on investing the Youth Corps with substantive powers. "This party," reads one such history, referring to the Kuomintang, "has had a bright and glorious history in leading the revolution. But this party has already engaged in over fifty years of struggle, and in truth there must be a consolidation of a new force to enhance and glorify this party's revolutionary spirit."[22]

Chiang Kai-shek's expectation that the Youth Corps would concentrate the revolutionary elements into a unified force was quickly disappointed. Soon the corps began fighting with the Kuomintang over jurisdictional authority, competing with it for recruits, and openly scoffing at it. So serious did the situation become that by March 1939, just one year after the official decision to form it, Chiang Kai-shek completely altered his conception of the Youth Corps. Whereas he had originally conceived it as assuming a leading—if not the leading—political role in the Nationalist regime, he now reduced it to indoctrinating and controlling the youth and preparing them for future membership in the Kuomintang. Inevitably, he said, the work of the corps had political implications, but it should consist primarily of education.[23] The corps' charter was also revised in June 1939, and the age limits of members were tightened to 16–25 *sui*.[24] Chiang Kai-shek and Ch'en Ch'eng, who had previously devoted much attention in their speeches to the shortcomings of the Kuomintang, now spoke instead of the moral shortcomings of youth and of the Youth Corps' task of training and leading the nation's young people.[25] The weaknesses and perversities of members of the Kuomintang were no longer stressed. Chiang and Ch'en continued to assert that the Youth Corps had an important role to play, but now they spoke of the primacy of the Kuomintang; now they averred that corps members were but the reserve army of the Kuomintang and the new "corpuscles" that would bring added vitality to the Kuomintang. They also declared repeatedly that the corps was to be "under the guidance of the Kuomintang."[26]

Having adopted this new conception of the Youth Corps, Chiang Kai-shek admonished corps members to accept their subordinate role. "If you think that the corps is intended to replace the party," he warned, "or that the relationship is between one that is important and one that is unimportant, or between one that is waning and one that is waxing, this is absolutely a mistaken concept. . . . I can say that . . . it is the corps of the party, and not some kind of organization outside of or in opposition to the party. Since it is the party's corps, corps members and party members are naturally comrades. . . . Between them, how can there be any suspicions?"[27]

The disease to which Chiang Kai-shek's original conception of the Youth Corps succumbed was factionalism. In forming the corps he had hoped to banish that political malignancy, conceiving of the Youth Corps as a new and unified revolutionary organization that would transcend the old factional rivalries. To draft the by-laws of the new corps, he had selected three men representing widely divergent wings of the regime: K'ang Tse, from the Blue Shirts; Ch'en Li-fu, leader of the CC Clique; and T'an P'ing-shan, a leftist and former leader of the illegal Third Party, who had only recently been readmitted to the Kuomintang. Members of the corps' 31-man Executive Secretariat (*kan-shih-hui*), equivalent to the Central Executive Committee of the Kuomintang, were similarly drawn from diverse segments of society and included youth leaders and such non-Kuomintang figures as Lu Tso-fu and Franklin Ho.[28]

These organizational measures had merely papered over the preexisting factional fissures, and the struggles that beset the corps during 1938–39 were essentially a continuation of the old rivalry between the Blue Shirts and the CC Clique. The Blue Shirts had disbanded in accordance with the resolution of the Extraordinary Congress, but from the beginning the working nucleus of the Youth Corps consisted predominantly of former members of that clandestine group—military officers, for the most part, and especially graduates of the Whampoa Military Academy, who aspired to a political role but for whom there was no place of influence within the Kuomintang itself.[29] Initially, the CC Clique had fought to establish a leading role in the corps,[30] but former Blue Shirts soon controlled the critical positions in the leadership. K'ang Tse, for example, headed the important Organization Department. And Liu Chien-ch'ün in 1939 became secretary of the Central Corps Headquarters, a position comparable to that of secretary-general of the Kuomintang.[31] Indeed, several people—including such former high officials in the corps as Huang Chi-lu (director of the Department of Propaganda) and Jen Cho-hsüan (better known as Yeh Ch'ing; a member of the Standing Committee of the Executive Secretariat)—today insist that the corps was simply a metamorphosis of the Blue Shirts.[32] In fact, however, the Blue Shirt faction was never able wholly to dominate the Youth Corps. Several members of the Standing Committee of the Executive Secretariat, for example— such as Ch'en Li-fu and Ku Cheng-kang—were members of the CC Clique.[33] Actual operations of the corps, nevertheless, were in large part directed by cadres associated with the former Blue Shirts.

## Activities and Membership

Following the reformulation of its goals in 1939, the Youth Corps focused especially on the nation's students. It organized branches in each of the higher-middle schools, technical schools, and universities to engage in what it very broadly defined as "propaganda" and political training. Among the more successful undertakings were month-long summer camps, where young people engaged in political study and swam, hiked, and played in attractive outdoor settings.[34] The corps also established drama and music societies, and provided vocational guidance. Publication of newspapers, journals, and pamphlets was strongly emphasized; in 1944 the corps issued 345 publications, 208 journals, 10 pamphlets, and 127 newspapers.[35] The corps also directed the Chinese Boy Scout Association.[36]

There were covert aspects to Youth Corps' activities. Its members allegedly "spied" on fellow students and teachers, reporting subversive sentiments or activities. In 1940, Chiang Kai-shek urged an end to such spying, but the practice continued in varying degrees on all campuses in the Nationalist area.[37]

Behind Japanese lines, Youth Corps activities tended to stress not just political indoctrination but espionage and terroristic operations, especially against collaborators with the enemy. Few details of these operations are known, although an official source states that in 1945 the corps had 128 units, with over 95,000 members, operating behind enemy lines. Corps operations were apparently most successful in the Shanghai area, but cells were established in most of the occupied provinces. A total of 272 corps members were reported killed in these covert operations.[38]

In the Communist areas, too, the corps was very active, the Communists complaining in 1943 that the corps was operating in all their "border areas." Most of the Youth Corps members in the Communist bases were, according to a Communist source, local ruffians (*liu-mang*) or children of the landlord class. In any event, the undercover operations of the Youth Corps included propaganda, destroying the reconstruction work of the Communists, sabotage, and even assassination.[39] Speaking about Kuomintang secret-service activities generally, and not solely about the Youth Corps' operations, a Communist source in 1943 admitted that their destruction was "very great."[40] In all likelihood, the clandestine operations of Youth Corps members were undertaken in cooperation with Tai Li's military secret service, which had spread a broad net of operatives behind enemy lines.[41]

Membership in the Youth Corps grew gradually but steadily. In late 1938 the corps had only 1,034 members, but it grew to

74,700 at the end of 1939; 232,245 at the end of 1940; 367,391 at the end of 1941; 423,144 in 1942; and just over a million in 1945. By 1947, when the corps was disbanded, it had reached a peak of about 1.4 million members. An analysis of membership figures in 1942 reveals that nearly half of the members (49 percent) were students, 38 percent were in government employ or private professionals, but a total of only 7 percent were employed in agriculture, industry, and commerce. Eighty-three percent were between the ages of 16 and 25 *sui*. The educational level was not notably high, with only 10 percent being university graduates, 62 percent having a middle-school education, and 28 percent having only a primary-school education. Seven percent of the members were women.[42]

The quality of the Youth Corps did not increase with its size. Although it was generally regarded as being more dynamic than the Kuomintang, it had many of the same organizational problems as the parent body. Resolutions presented by corps representatives to their First National Congress in 1943 complained, for example, that most members, and even some cadres, possessed an inadequate understanding of the corps' doctrines. Another resolution warned that discipline was so poorly enforced that "the unity [of the corps] is weak, the organization is lax, and some members regard the corps' commands as empty words. The ardor of the truly dedicated minority gradually turns cold."[43]

The brightest and most idealistic young people, moreover, shunned membership in the corps, which instead attracted the more opportunistic elements among the youth.[44] The editor of a Youth Corps periodical declared in 1941, for example, that "During the past several years, [the work of training the youth] has had some effect, but generally speaking we must say that it has failed." Chief among this editor's complaints was that the training provided the corps members had no relevance to the needs either of the youths themselves or of the nation, and that the members were simply using the corps to advance their careers. "To speak impolitely," he wrote, "the goal for most of them is simply to become acquainted with a few high officials and important people and with their circle of followers, in order to facilitate their struggle for position and their fight for the rice bowl."[45]

At the first corps congress, Chiang Kai-shek expressed his disappointment in similar terms. He complained that both ordinary members and cadres of the corps ignored the needs of the nation and used their positions in the corps simply for personal advancement. "This," he declared, "is the reason why society holds the corps in disrespect, and is also the greatest defect preventing the development of ardent faith among corps members."[46] Chiang also observed that the work of the corps had become formalized and bureaucratized. Corps cadres simply sat in their offices and handled official documents, and he implored them to get out and become familiar with actual conditions so that they could attain practical results.[47]

Sun Fo, son of Sun Yat-sen, suggested yet another reason the corps failed to attract a broad following among the youth. Speaking to a Youth Corps conference in 1944, Sun asserted that the corps' entire approach was wrong. Its method of political indoctrination was to teach the Three People's Principles by rote. It also placed an inordinate stress on military regimentation. As a result, he said, young people exposed to Youth Corps training "become rather like puppets. . . . The first thing they learned to perfection is how to click heels at the mention of, or mere reference to, the Supreme Leader [i.e., Chiang Kai-shek]."[48]

## Continuing Conflict with the Kuomintang

Although Chiang Kai-shek in 1939 had changed his conception of the Youth Corps—demoting it, in effect, from the leading agency of political leadership to a training vehicle for future members of the Kuomintang—friction and conflicts with the Kuomintang continued. In 1940, the corps headquarters published a short volume entitled *The Relationship Between the Party and the Corps (Tang yü t'uan te kuan-hsi)*, designed to resolve the conflicts between the two organizations. Two years later those conflicts still remained, for the volume was republished. In placating the competing organizations, the regime's leadership

stressed to both party and corps members that they were comrades dedicated to the same ideology and loyal to the same
leader, and that they therefore ought not slander each other or
struggle for power. Corps members were also reminded that
"This corps is the youth organization under this party's system—that is, it is the corps of the party—and definitely is not an
organization outside the party or opposed to the party."[49] An
ambiguity in the relationship nonetheless remained, for the
corps was not, strictly speaking, subordinate to the party. The
party ought not, therefore, "command" (*chih-hui*) the corps but
only "guide" (*chih-tao*) it. And the corps might, in turn, "guide"
the party.[50]

Admonitions did nothing to improve the corps' relations with
the Kuomintang, and in July of 1941 Chiang Kai-shek decried
the inability of these two organizations to cooperate. "Regardless of what we do," he lamented, "not only do we not attain the
utility of a cooperative division of labor, but virtually everywhere we conflict with each other. Thus we now have many
places where the corps and the party are unable to act in har-
mony, and even more commonly there is conflict between corps
members and non-corps members."[51]

A prime source of discord was the competition for members.
Although age limits for corps members had been fixed, neither
organization observed them. The result, according to a resolution presented to the corps' national congress in 1943, was that
the corps and the party "put all their efforts into absorbing new
members. But absorbing turns into struggle; struggle turns into
attacks; and attacks turn into slander. In this way, the party and
the corps become opposed to each other."[52]

Even among the top leadership of the corps the conflict was
intense, because some of the corps' leaders who were members
of the CC Clique felt greater ties of loyalty to the Kuomintang
than to the corps itself. Such people were called *tang-fang*, or
"party-side" members of the corps, and they stood in contrast to
*t'uan-fang*, or "corps-side" members, who were elements led by
the Blue Shirt faction. Presumably because of these internecine
struggles, the first national congress of the corps had to be re-

peatedly postponed with the explanation that conditions "were not yet ripe." When the congress finally did convene in March of 1943, the clashes between the tang-fang and the t'uan-fang were, as one participant recalled, "extremely heated."[53] In one episode, the two sides clashed over the fate of the corps' Cadres Training Class. The t'uan-fang proposed expanding it to the status of an academy, whereas the tang-fang wanted to *replace* it with a Central Cadres Academy. The difference between the two proposals, from this distance, appears slight, but substantive issues were presumably at stake. Finally, in a vote, the proposal to replace the old Training Class with a new academy carried the day. This revealed, Ch'en Tun-cheng asserted, "that the tang-fang [i.e., the CC Clique] stood supreme."[54] Ch'en's assessment pertained, however, only to the sessions of the national congress; among the rank and file of the corps, the t'uan-fang, or adherents of the former Blue Shirts, continued their preponderance.

As the numbers and strength of the Youth Corps increased, its conflicts with the Kuomintang intensified. In May 1945, for instance, when the Kuomintang finally convened a regular national congress, its sixth, after a hiatus of nearly ten years, Youth Corps leaders made a concerted effort to expand their influence within the party, especially by increasing their representation on the Central Executive Committee. By itself, the corps had only 60 representatives in that body, the total membership of which was over 600. The corps' representatives, therefore, formed an alliance with the Whampoa and Chu Chia-hua Cliques, and together these three factions controlled approximately half of the votes. By meeting each morning before the regular sessions of the congress, they were able to formulate common strategies and thereby mount a formidable challenge to their common rival, the CC Clique.[55] The struggle was acrimonious, and peace was restored to the congress only after Chiang Kai-shek personally intervened. "You should know," he reputedly told the Youth Corps representatives and other CC Clique rivals, "that I have handed the party over to them [i.e., the CC Clique] to manage. If not for them, the party would long ago have been finished.

Now, in making such a commotion opposing them you also oppose me. With regard to electing members of the Central Executive Committee, I will naturally look after people of all sides. Relax."[56]

By assuring the Youth Corps and its allies at the Sixth Party Congress that he would look after the interests of all factions, Chiang Kai-shek temporarily poured oil on the troubled waters. The basic sources of conflict and enmity between the Youth Corps and the CC Clique nonetheless remained, and the corps members' criticisms of the Kuomintang continued relentlessly.[57] The party, they charged, consisted of aged, superannuated, and corrupt bureaucrats, without energy or accomplishment. The Kuomintang had thus become an obstacle to the revolution, preventing the Youth Corps from attaining the goals of the Three People's Principles. Many corps members therefore advocated cutting loose from the Kuomintang, whereas others continued to think that the corps should replace the Kuomintang.[58]

At the second national congress of the corps, held at Lu-shan in September 1946, the question of the corps' future relationship with the Kuomintang became a topic of prolonged and heated debate. Some delegates, especially those representing students and local headquarters, advocated severing the relationship entirely and establishing the corps as a separate political party. Others, for the most part cadres in the corps' central headquarters, were somewhat more moderate. They argued that corps members should not concurrently hold membership in the Kuomintang, but they would not go so far as to form a separate party. Tang-fang, or members of the corps belonging to the CC Clique, however, bitterly opposed both these proposals, advocating instead maintenance of the status quo or even complete dissolution of the corps.[59]

At session after session of the Youth Corps congress, with General and Mme. Chiang Kai-shek observing the proceedings from seats among the representatives, the issue was vehemently and bitterly debated. Advocates of separation contended that at this critical juncture of history the nation needed a new and vital force to respond to the rebellion of the Communists. As long as the relationship with the Kuomintang continued, the old and ineffectual men in the party obstructed the revolutionary force of the Youth Corps. Arguing against separation, a representative named Huang warned that the corps, if it became a separate party, would probably rise in opposition to Kuomintang control of the government, just as the Communist Party had. Then, carried away by emotion, he shouted, "In my humble view, the party and the corps can never be separated. Mr. Chiang [Kaishek] is my venerated teacher. If he thinks that what I say makes no sense, then let him give me permission to commit suicide. I will hold no grudge. My coffin is ready." [60] Chiang, having listened to the debate in silence, was now challenged to resolve the issue. Standing, he declared that he fully agreed with Huang. A vote was taken, and the majority voted against separation. [61]

Elsewhere, however, the Youth Corps' struggle with the Kuomintang proceeded without letup. Following the Japanese surrender, the corps launched a major campaign to gain influence in local government. By March 1946, fully 62 percent of the corps members were reportedly engaged in work at the local level, some assuming posts as pao-chia chiefs, others as school principals. Many, too, won election to local representative assemblies. In Hunan, for example, 42 percent of the representatives in the provincial and hsien assemblies were members of the Youth Corps; in Fukien, the figure was 58 percent. [62]

## Merger with the Kuomintang

Elections to the National Assembly, the Legislative Yüan, and the Control Yüan scheduled for late 1947 provided the corps with an unprecedented opportunity to place its members in positions of political influence. But competition in the elections merely fueled the struggle with the Kuomintang. Details about the electoral campaigns are obscure. Liu Chien-ch'ün subsequently claimed, however, that the factional fighting generated by the elections was so disruptive that it contributed to the Communist victory. [63] Though electoral struggles between the corps and the Kuomintang erupted throughout the nation, they were most bitter in Hunan, where several party members were murdered by people acting on behalf of the corps. Indeed, the corps created such a reign of terror in Heng-yang that the party headquarters there demanded either adequate protection or permission for party members to withdraw from the entire area.[64]

These electioneering struggles infuriated Chiang Kai-shek, and he placed the blame for them on the Youth Corps leaders. "Their course," Chiang asserted, "is assuredly wrong, and their thought is absolutely mistaken."[65] The corps leadership, Chiang said, had committed two grave mistakes, which "are sufficient to bring about the complete defeat of the revolution." The first of these mistakes was the decision to participate in the elections. In pursuing their goal of *sheng-kuan fa-ts'ai* ("to become an official and grow rich"), Chiang claimed, the corps leaders used the members simply as "tools" of their own ambitions. By doing so, they caused the youth to lose faith in them and in the corps. It also transformed the "pure youth" in the corps into common bureaucrats and politicians, so that the corps lost its revolutionary character. Furthermore, by engaging in the elections, the corps created an enemy of the Kuomintang. "How then," Chiang asked, "can you have time to oppose the real enemy? The result of your actions, therefore, is simply to create struggle between the party and the corps and to sever the lifeline of this party's revolution."[66]

The second mistake was for the Youth Corps leaders to advocate the policy described by the phrase "maintain a not-too-close-and-not-too-distant (*pu-chi pu-li*) relationship with the party; develop mutual functions (*hsiang-hu te tso-yung*)." "I can definitely say," warned Chiang, "that if the party and the corps maintain a not-too-close-and-not-too-distant relationship, the result can only be mutual opposition and mutual obstruction, so that all power will be mutually dissipated."[67]

Convinced, therefore, that the struggles between the Kuomintang and the Youth Corps threatened the very existence of the Nationalist movement, and convinced also that the Youth Corps leaders were largely responsible for those struggles, Chiang Kai-shek finally determined to disband the corps. On June 30, 1947, he recommended to the Standing Committee of the Kuomintang's Central Executive Committee that the corps be absorbed into the party.[68]

The overwhelming majority of Youth Corps members were reluctant to merge with the Kuomintang. For years they had struggled with the party for political advantage, regarding the party as irredeemably corrupt and inefficient; now they feared that they would lose both power and positions if the two organizations were united. Chiang Kai-shek had, therefore, to plot the merger carefully. First he formed a broadly representative commission, headed by Ch'en Li-fu, Ch'en Ch'eng, and Wu T'ieh-ch'eng, to work out the sensitive issues involved in unifying the two organizations.[69] After nearly a month of intensive efforts, the commission completed its plan. Then, on September 5, 1947, Chiang convened a plenary meeting of the Youth Corps' Executive Secretariat. Arriving at the meeting, participants found the hall already decorated with slogans extolling the goal of the unity of the party and the corps.[70] There could be little doubt that they were being assembled to rubber-stamp a decision already made elsewhere. But Chiang was enough of a politician to know that the Youth Corps leaders, however strong their loyalties to him, would have to be cosseted if they were to acquiesce in the merger. In a written statement, he admitted that the party and the government suffered from a "deteriorating spirit."[71] But he beseeched the corps' leaders to accept the merger, promising them an important political role in the future. "Only if a seed is buried in the ground," he philosophized, "can it send forth sprouts and grow."[72] Moreover, as the editor of the *Chung-yang jih-pao* subsequently declared, the merger would constitute not simply a structural reorganization, but "a reconstruction of a revolutionary nature." It would mark the beginning of a new life for the party; the creation of a unity of spirit and purpose that would enable the revitalized party to defeat the Communists and complete the revolution.[73]

Despite Chiang Kai-shek's persuasion, the Youth Corps accepted the merger only after strenuous negotiations. Following the plenary meeting of the Executive Secretariat, a joint meeting of corps and party leaders convened on September 9. Both sides presented position papers setting out their programmatic and structural desiderata for the reorganization.[74] The agreement finally arrived at—ratified on September 12, 1947, by the Fourth Plenum of the Kuomintang's Central Executive Committee—carefully protected the political positions of Youth Corps cadres by assuring them comparable positions within the Kuomintang structure. Corps cadres at the hsien level, for example, would be reassigned to party headquarters at that level, and members of the corps' Executive Secretariat would receive appointments to the party's Central Executive Committee. The total number of staff positions would not be decreased, therefore, unless a cadre voluntarily resigned.[75]

In the wake of the merger, too, the Kuomintang would be radically reorganized. All corps and party members would have to reregister for party membership. This, in effect, would purge all undesirables from the party, including those who engaged in factionalism, were corrupt, or spoke or acted against the party. To deter future corruption, party members would have to record their property and wealth with the authorities. The merger plan also called for the implementation of land reform.[76]

## The Kuomintang After the Merger

Chiang Kai-shek professed himself deeply satisfied with the final agreement. "With the merger of the party and the Youth Corps," he declared, "everyone's ideas are reconciled and their spirits are united, and there is no struggle for power. The spirit of the conference moves me greatly."[77] But if Chiang truly believed that such a formal device as structural unification would end the fighting among his followers, he was doomed to disillusionment, for during the Nationalists' remaining two years on the mainland the conflict worsened. The merger itself, in fact, aggravated the struggles, since both sides fought for positions and power within the reconstituted Kuomintang.[78] Former Youth Corps members, for instance, contended that party reform should proceed "from the top down," because they dominated many of the local party branches and therefore wished to change the central organs, which were dominated by their rivals. By contrast, the CC Clique, whose power was preponderant in the party leadership, advocated reform "from the bottom up."[79] Each group, therefore, continued to place its own interests first.

The antipathy between the two factions was pervasive. During 1948, representatives in the Legislative Yüan with ties to the former Youth Corps openly formed a "club" that struggled bitterly with representatives linked to the CC Clique. Even as late as March 1949, an army newspaper reported that conflicts between former corps members and adherents of the CC Clique continued in several provinces with "undiminished violence."[80] Indeed, the struggle became so intense during 1948 and 1949 that Chiang Kai-shek was forced to postpone indefinitely the Seventh Party Congress, originally scheduled for March 5, 1948. "Unfortunately," Chiang later recounted, "the merging of the Party and the Corps . . . had not achieved the aim of a political revolutionary reform. On the contrary, factional conflicts within the Party, from central echelon down to local levels, became worse and worse. . . . It could well be said that the efforts of thoroughly reforming the Party by unifying the Party and the Corps have become abortive."[81]

## CHAPTER 5

# Politics Within the Regime:
# The Ko-hsin Movement

LARGELY BECAUSE OF General George C. Marshall's persua-
sive powers (backed, of course, by the prestige of the United
States), representatives of the Nationalists and the Communists
met together in a Political Consultative Conference on January
10–31, 1946, to try to forestall full-scale civil war and create a
unified, multiparty government in China. Despite the volatility
of the political situation and the critical nature of the issues discussed, the 38 delegates to the conference, representing diverse
and often antagonistic political interests, in just three weeks
hammered out an agreement that was a model of rationality and
mutual compromise. As a result, the conference resolutions,
though totally satisfying to none, offered—as General Marshall
accurately observed—"a liberal and forward-looking charter
which then offered China a basis for peace and reconstruction."[1]

Before the resolutions of the Political Consultative Conference
could be implemented, however, each of the several parties involved had to ratify them. For its deliberations on the resolutions, the Kuomintang convened the Second Plenum of the
Central Executive Committee in Chungking on March 1–17,
1946. There, despite Chiang Kai-shek's expressed support, the
resolutions encountered powerful opposition. U.S. State Department observers spoke vaguely and perplexedly about "reactionaries," "irreconcilables," and "disgruntled rightist elements"
within the Kuomintang who were attempting to sabotage the
agreements of the Political Consultative Conference.

It is now clear that these "reactionaries," who did indeed
wreck the government's negotiations for a peaceful settlement

with the Communists, were an organized coalition of diverse Kuomintang factions known as the Ko-hsin, or Renovationist, Movement. "The power of the Ko-hsin faction," remarked an observer in 1947, "already penetrates everywhere, and it has become the keenest competitor in politics today."[2] Thus, the Ko-hsin Movement was a weighty factor in the complex algebra of Kuomintang politics during the early postwar years, and a study of it reveals much about the condition of the Nationalist regime in the 1940's and about its factional strife.

## Origins of the Movement

The Ko-hsin Movement originated in early 1944, when the Nationalist regime's spiritual and material resources were at low ebb. The economy, ravaged by inflation, had seriously deteriorated; the army was exhausted; and war-weariness permeated the body politic. Dismayed by the situation, a small group of second-level Kuomintang cadres, members of the CC Clique, began searching for ways to revivify the government. One of that group, an agricultural economist named Hsiao Cheng, recalls his chagrin at hearing American criticisms of corruption and inefficiency in the Nationalist government. He was particularly exercised by the incompetence, indecisiveness, and lack of progressive spirit shown by the vice president of the Executive Yüan (and de facto premier), H. H. Kung, and by Minister of Economics Wong Wen-hao. "Most young comrades in the party," he observes, "were dissatisfied with them."[3]

Initially, this group of CC Clique malcontents—which besides Hsiao included P'an Kung-chan, Ku Cheng-ting, Ch'eng T'ien-fang, Yü Ching-t'ang, and Lai Lien—did little more than talk. On one occasion, Hsiao dispatched a letter advocating political changes to Chiang Kai-shek through Ch'en Kuo-fu, but Ch'en refused to pass it on, saying that its personal criticisms were too harsh.[4] In preparation for the Twelfth Plenum of the Kuomintang's Central Executive Committee, which was to meet in May 1944, the group increased their activity to the point of warranting being called a movement. To expand their political base they first enlisted the support of three prominent (but still second-ranking) party members outside the CC Clique: Liang Han-ts'ao and Ma Ch'ao-chün (members of Sun Fo's Clique), and Huang Chi-lu (a former Youth Corps cadre and follower of Hu Han-min). Then, on the very eve of the plenum, they formed an improbable alliance by enlisting the support of leading members of the Whampoa and Youth Corps factions. These were military men—Ho Chung-han, K'ang Tse, Hsiao Tsan-yü, and Cheng Chieh-min—who in the 1930's had been leading members of the Blue Shirts.[5]

At the plenary session of the Central Executive Committee on May 21, the now reinforced ranks of the Ko-hsin Movement launched an attack on the government. So forceful were they that after the meeting Chiang Kai-shek invited several of the Ko-hsin group to discuss their plan of political reform with him. In this meeting, Chiang appeared so receptive to the reformist proposals that Hsiao Cheng thought the Ko-hsin group had won a victory and that their proposals for reform would soon be adopted.[6] But to Hsiao's surprise, Chiang Kai-shek did not act on the group's recommendations. Kung and Wong, whose dismissals the group thought essential before any true political reforms could be launched, retained their posts. Nothing, therefore, had changed as a result of the group's activities in the Twelfth Plenum. Chiang subsequently let it be known that political reforms would have to be postponed until the military crisis created by Japan's Ichigo Offensive had eased. He promised, however, that the forthcoming Sixth Party Congress would consider thoroughgoing changes in the government's administration.

Through the rest of 1944 and into 1945, the Ko-hsin group increased their agitation for reform and established contacts with influential figures throughout the party. The climate was increasingly congenial to reformist sentiment, for the downward slide of the economy and the disastrous defeats in the Ichigo fighting convinced diverse political elements that reform was urgently needed. In September of 1944, for example, Fu Ssu-nien, who had participated in discussions of the Ko-hsin group even though he was not a member of the Kuomintang, led a campaign in the People's Political Council for political reform.[7] The

*Ta-kung-pao,* generally regarded as a mouthpiece for the Political Study Clique, also conducted a concerted editorial campaign for governmental reform. The government, it declared, was a nineteenth-century organization trying to fight a twentieth-century war, and, like an outdated piece of machinery, it was falling apart under the strain. "Beginning last year," the paper editorialized, "when the war entered a crucial stage, the government's weaknesses became even more evident, and such defects as corruption, the squeeze, and administrative and moral laxity came to the surface and became more serious, finally eroding the army's fighting strength."[8]

Chiang Kai-shek, too, expressed public support for reform, declaring in his 1945 New Year's address his determination to "ko-hsin" politics—his use of the verb could not have been accidental—during the coming year. The preceding month, H. H. Kung, a prime target of the Ko-hsin group, had gone to the United States, leaving the leadership of the Executive Yüan in the hands of his brother-in-law, T. V. Soong, whom the Ko-hsin group then regarded as a progressive and with whom they enjoyed good relations at the time. "It seemed," writes Hsiao Cheng, "that the future of Ko-hsin was becoming more hopeful."[9]

## Motivations and Targets of Attack

We have perhaps seen enough already to make preliminary observations about the motivations behind the movement. The Ko-hsin group were obviously dismayed by the deterioration and ineffectuality of the party and the government. In their eyes, the regime was blundering along haplessly, and the chief cause of the military defeats was a failure of government—reflected in the falling tax revenues and rising prices, and in the failure of the regime's grain policies (presumably meaning the tax-in-kind).[10] But since attacks were also directed at particular factions and specific individuals—thus far we have seen H. H. Kung and Wong Wen-hao singled out for criticism—the movement patently contained some ingredients of a struggle for power. A special target of the Ko-hsin group was the Political Study Clique, a loose-knit coterie of administrative and technical experts for whom ideology ranked low on their list of priorities. The members of this clique were linked to Chiang Kai-shek at least initially through Chang Ch'ün, who was Chiang's sworn-brother. Besides Wong Wen-hao, a few of the prominent members were Wu T'ieh-ch'eng (secretary-general of the Kuomintang's Central Executive Committee), Wu Ting-ch'ang (governor of Kweichow and chief secretary of the National Government), Chang Kia-ngau (minister of communications and adviser to the Executive Yüan), Ch'en I (governor of Fukien, secretary-general of the Supreme National Defense Council, and dean of the Central Training Institute), Hsiung Shih-hui (director of the Central Planning Board), and Shen Hung-lieh (secretary-general of the Party-and-Government Work Evaluation Committee).

Most Ko-hsin participants, by contrast, had found niches in the regime through association with its ideologically oriented organizations, such as the wing of the Kuomintang dominated by the CC Clique and the highly politicized Whampoa Military Academy. They felt that members of the Political Study Clique were simply unprincipled political parasites, ready to sell out the party and the nation whenever it served their selfish interests.[11] Members of the Ko-hsin Movement were, moreover, frustrated in their career ambitions. They were, as they called themselves, middle-ranking cadres of the regime (*chung-tseng chieh-chi*),[12] who had served in the party since the late 1920's and were getting on toward middle age; yet, because opportunists like Kung and Wong had for more than a decade played musical chairs with the top positions in the party and government, real power remained out of their reach.

Like the Maoists in the "Struggle Between Two Lines" in the Communist regime during the 1960's and 1970's, therefore, the Ko-hsin group generally represented the "ideologists" in a struggle against the "pragmatists." In both of these political contests, there clearly were differences of principle involved. But elements of career ambition and even personal dislike were interwoven inextricably with those questions of principle. This mix of motives became even clearer as the Ko-hsin Movement gained momentum following the defeat of Japan in August of 1945.

Two developments particularly outraged the Ko-hsin group in the immediate postwar period. The first was the conclusion of the Sino-Soviet Treaty of Friendship, signed coincidentally on the same day the Japanese surrendered, August 14, 1945. Among other controversial terms of this agreement was the recognition of the independence of Outer Mongolia, which the Nationalists had hitherto claimed was sovereign Chinese soil. The treaty was signed by Wang Shih-chieh, a prominent member of the Political Study Clique who had been named foreign minister specifically to sign the treaty after his predecessor, T. V. Soong, resigned rather than do so.[13] The second was the designation of two other members of the Political Study Clique, Hsiung Shih-hui and Ch'en I, to oversee the takeover of Manchuria and Taiwan, respectively. These were two of the richest prizes in the former Japanese-held areas, and Hsiung and Ch'en I were accompanied by trains of subordinates who filled positions to which, for example, the CC Clique aspired. As a result, both Manchuria and Taiwan witnessed intense factional struggles between the Political Study Clique and the other Kuomintang factions.[14]

To protest the Sino-Soviet Treaty and the selection of personnel to handle the takeover operations, the Ko-hsin group determined to send a letter to Chiang Kai-shek. Hsiao Cheng, Yü Ching-t'ang, and Hsiao Chi-shan were selected to draft the document. Hsiao Cheng, who at this stage seems to have been a key figure in the movement, recalls that the phrasing of his preliminary draft was again too extreme. Subsequent revisions, however, toned down the wording. When Chiang met with a delegation of the Ko-hsin group on December 10, 1945, he appeared to be deeply moved by the group's concerns and promised to do everything possible to adopt their ideas.[15]

## The Political Consultative Conference

The event that transformed the Ko-hsin group into a movement of truly national significance, however, was the Political Consultative Conference. The idea for such a conference, a multiparty instrument to establish guidelines for creating a unified and constitutional government, grew out of discussions between the National Government and the Communists in early 1945. Initially scheduled for November of that year, the conference had to be postponed because of the eruption of civil war and worsening relations between the two chief competitors for power. After the arrival of General Marshall, however, the two parties evinced a renewed desire for reconciliation, and the conference finally convened on January 10, 1946. Thirty-eight delegates attended: eight represented the Kuomintang; seven represented the Communists; and the remaining 23 either represented minority parties or were eminent personages without party affiliation.[16]

In three weeks of meetings, the Political Consultative Conference formulated a series of five resolutions designed to create a democratic, constitutional government and a united, nonpolitical, national army.[17] Many Chinese saw these agreements as offering the first distinct rays of hope for peace since the civil war had threatened in the fall of 1945, and they cheered the conference enthusiastically.

This approval of the conference was not universal, however, as evidenced by the Chiao-ch'ang-k'ou Incident. On Sunday morning, February 10, some 10,000 persons gathered in Chiao-ch'ang-k'ou in Chungking to celebrate the successful conclusion of the Political Consultative Conference. Such leading liberal and leftist figures as Li Kung-p'u, Lo Lung-chi, and Kuo Mo-jo were slated to address the mass meeting, which had been organized by the Democratic League and various local organizations. Even before the meeting began, however, a Kuomintang partisan attempted to seize control of the gathering by displacing Li Kung-p'u as chairman. Apparently a scuffle on the platform ensued. And then a gang of some 300–600 toughs, wielding benches and iron rods, stormed into the square, bloodying about 60 of the participants, including several of the intended speakers. Police and gendarmes at the scene conspicuously failed to interfere with the beatings.

Controversy has swirled around the Chiao-ch'ang-k'ou Incident, with the Nationalists blaming the Communists, and leftists accusing the Kuomintang and especially the CC Clique for the violence. A Kuomintang adherent involved in these events later recalled, however, that "the Kuomintang . . . planned to seize this opportunity [of a mass meeting], and to take control of the election of the meeting's chairman, in order to divert its purpose *and thereby render the Communists a merciless blow.*"[18] It is patent, therefore, that unspecified Kuomintang authorities were opposed to the meeting and had planned to interfere with it, even though the evidence that they actually called in the toughs remains inconclusive.

The same sentiments that inspired Kuomintang elements to interfere with the meeting at Chiao-ch'ang-k'ou served as a stimulus to the Ko-hsin Movement. Shortly after the conclusion of the Political Consultative Conference, Liang Han-ts'ao, Hsiao Cheng, and other leaders of the movement convened a public Ko-hsin symposium in the central party headquarters. The movement's previous symposia had attracted only some ten people, but over 100 attended this one. In four subsequent symposia in February and early March attendance at times grew to over 150, apparently because of the resentment many Kuomintang members felt about the resolutions of the Political Consultative Conference. The attendees were, for the most part, members of such leading Nationalist organs as the Central Executive Committee, the Legislative Yüan, the Control Yüan, the Executive Secretariat of the Youth Corps, and the People's Political Council.[19]

These symposia marked the true beginning of the Ko-hsin Movement's organized activities. At the third of these meetings, on February 27, the group adopted a document entitled "Our Cry" ("Wo-men te hu-sheng"), which proclaimed the major goals of the movement; and on March 4, the group prepared a provisional program that served as an organizational charter for the movement.[20] By March 1946, therefore, the Ko-hsin Movement had developed into an organized political force and had been substantially reinforced by growing numbers of adherents.

When the Second Plenum of the Central Executive Committee met in Chungking from March 1 to March 17, the Ko-hsin group threw the meetings into an uproar. On the one hand, they demanded reform, vehemently criticizing virtually every aspect of party and governmental activity, from the evils of bureaucratic capitalism to the failure to implement land reform, and from the regime's bureaucratic methods to its conduct of foreign policy. On the other hand, they attacked the resolutions of the Political Consultative Conference. Liang Han-ts'ao and Yü Ching-t'ang presented a joint statement, signed by 32 other Ko-hsin members, calling for complete rejection of those resolutions. Subsequently, 110 other delegates presented a similar demand. The Ko-hsin group even formally proposed that Chang Ch'ün, Wang Shih-chieh, and Shao Li-tzu—three of the Kuomintang's representatives at the conference—be expelled from the party on the grounds of disloyalty to the party, of compromising with other parties, and of willingness to hand over the ruling power to a multiparty government. Ku Cheng-kang, a prominent CC Clique member and a leader of the Ko-hsin Movement, emotionally cried out, "Save the Party!" The party leadership faced a veritable rebellion, and the secretary-general of the central headquarters, Wu T'ieh-ch'eng (who was a member of the Political Study Clique), was so stunned by the ferocity of the criticisms that he offered to resign.[21]

For Chiang Kai-shek, these criticisms were not just irksome; they also challenged his leadership. For he had placed himself squarely behind the Political Consultative Conference agreements, and the Kuomintang delegation there had acted entirely at his behest.[22] He therefore came to the defense of Chang Ch'ün and other Kuomintang delegates to the conference, asserting that the criticisms of them were unreasonable and excessive. Moreover, he said, "the mistakes of the government are my mistakes."[23] But he expressed no contrition. "At the time of our crushing defeat [during Japan's Ichigo Offensive in 1944], when China found herself in a most critical situation, all of you were shaken in your conviction, but I alone insisted on continued resistance. Now that the war has been won, you have so much to say."[24]

Still, Chiang could not wholly ignore the fractious Ko-hsin Movement, and at least four times he appealed to the delegates to support the agreements of the Consultative Conference.[25] He finally met secretly with eleven representatives of the movement and assured them that "as long as I am alive, the Communist party will never join the government."[26] That is, he expressed himself as being at one with the Ko-hsin Movement in his opposition to the resolutions of the Political Consultative Conference. Whether or not he was truly opposed to a coalition government—probable though that is—cannot be determined now. But if his opposition *was* genuine, it was impossible for him to acknowledge it openly, because to do so might have alienated George Marshall and thereby threatened the continuation of American political and material support. The Ko-hsin revolt in the Central Executive Committee plenary sessions, however, had forced him to reveal his hand, at least to these few Ko-hsin leaders.

Following that secret meeting, the Ko-hsin participants were noticeably quiet during the remaining sessions of the Second Plenum. And, at the conclusion, the Central Executive Committee unanimously ratified the Political Consultative Conference's resolutions in their entirety—albeit with a number of recommended revisions added with Chiang Kai-shek's blessing.[27] The intent of those recommendations was, on the surface at least, unclear. Publicly, the Nationalists contended that the recommended changes were only suggestions, and that, should the delegates to the Political Consultative Conference subsequently reject them, the Kuomintang would respect their decision.[28] Most outside observers, including the Communists and the U.S. embassy staff, however, thought that the members of the Second Plenum had raised detailed questions about the proposed constitution and about other highly technical matters in order to sabotage any agreement with the Communists.[29]

Having fathomed the real intent behind the recommended changes, the Communists quickly charged the Kuomintang with acting in bad faith. Whereas the Communists at the Consultative Conference had appeared willing—even anxious—to participate in a coalition government, they now shied away from a political settlement, postponing the March 31 meeting of their own Central Committee, which was to have ratified the resolutions of the Consultative Conference. They also resumed their military operations, capturing Changchun on April 18.[30] The Second Plenum was, therefore, a turning point in the postwar relationship between the Communists and the Nationalists. Perhaps those two contenders for power could never, in any case, have reconciled their differences. In the actual event, however, a now powerful segment of the Kuomintang, the Ko-hsin Movement, successfully stymied what at least appeared to have been an inspired attempt to forestall civil war.

## The Organization of Ko-hsin Seminars

During the months after the Second Plenum, the organization of the Ko-hsin Movement spread to many of the provinces. The movement's headquarters, called the "Capital Seminar" (*Shou-tu tso-t'an-hui*) was located first in Chungking and then, accompanying the government back to the east, in Nanking. Leadership was vested in 13 conveners (*chao-chi-jen*), who took turns attending to the daily administration of the movement's central office. Under the central office, there were to be four sections (General Affairs, Editing, Publications, and Correspondence) and five study groups (for Party Affairs, and for Political, Economic, International, and Special Problems). Although all Ko-hsin seminars were open to the public, and all Kuomintang and Youth Corps members who were committed to the cause of party renovation were invited to participate, any member who without justifiable cause failed to attend three meetings of the seminar, or three of the weekly meetings of their study group, would lose his membership in the movement. Similar "seminars" were to be established at the local levels.[31]

How closely the actual organization fit this blueprint is uncertain, but the movement soon spread widely. In addition to Nanking and Shanghai, Kwangtung, Kweichow, Yunnan, Chekiang, and Hunan were all the sites of Ko-hsin seminars during the summer and fall of 1946—and the seminars were usually held in the provincial headquarters of the Kuomintang. In Hunan, where the movement was particularly active, Ko-hsin seminars were also organized at the hsien level.[32]

Besides sponsoring public meetings, or seminars, a major activity of the movement was the publication of journals and pamphlets to spread the ideas of party reform. In July 1946, the central headquarters began publishing *Ko-hsin chou-k'an* (*Renovation Weekly*), of which the publisher was Liang Han-ts'ao and the editor Yang Yu-chiung. Several branches of the movement, including those in Hunan, Yunnan, and Kwangtung, also put out a variety of publications.[33]

## The Ko-hsin Critique of the Party and the Government

Writers in the Ko-hsin publications uniformly expressed dismay regarding the condition of the Kuomintang. It was, Ch'en Chien-fu stated, diseased and could not be saved without surgery. "I believe," he wrote, "that renovation [*ko-hsin*] is the same as revolution. If today our Kuomintang comrades do not arise to carry out a revolution, then in the future they will only be able to sit and wait while others carry out a revolution against them."[34] Ch'eng Yüan-ch'en expressed his disillusionment with the party even more bluntly:

That the Chinese Kuomintang must renovate itself is an ironclad fact. Futhermore, the need to renovate did not develop only today. Long ago, after the completion of the Northern Expedition, political power was usurped by the bureaucrats. Following the Northern Expedition and at the time of the Kuomintang's accession to political power, the Kuomintang should have begun implementing all its principles. But because political power has been usurped for close to twenty years, . . . the Kuomintang has been limited to pasting up written mottoes and shouting slogans, and it has lacked the capacity actually to govern. As a result, the people have derived only hope from the mottoes and slogans of the Kuomintang's principles; they have received no redress. With regard to actual governance, every place has been retrogressing. The Kuomintang advocates democracy, but the government stresses centralism and disregards elections; the Kuomintang advocates the principle of local self-rule, but the government maintains the specially privileged economic class, . . . assessing miscellaneous levies and taxes so that everywhere the people are dirt poor. All of this is enough to prove that the Chinese Kuomintang has already ceased to have any relationship with actual governance. A political party that has become separated from actual governance has lost its raison d'être.[35]

Such disillusionment filled the pages of the Ko-hsin publications. Ko-hsin writers professed not to be pessimistic, however, for—as Liang Han-ts'ao stated in the inaugural issue of *Ko-hsin chou-k'an*—"we believe that 'dissatisfaction' is truly an opportunity for renovation and an omen of a new life."[36]

In searching for the causes of the Kuomintang's weakened condition, many Ko-hsin writers agreed with Ch'eng Yüan-ch'en that the problems first appeared shortly after the party seized power in 1927. "The party has been in power for seventeen years," wrote Ho Yüeh-seng, "and it has been ill for seventeen years."[37] Li Ta similarly remarked that the Northern Expedition had resulted in a "military victory, but a political defeat."[38] Several Ko-hsin writers also stressed, however, that the strains of the war and the temptations after the war had greatly accelerated the process of deterioration.[39] In any event, all Ko-hsin participants in 1946 were united in the conviction that the Kuomintang was mortally ill and would be unable to compete for power with other parties during the constitutional era—unless their proposals for reform were quickly put into effect.

A basic cause of the Kuomintang's illness, thought the Ko-hsin participants, was the diverse character of its members. "Now," wrote Liang Han-ts'ao, "the membership and thought of the Kuomintang are 100 percent mixed up (*fu-tsa*)."[40] Party organization had always been lax, without adequate discipline, training, or propaganda. And, after the Northern Expedition, warlords and opportunists had flooded into the party. There was, therefore, no commonality of purpose among the party members. Many were totally indifferent to the revolutionary principles of the party and aspired only to attain power and wealth. This attitude corroded the revolutionary spirit of the party and resulted in widespread corruption, administrative inertia, and disregard for the welfare of the common people.[41]

The Kuomintang was also weakened, charged the Ko-hsin group, by its failure to practice internal democracy. Beginning in 1928, they said, the system of democratic-centralism had been replaced by that of "personal leadership" (*ko-jen te ling-tao chih-tu*). Thereafter, leaders of the party were no longer elected but were designated by higher levels of the party. Denied any responsibility and ignored by the party leadership, party cells below the hsien level atrophied; meetings became an empty formality, and the younger and more capable members consequently became inactive or even left the party. The Kuomintang therefore lacked a foundation in society or even among its own rank and file.[42]

Also because of the absence of democracy within the party, the leaders became a "special class"—aging, unimaginative, and jealous of their privileges. They maintained a monopoly on power, but they did nothing constructive with that power (*pao erh pu-pan*).[43] Cutting themselves off from the lower ranks of the party, they were never rejuvenated by the new blood and new ideas of younger members. The result by 1946, one Ko-hsin writer declared, was that the Kuomintang "now manifests a spirit of old age, of painfully maintaining the status quo; one does not see a youthful attitude of advancing optimistically into the future."[44]

A fatal flaw of the Kuomintang, thought the Ko-hsin group, was that it had failed to enforce party rule over the government (*i-tang t'ung-cheng*). According to Sun Yat-sen's prescription for revolutionary construction, the party during the period of political tutelage ought to be superior to the government, supervising it and giving it direction. This principle of party rule had, however, been disregarded. As Ch'eng Yüan-ch'en wrote, "the government long ago shed its relationship with the party."[45] And Liu Pu-t'ung observed that "Although the government is the government of the party, yet it has nothing to do with the political programs of the party. Although the party is a party of the Three People's Principles, yet it has nothing to do with the doctrines of the Three People's Principles."[46]

As a result of these several factors—the influx of opportunists into the party after 1927, weak party organization, the demise of the democratic spirit within the party, and the inability of the party to control the government—the party and government were now plagued by bureaucratism, factionalism, and bureaucratic capitalism. These were the Ko-hsin Movement's three principal targets.

Bureaucratism and factionalism, in particular, were the party's "mortal wounds," declared "Our Cry," a major policy statement of the movement. The poison of bureaucratism, it said, pervaded the regime.

Every government office is mostly pretense and perfunctoriness; they have lost the spirit of struggling for ideals. Officials at every level usually deceive their superiors and cheat their subordinates, and they engage in squeeze and corruption. Seldom does one perceive any ambition to save the nation and the people. Whether in governmental agencies or party offices, everything that is done is divorced from the people and society, and they become decadent *yamen* [old-style government offices]. With regard to the various conferences, they usually stress formalism, and rarely are there heated debates or the democratic practice of respecting the opinions of the majority. A revolutionary party, which was originally full of vitality, now merely evinces the psychology of old age, painfully maintaining the old facade; no longer does one see the demeanor of youth, charging optimistically ahead into the future.[47]

As for factionalism, although Chiang Kai-shek in 1938, at the Extraordinary Conference of the Kuomintang, had ordered all "small organizations" within the party to disband, competition continued to be rife. "Within the party," complained Jen Cho-hsüan (pseud.: Yeh Ch'ing), "there are many factions, and within the large factions there are small factions, and every faction competes with the others."[48] The Ko-hsin writers repeatedly complained that personnel selection in the regime was determined not by a person's merit or ability, but by his personal and factional relations.[49] Party members, therefore, "only know the factional organization, and do not know that there is a party organization. As a consequence, they do not begrudge destroying the party or sacrificing the party in order to expand the organization of the faction."[50] "Our Cry" concluded that, as a result of these factional struggles, "capable and honest persons can only feel depressed and discouraged. How can the life of the party not be suffocated by it?"[51]

Bureaucratic capitalism was an emotion-laden term, denoting the alleged practice on the part of high Nationalist officials of using political influence and ill-gotten wealth to invest in and dominate the nation's economy. Ironically, the phrase may have been coined by pro-Communist writers, but the Ko-hsin group adopted it as their own. In their hands, it was a blunt instrument of attack, employed to criticize a whole range of problems afflicting the nation. They charged, for instance, that bureaucratic capitalists manipulated the various state enterprises and used their control over foreign exchange to engage in market speculation. As a result, normal commercial and industrial enterprises failed to develop. Bureaucratic capitalists also sought only personal profit and had no sense of national welfare, so that the government was unable to improve the living standards of the common people. They manipulated prices, created high interest rates, exploited the peasants, and widened the gap between rich and poor. The methods of the bureaucratic capitalists also contributed to the corruption, inefficiency, and bureaucratism of the government.[52]

The Ko-hsin attacks on bureaucratic capitalism by and large lacked specificity. They did single out the Ch'ang-chiang and Yangtze Corporations, associated respectively with the families of H. H. Kung and T. V. Soong.[53] They also bitterly accused T. V. Soong of corruption. (Chiang Kai-shek publicly defended Soong, asserting that "Soong is not corrupt.")[54] For the most part, however, bureaucratic capitalism was simply a shibboleth employed by the Ko-hsin group to voice alarm about the economic crisis and the deteriorating living standards of the mass of the people. It also provided a base for their persistent demand that the party register the wealth and property of all its members in order to prevent the use of public office to amass personal fortunes.[55]

The specific remedy of the Ko-hsin Movement for the diseases of bureaucratism, factionalism, and bureaucratic capitalism was a party purge. Both the Sixth Party Congress in May 1945 and the Second Plenum in March 1946 had formally called for a "general review" (tsung ch'ing-ch'a) of the party members for the purpose of "thoroughly purging corrupt and evil elements."[56] During the months following the Second Plenum, however, the central party headquarters did not launch the called-for purge, and prospects for it dimmed. Ko-hsin participants in August and September of 1946 were losing enthusiasm as a result, for even six months after the Second Plenum the movement had accomplished nothing tangible. Indeed, the errors of the past were being perpetuated and conditions were worsening, so that, wrote Juan Hua-kuo, "most enthusiastic comrades suspect that our Ko-hsin Movement is nothing but talk." [57]

In September of 1946, however, the central headquarters finally ordered that the "general review" of party members begin on October 1. The news generated enormous excitement within the Ko-hsin group. "This is the greatest event in the Kuomintang since the party purge [of the Communists] in 1927," Juan Hua-kuo exulted. "We can view this as the first shot of the Ko-hsin Movement." [58]

During the first half of 1947, the Ko-hsin Movement continued to be a major force on the political scene. T. V. Soong was hounded from the premiership on March 1 after his fiscal policies led to a destructive gold panic in January and early February. Although published reports indicated only that Soong's chief critics were the Preparatory Committee of the Central Executive Committee's Third Plenum, the Legislative Yüan, and Fu Ssu-nien in the People's Political Council, little imagination is required to infer that the Ko-hsin group was in the vanguard of the attack. [59] During the sessions of the Third Plenum later that same month, such leading members of the Ko-hsin Movement as Ku Cheng-ting, Liu Chien-ch'ün, Lai Lien, Huang Yü-jen, and Jen Cho-hsüan were so strident in their attacks on bureaucratic capitalism, on peace talks with the Communists, and on various government officials—especially on members of the Political Study Clique such as Ch'en I and Wang Shih-chieh— that popular journals labeled them the plenum's "heavy artillery" (ta-p'ao). [60] Among the plenum's resolutions was a demand sponsored by a Ko-hsin participant that the property of corrupt officials be confiscated. [61]

## The Movement's Demise and an Autopsy

Following the Third Plenum in March 1947, the Ko-hsin Movement drops from view. *Ko-hsin chou-k'an,* the movement's journal in Nanking, ceased publication in August 1947, and that event probably marked the end of the movement as an effective political force, at least in the sense of an alliance of diverse factions. Many of the reasons for the demise of the Ko-hsin Movement can only be conjectured. Its members probably lost heart as a result of the lack of palpable achievement. The party purge instituted in October of 1946, for example, proved stillborn.[62] Chiang Kai-shek also evinced his limited sympathy for the movement in March 1947 when he named Chang Ch'ün—the most prominent member of the despised Political Study Clique—as T. V. Soong's successor as premier of the National Government. The most obvious reason for the passing of the movement, however, was the growing enmity between the Youth Corps and the CC Clique. The long-standing rivalry between these two factions had from the beginning made the Ko-hsin Movement an unnatural political marriage that had been possible only because the two were not monolithic entities but included people of varied political outlooks. Some CC Clique members, for instance, such as Hsiao Chi-shan and Wang Ping-chün, were adamantly opposed to the Youth Corps' participation in politics and therefore avoided treating it as a legitimate political force. Others, such as Lai Lien, Hsiao Cheng, and Yü Ching-t'ang, took the realistic approach that the Youth Corps was already involved in politics and that they therefore might as well try to work with it. During the electoral campaigns in 1947, however, conflicts between the two factions became so intense at both the central and the local levels that amicable cooperation became impossible. The Ko-hsin Movement therefore died, a victim of the factionalism that its adherents professed to deplore.[63]

The Ko-hsin concept did not, however, immediately disappear. The party resolutions that accompanied the merger of the Youth Corps and the Kuomintang in September 1947 were identical to those advocated by the movement. And some 200 members of the Legislative Yüan, including such former leaders of the Ko-hsin Movement as Hsiao Cheng and Ku Cheng-ting, coordinated their legislative activities through a Ko-hsin Club—a club that remains in existence to this very day. Members of this club were, however, in large part adherents of the CC Clique.[64]

Legislative Yüan members who continued to support the idea of the Youth Corps, and who had previously participated in the Ko-hsin Movement, organized a rival faction called the Hsincheng (New Politics) Club. This club, led by Liu Chien-ch'ün, Huang Yü-jen, and Liu Pu-t'ung, was described as "dead[ly] enemies" of the CC Clique.[65]

Throughout its existence, the Ko-hsin Movement had outspokenly criticized factionalism. Yet in fact, the movement had been simply another faction within the disorderly constellation of factions known as the Nationalist regime. Ko-hsin writers, of course, denied this. Jen Cho-hsüan, for example, argued that the movement was not a faction, because its goals were to eliminate factionalism and to unite all true revolutionaries into a purified Kuomintang.[66] It is true that the Ko-hsin Movement had brought together elements of such diverse segments of the regime as the CC Clique and the Youth Corps which, if they had not actually despised each other, had at least shared little in common. They had been able to form a temporary alliance, however, because the Political Study Clique and the agreements of the Political Consultative Conference represented more immediate threats to their political interests than they did to each other.

The Ko-hsin group also denied that in advocating reform they were motivated by selfish interests. "We insist," declared Ch'en Chien-fu, "that the motivations of those of us who participate in the Ko-hsin Movement must be pure and upright. That is to say, we must not possess any self-interest. The reason we seek renovation is purely for the party and for the nation, without a thread of concern for ourselves."[67] Despite this disavowal of personal interest, Ko-hsin participants were not indifferent to the effects that political reform would have upon their personal fortunes. Policy changes, they insisted, would necessarily entail changes of personnel, and they regarded the appointment of loyal and able party members as the obverse of the party purge. As Juan Hua-kuo observed, "loyal and able revolutionary comrades should be given the opportunity to advance, to display their abilities, and in large numbers to take on the responsibilities of every aspect of party and government."[68]

The careerist impulses animating the Ko-hsin Movement help explain its vitriolic opposition to the Political Consultative Conference. On first encounter, the fury the group vented on that conference and the Political Study Clique's representatives to it seems wholly unrelated to their demands for party reform. Yet their concern to maximize their political privileges makes that opposition perfectly logical. For the Ko-hsin participants were party professionals; the party sustained their careers. If the agreements of the conference were to take effect, the Kuomintang would lose its financial support from the government, and a whole array of government posts would thereafter have to be shared with non-Kuomintang people. The concessions made by Chang Ch'ün, Wang Shih-chieh, and Shao Li-tzu at the conference, therefore, threatened their very livelihood.

If renovation of the party had been the sole motivation behind the movement, then it is inexplicable why Ch'en Li-fu was spared the movement's attacks. Next to Chiang Kai-shek himself, no one was more responsible for the Kuomintang's lack of democracy, loose organizational discipline, and weaknesses at the local level. Yet not one word of criticism was uttered against Ch'en in the pages of the Ko-hsin publications. As a leader of the so-called CC Clique, he was, of course, closely associated with many of the Ko-hsin Movement leaders. The group even published an article of his, a philosophical essay of no particular political significance, in the *Ko-hsin yüeh-k'an*. But he had not participated in the movement; in fact, he regarded it as too radical.[69] His complete immunity from Ko-hsin criticism suggests that the movement was opposed less to the ills afflicting the Nationalist regime than to the Political Study Clique, T. V. Soong, and H. H. Kung, who were the principal political beneficiaries of Nationalist rule.

Throughout the life of the Ko-hsin Movement, Chiang Kai-shek's attitude was ambiguous. Several times he expressed approval of its ideas, but for him the movement itself was doubtless an irritation. Its overt opposition to the Political Consultative Conference, for instance, was contrary to his wishes. He also repeatedly defended Kung, Soong, and members of the Political Study Clique from Ko-hsin attacks; these men were his personal appointees whom he trusted and relied upon, and who were carrying out policies of which he approved.[70]

The Ko-hsin participants, for their part, invariably referred to Chiang in respectful terms, but their attacks placed him perilously close to their target area. A Ko-hsin writer in Hunan, for instance, charged that Chiang was surrounded by sychophants, and that it was therefore necessary to find honest cadres who would not fawn on him but would boldly tell him the truth. This writer also declared that Chiang Kai-shek could attain several of the movement's goals—such as purging the corrupt bureaucrats, dismissing the most noxious bureaucratic capitalists, and disbanding the Youth Corps (*sic*)—simply by issuing an order.[71] Advocates of a party purge must have been similarly disgruntled when Chiang delayed issuing the long-awaited order for a general review of the party. In like fashion, the Ko-hsin group's accusations of "dictatorial monopoly" and "personal leadership," although not explicitly directed at Chiang, surely reflected upon him and at least hinted at his diminishing prestige among the rank and file of the Kuomintang.

The Ko-hsin Movement and the Youth Corps were at once witnesses to and examples of the internal disintegration of the Nationalists' state apparatus. Members of those groups perceived the pervasive decay at the center of the party and government, and recognized that the regime could not long stand unless radical changes were quickly made.

Neither of these movements could have saved the regime, however, for each was as much a part of the disease as were the individuals and factions they attacked. As we have seen, when members of the Youth Corps gained cadre status, they displayed much the same bureaucratism, self-serving behavior, and disregard for the public weal as did members of the party. Several Ko-hsin leaders similarly ceased to be active in the movement after being promoted to higher positions in the government and party. "After they got into power," a former member of the Ko-hsin group acknowledged, "they naturally wouldn't speak out."[72]

The source of the problem was largely structural. Because there existed no effective, institutionalized means to make members of the regime accountable in their conduct of office to political constituencies or forces outside the government, most officials readily lost sight of the larger purposes of government. The attainment of power for its own sake, as well as for the prestige and wealth that accompanied it, became their preoccupation. To reach their goals, they participated in factions, which were the primary vehicles of political activity within the Nationalist regime.

Not policy, therefore, but power and position were the objects of political contention. This is the key to understanding the Youth Corps and the Ko-hsin Movement—and, indeed, to understanding Nationalist politics generally. This helps explain why so much of the political discourse was in terms of personal denigration rather than concrete policy proposals or structural analyses. The purpose of the moralistic rhetoric was to call into question the fitness of factional rivals to hold high and profitable office. Seldom, however, was the conduct of office or the course of government markedly changed when one faction displaced another, for the political system provided no means of pressuring those in office to place the mandate of their office above their personal and factional interests.

The fact that members of the Youth Corps and the Ko-hsin Movement were susceptible to the same pathologies as the rest of the Kuomintang does not vitiate the force or the accuracy of their criticisms. It does, however, reveal how shallow were the roots of their idealism. It further suggests that the fundamental weakness of the Nationalist regime lay less in the realm of ideas—for the criticisms of both the Youth Corps and the Ko-hsin Movement were, I believe, generally correct—than in that of structure. After some twenty years in power, during which time its leading organs had been neither revitalized by new blood from within nor refreshed by the breath of effective criticism from without, the regime had putrefied. This immeasurably eased the task of Mao Tse-tung.

## CHAPTER 6

# The Nationalist Army During the War of Resistance

THE ARMY WAS THE principal prop of the Nationalist regime. The political organs of the regime, the Kuomintang and the National Government, neither developed firm foundations in society nor created strong, autonomous institutions. They had gained a measure of power and influence after the victories of the Nationalist army in the late 1920's, but throughout the period of Nationalist rule they were overshadowed by the leadership and the policy demands of the army.[1] During the war against Japan and the civil war against the Communists, however, that prop of the Nationalist regime so decayed that, by 1948 and 1949, it could no longer support the political institutions of the regime.

Let the Nationalist army receive its due. It persisted for eight years in a war against an enemy force that was decidedly superior in organization, training, and equipment. By comparison with the French (whose resistance to the Germans collapsed after only six weeks of fighting) and the British (who received substantial material assistance from the United States), the resistance of the Chinese army was a marvel of determination and self-sufficiency. Completely frustrating Japanese expectations of a quick and decisive victory, it actively fought at Shanghai, at Nanking, and on the plains of North and Central China, incurring frightful losses. Then, having retreated from the coast, beyond the reach of the major transportation networks, the Nationalist army shifted to a strategy of attritional warfare that mired the Japanese army in the vastness of the Chinese nation.

This dogged resistance contributed significantly to the total

Allied war effort against the Axis powers. It tied up approximately a million Japanese troops on the continent of Asia—
troops that might otherwise have been used to combat the
island-hopping armies of the Western allies in the Pacific.[2] If in
some way history had been kinder to the Nationalists after
1945—if there had been no civil war, and if the Nationalists had
succeeded during the postwar years in creating a stable state on
the mainland—historians would now treat the Nationalists' resistance to Japanese aggression as a heroic epic of dauntless sacrifice. In the light cast by the postwar debacle, however, the positive contributions of the Nationalist army during the war are
inevitably overshadowed by the evidences of its deterioration.

## Shifting Strategies Against the Japanese

Even at the start of the war, the Nationalist army was unim-
pressive by Western standards. General Frank Dorn recalls that
"training would be characterized as unsatisfactory to nonexistent. . . . Equipment and weapons . . . were obsolete and in relatively poor condition. Ammunition was scarce."[3] Nor was it
administratively or politically unified. Instead, it was a coalition
of armies as diverse in their loyalties as they were in their equipment, training, and combat capabilities.

At the heart of this heterogeneous coalition was the "central
army" (*chung-yang chün*). In 1937, this force accounted for about
300,000 men, or probably no more than one-fifth of total Nationalist troop strength.[4] Its top commanders had joined the
army and the Kuomintang prior to the Northern Expedition of
1926–28, and usually were either former faculty of the Whampoa Academy (whose commandant had been Chiang Kai-shek)
or graduates of its first four classes. The central army was characterized chiefly by its loyalty to Chiang; in terms of tactical, lo-
gistical, and administrative skills, it generally was years out of
date. Within it, however, was an elite force created in 1934 known
as "The Generalissimo's Own." Trained under the direction of
German advisers, and armed with German-made automatic
weapons and mortars, the 80,000 men in these elite divisions
constituted the core of Chiang Kai-shek's military modernization

program. Indeed, faith in the considerable fighting abilities of these divisions had emboldened Chiang to assume an unyielding attitude toward the Japanese after the Lu-kou-ch'iao, or Marco Polo Bridge, Incident of July 7, 1937.[5]

The remainder of the Nationalist army was made up of provincial armies that were the remnants and direct descendants of the warlord armies, commanded by men who had risen to power and prominence independently of the central government. The loyalty of these commanders to Chiang Kai-shek and to the National Government was therefore conditional, and they were often jealous and fearful of Chiang's growing power. As a consequence, the conduct of the provincial armies sometimes proved quite baffling to outside observers. As Aleksandr Kalyagin, a Russian adviser to the Nationalist army during 1938–39, subsequently remarked, a commander "might receive an order to attack, but would withdraw his troops to the rear, surrender a city, and not even receive the slightest punishment. What was one to make of this? [To learn the answer,] one must look into the 'Church calendar,' see what sort of general this is, which province's troops he is commanding, in which province he is fighting, which troops he is cooperating with, etc., and then everything will become clear."[6] In other words, Chiang Kai-shek and the Nationalist high command did not wield sufficient power to impose their will in every instance upon the provincial armies. One thing a provincial commander knew well: his military position, political power, and economic well-being were dependent upon the preservation of his military force. Thus, whenever he received orders from the high command to engage in combat, his decision whether to obey or not—whether to fight or not—was based upon calculations of personal as well as national interest.

When the war erupted, the Japanese high command held this patchwork army in disdain. They had easily defeated Chinese forces in Manchuria in 1931, and the memory of that victory deeply colored their evaluation of the Nationalist army in 1937. They were therefore convinced, after the fighting erupted, that they could quash Chinese resistance in just three months, or at most six months. What they did not realize was that the political equation in China had changed, and that Chiang Kai-shek and important segments of the Chinese nation were now resolved to resist Japanese aggression as they had not been in 1931.

Chiang Kai-shek's strategy in resisting the Japanese invasion was essentially one of trading space for time. He recognized the superiority of the Japanese army to his own and therefore accepted the loss of large areas of North and Central China as he and his government retreated to the west. He had conceived this strategy at least as early as August 1935, for he had then told a gathering of political cadres that "Even if we lose fifteen . . . of the eighteen provinces of China proper, with Szechwan, Kweichow, and Yunnan provinces in our control, we definitely will beat any enemy and recover all the lost territory."[7] Chiang's confidence was built on the realization that China's economy and society were still in a pre-modern, pre-industrial stage. He believed, therefore, that the nation's resistance could continue regardless of how many cities and factories fell to the enemy. Moreover, the invading armies would be exhausted and separated from their sources of supply should they advance into China's virtually unlimited hinterland. Occasionally, as at Shanghai, he did not adhere to the principle of trading space for time. In the long run, however, the principle succeeded much as he had anticipated.[8] The Japanese did seize, with relative ease, the urban centers of North and East China. But after they captured Wuhan and Canton in October of 1938, the character of the war fundamentally changed. By then, the Chinese defenders had taken up positions in the hills and mountains of the interior, where the Japanese could no longer bring to bear the full power of their artillery and motorized troops. The Japanese advance therefore stalled, and from then until mid-1944 the lines between the two combatants remained essentially unchanged.

By avoiding a knockout blow during the first year of the war, Chiang Kai-shek had scored a strategic victory. On October 25, 1938, as Wuhan fell to the Japanese, he exulted that this "marks a turning point in our struggle from the defensive to the offensive. It also marks a beginning of a change of tide in the war. It must not be mistakenly viewed as a military reverse or retreat."[9] To many, this declaration must have sounded like sheer bravado. But Chiang believed that the Japanese were spreading their resources of men and equipment thin by advancing across the expanse of China. This, he thought, rendered them vulnerable to attack all along the front as well as in the rear. He also professed to see the Japanese people, suffering from political repression and a collapsing economy, increasingly opposed to the war policies of their leaders. Thus, he declared, "the longer our enemy struggles, the more he involves himself in difficulties; while the longer we struggle the stronger and more determined we become."[10]

The Japanese, meanwhile, similarly shifted to a strategy of attritional warfare. They too realized that they would vainly exhaust their resources if they attempted to pursue the Nationalist forces farther into the interior. Their new strategy, therefore, was to precipitate the collapse of Chinese resistance through "internal disintegration."[11] To accomplish this goal, they tightened the noose of their economic blockade on the Nationalist area. Their army operations during this period were designed to constrict the Nationalists' lines of supply. In the spring of 1939, for example, they attacked and seized Nanchang in Kiangsi province, thereby cutting the important Chekiang-Hunan railway. In November of the same year, they landed an amphibious force at Pohai (Pakhoi) in western Kwangtung and advanced a hundred miles to take Nan-ning, a rail center and the capital of Kwangsi. Then, in September of 1940, they occupied the northern part of French Indochina, closing the important supply line between Hanoi and Kunming. Thereafter, the Nationalists were dependent for supplies from the outside world on the newly opened but barely passable Burma Road, on air transport from Hong Kong (until the Japanese occupied the city in December 1941), and on the long caravan and truck route from Russia.

The Japanese also launched destructive air attacks, their bombers striking indiscriminately at military and civilian targets. Their purpose was less to destroy military installations and factories than to demoralize the population. Virtually all cities in the Nationalist area, including Kweilin, Kunming, and Sian, were hit. Chungking, however, suffered most severely. Bombed 268 times from 1939 to 1941, the city was largely gutted, and many thousands died (4,400 were killed in just the first two days of heavy raids in May 1939).[12]

Yet neither the air raids nor the blockade broke the Chinese will to resist. Perceiving this, the Japanese high command in July 1940 made a momentous decision. Believing that success in China would continue to elude them unless they obtained access to the rich natural resources of Southeast Asia, and convinced that the Western powers were preoccupied with the war in Europe, the Japanese leaders agreed to broaden the scope of imperial expansion beyond the China theater. This decision inevitably altered the character of the China war and also led, a year and a half later, to the attack on Pearl Harbor.[13]

During this second period of the war, from the fall of Wuhan to 1941, the Japanese usually held the initiative; usually, too, they were victorious. But for the Japanese, the Nationalist strategy of actively counterpunching was costly and frustrating. To disperse potentially dangerous formations of Nationalist troops, for example, they launched attacks into northern Hupeh in May 1939 and again in May 1940, and into southern Honan in January 1940. Although the battle lines remained relatively static during this period of the war, the intensity of the fighting was high, as suggested by the heavy casualty figures for both combatants (see Table 5).

As the war dragged on, the Nationalist army suffered losses in more than just men; shortages of weapons and equipment became severe, and it was not uncommon for two, three, or even more soldiers to have to share one rifle.[14] Replacing matériel was difficult, because the Japanese blockade obstructed supply routes, foreign nations (except Russia) that might have provided aid felt they had more pressing concerns, and domestic production was never adequate to meet the army's needs.[15] Furthermore, the inflation—which progressed slowly at first, but with growing momentum after 1940—cut sharply into the government's real expenditures on the army and eroded the economic well-being of both officers and ordinary soldiers.[16]

Changing political relationships also weakened the National-

TABLE 5

*Japanese and Chinese Casualties, 1937–45*

| Year | Killed | Wounded | Missing | Total |
|---|---|---|---|---|
| JAPANESE | | | | |
| 1937 (July to Dec.) | 51,220 | 204,880 | — | 256,100 |
| 1938 | 88,978 | 355,912 | — | 444,890 |
| 1939 | 82,019 | 328,076 | — | 410,095 |
| 1940 | 68,327 | 273,309 | — | 341,636 |
| 1941 | 36,209 | 144,836 | — | 181,045 |
| 1942 | 27,841 | 111,362 | — | 139,203 |
| 1943 | 31,905 | 127,609 | — | 159,514 |
| 1944 | 50,158 | 200,632 | — | 250,790 |
| 1945 | 47,051 | 188,204 | — | 235,255 |
| TOTAL | 483,708 | 1,934,820 | — | 2,418,528 |
| CHINESE | | | | |
| 1937 (July to Dec.) | 125,130 | 242,232 | — | 367,362 |
| 1938 | 249,213 | 485,804 | — | 735,017 |
| 1939 | 169,652 | 176,891 | — | 346,543 |
| 1940 | 339,530 | 333,838 | — | 673,368 |
| 1941 | 144,915 | 137,254 | 17,314 | 299,483 |
| 1942 | 87,917 | 114,180 | 45,070 | 247,167 |
| 1943 | 43,223 | 81,957 | 37,715 | 162,895 |
| 1944 | 102,719 | 103,596 | 4,419 | 210,734 |
| 1945 | 57,659 | 85,583 | 25,608 | 168,850 |
| TOTAL | 1,319,958 | 1,761,335 | 130,126 | 3,211,419 |

SOURCE: *China Handbook, 1950*, p. 182.

ists' resolve to fight actively against the Japanese. Enmity toward the Communists had been building since 1938. Especially after the New Fourth Army Incident in January 1941, the Nationalist leaders felt that they were engaged in a two-front war. After the Americans entered the war, the Nationalists regarded the Communists as the more dangerous of their two enemies, for they anticipated that the United States, with its enormous material resources, could defeat the Japanese alone and that further Chinese sacrifices would be unnecessary.[17]

All these factors contributed to the declining effectiveness of Nationalist resistance to Japan. As early as November 1939, an official army journal complained of shortages of equipment, inadequate replacements for casualties, and poor morale. "With this kind of army," it concluded, "how can we fight off an enemy?"[18] Chiang Kai-shek, too, noted the deterioration of his army in the early part of the war. In late 1939 he launched a large-scale winter offensive intended to deny the Japanese the use of the Yangtze River. The result was a devastating defeat. Reviewing the reasons for the debacle, Chiang in February of 1940 noted that the morale of the common soldiers had declined sharply since 1937, and that "the spirit and the work of high-level commanders . . . is even less positive and enthusiastic than during the past two years." He criticized the officers, for example, for neglecting troop training and staff planning, for failing to gather intelligence about the Japanese, and for fearing to engage the enemy in battle. Most distressing to Chiang, however, was the disease of the spirit that had infected the high-ranking officers. They were, he said, concerned only to preserve their own lives and positions. As a result, they fought hesitantly and without determination, failed to cooperate with other units, neglected their work, and engaged in gambling, whoring, and smuggling.[19] (Japanese intelligence confirmed Chiang's negative assessment, reporting in 1941 that the fighting efficiency of the Nationalist army had declined 20–30 percent during the preceding year.)[20] After the winter offensive of 1939–40, therefore, Chiang Kai-shek at least temporarily reverted to a purely defensive stance.[21] And after the Japanese attack on Pearl Harbor, he abandoned completely any idea of conducting sustained offensive operations against the Japanese.

During the third period of the war, beginning with Pearl Harbor and lasting until the Ichigo Offensive in 1944, the process of deterioration in the quality of the Nationalist army proceeded apace. The China war had stalemated, and the level of hostilities were generally low. In the summer of 1942, after General James H. Doolittle's famed bombing of Tokyo, the Japanese did strike into Chekiang and Kiangsi with a force of 100,000 men to destroy air bases that might be used in future raids against the home islands. Periodically, too, they launched attacks against the Nationalist lines, less to occupy new territory than to ravage the countryside, seize or destroy recent harvests, or train recent recruits in actual combat. Occasionally the Chinese still fought tenaciously, as they did in the defense of Ch'ang-te in northern Hunan, where three divisional commanders were killed and the 57th Division suffered 90 percent casualties.[22]

Such instances of fierce fighting were infrequent, however, during this third period of the war. Rather, operations were customarily small-scale and limited to local or tactical objectives. The situation in Hupeh was probably typical. During the period from April to October of 1942, for instance, the Hupeh provincial government reported two "relatively large battles" against the Japanese. In one of these, 1,000 Japanese seized the hsien capital of Kuang-chi; a month later, the Chinese recaptured the city, killing over 20 Japanese and capturing over ten guns. In the other, in June, some 700 Japanese attacked the town of Hao-hsüeh; in the counterattack, an entire Chinese company, numbering more than 100, was lost.[23]

This contrasts with Nationalist operations against the Communists. During the same period, Nationalist troops attacked a Communist force that had infiltrated the province, killing and capturing over 1,000 "bandits" and capturing several hundred weapons. In central Hupeh, too, they engaged the main force of the Communist New Fourth Army's 5th Division, which numbered more than 10,000 men. Generally speaking, Hupeh provincial reports covering the period from early 1942 to late 1943 leave the distinct impression that Nationalist operations against the Japanese were defensive and reactive in character, whereas those against the Communists were offensive in nature, involved significantly larger numbers of troops, and resulted in markedly heavier casualties.[24]

## Deterioration of the Army's Fighting Capabilities

During this third period of the war, the criticisms of Western observers regarding the passivity and corruption of his army stung Chiang Kai-shek to the quick.[25] But he believed that his army was no longer combat-worthy. When Roosevelt pressed him in March of 1944 to order a Nationalist force in Yunnan, overwhelmingly superior numerically, to attack just one Japanese division in north Burma, Chiang demurred. Nationalist

China, he admitted, had become so militarily impotent and politically fragile that even such a minor task was beyond its capabilities. "Seven years of war," he told Roosevelt, "have taxed China's material and military strength to such an extent that to insist upon her doing something beyond her power would be to court disaster."[26] As a consequence, Chiang's strategic goals were now limited to maintaining the existing battle lines and to preparing for a future Allied landing on the China coast.[27]

The full extent of the Nationalist army's debility was exposed during Japan's Ichigo Offensive. Suffering from the air strikes of Chennault's 14th Air Force, and especially fearful that the Americans would soon launch B-29 bomber raids against the home islands, the Japanese determined to seize or destroy the air bases in south-central China. Beginning in April, and advancing to their farthest extent in December, the Japanese swept through six provinces, cleared a transportation corridor from Manchuria to Vietnam, and destroyed the offending air bases. Only at Heng-yang did the Japanese forces meet prolonged, meaningful resistance. There, the Tenth Army, commanded by General Hsüeh Yüeh and supported by Chennault's fighters and bombers (but denied fresh supplies by Chiang Kai-shek), held off the aggressor during six weeks of bloody, determined fighting. Elsewhere, the Japanese moved virtually at will; the Chinese troops had become too weak in body, spirit, and weapons to mount an effective resistance.[28]

During the first phase of the Ichigo Offensive, the Japanese struck into Honan to take control of the full length of the Peiping-Hankow railway and thus protect their rear during the ensuing major phase of the campaign in South China. In this battle—known as Kogo by the Japanese and as the Battle of Central Honan by the Chinese—a Japanese force of about 60,000 men in just two months completely shattered a Nationalist army five times its size. Only once, at the town of Ssu-shui just west of Kaifeng, did the Nationalists put up any real resistance; elsewhere, the Japanese advanced almost unimpeded. It was a sudden and crushing blow to the Chinese.[29]

After the battle, the Nationalist commander in Honan, T'ang En-po, convened a three-day conference to hear the reports of his top officers and to evaluate their performance. His lectures during that conference revealed the pathetic condition of the Nationalist army in Honan. "During the past two years and more," T'ang told his officers, "our troops have been stationed in Honan and have not fought any large-scale battles. Their life became soft, and they were concerned only with pleasure. There were all kinds of temptations inherent in a bad environment. Moreover, everyone lacked determination; they lacked a clear comprehension [of what needed to be done]. As a result the troops gradually deteriorated." [30]

Turning to specific manifestations of that deterioration, T'ang identified important ingredients in the defeat:

(1) *Poor intelligence.* We planned our defense as though in the dark. We misjudged the objectives of the Japanese, and did not even know how many or what kind of troops the Japanese were mobilizing for the attack. We must ask, why was the intelligence so inadequate? To be frank, it was entirely because we high-ranking officers ordinarily do not emphasize intelligence work and because our collection of intelligence is too haphazard. As a result, the headquarters staff did not know what the situation of the enemy was, and all our troop deployments, battle preparations, and tactical commands were wrong.

(2) *Lack of morale.* With the exception of the New 29th Division, our troops hardly performed any meritorious acts in battle. The troops lacked combat spirit and there was no willingness to sacrifice. Some cadres even avoided combat. This lack of fighting spirit was the most obvious and serious defect among our troops.

(3) *Inept commanders.* Poor staff work is a major cause of our mistakes. Staff officers do not adequately collect information about the enemy or even about ourselves. Planning of operations was therefore wholly inadequate. In the field, commanders at all levels failed to make the best use of their troops. A few officers even deserted their units.

(4) *Failure to carry out orders.* Most cadres at all levels do not thoroughly carry out their superiors' commands, and some even completely ignore them. For instance, during this campaign, the commander of the Twelfth Army was ordered to attack Lung-men, but for three days he failed to advance. Disregard of orders was truly a most important cause of our defeat. In the past, in such battles as those at T'ai-erh-chuang, Shanghai, Wuhan, and Hsü-chou, we exacted a price from the enemy even though we were ultimately defeated. "But in the

defeat in this campaign, no one was able to exact much of a price, and no one carried out the orders of their superiors or fulfilled their responsibilities. This kind of defeat is shameful!"

(5) *Insufficient cooperation.* Our chief concern should be to attain victory in battle, even if we must sacrifice ourselves. But now, because of jealousy and delight in the tribulations of others, we failed to cooperate or come to the assistance of one another. This was true not just among the different armies in the war zone, but even among individual commanders within the same army.

(6) *Inattention to battlefield evacuation of the wounded.* Unit commanders ordinarily give no attention at all to the organization, personnel, or equipment of the medical staff in our units. So how could there be any first aid or evacuation of the wounded during battle? The failure to provide medical assistance for the wounded is a great cruelty on the part of the unit commanders.

(7) *Lack of regard for weapons and equipment.* In this battle, we lost half our backpacks and not a few of our weapons. Some people asked me after the fighting why I did not request replacements for this equipment, but I was so ashamed that I did not have the "face" to report the losses.

During the Battle of Central Honan, Chinese peasants armed with farm tools and crude weapons attacked T'ang En-po's Chinese soldiers as they retreated before the Japanese. They disarmed an estimated 50,000 of those soldiers and even murdered some of them.[31] With his subordinates, T'ang candidly discussed this astounding phenomenon:[32]

Ordinarily, our troops made no effort to communicate with the public; they even ignored the local elites. We did strike down the local bullies and evil gentry, but we failed to establish a relationship with the masses. For instance, the Twenty-ninth Army was stationed at Yü-hsien for over two years and learned nothing of local conditions, and as a result they suffered greatly at the hands of the local population. This was all of their own making. "If in ordinary times we pay no attention [to the civilian population], then as soon as we get into difficulties or betray the slightest weakness, the Japanese puppets and the traitor bandits attack us. Even the local government, the local elites, and the people come to attack us."

Moreover, the reason our army had a poor reputation in this battle was chiefly owing to our dependents and our personnel in the rear.

Only the Thirteenth Army properly took care of its families and dependents beforehand; all the rest moved in a panic at the last moment, everywhere creating disturbances among the civilian population. According to reports, our troops confiscated many ox carts, but in fact few of these were used to transport the army's matériel. By far the greater number were used to transport families and dependents. "You think about it. With such large losses among the local people, how could the commoners not hate us?"

In the past, I repeatedly ordered that dependents be settled far in the rear, and I provided accommodations there. But none of you sent your dependents there. Tell me, at this time of national crisis, are your families or the nation more important? As for military personnel in the rear, their training and discipline were neglected. As a result, an important reason for the poor reputation of our army was that some bad elements among the officers and men did not maintain discipline.

## The Quality of the Officer Corps

The inept leadership, the absence of troop discipline, and the lack of fighting spirit displayed in the Battle of Central Honan were not restricted to the troops in that province (T'ang En-po was one of the more competent Nationalist generals), nor were they found only during the last year of the war. Although these defects were magnified during the period of stalemate, they were characteristic of the Nationalist army throughout most of the war. The officer corps, for example, had from the beginning sadly lacked professional skills. The senior officers who had graduated from the Whampoa Academy were almost innocent of a military education; most were graduates of the period 1924–26, when training had been elementary and had lasted for from less than six months to at most a year. They seldom benefited thereafter from the rotating assignments in administration, teaching, or the specialized branches of the army that were customary in the modernized Western armies. During the 1930's, these officers might have taken advantage of advanced training in the Chinese staff college. Few Whampoa graduates, however, deigned to return to the classroom; in any case, the training provided by the staff college was embarrassingly inadequate when measured by international standards.[33]

A few of the generals nonetheless stood out from their peers and were commanders of genuine talent. Paradoxically, however, Chiang Kai-shek seldom made full use of them, because he valued the quality of loyalty more than ability and incorruptibility in his subordinates. Pai Ch'ung-hsi, for instance, may have been the most able officer in the army, and Joseph W. Stilwell urged that he be named army chief of staff. But Chiang could not tolerate Pai in any post where he held substantive and independent military power because—even though Pai's commitment to the National Government could now hardly be doubted—he had a history before 1937 of rebelling against Chiang. Ch'en Ch'eng was another skilled commander who was long denied positions worthy of his abilities. In his case, he enjoyed the trust of Chiang, but he had the misfortune of having lost a factional dispute with the incompetent minister of war, Ho Ying-ch'in.[34]

A further problem was that fully a third—and some estimates go as high as two-thirds—of the central army had been destroyed in the fighting at Shanghai and in the lower Yangtze during the first months of the war. As a consequence, the balance of military and political authority within the Nationalist regime shifted perceptibly from Chiang Kai-shek and the central leadership to the provincial armies and their commanders.[35] Even less than before the war, therefore, could Chiang issue orders to, and expect to be obeyed by, such independent-minded commanders as Lung Yün and Yen Hsi-shan.

Chiang subsequently attempted to right the balance, adding steadily to the central army's numbers and building it up again to about 300,000 men in 1941, and then to some 650,000 by the end of the war.[36] Whenever possible, he ordered the regional forces into combat with the Japanese while holding the central-army divisions in reserve, protecting their personnel and precious equipment.[37] In distributing weapons and equipment, he invariably favored his central forces over the provincial armies. This practice could have ironic consequences: in 1944, for instance, Chiang's representatives hotly protested the United States's distribution of Lend-Lease equipment to General Hsüeh Yüeh—whose loyalty Chiang doubted—at the very time that

Hsüeh's forces were fiercely resisting the Japanese at Heng-yang.[38]

The regional commanders were, however, loath to sacrifice their armies on the altar of Chiang's political ambitions. In May 1939 at the battle of Sui-Tsao in northern Hupeh, for instance, a large Japanese force was suffering shortages of food and ammunition and could have been routed, but Li P'in-hsien of the Kwangsi Clique let it escape rather than engage it in battle. Then, too, the winter offensive of 1939–40 failed in large part because the regional armies responded so grudgingly and ineffectively to Chiang's orders to attack.[39]

The mutual distrust between the central government and the regional commanders profoundly affected the Nationalists' battlefield planning and overall strategy in the war. Ch'en Ch'eng in 1938 had stressed the need "to eliminate the concept of private interests, to convert all armies into genuine national armies, and to thoroughly eliminate the erroneous notion of self-preservation and self-protection."[40] This goal was never realized, however, not even by 1949.

When the war began, lower-ranking officers were generally better trained than their superiors. But fully 10,000 of the approximately 25,000 men who graduated from the Central Military Academy between 1929 and 1937 were killed during the first four months of the fighting.[41] The central army never really recovered from these losses. The academies continued throughout the war to turn out new lieutenants, but they were poorly prepared for their duties. Entrance requirements at the academies had to be lowered, and the period of training was reduced to just one year. The quality of training at the academies, moreover, deteriorated. The Russian adviser Kalyagin found, for example, that the faculty in 1939 had no combat experience and taught entirely by lecturing; they used neither equipment nor practical exercises. The artillery academy used similar methods of instruction, although it did have a training regiment, which provided the students some practical experience in firing and concealment. Although the Central Academy, including its nine branch campuses, graduated nearly 120,000 officers during the war, the army still had to promote large numbers of men from the ranks. By 1945, therefore, only 20 percent of the officers in a typical battalion of infantry were academy graduates; before the war, that figure had been 80 percent.[42]

The Nationalist officer corps at both the senior and junior levels received poor marks during the war from expert military observers. Officers were, General Wedemeyer declared, "incapable, inept, untrained, petty . . . altogether inefficient."[43] Their staff work and administration were bureaucratized and often impractical; and, Wedemeyer added, "the disorganization and muddled planning of the Chinese is beyond comprehension."[44] Even when plans were prepared, the tendency of field commanders to act independently, their reluctance to cooperate with other commanders, and their desire to preserve their strength, meant that the plans frequently went awry.[45] Officers were also notoriously unaggressive. "The Guomindang generals," Kalyagin complained, "were forever finding reasons not to send their troops into battle."[46]

Curiously, however, once engaged with the enemy, Chinese officers sometimes fought heroically, with a startling abandon and disregard for human life. Chiang Kai-shek purposely instilled an attitude of selfless sacrifice in his officers. An American who witnessed the Salween campaign in western Yunnan in April 1944 described the results:

Several days were wasted and heavy losses incurred . . . in suicidal charges by a succession of squads against enemy pillboxes. Teamwork in the use of weapons and supporting fire and the use of cover were conspicuously lacking . . . most casualties resulted from attempts to walk or rather climb up through interlocking bands of machine-gun fire. As a demonstration of sheer bravery the attacks were magnificent but sickeningly wasteful. Some platoon leaders were killed within one or two meters of the enemy embrasures and several of the best company and battalion commanders were killed and wounded in personal leadership of their troops. A general coordinated assault might have overrun the positions by sheer esprit and weight of numbers, but adjoining or supporting units would idly watch some single squad or platoon get mowed down in a lone advance, then try it on their own front.[47]

Thousands of Chinese soldiers sacrificed their lives in such fool-hardy displays of bravery; the Nationalist army incurred what was—considering the long periods of inactivity during the eight years of war—an appalling casualty rate of 23 percent.[48]

Officers also disregarded some of the basic principles of their trade. They neglected the maintenance of weapons and equipment. They disdained concealing or camouflaging their positions, even putting gunners along the crests of mountains.[49] The gathering and protection of intelligence were conducted haphazardly. Kalyagin found that "battle intelligence was not carried out and aerial intelligence was lacking. Commanders made decisions blindly."[50] Safeguarding intelligence from the enemy was similarly ignored. As Kalyagin observed, "Usually everything that went out from headquarters became known to Japanese intelligence."[51]

No one was more conscious of the shortcomings of the Nationalist officer corps than Chiang Kai-shek. Indeed, he often personally took a hand in commanding the army, ordering units even at the regimental level to move or take a specified action, although he might be unfamiliar with the terrain, condition of the troops, or disposition of the enemy forces. He often did this without informing high-level commanders, and utter confusion easily resulted.[52] Chiang's interference in his army's field operations may have sprung from hubris, bred by long years in power, but he justified the practice by asserting that his generals were utterly incompetent. To General Joseph W. Stilwell, he explained: "I have to lie awake nights thinking what fool things they may do. Then I write and tell them not to do these things. But they are so dumb, they will do a lot of foolishness unless you anticipate them. This is the secret of handling them—you must imagine everything that they can do that would be wrong, and warn them against it."[53] In all probability, however, Chiang's interference in field operations did more harm than good, creating confusion and stripping his officers of initiative.[54]

## The Enlisted Men: Conscription and Training

The common soldier in the Nationalist army, by contrast with his officers, won the admiration of the foreign experts. As Stilwell remarked, "Chinese troops if well trained, equipped and led can match the valor of soldiers everywhere."[55] Usually, however, the Nationalist soldiers were so ill-treated and ill-fed that they lacked both the ability and the morale to fight effectively.

Most of Nationalist China's soldiers were conscripts. According to the conscription law, all men between the ages of 18 and 45 *sui*—with the exception of only sons, students, and hardship cases—were eligible for the draft.[56] The government strongly propagandized the "Principle of the Three Equals" (*san-p'ing yüan-tzu*), whereby responsibility for military service would rest equitably upon all areas and economic classes of the nation. To realize that principle, quotas were allocated to the local authorities on the basis of population, and the conscripts were then to be selected by drawing lots.[57]

So much for principle. Practice was different. Chiang Kai-shek himself declared, "Military conscription is now managed badly; this is truly the chief reason why discipline in our armed forces has collapsed and why our fighting ability has deteriorated."[58] The deepest flaw in the system was that it depended ultimately upon local authorities to carry out the work of selecting and assembling the draftees. But the Nationalist government exercised little control over these authorities, who invariably represented the interests of the wealthy and powerful elites in each locality. Sons of the elite consequently avoided the draft, whereas the poor and weak were press-ganged into the army in utter disregard of the Principle of the Three Equals.[59]

Seldom was the system of lottery employed. For reasons that remain unclear, attempts to select conscripts through the lottery frequently provoked riots.[60] One wonders if the riots were incited by local elites, who might have felt it difficult to manipulate the lottery in their favor. In any event, the responsibility for selecting the new soldiers fell largely upon heads of the *pao* and *chia*, those neighborhood administrative units comprising about 1,000 and 100 households, respectively.

The pao-chia heads have been thoroughly vilified for their role in conscription. Nationalist conscription officials complained that they changed the population registers, or increased or decreased the recorded ages, so that members of their families and their friends could avoid the draft. They were, declared a con-scription official in Kweichow, arbitrary, ignorant, and corrupt.[61] Such indictments of the pao-chia heads doubtless were often ac-curate. In Li-ling hsien in eastern Hunan, however, the pao-chia heads were described as hapless tools of the local elites. There, the t'u-hao lieh-shen (local bullies and evil gentry) and secret so-cieties controlled all aspects of government. Thus, when the pao-chia heads received a draft call, they would have to convene a meeting of the local power-holders to decide who would, and who would not, be drafted.[62]

Not only political power but wealth obtained exemptions from the draft. Many rich families sent their sons to the univer-sities, where they would be exempt from the draft. More com-mon was the practice of purchasing substitutes. Riffraff of rural society offered—for a price—to serve in the army in the place of legitimate conscripts. This, for many, became their profession; they would desert from the army at their first opportunity and then offer themselves for sale again and again. Some 80–90 per-cent of the recruits in Li-ling hsien were reputedly obtained in this fashion—though that figure would appear to be either exag-gerated or atypical.[63]

By about 1941, the reservoir of draft-eligible males was run-ning dry. The number of families with more than one son still at home had declined; the rich had learned to obtain exemptions; and many young men had simply fled, feigned sickness, or mutilated themselves.[64] Thereupon, wrote the head of conscrip-tion in Szechwan, the practice of dragooning soldiers (la-ping) "filled the entire nation."[65] When the formal conscription sys-tem proved inadequate, army units in the field dispatched press-gangs (chieh-ping-tui) to pick up the needed replacements. The result was wholesale abductions of the poor (the rich could pur-chase their release). A memorandum sent by General Wede-meyer to Chiang Kai-shek in 1944 described how the system might work: "For example, you are working in a field looking after your rice . . . [and there come] a number of uniformed men who tie your hands behind your back and take you with them. . . . Hoe and plough rust in the field, the wife runs to the magistrate to cry and beg for her husband, the children starve."[66] Milton Miles, commander of an American clandestine unit in China and an ardent admirer of the Nationalist government, also reported seeing a press-gang stage a street performance of juggling and acrobatics. It then seized able-bodied members of the audience "on the theory that any man with time to watch a street show had better be in the Army!"[67]

"The people," observed an official journal, "look upon [conscription] like death."[68] Not only were the men taken from their fields, causing untold hardships on the dependents left at home, but the feeling was widespread that, once drafted, they would never return home. The absence of any system of retirement or discharge from the army, the rarity with which soldiers corresponded with their families after entering the service, and, indeed, the high mortality rates in the army—all lent a degree of credibility to the peasants' fears.[69]

For the first several months of their military service, life for the new soldiers was especially hard. They were marched to reception centers where, following a perfunctory medical examination, they were assigned to replacement units to undergo three months of basic military training. In fact, because of either financial shortages or the pressing need for troop replacements in the field, the period of training was frequently much shorter than that prescribed. Sometimes, indeed, the recruits were marched directly to service at the front. So inadequate was the training given the new soldiers that an official publication even suggested that for them to go into battle was "truly like being sent to die."[70]

As a result of limited funds, official corruption, and sheer callousness, conditions in the reception centers were often appalling. Colonel Lyle Stephenson Powell, a U.S. Army medical officer on liaison duty with the Nationalist army, provided the following description of such a "camp" in February 1945 near Kweiyang:

This recruiting center consisted of a number of buildings sequestered in different villages lying within sight of each other in a little valley a few miles from the city. . . . We proceeded first to the so-called hospital or dispensary. . . . I have seen a good many ghastly sights, but I have never seen anything that gave me such a complete turn as did this "hospital." The building consisted of a long, earthen-floored, thatched-roofed hut, the sides of which had practically all disappeared, presumably as firewood. Lying on boards in this hut were some seventy to eighty men. Two or three had old overcoats of some sort pulled up over them; the rest had only shirt, trousers, and either bare feet or straw sandals. For warmth they were lying as close together as possible and were too sick to get up to answer the calls of nature; as a consequence, the foulness of the place was beyond belief. As I went along looking at these people I counted several that were dead, some already as stiff as the boards they were lying on. Some were obviously about to expire, and the others were in various stages of questionable animation.

We went on to the villages to look at some of the quarters. We found that the system was to sequester the village houses that had boards on the ceiling of the ground floor. This left a cozy little room under the thatched eaves, filthy with the dirt and dust of the ages, where the recruits slept. We inquired why they used the upper story, and the Chinese sergeant told us that if they didn't put the men in the upper story they would all run away during the night. "In fact," he said, "it is necessary for us to take all their clothes away from them at night to keep them from getting out through the roof and escaping in spite of the guards that we have posted around the house. And even then, occasionally one gets away." It was February and I had been freezing cold every day, though well clad in good woolen clothes. At night I had been sleeping under four blankets and had had a hard time keeping warm. These poor fellows slept naked in a leaky attic, some forty or fifty crowded into a space approximately ten by fifteen feet. The sergeant told us that they kept warmer and slept better if they were crowded close together.[71]

Although not all reception centers were as noisome as this one, it was not wholly atypical, as shown in a report by a Nationalist official inspecting conscription conditions in late 1940: "Filthy and in disorder, the quarters were crowded. As for the troops, they were emaciated and gaunt, and their clothes were in rags. They were just like a group of beggars. As for the squalor of the sleeping quarters, the filth of the toilets, the cries of the sick, and the grievances of the deserters, all were excessive. No wonder the men regard the training units as hell; they all wish to risk their lives on the battlefield but are unwilling to endure suffering here."[72]

After completing "training," the conscripts were assigned to units in the field. Because of the paucity of transportation, they customarily had to march to join those units, which were often hundreds of miles away. These marches were the most terrible part of the conscripts' introduction to the army. Fearful that the conscripts would try to escape, the guards treated them like prisoners; frequently they roped the recruits together, linking them like pearls on a string. Conscription officials at higher administrative levels deplored this practice, but—arguing that the conscripts were parochial in outlook and therefore not capable of comprehending the importance of military service—they also condoned it as an emergency measure.[73] For food, the conscripts received only small servings of rice gruel, partially because of the skimpy budget provided by the government, but often because the officers in charge had "squeezed" most of the rations for their own profit. For water, they might have to drink from puddles at the roadside—a common cause of diarrhea.[74] Physically weakened, the conscripts became easy victims of disease. Denied medical attention, many died. Chiang Kai-shek even told of conscripts, so ill that they could no longer move, who were shot to death by the guards along the roadside.[75]

Some recruits on this hellish march to war luckily escaped. Some bribed their way free; others tried to run. Those who were caught were usually beaten. Then, according to Wedemeyer's memorandum to Chiang Kai-shek, the unfortunate recruits would be "carried along with broken limbs and with wounds in maimed flesh in which infection turns quickly into blood poisoning and blood poisoning into death."[76] The dead were sometimes placed in shallow graves; many were simply left where they fell, unburied.[77]

Repeatedly the government issued orders to improve these conditions. It ordered that water stations and medical clinics be set up along the routes followed by the conscripts. It also proscribed physical punishment and other forms of brutality.[78] Indeed, in 1945, following a visit to a conscript reception center,

Chiang Kai-shek was so appalled by conditions that he ordered that the director of the Conscription Bureau, the commanding officer of the reception center, and several lesser officers be summarily executed.[79] Such remedial measures had little if any effect, however, and many young men continued to die ghastly deaths during those few weeks following their first encounters with the conscription officers. Chiang Kai-shek related that fewer than 100 recruits of a group of 1,000 survived a march from their starting point in Fukien to Kweichow.[80] Only seventeen of 700 recruits lived through a 500-mile trek from Kwangtung to Yunnan.[81] These were, no doubt, extreme examples. Yet nearly half—44 percent—of the 1,670,000 men drafted during 1943 either perished or deserted on the march to their units.[82] The total number of conscripts who died during the eight years of the war *before they reached their assigned units in the field* was about 1,400,000—or one out of every ten men drafted.[83]

## The Enlisted Men: Food and Medical Treatment

Conscripts who survived their initial training and the perilous trek to their assigned units soon faced other challenges more deadly even than the Japanese. These were hunger, cold, and disease. Actually, the soldiers' food rations would have been adequate if the regulations had been enforced. Troops in the central army, for instance, were allocated 24 ounces of rice daily and sufficient money to buy a pound of pork each month. (Rations of provincial troops were substantially less.) But corruption up and down the chain of command regularly siphoned off a portion of these food and money allowances. Then meat, salt, and oil would disappear from the soldiers' diets for months at a time, and they would have only a few boiled vegetables to add taste and nutrients to their staple of grain.[84]

Fed inadequately by the army, the soldiers often became scavengers, stealing from whatever villages or peasants they happened to encounter. As a result, the common people viewed Nationalist soldiers as they would a plague or any other natural disaster, often fleeing at their approach.[85]

Despite all such efforts to supplement their diets, most Nationalist soldiers during the latter half of the war suffered nutritional deficiencies that seriously affected their ability to function as soldiers. As early as 1941, General Hsiung Shih-hui reported that soldiers in Chekiang, without meat or oil to eat, generated so little body heat that they insisted on wearing winter uniforms even in hot weather. General Wedemeyer, when he took up his duties as Chiang Kai-shek's chief of staff in October 1944, at first concentrated his attention primarily upon problems of troop movements and dispositions. Within a month, however, he realized that the soldiers were too weak to march and were incapable of fighting effectively, largely because they were half-starved.[86]

Hardly less debilitating to the army were the abysmal sanitary conditions and woefully inadequate medical treatment available. Soldiers wore their uniforms throughout the winter without changing; soap was not issued; and there existed no facilities in the army camps for bathing. Kitchens were frequently located beside latrines; drinking water was seldom boiled; and the troops—many of whom carried communicable diseases—as a matter of course dipped their germ-laden chopsticks into one common pot. These conditions of inadequate food and clothing and unsanitary living conditions left every soldier an easy mark for disease. Malaria took the largest toll. Seldom were mosquito nets used, and the disease, which before the war had been prevalent only in South China, spread even to the northern provinces as a result of the movements of population during the war. Because quinine was in short supply, the authorities were sparing in its use. As a consequence, individuals and sometimes entire regiments shuddered and shook from the fever. Only when the troops were about to go into battle was quinine distributed. Sometimes, though, it was even then held back for an "emergency."[87]

Other common scourges were intestinal and skin afflictions. Dysentery, which spread widely because of the troops' otherwise weakened condition, was often fatal because of ignorance and shortages of medicine. Scabies and tropical skin ulcers were common, and if the soldiers took off their long, cotton-padded winter uniforms in summer, the suppurating sores on their bare legs became visible. Eye infections were also widespread, most notably in the northwest. Near Lanchow, more than half of the troops suffered so severely from eye infections (such as trachoma and gonorrheal conjuctivitis) that they could not effectively aim their rifles. Tuberculosis was common, as was venereal disease, despite Theodore White's statement that it was relatively rare because the soldiers lacked the vitality and opportunities for sexual activity. Between 1939 and 1940, the incidence of venereal disease reportedly increased three times; and in the Lanchow area an estimated 90 percent of the troops suffered from gonorrhea and 30 percent from syphilis.[88]

Disease and malnutrition seriously reduced the fighting capabilities of the Chinese army. During the fighting in the southwest in 1945, American observers found that the Thirteenth Army was unable to hike even a short distance "without men falling out wholesale and many dying from utter starvation."[89] Another American officer, Colonel David D. Barrett, reported seeing Nationalist soldiers "topple over and die after marching less than a mile."[90] Some of the sick and weak would for a time be carried on stretchers. But "it is not unusual," read another American report, "to see the occupants of the litters dumped by the road either dead or soon to die."[91] A reporter for the highly regarded *Ta-kung-pao* (*"L'Impartial"*) observed that "where troops have passed, dead soldiers can be found by the roadside one after another."[92] A few elite troops, most notably the Youth Army and divisions of the Chinese Expeditionary Force, which had received training from U.S. forces, were still adequately fed. But when soldiers in a substantial part of the army were barely able to walk and when even short marches left the roadsides littered with bodies, the Nationalist army could not be reckoned an effective fighting force.

Medical treatment was ostensibly provided Chinese troops by the Army Medical Corps. However, Dr. Robert Lim (Lin K'o-sheng), chairman of the Chinese Red Cross Medical Relief Corps, depicted its services as "pre-Nightingale."[93] Wedemeyer's memorandum to Chiang Kai-shek even compared the army hospitals to German extermination camps.[94] The comparison had a basis in fact.

On paper, the organization of the medical corps—with its first-aid teams, dressing stations, field hospitals, and base hospitals—appeared unexceptionable. The organization was undermined, however, by inadequate and incompetent personnel, by insufficient equipment and medicines, and by neglect and corruption. There were only 1,000–2,000 reasonably qualified doctors in the entire army, so that there was one qualified doctor available for every 1,700 to 3,400 men—whereas there was one doctor for every 210 men in the British army and for every 150 men in the U.S. army.[95] Some 28,000 additional "doctors" served in the Medical Corps, but most of these were grossly incompetent, having been promoted to "doctor" solely on the basis of their experience as stretcher-bearers or field nurses.[96] Lyle Powell found in 1944 that in the entire 46th Army Corps, consisting of three divisions, there was not even one qualified physician; the chief medical officer was an inexperienced graduate of a short-term army medical school.[97] Even when there were competent doctors, they were handicapped by severe shortages of equipment and medicines. A field hospital, Powell reported, "did not have beds or cots and had few blankets, few sheets, a limited number of dressings, few drugs, and no sterilizers, operating-room kits, electric lights, operating tables, or X-ray machines."[98] One of the persistent problems, moreover, was that corrupt officers frequently sold the few medicines that were available; and much of the medicine that was used was phony or watered-down.[99]

Medical assistants were even less competent than the doctors. Because of the low regard in which the medical services were held, the typical unit commander transferred his most ignorant or weak soldiers—those incapable of holding a rifle—to serve as medical corpsmen. Since stretcher-bearers were often civilians paid or conscripted for the job, they tended to take flight as soon as fighting began.[100] The result, reported an official journal, was that the wounded could get no first aid. On the battlefield, continued the journal, the sound of cries for help was terrible.[101] Even a medical-corps journal charged in 1938 that the wounded often struggled on their own to reach the railway depots where, without care or medicines, their wounds soon filled with maggots.[102] The Russian adviser Kalyagin observed that, without dressing or feeding stations, the wounded "died from hunger and wounds right there beside the road."[103]

The seriously wounded were usually left to die on the battle-field. Those who were evacuated had to endure long waits before receiving something like professional care. This was because the medical corps was desperately short of transportation, and because the hospitals were located well away from the front, where the doctors felt secure.[104]

Few if any reforms were undertaken in the medical corps during the course of the war. Civilian organizations such as the Chinese Red Cross Medical Relief Corps did attempt to mitigate the inadequacies of the official medical service. Yet throughout the war a seriously wounded soldier had but a slight chance of recovery, and mortality rates even among those with minor wounds were appallingly high. "Not many cripples," Rhodes Farmer wrote after witnessing the early years of the war, "are to be seen in China."[105]

Chinese soldiers, poorly fed and badly treated, had little enthusiasm for combat; many deserted. Indeed, half of China's troops—over eight million men—simply disappeared and were unaccounted for during the course of the war.[106] Some of these doubtless died of disease, but a high proportion of them deserted. A typical unit was the 18th Division of the Eighteenth Army; being a part of the central army, conditions in it were relatively good. Yet during 1942, even though not engaged in combat, 6,000 of its complement of 11,000 men were lost, either through death or desertion. Even General Hu Tsung-nan's forces in 1943, which were particularly favored because they were being used to blockade the Communists in North China, reportedly lost an average of 600 men from each division (of about 10,000 men) every month.[107]

During the latter half of the eight-year war with Japan, the Nationalist army was in an advanced state of disintegration. However substantial its achievements against Japan early in the war, it was manifestly incapable, at least after 1942 and probably earlier, of sustained, effective military operations. The army at the end of the war was, to quote General Ho Ying-ch'in, "exhausted in the extreme" (*p'i-pei chih yü*).[108] There were, to be sure, exceptions. Eight divisions had recently completed a 13-week program of American-style training; 22 other divisions were in various stages of that training; and these, being well-fed and well-equipped, were relatively efficient fighting units.[109] The remainder of the 300-odd Chinese divisions, however, remained untouched. This exhaustion and decrepitude were to be of supreme significance, for the army was soon called upon to fight a civil war with the Communists.

## CHAPTER 7

# The Nationalist Army Against the Communists

WHEN THE JAPANESE surrendered in August 1945, the Nationalist army, though weary and battered, still appeared far superior to the Communist forces.[1] Indeed, during the early stages of the civil war, in 1946 and early 1947, the government's armies pushed forward, seemingly irresistibly. They advanced deep into Manchuria, past Changchun on the road to Harbin; large areas of Shantung were retaken; and on March 19, 1947, in a loudly proclaimed victory, they captured Mao Tse-tung's headquarters at Yenan. Exultantly the Nationalist high command predicted victory over the Communist "bandits" within six months.[2] But from the second half of 1947 on, the strategic advantage shifted inexorably to the Communists.

The search for an explanation of this dramatic change in the character of the civil war has for decades provoked heated—often embittered—debate. Partisans of the Nationalists have pointed an accusing finger at the United States, claiming that it failed to supply Nationalist forces with adequate weapons, ammunition, and equipment. They have contended, for example, that General George C. Marshall imposed an embargo that for ten months, from July of 1946 to May of 1947, prohibited the shipment of munitions from the United States to China. Subsequently, it was charged, shipments of war matériel authorized by the China Aid Act of April 1948 reached the Nationalist forces only after long and seemingly inexcusable delays.[3]

Curiously, the debate over the question "Who Lost China?" has been based not on Chinese sources, but almost entirely on

English-language documentation, particularly from the State Department and from Congressional investigations. The testimony in that documentation is so filled with innuendo that some scholars, despite overwhelming evidence to the contrary, continue even today to argue that pro-Communist elements in the United States determined the political and military outcome of the Chinese Communist revolution. A variety of Chinese sources suggest, however, that the Nationalist army was defeated for reasons other than the actions of Communist fellow travelers in the State Department and the betrayal of China by the American government. These sources, upon which the ensuing discussion is largely based, include the memoirs of Nationalist generals and official Nationalist publications. Most notable among the latter is a six-volume study entitled *Recollections and Evaluations of Important Communist-Suppression Campaigns* (hereafter referred to as *Recollections*).[4] This study was prepared in 1950, immediately following the debacle on the mainland, by seventeen high-ranking Nationalist officers, including Hu Tsung-nan and T'ang En-po, and published presumably by the Ministry of National Defense. It was undertaken explicitly to provide the Nationalist leaders with the lessons of the past in order to serve as a guide in the future. Together with the other Chinese sources, it clearly reveals that the Nationalist army was defeated as a result of its own ineptitude and of being pitted against a vastly more effective fighting force.

## The Availability of Arms and Equipment

The American embargo on arms to the Nationalists was in effect until May 1947. If this embargo had seriously affected the operations of the Nationalist army, the shortages of weapons would have been apparent by the latter part of 1947. Yet in September of that year, the Ministry of National Defense reported that since August 1945 it had been actively rearming its second-line troops. From that time to June 1947 it had provided 423,422 rifles and 17,253 light and heavy machine guns to second-line units. During that period, troops in all the important provinces had been fully supplied, and over 60 percent of the troops in the lesser provinces had also received weapons. The Ministry added that this work of supplying all the second-line troops in the nation would be completed by the end of 1947.[5] One may infer that if the second-line units were being adequately provided with arms, shortages among the first-line forces could not have been acute.

In fact, *Recollections* does not mention shortages of equipment as being a factor in any of the anti-Communist campaigns until early 1949, when Nationalist forces were preparing to defend against a Communist crossing of the Yangtze River.[6] The 1949 shortages, moreover, were attributable not to inadequate shipments from abroad, but to disastrous losses earlier in Manchuria and North China. The Communists claimed that during a period of four and a half months from September 1948 to February 1949 they captured 1,709,000 rifles, carbines, and pistols, 193,000 automatic rifles, 37,000 artillery pieces, and 12,000 motor vehicles.[7]

The Ministry of National Defense, moreover, explicitly confirmed that shortages of ammunition and weapons were not a cause of the military debacle. In 1950, in a document classified "Top Secret," the Ministry remarked on the plenitude of American aid: 39 divisions had been completely equipped with U.S. arms, and many other divisions had received surplus American supplies. The problem, then, had not been a lack of American aid. "We have never heard it said," concluded the Ministry's report, "that our military defeat in recent years resulted from a lack of ammunition or an insufficiency of other supplies. Rather, we inadequately understood bandit-suppression and anti-Communism; we had insufficient morale; and our government, economy, and programs completely failed to provide close support for the bandit-suppression military effort. This was an important factor in our defeat."[8]

## Erroneous Tactics and Strategy

Nationalist troops fighting in the civil war, noted the *Recollections*, were fearful of hand-to-hand combat, dared not engage in nighttime fighting, exercised poor fire-discipline, and lacked mobility. They also failed to reconnoiter their positions adequately, and they disliked fighting in mountainous terrain.[9] Serious though these criticisms were, the principal causes of the Nationalist military defeat were not tactical but strategic. As General Liu Chih wrote of the Battle of Hwai-Hai, "the strategic failures were greater than the tactical, and the tactical failures were greater than [those committed in individual] combat."[10]

From the onset of the civil war, the Nationalist high command overextended its forces. By attempting to control too large an area, the army was weak everywhere. Its strategy of "extended lines and occupied points" (*yen-hsien chan-tien*), wrote the *Recollections*, was initially the result of "political demands"—presumably referring to the truce arranged by General Marshall. As a consequence, the Nationalist army had not pressed its advantage and had not pushed for a victory when, the authors of the *Recollections* stated,[11] it held a decisive advantage over the Communists.* Having spread itself thin along the "lines and points," the *Recollections* continued, the Nationalist army then committed

---

*The assertion that the Nationalist army could easily and quickly have exterminated the Communist forces—but for the truce arranged by Marshall in January 1946—is still popular in pro-Nationalist circles. It is entirely fallacious. Since at least 1930 the Nationalist authorities had repeatedly proclaimed that they would annihilate the Communist bandit forces in three months, six months, or a year. In 1947 and later, they continued to make such predictions—each time, of course, without result. That they would have been any more successful in making good on that promise in early 1946 is, therefore, unlikely.

Moreover, the assertion that they could have quashed the Communists in January 1946, but not in April, implicitly admits that the Nationalists were incapable of defeating a Communist force that posed any significant challenge at all. For even if the Communists were somewhat stronger in April than they had been four months earlier, they were still far weaker, as measured by all objective criteria, than the Nationalists. Their army was smaller and less well armed, they controlled a lesser and poorer area of the nation, and they were the recipients of much less international assistance than the Nationalists. Indeed, the frailty of the Communists is suggested by Steven I. Levine's conclusion, after a detailed study of the Communist movement in Manchuria, that "As late as mid-1947, Communist power in much of northern Manchuria rested upon extremely shaky foundations, and only a slightly better organized and better-led opponent might at a minimum have fought the Communists to a standstill in the region" (Levine, "Mobilizing for War," p. 5). The argument that the 1946 truce was critical to the outcome of the civil war is, therefore, utter sophistry.

the grave error of allowing the initiative to slip to the Communists. Instead of attacking the Communists, the Nationalist commanders remained within their fortified garrisons—usually in cities and towns astride lines of communications—where they were more concerned with their own safety than with eliminating the enemy. Most commanders, stated the *Recollections*, "excessively emphasized their personal security, so that everyone became hesitant and infected one another with a sense of the ferocity of the Communists. As a result, they abandoned the initiative on the battlefield and allowed the Communists to come and go as they pleased." [12]

This strategic passivity, when combined with the Communist forces' offensive spirit and high mobility, placed the Nationalist forces in an impossible dilemma:

Because our army defended points and protected lines, [observed the *Recollections*], our military forces were stuck; mobility was lost and assuming the initiative was difficult. When attacking the Communists, for instance, if we cut back on the number of troops at the various fortifications, then the bandits would avoid decisive battle with our main force and would instead strike at the weak points in the rear of our troops. . . . If we were concerned about security everywhere, then we did not have sufficient troop strength to attack. This was not only ineffective but also harmful. Furthermore, when the main force of the bandits attacked one of our positions, then—if our reinforcements did not arrive on time—the position would be in danger of being wiped out; and if reinforcements did arrive on time, then the bandits would turn and attack a different position. As a result, this caused us always to lag behind the enemy and everywhere to lapse into passivity. [13]

## Lack of Cooperation

Personal relations and factional alignments always played a weighty role in Chinese society and politics. In the army, however, they were accentuated by the diverse character of the various units. Whatever their source, the old enmities and suspicions—especially among the several provincial commanders on the one hand, and between the provincial commanders and the central-army commanders on the other—always remained strong. Yet even among graduates of the Whampoa Academy, jealousies and animosities created broad rifts in the command structure.

During the civil-war period, the dominant clique in the army, which determined all other clique orientations, was that of Ch'en Ch'eng. Ch'en, who served first as minister of war (December 1945–June 1946) and then as chief of the general staff (June 1946–April 1948), had broad authority in personnel matters. Generals not belonging to his coterie claimed that he gave top appointments in the army to Whampoa graduates belonging to his clique, even though most of them had limited combat experience,[14] while commanders with skill and experience were relegated to insignificant jobs in administration or training. General Sung Hsi-lien, for instance, who had been a group-army commander in the U.S.-trained Chinese Expeditionary Force in Burma, was transferred to Sinkiang, where he was obliged to direct a branch of the military academy that had but 200 students.[15] Allegedly because of jealousy, Ch'en Ch'eng relieved General Ch'en Ming-jen of his command, even though he had won the Battle of Ssu-p'ing-chieh, the Nationalists' principal victory in Manchuria.[16] Kuan Lin-cheng, Chiang Kai-shek's successor as commandant of the Central Military Academy, felt that Ch'en Ch'eng finally offered him command of a badly tattered and demoralized army only because Ch'en expected him to be defeated by the Communists and thereby to fall into disgrace.[17]

In combat, these enmities and rivalries often had disastrous consequences. During the celebrated Battle of Hwai-Hai in late 1948, for example, General Ch'iu Ch'ing-ch'üan was ordered to relieve General Huang Po-t'ao's army corps, which had been enveloped by the Communists. But Ch'iu advanced only eight miles in ten days, and was still twelve miles distant when Huang committed suicide and a large part of his force surrendered to the Communists. Ch'iu, it is claimed, had been envious ever since Huang had received special honors from Chiang Kai-shek. When he first received word that Huang's army corps was surrounded, he allegedly remarked with satisfaction that now Huang could prove whether or not he was indeed worthy of the honors bestowed upon him.[18]

In battle, stated the *Recollections*, our commanders "frequently were concerned [only] with their own interests, so that the entire situation was damaged."[19] This disinclination of Nationalist commanders to cooperate on the battlefield, to coordinate operations, or to come to one another's assistance, magnified the force of the Communists; it frequently enabled them to wipe out Nationalist units piecemeal, and thus contributed significantly to the final Nationalist defeat.[20]

## Defections and the Difficulties of Troop Replacement

The first major defection of a Nationalist military unit to the Communists after the Japanese surrender occurred on October 31, 1945, when General Kao Shu-hsün, together with his entire division, surrendered to the Communists in Hopei. Thereafter, the list of defecting units increased rapidly.[21] The Communists claim to have taken about 3,700,000 prisoners between July 1946 and January 1949, but many of these prisoners had actually defected. The defections frequently occurred in the midst of combat, and the outcome of many a battle was determined by these precipitate surrenders.[22]

The Communists made defection for the Nationalist troops easier with their well-known policy of kindly treatment of prisoners-of-war. All prisoners and defectors who consented were incorporated into the Communist army as either front-line or service personnel. Others who were too infirm or for some other reason could not be employed, noted the *Recollections*, were given passes and travel expenses and then released, so that they might return to the Nationalist areas. To induce officers possessed of specially needed skills to join them, the Communists offered higher ranks and increased salaries. Such treatment of prisoners, the Nationalist authors of the *Recollections* noted, was very different from their own, and represented a psychological advantage for the Communists. Such methods, too, enabled the Communist army to attain numerical parity with the Nationalists during the course of 1948.[23]

Nearly all defecting Nationalist units were provincial, not central-army, forces. Commanders in the provincial armies were particularly prone to defect because they felt discriminated against, many being convinced that the central authorities had removed them from their provinces and sent them into battle against the Communists with the expectation that they would be annihilated. As early as 1946, therefore, opposition to the civil war was strong among the provincial forces, especially among those from Kwangsi and Yunnan. This heightened the central authorities' distrust of them, and to prevent defections they planted agents within the ranks of the provincial units. The central authorities also broke up the larger provincial armies, scattering the constituent units, of divisional size or smaller, among the more loyal central-army forces. Such measures slowed the rate of defection among the provincial troops, but did nothing to fire their fighting spirit.[24]

Low morale in the Nationalist forces, of course, lay at the base of most defections, and nowhere was the lack of morale more evident than in the army's lower ranks. The conscription system was at least as corrupt as it had been during the war, with the result that the army could not obtain adequate troop replacements. Most units were therefore far below authorized strength. The *Recollections* complained that the Communists had much less difficulty mobilizing men into their army, and that this difference significantly influenced the outcome of the war.[25] Dragooned into the service, Nationalist soldiers felt little commitment to the cause for which they were supposedly fighting. They were, if possible, fed even less adequately than during the war.[26] The fighting spirit of the troops during the civil-war period was therefore almost nil. Ho Ying-ch'in recognized this in mid-1948 when, upon assuming the post of minister of national defense, he declared that his first task was to revive army morale, from top to bottom: "Hungry, poorly clothed men," he said, "cannot fight."[27]

The Communists skillfully exploited the Nationalist troops' discontents. They directed barrages of propaganda at the weak spots in the Nationalists' psychological and political armor. Propaganda leaflets emphasized the harshness of life under Nationalist rule, noting that the government seized the people's grain, that there were continuous famines and floods, and that the rich lived in comfort and luxury while the poor had to serve in the army. The leaflets stressed that soldiers in the Nationalist army received inadequate food, and that they were maltreated by their officers. To the provincial troops, the Communists wrote that Chiang Kai-shek sent them to battlefields far from home and sacrificed them there while favoring and protecting his central-army forces. In the Communist areas, said the propaganda pamphlets, there was unity of spirit and economic plenty; there were no beggars, thieves, or bandits, as in the Nationalist areas. The Nationalist soldiers should therefore stop killing fellow Chinese, and those who surrendered would be well treated. One pamphlet assured the Nationalist soldiers that the Communists did not—as Chiang Kai-shek's propaganda claimed—bury prisoners alive or strip off their flesh.[28]

## Spies and Agents

A persistent complaint in the *Recollections* concerned the paucity of information about the Communists. Intelligence work, it asserted, was formalistic and bureaucratized; it was "nothing more than paper discussions of troop deployment."[29] Nationalist agents were unable to penetrate the Communist apparatus, and as a consequence the Nationalist army frequently marched unwittingly into Communist traps.[30] Communist agents, by contrast, were notoriously successful. "From the office of the commander-in-chief to the various levels of army headquarters," recalls General Teng Wen-i, "all were infiltrated by Communist agents, spying and creating disinformation, so that the enemy were fully apprised about our situation as well as their own, whereas the Nationalist army knew neither its own situation nor that of the enemy. Naturally our forces could not avoid being surrounded and captured by the Communists."[31]

Although Teng Wen-i, like many Nationalist authorities, may have been excessively concerned about Communist undercover activities, Communist agents did in fact contribute critically to the Communist victory. Many held key positions. At the important battle of Wei-hsien in Shantung in April 1948, for example, the chief of staff of the Nationalists' 96th Army was a Communist agent. At the battle of Tsinan in September 1948, the head of

the 2d Pacification Command's Office of Military Operations reportedly revealed the Nationalists' entire battle plan to the enemy. (This, together with the defection at a critical moment of
the 84th Division, contributed in a major way to this first loss by
the Nationalists of a provincial capital within China proper.)[32]

The most dramatic instance of Communist infiltration, however, was the amazing General Liu Fei. Liu throughout most of
the war and civil-war periods served as assistant chief of staff of
the entire Nationalist army; he was, at the same time, a Communist agent.[33] From his high-level office, he could report to the
Communists virtually every major move the Nationalist army
would make. He also arranged for the appointment of another
Communist agent, Kuo Ju-kuei, to the important post of chief of
the War Planning Board. During the Nationalists' catastrophic
defeat in the Battle of Hwai-Hai in November 1948–January
1949, these two officers came under suspicion because, according to the top Nationalist commander in the campaign, General
Liu Chih, "our army's every move was often known in advance
by the Communists."[34] No investigation was undertaken, however, possibly because Liu Fei was a stereotypical Nationalist
officer—pompous, bureaucratic, and with a reputation for criticizing everyone.[35]

In the spring of 1949, Liu Fei was assigned yet another sensitive task. Still trusted by the top Nationalist leadership, he was
named a member of the six-man delegation that on April 1,
1949, flew to Peiping to seek peace with the Communists. With
Liu on the Nationalists' negotiating team, the chief Communist
negotiator, Chou En-lai, was in the enviable position of being informed of his counterparts' every consideration and maneuver.[36]

After these negotiations broke down, Liu Fei and the rest of
the delegation remained in Peiping rather than return to Nanking. Subsequently, Liu lived in considerable comfort and with
some honor under the Communists. Indeed, after Liu had been
specially appointed as a representative to the Communists' Political Consultative Conference in 1949, Mao Tse-tung took note
of his undercover activities, publicly hailing him as "a citizen
who contributed meritoriously to the establishment of the People's Republic of China."[37]

During the final stages of the civil war, Communist agents proliferated. Particularly in 1949, following the Nationalists' loss of Manchuria, the defeat at the Battle of Hwai-Hai, and the failure of the gold yüan reforms, morale in the Nationalist area plummeted. Even within the army and the government, observed the *Recollections*, "there imperceptibly developed the phenomena of opportunism, disunity, and defeatism."[38] As a consequence, the Communists easily recruited agents within the ranks of the Nationalist army. One of those recruited was Tai Jung-kuang, a Whampoa graduate who enjoyed Chiang Kai-shek's complete trust. Yet when the Communists staged their amphibious attack across the Yangtze on the night of April 20, Tai ordered his troops at the key fortification of Chiang-yin, midway between Shanghai and Nanking, to turn their guns not at the Communists, but at the other Nationalist defenders.[39] The Communist assault across this mighty river had been chancy; Wedemeyer said that the Nationalists "could have defended the Yangtze River with broomsticks if they had the will to do so."[40] But, assisted by Tai Jung-kuang's betrayal, the Communists swept across the river and entered Nanking, the Nationalists' capital, on April 23. The end of Nationalist rule was at hand.

Communist agents within the ranks of the Nationalist regime manifestly played an extremely important role in determining the outcome of the civil war. Yet scholars attempting to explain the Nationalist defeat have completely ignored this aspect of history. Instead they have repeatedly searched for the slightest hint of Communist influence on American policy, direct or indirect, that might have led to the debacle of 1949. It is hard to imagine a more striking case of present political concerns distorting the historian's enterprise.

## The Superiority of the Communists

By contrast with their criticisms of their own army, the authors of the *Recollections* had considerable praise for their Communist opponents. Their observations clearly show that the Nationalist army was both outwitted and outfought on the battlefield. Prior to battle, according to the *Recollections*, the Communists made extensive preparations; they "fully expressed their ideas, unified their will, . . . studied the terrain, and grasped the enemy's situation."[41] These thorough discussions contrasted with the Nationalists' vain efforts to maintain secrecy. "As for our side," reads the *Recollections*, "because of a concern for maintaining secrecy, nothing at all was said of preparations just prior to a campaign. And because of this internal concealing of information, all fighting was done stupidly. We were even less sophisticated about studying and analyzing the enemy's situation."[42]

The Communists, said the *Recollections*, only engaged in combat when they held the advantage. Then they "avoided no difficulties and begrudged no sacrifices, and with daring and determined attacks they did not cease until they had attained their goal of annihilating us. But when the situation was not to their advantage, they quickly and unhesitatingly disengaged and turned to attack us elsewhere."[43] In this way, wrote the Nationalist authors of the *Recollections*, the Communists always held the initiative, keeping the Nationalist army off-balance and on the defensive.[44]

Tactically, the Communists stressed surprise, attacking when and where attack was unanticipated. In each battle, the *Recollections* stated, the Communists "first employed surprise strikes (*ch'i-hsi*), and then they employed large-scale assaults (*ch'iang-kung*). . . . And in the midst of the large-scale assaults, they created opportunities for surprise strikes." But we, added the Nationalist generals, "always employed frontal attacks; seldom did we prepare or deploy for surprise strikes or large-scale assaults."[45]

A particular strength of the Communists, the *Recollections* stressed, was the broad latitude of decision allowed their commanders in the field. Thus, if they faced defeat, they could quickly withdraw, thereby keeping their losses to a minimum. The Nationalists, by contrast, "often fell into situations [where the soldiers had to] fight to the death. . . . High-ranking commanders lacked the authority to act independently or to change plans on the spur of the moment." This was especially regrettable, because higher-echelon planning staffs were ignorant of precise conditions in the field; yet they often issued orders in a bureaucratic way that allowed for no discussion or modification.[46] As a result of these contrasting methods, the Communists avoided heavy losses even when they were defeated; yet when they were successful, their victories were decisive and Nationalist casualties were large. This, remarked the *Recollections*, was a primary reason why the Communists were able to turn their position of inferiority into one of superiority.[47]

The ingredients of military success are, of course, complex, and the *Recollections* in passing noted other factors that contributed to the outcome of the civil war. The Communists, for example, promoted or demoted their troops entirely on the basis of "fighting merit." "But we used academic and financial background, and social and political backing, as the bases for promotion. Fighting merit was secondary."[48] The *Recollections* also remarked that the Nationalist military effort had been hamstrung by bureaucracy. In the Manchurian fighting, for instance, the Communists had used sleds and horses to move about. Only after countless meetings, however, were the Nationalist forces able to acquire those things. Communist troops also had shovels and camouflage for use in snow; but the Nationalists, hampered by convention and financial shortages, could not adjust to the demands of the environment.[49]

Finally, the *Recollections* admired the support given the Communist army by the civilian population. For instance, the Communists used old and young as lookouts, and the whole population served as an intelligence network. If they ran short of food, the Communist soldiers could eat with civilian families. Because of mass mobilization, too, the Communists seldom left wounded soldiers on the battlefield. But in the Nationalist area, observed the *Recollections*, "politics did not support the military," and therefore "we could not but rely purely on military force to do battle."[50]

The Political Bureau of the Ministry of National Defense reflected even more poignantly upon the importance of popular support for the outcome of the civil war. "Frankly speaking," declared the Bureau in 1950, "it is impossible to crush the Communist bandits by relying only on the government and the army, without the help of the *lao-pai-hsing* [the common people]. The reason we were defeated on the mainland was precisely because we did not intimately join hands with the lao-pai-hsing." [51]

Here again we have evidence that military and political disaster, with the efficacy of a Zen *kōan*, had brought enlightenment to at least some of the Nationalist leaders. How the thought must have mocked them: "The reason we were defeated on the mainland was precisely because we did not intimately join hands with the lao-pai-hsing"! Joining hands with the lao-pai-hsing would have required, of course, a political, not a physical act. It would have required fundamental reforms. It would have required a government that was open to public opinion, policies that were beneficial to the lao-pai-hsing, and an administration and leadership capable of transcending personal and factional interests in pursuit of broad national goals. Those were characteristics, however, that the Nationalists had never in any large measure displayed. Thus, while the war with Japan had grievously weakened the Nationalist army, the real source of its defeat lay in the very nature of the regime.

## CHAPTER 8

# Chiang Ching-kuo and the Gold Yüan Reform

A CONTRIBUTOR TO *Chuan-chi wen-hsüeh* (*Biographical Litera-ture*), writing in 1979, asserted that he firmly believed the Na-tional Government would still be in Nanking if the gold yüan reform had not been instituted.[1] In the same vein, Shen Yün-lung, one of Taiwan's leading students of modern Chinese his-tory, has written: "After only forty days, the value of the gold yüan declined so that it was almost the same as scrap paper. The property of tens of millions of people was suddenly transformed into nothing, not worth a cent. This enormously affected the people's morale and the fate of the nation, and was the chief rea-son for the loss of the mainland."[2] As a result of this widely held view, the minister of finance at the time of the reform, Wang Yün-wu, has since his death in 1979 been labeled the principal author of the Nationalist defeat.[3]

The sequence of events following the gold yüan reform of Au-gust 1948 lends some plausibility to these interpretations and criticisms, for within three months of the promulgation of the reform the economy was in a state of final collapse and the central-government armies were being backed against the Yangtze River. Just two months later, in January 1949, Chiang Kai-shek was pressured to resign as president of the National Government. Thereafter, the situation degenerated into a com-plete rout.

To lay the blame for the Nationalist defeat on the gold yüan reform or on a single cabinet minister, however, confuses cause and effect. The reform was not the cause of the economic col-lapse in 1948; it was rather a calculated, though desperate, gamble to impede a collapse that had begun before the reform was inaugurated. The gamble, it is true, failed. And by creating disillusionment and anger among significant sectors of the population—particularly the middle classes, who had long been among the principal supporters of the regime—the attempted currency reform doubtless hastened the Nationalist political collapse. But it was a gamble that Chiang Kai-shek, as well as Wang Yün-wu, correctly perceived as being justified and as having at least some chance of success.

## The Adoption of the Reform

The economy of Nationalist China during 1947 and much of 1948 was in a terrible state: the fabric of rural society was becoming unraveled; industrial production was faltering; the transportation system was in a state of continual disrepair (largely owing to Communist sabotage); and inflation was daily eroding the value of the fa-pi, the national currency.[4] (See Table 6.) During the summer of 1948, however, the economic situation worsened, and the nation seemed to be plunging toward utter collapse. Owing to the large budgetary deficits necessitated by the war against the Communists, the volume of fa-pi in circulation had risen from Y34 trillion in December 1947 to Y250 trillion in June 1948. Then in just a month and a half that figure rose to somewhere between Y600 and Y700 trillion.[5] Because of the expanding battle zone, too, fa-pi flowed in a growing torrent from North China to Central and South China.[6]

As the volume of currency swelled, public confidence in the future of both the government and the fa-pi diminished. People therefore raced to buy goods—any kind of goods—before their money lost what little value it still retained. This rapid circulation of the currency added fuel to the inflation, so that prices shot upward faster than the government issue of fa-pi. (In December 1947, prices were increasing 3.5 times faster than the increase in new money; in June 1948, 5 times faster; and in early August, 11 times faster.)[7] The result was that the inflation skyrocketed at an unprecedented rate. During just the two and a half months from late May to mid-August, prices in Shanghai

TABLE 6

## The Course of Fa-pi Depreciation,
## September 1945 – August 19, 1948

(September 1945 = 100)

| | Month | Note issue | Shanghai whole-sale price index |
|---|---|---|---|
| 1945 | September | 100 | 100 |
| | October | 120 | 110 |
| | November | 134 | 288 |
| | December | 153 | 257 |
| 1946 | January | 171 | 269 |
| | February | 187 | 509 |
| | March | 200 | 742 |
| | April | 227 | 748 |
| | May | 266 | 1,103 |
| | June | 313 | 1,070 |
| | July | 320 | 1,180 |
| | August | 352 | 1,242 |
| | September | 401 | 1,475 |
| | October | 443 | 1,554 |
| | November | 489 | 1,541 |
| | December | 553 | 1,656 |
| 1947 | January | 669 | 1,990 |
| | February | 718 | 3,090 |
| | March | 852 | 3,248 |
| | April | 1,024 | 4,130 |
| | May | 1,243 | 7,045 |
| | June | 1,453 | 8,673 |
| | July | 1,746 | 9,032 |
| | August | 2,211 | 9,557 |
| | September | 2,526 | 12,534 |
| | October | 3,106 | 17,352 |
| | November | 4,012 | 19,296 |
| | December | 4,941 | 24,282 |
| 1948 | January | 5,191 | 36,939 |
| | February | — | 52,900 |
| | March | 10,383 | 85,502 |
| | April | — | 99,117 |
| | May | 20,024 | 142,468 |
| | June | — | 256,397 |
| | July | — | 755,165 |
| | August | 296,648 | 1,368,049 |

SOURCE: Wu Yuan-li, pp. 50–51.

TABLE 7

Selected Prices, Shanghai, May–August 1948

(thousands of fa-pi)

| Date | White rice (first) | Wheat flour | Peanut oil | Cotton yarn (fine) | Cotton yarn (coarse) | Koo Pan soap |
|---|---|---|---|---|---|---|
| May 26 | 6,300 | 2,050 | — | 305,000 | 204,000 | 7,000 |
| June 2 | 6,700 | 1,950 | 18,500 | 302,000 | 194,000 | 7,030 |
| June 9 | 8,000 | 2,530 | 22,500 | 442,000 | 262,000 | 9,100 |
| June 16 | 10,000 | 3,310 | 31,000 | 500,000 | 298,000 | 17,000 |
| June 23 | 13,900 | 4,280 | 40,500 | 655,000 | 450,000 | 20,100 |
| June 30 | — | — | — | 830,000 | 800,000 | 32,500 |
| July 7 | 20,000 | — | — | 1,000,000 | 800,000 | 36,000 |
| July 14 | 29,500 | 8,120 | 76,000 | 1,350,000 | — | — |
| July 21 | 37,000 | 11,300 | 102,000 | 1,700,000 | 1,150,000 | 75,000 |
| July 28 | 37,000 | 10,700 | 95,000 | 1,800,000 | 1,370,000 | 75,000 |
| Aug. 4 | 39,500 | 12,650 | 107,000 | 2,000,000 | 1,420,000 | 65,000 |
| Aug. 11 | 50,000 | 18,150 | 165,000 | 2,880,000 | 1,850,000 | 76,000 |
| Aug. 18 | 63,000 | 22,700 | 195,000 | 3,200,000 | 2,130,000 | 83,500 |

SOURCE: Compiled from the weekly section, "This Week's Business," *China Weekly Review*, June 5–Aug. 21, 1948. (The source does not give units for the commodities listed.)

increased approximately ten times. Rice, which had sold for Y6.3 million on May 26, sold for Y63 million on August 18; peanut oil during the same period increased from Y18.5 to Y195 million; and soap rose from Y7 to Y83.5 million. (See Table 7.)

Evidence of economic collapse resulting from the hyperinflation became increasingly apparent between June and mid-August. Rice riots, which began in Ningpo on June 14, spread rapidly across the country during the ensuing month. Prices of other goods rose so fast that shopkeepers changed price tags several times a day. On June 25, and again on July 10, prices spurted about 30 percent during just one working day. With prices and production costs shifting almost hourly, normal business calculations became impossible. Increasingly, shopowners simply shuttered their stores rather than risk reducing their inventory in exchange for fa-pi at any price.[8] At one point, flights between Shanghai and Nanking were canceled because the price of tickets, which required government approval, could not keep up with the ever-rising cost of fuel.[9] The government's printing presses could not produce currency notes fast enough to meet the needs of the economy. Employers, for example, had difficulty accumulating sufficient cash to meet their payrolls. Most fa-pi notes were in denominations of Y100,000 or less—it was not until late July and August that Gold Customs Unit notes worth from Y500,000 to Y5 million appeared—so the sheer bulk of money needed for even a moderate-sized purchase was becoming a concern.[10]

As the economy deteriorated, the public felt uncertainty, fear, and despair. "Especially serious," editorialized the *Ta-kung-pao* on August 5, "is that everyone believes nothing can be done about [the economic crisis]. So they live from day to day, without thought of the future, as though awaiting the onset of collapse."[11] As all efforts to control the economic decline failed, popular discontent with the government increased. Rumors spread that the government was going to seal up safe-deposit boxes, close half the country's banks, or nationalize gold; it was even reported that Chiang Kai-shek had been detained in North China.[12] People were prepared to believe the worst.

Within the government, leading officials had long downplayed the seriousness of the economic situation;[13] but after the crisis worsened in June, the facts could no longer be explained away. Cyril Rogers, a Briton who was a leading adviser to the Central Bank, reported in mid-July that "realization of seriousness of situation has finally seeped up to the highest levels [of government], with result that near panic reigns on Olympus."[14] A month later, on August 11, Prime Minister Wong Wen-hao apprised the United States that China faced bankruptcy "apparently only a few months ahead."[15] Confronted with imminent financial collapse, the government took what was perhaps the only course left to it (other than abandoning the fight against the Communists): it replaced the virtually worthless fa-pi with a new paper currency, the gold yüan note (*chin-yüan ch'üan*).

For several years, various economists and laymen had argued for currency conversion, contending that popular psychology— i.e., the people's loss of confidence in the fa-pi—was the chief cause of the runaway inflation.[16] Inflation could be slowed, they claimed, simply by adopting a new unit of currency to replace the fa-pi. This notion was seductive in its simplicity, and large quantities of new currency notes had in fact been printed during the war and again in 1945 in anticipation of such a conversion.[17] Wiser minds had always countered, however, that the inflation could not be stopped—whatever the unit of currency—unless the government balanced its budget.

The worsening economic crisis in the summer of 1948 forced the government to look again at currency conversion as a cure for the now virtually uncontrolled inflation. Wong Wen-hao— reportedly with Chiang Kai-shek's approval—formed a committee in early July to prepare a plan for the immediate switch of currencies. In its report a week later, the committee warned the prime minister against conversion at that time, reminding him of the obstacles and perils associated with the move. Wong conveyed this report to Chiang, who consequently dropped the idea of abandoning the fa-pi just then, although he commented that "something may have to be done soon nevertheless."[18]

By early August, the crisis had so deepened that Chiang became convinced that currency conversion, whatever the dangers, must be attempted. To his summer retreat in Ku-ling he called the government's leading financial advisers for consultation. T. V. Soong, Chang Kia-ngau, and Yü Hsia-ch'ing reportedly warned him against the reform, arguing that the value of the new currency could not be maintained if military expenditures were not first reduced. Premier Wong and Finance Minister Wang Yün-wu, however, favored conversion.[19]

Despite the divided counsels, preparations for currency reform advanced rapidly, if uncertainly. As early as about August 7, the Central Bank began distributing issues of the new paper currency to branch offices throughout the country. By the evening of August 13, the decision to launch the reform appeared so imminent that officials in the Central Bank in Shanghai were placed on standby in anticipation of the conversion order.[20] Indecision, however, still marked the planning process. On August 16, Yü Hung-chün (O. K. Yui), director general of the Central Bank, brought a new conversion plan, labeled Plan "B," from Shanghai to Nanking. Wong Wen-hao, Wang Yün-wu, and Foreign Minister Wang Shih-chieh gave their approval to it, whereupon the earlier plan, now labeled "A," was shelved while Wong and Yü flew to Ku-ling to present the new plan to Chiang. Chiang made a major modification in the plan, ruling against the proposed free convertibility of the new currency into gold.[21] After discussing the matter with T. V. Soong, who supported the new plan, Chiang on August 18 suddenly flew back to Nanking. In the capital, opponents of the reform again warned Chiang of the loopholes and inadequacies in the plan, but the president now believed the crisis to be so grave that he could tolerate no further hesitations or opposition. Already the measure had been examined repeatedly, he asserted, and it must be promulgated immediately. If there were indeed' defects in the plan, they could be rectified later.[22] Following approval by the Central Political Council and the Executive Yüan, and using the emergency powers vested in him during the struggle against the Communists, President Chiang promulgated the Financial and Economic Emergency Measures (*Ts'ai-cheng ching-chi chin-chi ch'u-fen ming-ling*) on the evening of August 19, 1948.[23]

These Emergency Measures slowed the inflation for barely five weeks. Moreover, 70 days after the reform was launched, the government was forced to admit that it had failed. Was not this clear evidence that the currency-conversion plan had no chance even from the beginning?

In adopting the policy of currency conversion, one set of facts undoubtedly colored all of Chiang Kai-shek's calculations: the inflation in August was utterly out of control, and the entire economy was collapsing; if the economy collapsed, political and military collapse would soon follow. The conversion plan offered at least a glimmer of hope in an otherwise hopeless situation.

Proponents of currency conversion were correct that the explosive price increases were in substantial degree the result of the people's loss of confidence in the fa-pi—as evidenced by the fact that prices were rising much faster than the creation of new money. Chiang, Wong Wen-hao, and Wang Yün-wu were now hoping that the new currency would win the public's confidence at least temporarily—if only for about six months. If the collapse of the economy could be averted for even that brief period, the government could in the meantime formulate more permanent solutions to the monetary crisis.

The fundamental long-term solution envisioned by the government leaders was to balance the budget. Neither Wong Wen-hao nor Wang Yün-wu, for example, deluded themselves that the root of the inflationary problem was other than the budgetary deficit and the consequent need continually to create new money.[24] They therefore proposed that the deficit not exceed 30 percent of total expenditures—as compared with the more than 66 percent deficit then current.[25] The Emergency Measures accordingly stipulated that revenues be increased (largely by increasing taxes—including, for instance, a 40 percent surcharge on imported goods) and expenditures reduced (for example, by eliminating excess military and government personnel, and by requiring that state-run enterprises and transportation agencies become self-sufficient). General Ho Ying-ch'in, the minister of national defense, was also reported to have promised to reduce military expenditures substantially as long as future price levels remained stable.[26]

A second part of the solution envisioned by the Nanking leaders was to obtain a currency-stabilization loan from the United States. With such a loan, the government would hold sufficient reserves to permit the convertibility of the gold yüan to dollars or bullion, thereby shoring up public confidence in the new currency. Earlier in the year, during negotiations preceding the passage of the China Aid Act of April 1948, Washington had rejected a Chinese request for a stabilization loan on the grounds that the enormous sums needed would simply be dissipated under the existing conditions of war and inflation. In August, however, the Nationalist leaders had two reasons for thinking that decision might be reversed: first, if the currency reform halted the inflation even for a few months, this would demonstrate the Chinese capacity for "self-help" that Washington was demanding as a precondition for further aid; and, second, the November elections in the United States might bring in a Republican administration and Congress, which were likely to be more sympathetic to the National Government than the Democrats had proved.[27] As Ambassador John Leighton Stuart observed on August 23, "there is surprisingly frank admission in official circles that Government's eyes are glued to a sympathetic Republican Congress in January and that this [reform] program is plank thrown across intervening chasm."[28] The Nationalists were to be disappointed on both counts: the favorable effects of the currency reform did not last several months, and the Republicans lost the 1948 elections.

## Chiang Ching-kuo in Shanghai

The Emergency Measures applied to all areas under the jurisdiction of the National Government. In fact, however, the government focused on the major cities, and particularly on the coastal metropolises of Shanghai, Canton, and Tientsin. In each of these three ports, an Economic Supervisor's Office was established to coordinate and implement all phases of the reform program. The Economic Supervisor in Canton was Kwangtung Governor T. V. Soong; in Tientsin it was Chang Li-sheng, who was also vice-premier of the central government; and in Shanghai it was Yü Hung-chün.[29]

As events soon revealed, T. V. Soong and Chang Li-sheng were something less than vigorous in their enforcement of the Emergency Measures, and by the end of September prices in their areas of jurisdiction were approximately double the levels of August 19. Prices elsewhere in the country rose at least as fast.[30] Shanghai consequently became the test case for the entire reform program. Here, in the nation's financial, commercial, and industrial center, where hoarding and speculation had become a way of life among the most wealthy and influential entrepreneurs, the reforms were pushed with a fervor and relentlessness evident nowhere else. The reason was the dedication of one man, the Deputy Economic Supervisor, Chiang Ching-kuo.

Chiang Ching-kuo was a most uncommon bureaucrat. Only 39 years old in the summer of 1948, he was the eldest son of the president and had lived in the Soviet Union for over eleven years. After his return from Russia in 1937, his father had him undertake an apprenticeship in Chinese politics, beginning with a series of middle-ranking posts in Kiangsi province. There he established a reputation as a highly authoritarian, but effective, administrator. He also became a leader in the Youth Corps, where he attracted a group of young and dedicated followers who remained close to him through the ensuing years. During these years, too, young Chiang impressed his father with his capabilities as an administrator, as well as with his strong filial loyalty.[31] Thus, the fact that Chiang Kai-shek selected Ching-kuo for the job in Shanghai was not adventitious. Chiang Kai-shek could now rely on few men, and he needed someone in Shanghai who shared his sense of commitment, who was incorruptible, and who could act courageously, without fear of criticism or opposition. Ching-kuo met those requirements, and he quickly became the dominant personality in Shanghai.

Although Yü Hung-chün held the title of Economic Supervisor, his role in the reforms was secondary and shadowy. Indeed, Wu Kuo-chen, who was at the time mayor of Shanghai and also an official in the Economic Supervisor's Office, has remarked that Yü "was just that type of man who would do everything that he was told to do by Ching-kuo."[32] The institutional basis of Ching-kuo's power seems to have been established at a meeting of the Shanghai Economic Supervisor's Office on August 26, when he was given authority over all economic control and investigative work in the city, with the power to coordinate all political, military, and other governmental agencies in that endeavor.[33]

Chiang Ching-kuo brought with him to Shanghai a deep concern for the common man in China and, conversely, a strongly antielitist political philosophy. He expressed dismay that the mass of Shanghai's residents lived in wretched poverty while a few dressed extravagantly, rode about in limousines, and lived in splendid residences. "The vast majority of the people," he declared, "still live in crude sheds and cubbyholes, and further thousands and tens of thousands are homeless, wandering about the streets and alleyways or writhing in fields and ditches.

They have truly become a horde of beggars for whom even wearing a pair of grass sandals seems a rare luxury."[34] In the journal he kept during the period of the economic reforms, he repeatedly expressed appreciation for the simple, long-suffering qualities of the common man. On August 31, for instance, he recorded: "In the afternoon I met with over forty members of the masses, and what they said was all very ordinary (*p'ing-fan*). I discovered that the common people are extremely lovable."[35] On September 10 he wrote: "China's commoners are really good (*shan-liang*). If in the future I can but have a bit of strength, I must do something for them."[36]

Not only, in Ching-kuo's view, were the common people objects of pity and sympathy; they were also a source of political power. "Regardless of what one does," he declared, "if only one stands together with the people . . . one will never be defeated." And he also wrote, "In the whole world, there is no force greater than the force of the people, and there are no words more truthful than the words of the people."[37]

Chiang Ching-kuo viewed Shanghai's big moneymen, by contrast, as deceitful evildoers who were the cause of the common man's suffering. "Their wealth and their foreign-style homes," he said, "are built on the skeletons of the people. How is their conduct any different from that of armed robbers?"[38] And, "automobiles, refrigerators, perfumes, and nylon hosiery imported from abroad [for the wealthy classes] are like cells that thrive parasitically on this impoverished nation, or like opium that destroys the national economy, because using foreign currency to obtain high-class luxuries is a suicidal policy for the nation."[39]

Possessed of this image of society, Chiang Ching-kuo did not approach the tasks of currency conversion and price control as a tired and jaded bureaucrat going through the motions of enforcing yet another set of government regulations. That, he asserted, had been the fault in the past, and thus previous attempts to solve the economic crisis had repeatedly failed. Instead, he perceived that his task in Shanghai was to launch "a kind of social revolutionary movement" employing "revolutionary methods." "The policy today of holding down prices is merely a technical matter, and the real goal is to destroy all manifestations of economic inequality in society."[40]

The targets of his social revolution were the big, wealthy, "traitorous merchants." "Those who disturb the financial market," he declared during his third day in Shanghai, "are not the small merchants, but the big capitalists and big merchants. Therefore, if we are to employ severe punishments, we should begin with the chief culprits (*huai-t'ou*)."[41] He held meetings with these financial magnates, but came away with impressions starkly different from those derived in meetings with the commoners. The capitalists, he said, were friendly toward him in person, "but behind one's back there is no evil that they do not commit."[42]

Throughout the period of the Emergency Measures in Shanghai, Ching-kuo had to work hand in hand with the existing governmental and police agencies there. But his relations with the top officials in those agencies were often strained, because he felt they were less than enthusiastic in their support of his "revolutionary" methods and goals.[43] He consequently relied heavily upon two organizations that were linked to him by close personal ties. The first of these was a paramilitary unit called the Bandit-Suppression National-Reconstruction Corps (K'an-luan chien-kuo ta-tui), which had been organized, probably in early 1947, to assist in the administration of areas close to the battle lines or recently recovered from the Communists. In these areas, Communist agents were actively working underground, the pao-chia chiefs were corrupt, and relations between the central-government troops and the people were frequently bad. To remedy these defects, cadres for the new corps were trained at the Central Training Institute under the direction of a committee whose chairman was Chang Li-sheng and whose vice-chairman was Chiang Ching-kuo. Commander of the Bandit-Suppression National-Reconstruction Corps was General Hu Kuei, a graduate of the third class at the Whampoa Academy and one of Chiang Ching-kuo's "brain trusters."[44]

In Shanghai, however, the most prominent officer of the corps was Wang Sheng, a longtime close friend of Ching-kuo (their friendship was apparently established during the war against Japan, when both were working in the Youth Corps). Wang was commander of the Sixth Ta-tui (Large Corps), which was the first unit of the Bandit-Suppression National-Reconstruction Corps to be transferred to Shanghai. By late October, four of the six Ta-tui had already been brought to Shanghai and the last two were preparing to leave the front to join the work under Chiang Ching-kuo. Altogether, the corps probably numbered about 30,000 men.[45]

The work of the corps was to assist existing police and garrison forces in the Shanghai area in enforcing the Emergency Measures. They participated, for example, in searches of warehouses for hoarded goods. They also put up "secret-report boxes" in each city ward for citizens to report violations of the economic regulations to the authorities. The corps members were not, however, empowered independently to make arrests; that was left for the regular enforcement agencies.[46]

The second organization supporting Ching-kuo's endeavors was the Greater Shanghai Youth Service Corps (Ta-Shang-hai ch'ing-nien fu-wu tsung-tui). This was a form of mass political organization, similar in many ways to the Kuomintang's Youth Corps. It was, in effect, an extension of the Bandit-Suppression National-Reconstruction Corps, for it was commanded by Wang Sheng and trained by members of that corps. Formation of the Youth Service Corps began on September 9, 1948, with an appeal to "those members of the youthful community in Shanghai who are fired with a sense of righteousness, equipped with courage and farsight[edness], promising and idealistic, to rise together and participate in the 'Greater Shanghai Youth Service Corps' so that with our united and joint efforts we may thoroughly cleanse the dregs of the current age, and proceed to build the New China of the Three People's Principles." On September 25, during the formal inaugural ceremonies of the corps, over 12,000 members were enrolled.[47]

Chiang Ching-kuo placed high hopes on this new organization, regarding it as an instrument for achieving his ultimate economic and political goals in Shanghai and, indeed, the nation as a whole.[48] According to Wang Sheng, the purposes of the Youth Service Corps were:

(1) to overthrow the evil forces that violate the well-being of the nation and race; (2) to be without desire for privileges, to do work that others do not wish to do, to endure the suffering that others do not wish to endure with no thought of struggling for positions as members of the Legislative Yüan or the National Assembly; (3) to aid our impoverished and suffering countrymen; and (4) to be nameless heroes in fulfilling our supreme duty to the nation. In short, we seek to eliminate two groups: one is an evil group, the Communist Party; one is a decadent group, the corrupt officials and traitorous merchants.[49]

The concept of a selfless, dedicated group of youth striving to improve the lot of the mass of the people, against the machinations of both the Communists and the decadent elements in society, may have been a noble and ambitious one. But the concept tells more about Chiang Ching-kuo's sense of purpose than it does about the corps or conditions in Shanghai, for the reform movement soon ended and the corps' achievements—so far as is discernible from available materials—were negligible.

## The Implementation of the Reform

The first stage of the gold yüan reform in Shanghai, that of converting the old fa-pi into gold yüan, proceeded smoothly. Banks closed for three days following the promulgation of the Emergency Measures in order to convert their accounts into gold yüan units. On Monday, August 23, the banks reopened and began exchanging the new currency for the old fa-pi notes at the rate of GY1:Y3,000,000. The public cooperated, often with surprising good grace, standing in queues for hours at a time to turn in their suitcases and basketloads of fa-pi for the new gold-and-brown gold yüan notes. Becoming accustomed to the new currency required a degree of mental effort: a tram ticket now cost only ten cents, instead of Y300,000; a copy of the *North China Daily News* cost twenty-five cents by contrast with Y800,000 the previous day; and a month's subscription for the same paper fell from Y19,000,000 to GY6.[50] Hitherto, everyone in China had been a millionaire; most lost that lofty-sounding status with the currency conversion. They nevertheless accepted the new currency without opposition, for no one any longer had confidence in the inflated fa-pi.

Other aspects of the reform program proved to be more difficult to carry out. Although members of the lower and middle classes generally complied with the order to turn over their gold and silver to the government, those possessing large holdings of the precious metals and foreign currencies—private banks and the "big families" (*ta-hu*, i.e. very rich and influential people)—frequently resisted, suspicious now of any form of paper currency. Many of these converted only a small part of their caches, thereby obtaining certificates that they could produce to demonstrate their compliance with the regulations. The bulk of their holdings, however, they concealed or smuggled to Canton or Hong Kong.[51]

Chiang Ching-kuo made concerted efforts to pressure the wealthy to turn in their holdings. Trucks equipped with loudspeakers cruised the streets, stopping in front of the homes of the rich and urging them to turn in their gold. The government also promised anonymity to informers who reported violations to the police.[52] Some arm-twisting was necessary. On September 18, Ching-kuo suspended operations of the city's four leading commercial banks for their failure to convert their holdings into gold yüan.[53] He also ordered the arrest of no less a personage than Aw Haw (Hu Hao)—son of the famed "Tiger-Balm King," Aw Boon Haw (Hu Wen-hu)—for gold and foreign-currency smuggling.[54] As a consequence of these forceful measures, Shanghai residents had by the end of September turned in at least 64 percent of all the gold, silver, and foreign currency that the government collected throughout the nation.[55]

Despite these efforts, no aspect of the reform received more criticism from the press and the public than the government's inability to enforce its regulations upon the nation's wealthy classes. The government failed completely, for example, to enforce its requirement that citizens register all their foreign assets above the value of U.S. $3,000—partly because the U.S. government refused to cooperate in identifying those assets in the

United States.[56] According to a Kuomintang-related newspaper, no more than 20–30 percent of the gold, silver, and foreign currencies in the country as a whole had been exchanged for gold yüan by the deadline, September 30.[57] Most of that, too, was turned in by the middle classes, not by the plutocrats.[58]

The most publicized of Chiang Ching-kuo's efforts in Shanghai was his use of force and the threat of force to hold commodity prices to the level of August 19. For this, he has been both praised and vilified—praised, because prices held firm in Shanghai longer than elsewhere; and vilified, because the attempt to employ political methods to restrain economic forces ultimately failed.

During the 70 days of the Emergency Measures, several hundred people in Shanghai were arrested and one civilian was executed for economic crimes. Most of those arrested were charged with overpricing, scalping, or hoarding.[59] On August 25, for instance, two days after the new regulations went into effect, the Economic Police arrested twenty vendors of vegetables and meat for charging prices higher than those of August 19. During the following week, several dozen more were apprehended. The most serious offenders were referred to the Special Criminal Court; most, however, were detained in jail for periods of two to seven days and then released.[60]

Chiang Ching-kuo was, however, only marginally concerned with the small shopkeepers who added a few cents to the price of a catty of pork or a pack of cigarettes. It was the large-scale hoarders, speculators, and market-manipulators who, in his view, created the commodity shortages and worsened the inflation. These, in local parlance, were the "Big Tigers" (*ta-lao-hu*), and Ching-kuo soon acquired the reputation of being a fearless and resolute "Big Tiger Hunter." In his private journal, beginning on September 1, Ching-kuo recorded the preparations for his initial hunt: "In the afternoon I decided to present a list of the big hoarders, and began taking action." The next day: "Yesterday evening, I received a telephone call from Nanking [from his father?] desiring a quick settlement of cases involving violations of the economic laws, and also urging strict handling of the big speculators. . . . Today I have determined to act firmly against the traitorous merchants."[61] The next day, September 3, seven "Big Tigers"—including some of the most famous names in Shanghai—were arrested. Tu Wei-ping, a son of the famous Tu Yüeh-sheng, was charged with black-market stock transactions after the Shanghai Stock Market had been shut down; Jung Hung-yüan, head of the Jung (also read "Yung") family's extensive interests in cotton and flour mills and a member of the National Assembly, was charged with illegal foreign-exchange remittances; the others, such as Huang I-ts'ung (manager of a cigarette company) and Chan P'ei-lin (chairman of the Paper Guild), were mostly accused of having hoarded goods and refused to sell them at the official price.[62] The same day, one Wang Ch'un-che, arrested more than two months previously for large-scale speculation in foreign currencies, was sentenced to die.[63] "This kind of thing," Ching-kuo recorded in his journal, "is of the utmost significance in changing the psychology of the people of Shanghai."[64]

Through late August and all of September, prices in Shanghai generally held steady. There was, indeed, a burgeoning black market: food retailers sold their choicest articles under the counter, at prices above the official ceiling; and the quality of goods sold at official prices deteriorated (patrons complained that now the meat had more bone, and that hens apparently no longer produced normal-sized eggs).[65] But, as Indian Ambassador K. M. Panikkar remarked, "For over four weeks Shanghai was practically terror-stricken into good behaviour."[66]

Chiang Ching-kuo's success in holding prices to approximately the August 19 levels was, paradoxically, the cause of his most worrisome problem. For with prices elsewhere in the country rising, commodities fled from his area of control. The consequent shortages became progressively more acute, causing distress among both consumers and manufacturers. The shortages also created a constant upward pressure on prices. The scarcity of rice, for instance, was felt as early as September 4, and thereafter was a source of severe concern. Vegetables and meat disappeared quickly from the markets each morning; and the dwindling supply of coal created anxiety as the arrival of cold weather became imminent. In industry, manufacturers were faced with growing shortages of both raw materials and fuel. Most serious for them, however, was the disparity between the fixed prices of finished goods and the cost of the raw materials they had to purchase outside the city, where prices were not effectively controlled. In early October, for example, the cost of producing each *chien* of cotton yarn was GY780, but the ceiling price was only GY707.[67] As a result, manufacturers threatened to cut back on production and simply hoard their current inventories. If they were allowed to do so, unemployment in the city would rise, and consumer shortages would worsen. Here was a situation that, as Ching-kuo noted in his journal on September 24, "needs urgently to be corrected."[68]

Attempts to resolve the supply problem took many forms. Hoarders were vigorously prosecuted, and the Bandit-Suppression National-Reconstruction Corps, Youth Service Corps, and Shanghai Economic Police launched repeated citywide searches of warehouses, factories, and even residences to flush out commodities that had been held in storage more than three months (the official definition of hoarded consumer goods). These measures forced some commodities onto the market, but they only momentarily relieved consumer demands. To keep goods in the city, stringent restrictions were imposed on the export of food, clothes, fuel, and other goods such as soap, shoes, and paper. And, to resolve the acute shortage of raw cotton, both state-run and private spinning mills established a joint procurement agency in mid-September to buy cotton in the interior and then distribute it among all the mills.

Despite all these measures, an adequate supply of goods still did not flow into Shanghai. The city had become a tiny island of controlled prices in the midst of a sea of raging inflation.[69] The situation was obviously impossible, and on September 30 the Executive Yüan confronted the problem by expanding the areas of jurisdiction of the Economic Supervisors' Offices. Thereafter, Ching-kuo held the authority to enforce price controls in the city of Nanking and the three provinces of Kiangsu, Chekiang, and Anhwei, as well as in Shanghai.[70] This measure proved to be ineffectual, however. It also came too late, because the inflation even in Shanghai was soon out of control.

The turning point in Shanghai came on October 2, when the central government committed what proved to be a monumental blunder. In an understandable attempt to reduce the budgetary deficit—an attempt that in other circumstances would have been laudable—the government raised the taxes on tobacco, alcoholic beverages, tin foil, and joss paper, and permitted merchants to adjust the sales prices on these items upward accordingly. The tobacco shops closed for two days to adjust their prices; when they reopened, the price of cigarettes had risen between 100 and 120 percent. This was the first time that the authorities in Shanghai had officially approved a price hike above the August 19 level, and the public was stunned. Long sensitized to hints of future inflation, the people surmised that similar taxes, and hence price increases, would soon affect items of daily consumption.[71]

The result was that the people went on a wild buying spree, buying up goods before the anticipated increase of prices. Woolen and silk cloth, shoes, ready-made clothes, canned goods, and imported goods of every description were among the first to go, but soon all commodities began to disappear. To the shopkeepers each sale represented a loss, for the selling price was surely lower than the cost of replacements; so they hid their stocks and shortened their business hours, opening late, halting sales during lunch, and closing early in the evenings. This sharpened the consumers' panic. By October 7, the commodity shortage had become critical. Factories were producing only limited amounts of new goods. The flow of food and raw materials to the city had dwindled to a trickle. Shop shelves were empty, and even the itinerant food stalls—which the city authorities had long tried in vain to eliminate—finally disappeared for want of products to sell.[72]

Within three weeks the buying spree had abated, for virtually nothing remained to be purchased. Then Shanghai became like a besieged city, shortages being far more critical than at any time within memory, including the last stage of the war with Japan. The poor went for weeks without rice, meat, or cooking oil. Only a few vegetables were available in the markets; queues were long; prices were far above the official ceilings. Hospital officials, unable to procure food, were talking of closing their facilities. Medicines were unavailable for the sick; powdered milk for infants vanished; there were not even coffins for the dead— everything disappeared from the shops as people desperately purchased goods as a hedge against the anticipated inflationary spurt.[73]

The rich weathered the crisis better than the working classes, but even they experienced relative hardships. Their servants started lining up in the food markets as early as three in the morning to obtain, at ever-rising prices, the little meat or rice that did appear in the city. The more affluent began taking their meals at restaurants, which could still buy meat and vegetables (at premium prices, to be sure) because of their long-standing relationships with food suppliers. As customers jammed the restaurants, however, the servings became smaller, and by the end of October the restaurants, too, were closing. Dance halls and bars were similarly filled to capacity as a fever of hedonism afflicted a population that had more money to spend than there were goods to spend it on. For the same reason, outbound trains to Hangchow and Soochow were filled with pleasure-seekers.[74] In painful contrast were the thousands of unemployed and hungry factory workers, the vendor who committed suicide because he could obtain no flour to make *ta-ping* (big cakes), and the emaciated blind man gnawing the bark of a tree on the Bund, in the very shadow of Shanghai's biggest banks.[75]

Chiang Ching-kuo agonized as the economic situation deteriorated. The fate of his father's regime, he believed, depended on the outcome of the Emergency Measures, which in turn depended on the success or failure of his efforts.[76] He struggled, therefore, to resolve the supply crisis. In October, for example, thinking that market manipulators and hoarders were causing the rice shortage, he threatened the head of the rice guild and the heads of the two big rice markets in the city with dire punishments if shipments to the city fell short of 200,000 piculs a month.[77] In fact, however, rice did not reach Shanghai because of the unfavorable price differential between the city and the producing areas. Moreover, many local governments in the rice-producing areas were preventing shipments from leaving their districts altogether.[78] Ching-kuo consequently devised a more positive plan, whereby the city would send cotton goods and sugar to the interior, and there barter them for rice and other foods.[79] He also prepared a plan of rationing, to begin in November, that would assure the adequate and equitable distribution of rice, cooking oil, cotton cloth, coal, and sugar throughout the city.[80]

None of these measures was effective, however, and by late October virtually all essentials had disappeared from the markets, and commercial and industrial activity had come to almost a complete halt.[81] In view of the desperate nature of the situation, the government's top administrators convened in Nanking on October 27–28 to reassess their economic policies. (Chiang Kai-shek was absent in North China inspecting the military situation.) Most participants in these meetings now bitterly opposed the Emergency Measures, and Chiang Ching-kuo was the target of venomous criticism. Only Chang Li-sheng, the Economic Supervisor in Tientsin, joined Ching-kuo in arguing in favor of continued economic controls.[82]

Three days later, on October 31, the government revoked the policy of price controls. The same day, Wong Wen-hao and Wang Yün-wu submitted their resignations to President Chiang.[83] As for Chiang Ching-kuo, he publicly apologized to the people of Shanghai, saying "not only have I failed to carry out my plans and responsibilities, but in some places . . . I have even increased the suffering of the citizens of Shanghai." He therefore requested that the central government punish him, in order to make evident that it was he who bore responsibility for those sufferings. At the same time, however, he expressed the hope that the people would "not again allow traitorous merchant-speculators, bureaucratic politicians, and ruffians and scoundrels to come and control Shanghai."[84]

Soon the government returned to the original owners the hoarded goods that had been confiscated and released on bail those who had been arrested for economic crimes. It retreated further on November 11 by permitting citizens to hold gold, silver, and foreign currency, and by adjusting the exchange rate of the U.S. dollar to GY20 (in contrast to GY4 during the period of the reform) in recognition of the new economic realities.[85] Inflation was thus again the order of the day. The gold yüan reform of August 19 had been a quick and complete failure.

## In the Wake of the Gold Yüan Reform

The termination of price controls on October 31 marked the beginning of the final collapse of the National Government on the mainland. Little wonder, therefore, that observers have concluded that the gold yüan reform was *the cause* of that collapse. Largely by coincidence, the full extent of the debacle on the battlefield also became apparent at precisely this time. The Communists had begun their decisive offensive in Manchuria on September 12, and they had gone quickly from victory to victory—Changchun fell on October 20, Mukden on October 30, and Yingkow, the last remaining Nationalist stronghold north of the Great Wall, on November 5. During this same period, Nationalist defenses south of the Great Wall began disintegrating. The loss of Tsinan on September 25 was a critical strategic defeat that severely damaged the government's prestige and the people's morale. Six weeks later, on November 8, the Communists attacked Hsü-chou, which was regarded as the last defense obstructing the Communist approach to the Yangtze River and the Central China cities of Nanking and Shanghai. The battle of Hsü-chou (or Hwai-Hai) lasted 65 days, and it ended in a crushing defeat for the Nationalists. But so fragile was public confidence in the army that Shanghai reverberated with rumors of impending defeat at Hsü-chou as early as November 9.[86]

Following the unfreezing of prices on October 31, the economy deteriorated no less rapidly than the military situation. Prices increased, of course, but far more rapidly than anticipated. In just two weeks the wholesale price index rose over sixteen times. Many goods that shopkeepers had kept out of sight during the period of price controls now reappeared on the shelves, but customers were few, because—or so it was explained—most Shanghaiese had spent all their money during the October buying spree. Apparently for the same reason, patronage in restaurants also declined, and dance halls and other places of entertainment were practically deserted.[87]

For all but the very rich, the most exigent problem continued to be that of finding food. Removing price controls had not substantially restored the flow of rice and other necessities into the city. Farmers near Shanghai had just reaped a good harvest, but they were reluctant to sell. They did not want to hold gold yüan notes, and there were no commodities for them to buy. So they hoarded their rice, and continued to feed rather than slaughter their pigs.[88] Food prices in Shanghai consequently soared, and shortages were widespread. The situation provoked yet another wave of panic. Thus, when rice shops boosted their prices by as much as ten times, hungry and frightened customers stormed the shops, looting them of rice. The first of these rice riots in Shanghai was reported on November 4. They reached a peak on November 8. By November 10, with the rice shops completely emptied, the rioters turned against shops and mills with wheat flour. Some rioters during these events shouted or carried slogans appealing for the return of price controls: "Why should Chiang Ching-kuo abandon the ceiling prices? Why should he leave Shanghai?"; or "All the workers of Shanghai request Chiang Ching-kuo to remain at his post." Frightened by the rioters, rice merchants stopped even trying to bring rice into the city. Not until November 12 did the crisis ease. By then, special government shipments of rice from Hong Kong and Kiangsi, some of it by air, reached the city. More important in the long run, though, was the fact that farmers soon began selling their hoards of grain, apparently tempted by the undreamed-of prices being offered them.[89]

By the latter half of November, the economy was a shambles. Industrial production in Shanghai in November and December was down to 50–60 percent of what it had been in the first part of the year; cigarette, silk, and paper factories had largely suspended operations; industrial use of electricity was down sharply; and labor discontent was widespread. Interest rates reached 500 percent a month. Money was in such short supply that a premium of 20 percent was being paid just to obtain the currency notes.[90]

In a last, desperate attempt to restrain the inflation, the new finance minister, Hsü K'an, on November 23 began selling gold and silver to the public in an effort to reduce the volume of inflation-producing gold yüan and to restore confidence in the currency. The price of one ounce of gold was fixed at GY1,000, but purchasers were required to deposit an additional GY1,000 in the Central Bank for one year at a nominal interest rate of 2 percent a year. Each ounce of gold thus in effect sold for GY2,000.[91] There was a bitter irony here that did not escape the public: only three months earlier, the government had bought this same gold from them at only GY200 an ounce. Even at the price of GY2,000, however, the public stormed the banks to buy the precious metals, queuing up overnight by the tens of thousands. Sales were halted at least twice as a result of pandemonium, but on the second occasion only after 45 people had been injured and seven had been crushed to death.[92]

Early in 1949 the gold yüan began to depreciate uncontrollably. The price index in Shanghai, which at the end of November stood at 2,199, rose to 3,483 in early January 1949 and skyrocketed to 35,774 by early February. By April, the price index stood at over 3,000,000 and the National Government—now having fled to Canton—desperately attempted yet another currency conversion, replacing the gold yüan with a new silver yüan. In just eight months, therefore, the gold yüan had lost virtually all value, just as the fa-pi had before it.[93]

Already in November 1948, however, with the economy collapsing and the Communist advance on Nanking and Shanghai seemingly imminent, a terrified flight had already begun. Prominent political figures and wealthy merchants, together with their families, led the way. Announcements of their arrival in Hong Kong, Taiwan, Canton, Amoy, Swatow, and Kweilin read like a *Who's Who of China*: Wang Yün-wu, Chiang Ting-wen, Li Shih-tseng, and the families of T. V. Soong and H. H. Kung. Some 31,000 refugees arrived in Taiwan, through Keelung and the Taipei airport, during November; 50,000 arrived in Hong Kong during just one week that month. These figures increased exponentially during the ensuing months. The government facilitated the flow, informing officials on December 1 that they could borrow two months' pay to finance the evacuation of their families (though the officials themselves were to stay on the job). Ships from Shanghai were booked solid, the China Merchants' Steam Navigation Company announcing in early December that it would accept no more reservations that month. Real estate prices in Shanghai slumped to half of normal levels as owners scurried to salvage whatever they could before taking flight. Those failing to find buyers sought out foreigners—preferably Soviet or Czechoslovak nationals—to hold the property titles on their behalf. In the wake of the gold yüan reform, therefore, pessimism, despair, and defeatism pervaded the cities of Central China.[94]

\*

You see [remarked Wu Kuo-chen in 1953], the whole trouble about the gold yüan was that it embittered every part, every segment, of the Chinese people against the government. The intellectuals, of course, they knew it would not work, thought it was just sheer stupidity. The bankers and businessmen like Li Ming got embittered and hated the government. And the middle class got entirely bankrupt because they surrendered what little savings they had. The shopkeepers had to sell all their goods at the fixed prices, gold yüan prices, and lost their properties that way. And then even the poor people. You see the Chinese poor people always had some ornament, gold you know, and so on, but they had to surrender those things too and then finally the currency they got became worthless. So you may say this gold yüan was a fatal blow.[95]

This statement typifies the view of Chinese who lived through the period of the gold yüan reform. For them, it had been a traumatic experience, with wrenching political and personal consequences. Most people thereafter abandoned all hope for economic recovery; the failure of the reform seemed to demonstrate that the National Government was totally without resources to

control the inflation. People also felt aggrieved that the government had bought their treasured gold, silver, and dollars with
worthless paper money.

This popular resentment was initially directed at Wong Wen-
hao and Wang Yün-wu. But Chiang Kai-shek was too closely associated with the reform to avoid all taint. As the Catholic daily
*I-shih-pao* wrote, the cabinet of Wong Wen-hao was merely the
"secretarial office of the President," and "decisions on every issue were sought from President Chiang." The *I-shih-pao* asserted
that it continued to believe in Chiang's "greatness of character"
but felt he was taking upon himself too much responsibility.[96]
This waning of popular confidence in Chiang after the failure of
the reform was undoubtedly an important factor in his decision
to retire from the presidency on January 21, 1949.

In historical perspective, it is obvious that the gold yüan reform did hasten the political collapse of Nationalist rule on the
mainland. The National Government had not erred, however, in
attempting the currency reform. Critics of the reform usually ignore the fact that the economy was already, in early August
1948, rushing pell-mell toward collapse, and that the fall of the
government itself was already foreseeable.[97] In these circumstances, not to have attempted the reform would have been
more blameworthy than attempting it and failing. For, as indicated earlier, several factors in mid-August seemed to promise at
least a chance of success. Why, then, did the reform fail?

The chief reason was that too much gold yüan currency was
created, thus stimulating a renewal of inflation. This in itself is
not surprising. What is striking, however, is that as of September 30, only 23 percent of the new gold yüan notes created were
to finance the government and its military operations, whereas
at least 63 percent were printed to redeem the gold, silver, and
foreign currencies that were turned in to the Central Bank. (See
Table 8.) The chief inflationary push, therefore, resulted from
the government's policy of nationalizing those items. But for
that policy, the post–August 19 inflation would have proceeded
considerably more slowly than it did. Deficit funding for the military and other government expenditures would also have been

TABLE 8

*Aggregate Issues of Gold Yüan, August 23–October 31, 1948*

(million gold yüan)

| Issue and purpose | Issued during period ending: | | |
|---|---|---|---|
| | August 31 | September 30 | October 31 |
| To redeem gold, silver, and foreign currency | 108.8 | 600.0 | 760.0 |
| To redeem fa-pi and Northeastern currency | | 50.0 | |
| To pay military and other governmental expenses | | 220.0 | |
| Total issue | 296.8 | 958.8 | 1,595.4 |
| Increase over August 23, 1948 | 50% | 500% | 800% |

SOURCE: "Tsung-chieh che ch'i-shih-t'ien," p. 360.

correspondingly less than the GY220 million expended by September 30.

The problem here was that the value of the gold, silver, and foreign currencies had hitherto been stored in forms that had not constituted an inflationary force. Indeed, during 1946 and early 1947 the government had purposely *sold* large quantities of gold to take paper currency out of circulation and dampen the inflation. After August 19, that policy was reversed; the government now purchased precious metals and thereby put large amounts of paper currency into circulation.

This had not been the government's intent. Persons surrendering gold, silver, and foreign currency had been offered three alternatives: to deposit the gold yüan equivalent in the Central Bank; to purchase government-issued U.S.-currency bonds; or to receive gold yüan notes as cash.[98] But, as Premier Wong explained in late October, far more people than expected had selected the third alternative—thus forcing the government to issue more currency than it had planned or wished to do.[99] Presumably the people's confidence in the government—in this case represented by the Central Bank and government bonds—was so low that they preferred cash (even though they feared it would soon lose value) to some paper representation of cash. In any event, the result was that U.S. $190 million worth of gold, silver, and foreign currencies that had hitherto been held off the market were now suddenly converted into money and became an active inflationary ingredient. Or, in the terminology of the time, it became "floating capital" (*yu-tzu*) seeking objects of purchase and investment.

To absorb this excess currency, the government tried to sell former enemy properties and shares in five of the major government-run enterprises (the China Textile Development Corporation, the China Merchants' Steam Navigation Company, the Taiwan Sugar Corporation, the Taiwan Paper Corporation, and the Tientsin Paper Corporation). The public, however, expressed little interest in these investments; after nearly a month, sales had absorbed only GY4 million (by contrast with the projected GY564 million).[100] At the same time, commerce and industry were suffering, and thus the normal investment markets failed to channel off significant amounts of idle capital. Money consequently became a glut on the market, evidenced, for example, by the fact that the black-market interest rate in Shanghai on September 26 fell to 5 percent a month (as compared with an average of 55 percent a month prior to August 19).[101] This glut of currency was, of course, the chief fuel for renewed inflation.

A second reason for the failure of the Emergency Measures was the National Government's weak and territorially limited administrative control. If the policy of price controls had been enforced as vigorously throughout the Nationalist area as it was in Shanghai, the government might have realized its hope that the inflation would be alleviated for at least six months. But even after the jurisdiction of the Shanghai Economic Supervisor's Office was extended on October 1, and Chiang Ching-kuo theoretically had the authority to accomplish throughout Kiangsu, Chekiang, and Anhwei what he had already accomplished in Shanghai, nothing changed. The National Government simply did not possess the administrative vigor to assert economic control over the vast interior of the country. And without that vigor, political attempts to hold back the inflation were doomed.

Finally, the Emergency Measures failed because the people

lacked confidence in the gold yüan. Basically, this was attributable to their unhappy experience with the paper currency over the preceding ten years. But two factors during the reform shattered whatever remnants of trust in the currency remained. The first of these was the deteriorating military situation in Manchuria and North China. Beginning on September 12, the battle reports were unrelentingly dismal. As never before, the public began seriously to contemplate the possibility that the Communists would win the civil war. Public confidence in the National Government's currency diminished proportionately. The second factor was the tax increases on October 2, which dealt a severe blow to the people's faith in the currency. The government was no doubt mistaken (as became evident after the event) in imposing the new taxes. Yet the public's reaction was totally out of proportion to the inherent significance of those taxes, demonstrating just how frail the public's confidence in the gold yüan was at that time.

If the chief stimuli to inflation after August 19 were the policy of nationalizing gold, silver, and foreign currencies and the low popular confidence in the new currency, had Chiang Kai-shek erred when he modified Plan "B" so that gold yüan could not be freely converted to gold? Chang Kia-ngau, whose judgment in these matters must be taken seriously, has answered "Yes." "If the government could have prevented a further major expansion in the supply of money," he wrote, "it could have made the gold yüan freely convertible into bullion, and confidence in the currency might have been restored." [102]

One might also argue, however, that—as Chiang Kai-shek believed—it would have been reckless and irresponsible to allow convertibility when the government's reserve of specie and foreign exchange would have been threatened by a large public demand. In early 1947, Chiang had witnessed a gold panic that threatened the government's financial stability. [103] To have risked another gold panic now in 1948, in the light of that experience and with such a small bullion reserve—even though convertibility would clearly have helped shore up public confidence in the gold yüan—would have been an even more risky gamble than the gold yüan reform without convertibility.

To the largely economic reasons for the failure of the gold yüan reform just enumerated, Chiang Ching-kuo added a political explanation. Though he took note of the effects of excessive issues of gold yüan notes and of the unfortunate decision to increase the tobacco and alcohol taxes, he laid most of the blame on the spineless and uncooperative officials in the government. Even at the beginning of the reform, on August 22, he complained that "most government officials hold a doubting attitude." [104] By early September, he was reflecting that "the most worrisome thing today is that most high-level officials maintain attitudes of 'watching,' 'doubting,' and 'opposing' this policy. They are not like most of the people who earnestly seek a peaceful life and who sincerely support the success of the policy. As a consequence, I am isolated in my work and not a single high-level official wishes to assist me." [105] Some officials argued against his policy of harsh enforcement of the reform, asserting that his measures were frightening the industrialists into closing their factories. Others, Ching-kuo thought, were simply going through the motions of carrying out the reform, speaking without conviction and dragging their heels. [106] Among the worst of these was Mayor Wu Kuo-chen. Ching-kuo despised what he thought was Wu's stultifying bureaucratism. Wu, for his part, repeatedly submitted his resignation—although Chiang Kai-shek just as often rejected it. [107]

No less worrisome to Ching-kuo than the officials in Shanghai were those in the central government. Premier Wong Wen-hao and members of the Executive Yüan, for instance, continually wavered. Ching-kuo repeatedly complained that they had no concept of an overall policy and no confidence in the price-control program. [108] As his frustration mounted, so did his anger. "The merchants are hateful," he recorded in his journal on October 26, but "politicians within the party are even more hateful." [109] After the controls were abandoned, he further ruminated that "the issue is not whether or not there are price controls, but [what the removal of controls] reveals about the government's ineffectiveness [*wu-neng*], fear of adversity, and lack of conviction." [110]

Actually, the politicians and bureaucrats were probably less villainous than Chiang Ching-kuo depicted them. To officials like Wong Wen-hao and Wu Kuo-chen, for instance, it was obvious that the inflation could not be halted so long as the government continued to employ deficit financing to pay for the war with the Communists. If they did not cooperate with young Chiang, therefore, it was at least partially because they regarded his efforts to work an economic miracle by means of moral resolve and political coercion to be, at best, quixotic. There were no real villains, then, in the events surrounding the gold yüan reform, because at that stage of the revolution all participants were more like victims in a tragedy than heroes or villains in a melodrama. The villains, if there can be said to be such in history, were those who, a decade or two earlier, had failed to devise a system of government that would have obviated the necessity of a political and social revolution by the Communists.

## CHAPTER 9

# Who Lost China?
## Chiang Kai-shek Testifies

"To tell the truth, never, in China or abroad, has there been a revolutionary party as decrepit and degenerate (*t'ui-t'ang ho fu-pai*) as we [the Kuomintang] are today; nor has there been one as lacking in spirit, in discipline, and even more in standards of right and wrong as we are today. This kind of party should long ago have been destroyed and swept away!"[1]

The time was January 1948; the speaker was Chiang Kai-shek. Frequently during 1947–50, the climactic years of struggle with the Communists for control of the Chinese mainland, Chiang addressed his military commanders and civilian cadres in similarly scathing language. His purpose, he asserted, was to identify the causes of Nationalist errors and weaknesses so that he could "turn defeat into victory." Chiang's speeches from this period—readily available in published form for years, but until now ignored by all—constitute in all probability the most compelling testimony on why the Nationalists were defeated by the Communists.

During the civil war years, as the strategic advantage passed to the Communists, Chiang Kai-shek was both surprised and humiliated by the accumulating series of defeats. "Regardless of what aspect we discuss," he declared in June 1947, "we hold an absolute superiority; in terms of the troops' equipment, battle techniques, and experience, the Communists are not our equal. . . . We are also ten times richer than the Communist army in terms of military-supply replacements, such as food, fodder, and ammunition."[2] Seven months later, in January 1948, Chiang still claimed that "with regard to matériel, we have very good equipment and excellent weapons; one could say that we possess all the conditions necessary for victory."[3] "But why," he continued, "does our Communist-suppression [campaign] still suffer defeats and suffer losses?"[4] During 1947 and 1948, Chiang examined this question repeatedly and from different perspectives. With regard to the military, he observed that the chief weaknesses were a lack of knowledge and skill on the part of officers, poor conditions for the common soldiers, and moral and spiritual shortcomings at all levels.

The officers, Chiang declared, were utterly lacking in professional competence. Most commanders, from the highest to the lowest level, "fight muddleheaded battles" (*ta hu-t'u chang*). "No one studies theory or the basic training manuals (*tien-fan-ling*); even less do they pay attention to reconnoitering the enemy's situation or the lay of the land; they draw up plans with an air of indifference and casually issue orders, and they are unable to study carefully or make thorough preparations."[5] In January 1948, Chiang complained that most of his officers "don't use their brains and are unwilling to study. Regardless of what the problem, they are invariably careless and do not seek a thorough understanding. In administration, they are even more perfunctory and superficial, and do not attempt to be thorough. . . . Now, the brains of most of our soldiers are actually asleep."[6]

Just how disgusted he was with his top officers' lack of military skill is indicated by this scorching diatribe: "You should know, those of you who today serve as army commanders and division commanders, if you were in a foreign country and really had to rely just on your own knowledge and ability, you would not be qualified to serve as regimental commanders. It is only because everything in our China is backward and there is a shortage of talent that you, with minuscule abilities, bear such heavy responsibilities."[7]

Chiang also scolded the officers for their indifference to the condition of their men. Officers ignored such basic elements in training as aiming, firing, reconnoitering, and liaison, with the result that "the soldiers' combat skills are so poor that they cannot fight."[8] Nor did officers provide the troops with adequate food, clothing, or medical care, even embezzling supplies meant for the men. Chiang's solution was for the officers to "eat what the troops eat, wear what the troops wear, and live in the troops' barracks." He added: "We can say that the Communists' military cadres have already completely attained this. Between their officers and men there are only differences of function, but there is no gap in their living conditions."[9] In the Nationalist army, by contrast, given the treatment of the men "it must be considered very good if they do not mutiny or desert."[10]

"It cannot be denied," Chiang observed in June 1947, "that the spirit of most commanders is broken and their morality is base." High-level officers, complacent in their posts, were encumbered by family members and began acting like warlords. "As a consequence, their revolutionary spirit is almost completely dissipated, and they are concerned only with preserving their military strength and resources (*shih-li*)."[11] Chiang was especially critical of his commanders for their failure to cooperate with one another.[12] "Everyone nourishes the evil habit of caring only for himself and is concerned only for the advantage of his own unit; toward the perils and difficulties of other troops, or the success or failure of the whole campaign, they give almost no thought. . . . With the discipline of our troops so lax and morale so low, there is absolutely no way even through luck that we can avoid defeat when we do battle with the tough and resourceful (*hsiung-wan chiao-hua*) Communist army."[13]

Foreshadowing John F. Kennedy's remark after the Bay of Pigs fiasco that "victory has a hundred fathers and defeat is an orphan," Chiang also complained of his commanders' selfishness in grasping for honors and shunning blame. "If we are defeated in battle, then they are mutually resentful and criticize one another, but they conceal their own errors, absolving themselves completely of responsibility for the defeat." But "if victorious, they fight for honors."[14]

The commanders, moreover, were corrupt, overstating the number of men in their units and embezzling the grain and money consigned to their troops.[15] They also failed to carry out orders: "Now, at all levels of command, most feign obedience to their superiors' orders, sometimes not implementing them at all, with the result that the value of the orders is completely lost." [16]

Chiang felt that his commanders deceived him in their reports from the battlefield. One of their most serious deceptions occurred on arriving at the front: even before actually establishing contact with the enemy, Chiang complained, "they say that such-and-such an enemy troop column has arrived at their front, and such-and-such a column at their flanks, so that it seems as though the situation is absolutely critical. But if you go and investigate the actual situation, there are only a few enemy troops, and perhaps no such unit at all at their front. And after establishing contact, they often exaggerate victory, saying that they have killed so many thousands or tens of thousands of the enemy. They should know that the Communist army's principles of combat stipulate that they avoid decisive battle with our main forces and that it is practically impossible for us to annihilate thousands or tens of thousands of them. One look at this kind of exaggerated report and you know it is inaccurate." [17]

"If," Chiang declared in June 1947, "we speak about the level of most officers' spirit and morality, knowledge and ability, and the level of understanding of ourselves and of the enemy, then we should long ago have been defeated by the bandit army." [18]

Chiang Kai-shek was even more disillusioned about the civilian branches of the regime than he was about the army. Never in his 40 years of participating in the revolution, he asserted in July 1947, had he felt more disheartened, or more pessimistic about the future of the revolution. The reason was not that the economy was in crisis, or that politics were at an impasse, or that the Communists were growing daily in strength. No, he said, the reason was the sad state of the Kuomintang and the Youth Corps: "Our strength is completely superficial; in actuality, it is nonexistent in the extreme. Our party and corps possess no basic-level organization; they possess no new blood; and members of the party and the corps perform no function among the masses or in society. The existence of the entire party depends almost completely upon visible military strength. This is our true crisis. This is my sole concern!" [19] Two months later, at the time of the merger of the party and the Youth Corps, he again spoke of their lack of organization, training, and discipline; they "can be said to be only empty shells, without any real strength."[20]

But the merger of the corps with the Kuomintang produced no tangible results, and in January 1948 Chiang was still complaining that "our revolutionary work is conducted carelessly and perfunctorily so that there is absolutely no progress." Because of the party's mistakes, he said, "most people in society attack the party unsparingly, even viewing party members as offenders against the state and the nation."[21]

Amazingly, Chiang expressed unabashed admiration for the Communists. They represented everything he admired and everything the Nationalist regime lacked: organization, discipline, and morality. The Communists, he noted, not only studied and discussed problems exhaustively, but also implemented their plans completely. "They do not permit even the slightest muddleheadedness or vagueness of ideas, . . . and by no means can they be superficial, stopping halfway." By contrast, he asserted, "nowhere are our methods or actions the equal of theirs." "Most of our cadres do not use their brains and are unwilling to study, are neither careful nor reliable . . . and thus we sink in defeat."[22]

The difference, Chiang said, was that the Communists employed the "scientific method." This approach, he thought, had been inculcated largely through the *cheng-feng* (party reform) movement, and he urged his own followers to emulate that movement in order to strengthen the organization of the Kuomintang and increase the fighting strength of the Nationalist army.[23]

Despite his pessimism about the condition of the Kuomintang and his army in 1947–48, Chiang Kai-shek was not, of course, prepared to abandon the field to Mao Tse-tung. "Although [the Communists' organization, training, and propaganda techniques] are all superior to ours," said Chiang in September 1947, "our ideology, thought, and [political] line are nevertheless definitely more correct than theirs and are, moreover, more suited to the needs of the nation. Therefore, if only we can study everything of theirs and comprehend everything of theirs, we can then be assured of annihilating them."[24]

The march of events did not, however, allow the Nationalists the leisure to "study everything of theirs and comprehend everything of theirs." On January 21, 1949—with the economy nearing total collapse, with the army being pushed back to the Yangtze, and with the people feeling disillusioned with or even contemptuous of the government in Nanking—Chiang Kai-shek resigned the presidency. Retiring to his native village of Hsi-k'ou in northeastern Chekiang, he kept one eye on political developments but also toured the area's many scenic spots and relaxed with his family in the country.[25] This might have been an idyllic retirement. For Chiang, however, it was—in the words of a chronicler, Ts'ao Sheng-fen—"the most troubled and strenuous period of self-examination in his life."[26] The movement that he had led for over twenty years now lay in shambles. He felt humiliated. What, he wondered, were the reasons for the defeat?

With a succession of visitors to Hsi-k'ou—including Ch'en Li-fu, Wang Shih-chieh, Chang Tao-fan, T'ao Hsi-sheng, Ku Cheng-kang, Chang Ch'ün, Wu Li-ch'ing, and Chang Ch'i-yün—Chiang Kai-shek pondered this question. After three months, wrote Ts'ao Sheng-fen, Chiang's answer was that "the military and governmental branches both bore a responsibility for the past defeats. But the chief reason, which cannot be denied, arose from the paralysis of the party: the membership, organizational structure, and method of leadership all created problems. Thus, the party became a lifeless shell, the government and military also lost their soul, and as a result the troops collapsed and society disintegrated."[27]

During the summer of 1949, Chiang again plunged into the maelstrom of Chinese politics. Using as his chief weapons his director-generalship of the Kuomintang (which he had retained, even though resigning as president) and his control of the government's gold reserve (which he had secreted out of Shanghai to Taipei), he engaged in a bitter power struggle with Acting-

President Li Tsung-jen. Finally, as Communist armies consolidated their control on the mainland, Li flew to the United States in December 1949, and Chiang Kai-shek, taking refuge in Taiwan, resumed the office of president of the National Government in March 1950.

After returning to the political stage in late April 1949, Chiang had immediately begun acting upon the insight he had arrived at during his brief retirement that the "paralysis" of the Kuomintang had been the ultimate source of the deterioration and collapse of Nationalist power. At a Central Executive Committee meeting of the Kuomintang in Canton in July, he presented a proposal for party reform. Because of the rush of events caused by the military debacle on the mainland, no action was taken on the proposal until a year later. Then, as president in Taiwan, Chiang formed a top-level Central Reform Commission, headed by Ch'en Ch'eng, to plan and oversee a fundamental overhaul of the party, including a purge of members who had compromised with the Communists or had fled for safety abroad.[28] At the same time, he attempted to revitalize the hapless remnant of his army through intensified military training and political education.

During this period of rebuilding, Chiang frequently spoke with his chief officers about the reasons for the recent defeats. "Today I must painfully point out," he asserted, "[that] from the latter part of the war against Japan to the present, the corruption and degeneracy (*t'an-wu fu-pai*) manifested within our revolutionary army has been truly fantastic, simply unimaginable!" The army had been "soulless," without fighting spirit or discipline, and plagued with incompetent, uncooperative commanders. Such an army "could not but take the road to defeat."[29]

Thus during late 1949 and 1950, Chiang's criticisms of the army, the government, and the party were essentially similar to those he had voiced in 1947 and 1948. More than previously, however, he now emphasized how the weak and faulty organization both of the regime and of society as a whole had contributed importantly to the collapse. A major organizational defect, he declared, was the absence of a system of political commissars in all army units. Such a system had existed in the 1920s but had been abolished after the Northern Expedition in order to unify military command. Because there were no political commissars, Chiang declared, there was inadequate surveillance of, or checking upon, the military commanders. As a result, there were "even fewer means of judging the accuracy of [reports on] combat achievements; all kinds of . . . corrupt and degenerate phenomena developed."[30] Without political commissars, too, the political education of the troops had been neglected, so that "the will to fight the enemy was weak, and fighting spirit was entirely lost. And, especially, [the troops] were ignorant of the need to protect and unite with the people, even unrestrainedly harassing them, so that military discipline was completely nonexistent."[31]

Also as a result of lax organization, Communist spies and agents had penetrated everywhere—"there is no hole they do not enter" (*wu-k'ung pu-ju*). They infiltrated particularly the leading organizations of the government and the army, gaining accurate information and at the same time spreading false rumors. As a result, said Chiang, the collapse of the mainland was wrought not so much by enemy military actions as by the confusion, fear, and trouble created within the Nationalist ranks by these Communist agents ("even to the extent that our several million troops, without even experiencing fierce battle, were shattered by the enemy, and innumerable excellent weapons were presented to the Communists and used to massacre us").[32]

In his postmortem analysis, Chiang indicated repeatedly that the army was technologically superior to the Communists; never did he complain of shortages of weapons or ammunition caused by inadequate or dilatory American aid. He did, however, occasionally voice grievances against the United States. He claimed, for example, that "our government mistakenly believed in Marshall's mediation." As a result, the Nationalist army committed a strategic error in sending crack troops to Manchuria, thereby leaving China proper vulnerable to Communist attack.[33] (This complaint overlooked the fact that General Albert Wedemeyer in November 1945 had advised Chiang against sending large military forces into Manchuria, arguing that the Nationalists should first consolidate control of China south of the Great Wall.)[34]

Chiang also regretted the psychological effects upon his followers of the alliance with the United States. The army, he declared, acquired numerous dissolute tendencies from contact with U.S. troops, becoming soft and luxury-loving.[35] In society as a whole, the people abandoned their traditional sense of self-reliance and became dependent upon U.S. aid. As a consequence, said Chiang, when the State Department's *White Paper* appeared in August 1949, indicating that the United States would send no more aid, "everyone felt that the hope of victory against the Communists had already been practically lost."[36]

Clearly, then, Chiang in 1949 and 1950 was not entirely happy with his onetime ally. Yet little space in his collected speeches is devoted to recriminations against the United States. The weight of his remarks, taken as a whole, clearly indicates that he believed the collapse on the mainland to have resulted from weaknesses of and mistakes made by the Nationalists themselves, rather than from the impact of foreign influences.

How accurately does Chiang Kai-shek's testimony reflect actual conditions in the Nationalist movement? Were his criticisms perhaps simply rhetorical statements intended to stir his followers to even greater efforts? There exists some basis for this suspicion, because Chiang for over twenty years periodically castigated the Kuomintang for having abandoned the revolutionary struggle in terms virtually identical to those he used in the late 1940's. In 1928, for example, he exclaimed that "party members no longer strive either for the principles [of Sun Yat-sen] or for the masses. . . . The reason is that the revolutionaries have become degenerate, have lost their revolutionary spirit and revolutionary courage."[37] And we have seen in Chapter 4 his scathing remarks about the Kuomintang when he organized the Youth Corps.

Despite Chiang's seemingly habitual tendency to scold his subordinates and to deplore the absence of revolutionary fervor in the Kuomintang, his criticisms usually accurately reflected the general state of affairs in the regime. The loss of revolutionary enthusiasm that he deplored in 1928 was indeed a fact. His philippics during the 1940's were also amply corroborated by other sources, such as the writings of the Ko-hsin movement.

His denunciations of his army officers in the civil war period, too, bear a striking similarity to the observations of General David Barr. Barr, who headed the U.S. Military Advisory Group, reported to Washington in November 1948 that "No battle has been lost since my arrival due to lack of ammunition or equipment. [The Nationalist] military debacles in my opinion can all be attributed to the world's worst leadership and many other morale destroying factors that lead to a complete loss of will to fight. [There is] complete ineptness of high military leaders and . . . widespread corruption and dishonesty throughout the Armed Forces. . . ."[38] In an earlier day, such a disparaging judgment by a foreigner would inevitably have been suspect; but Barr's and Chiang's assessments are mutually corroborating.

That Chiang's speeches had not been merely exhortative, but represented his considered assessment of the Nationalist movement during those years of defeat, is further borne out by his book *Soviet Russia in China*, published in 1956. There he devoted more attention to economic factors and the duplicity of the Communists in explaining the defeat on the mainland than he had done in his 1947–50 speeches. Even in that work, however, his concluding analysis was congruent with his earlier assessment. "Admittedly," he asserted, "many factors have contributed toward our defeat. The mortal blows to our anti-Communist struggle when we were still on the mainland, however, did not come from administrative shortcomings alone. . . . *The mortal blows sprang from serious defects in organization and technique, from serious errors in policy and strategy, and, above all, from the weakening of our national will power* at the time when it most needed to be strengthened."[39]

Clearly, then, Chiang Kai-shek did not attribute the defeat of his regime to a betrayal by the American government, to shortages of ammunition, or even to the force of Communist arms. In his view, the causes of that defeat lay within the Nationalist regime itself, which he believed had become during the civil war period not just corrupt and inefficient, but virtually moribund.

Chiang had, over the years, attempted to eliminate the decrepitude, corruption, and lack of discipline that were sapping the spirit of the Nationalist movement. In 1932, for instance, he had created the Blue Shirts, and in 1938 the Youth Corps, organizations that he thought would restore revolutionary vitality to the faltering regime. In 1946, too, he launched a purge to eliminate from the Kuomintang all those who lacked the desired revolutionary zeal and virtues. None of these attempted remedies succeeded, any more than did his perpetual scolding of his subordinates—and some of them, by stimulating factional enmities, may even have made matters worse.

Chiang's efforts to eliminate inept and corrupt subordinates were confounded, at least in part, by his belief that there were no capable people to take their place. General Claire Chennault once complained at length to Chiang about the ineffectiveness of the Chinese air force and the incompetence of its commanders. As Chennault subsequently recounted the scene:

He [Chiang] listened patiently to Madame's translation for about thirty minutes and then cut me short with a shrug of his shoulders and a short grunted sentence, leaving the room abruptly.

"He says he knows all about the things you have told him, and he knows the men you have reported are no good," Madame translated.

"If he knows all about them, why doesn't he do something to them," I exploded.

"He says that the Chinese are the only people he has to work with, and if we get rid of all those people who are at fault, who will there be left?" Madame replied. Not until years later, when I was struggling to organize an American air force in China, did I really appreciate the Generalissimo's dilemma. *Lack of honest, technologically competent, loyal subordinates was his worst problem.* He managed by playing off one against the other, getting what he could from them, and every now and then lopping off a few heads as a warning that there was a limit to his patience.[40]

That there was in China a shortage of highly qualified personnel in such a technologically advanced organization as the air force comes as no real surprise. What is striking is that Chiang and his closest associates felt a severe shortage of skilled and dependable personnel in all areas of endeavor—military, political, and governmental. Wu T'ieh-ch'eng, who served in the key post of secretary-general of the Kuomintang throughout the period 1941–48, lamented on his deathbed that "within the party, talented persons (*jen-ts'ai*) did not appear in significant numbers; and outside the party, talented persons were unwilling to set aside their prejudices and come together [in the service of the regime]. As a consequence, the mainland was lost."[41] Ch'en Pulei, Chiang Kai-shek's longtime confidential adviser and assistant, likewise bemoaned China's lack of skilled and knowledgeable people who were, at the same time, willing to serve the state selflessly.[42]

Because Chiang felt that there was such a dearth of qualified personnel, he was indeed caught, as Chennault said, in a dilemma. If, for example, he dismissed all military commanders who were of only marginal ability, with whom would he replace them? Such dismissals, Chiang doubtless thought, would only have exacerbated an already grave situation. That line of reasoning, too, may have been why he did not accept the Ko-hsin group's demands that he eliminate the allegedly corrupt and incompetent members of the Political Study Clique; even if he had agreed that they were corrupt and incompetent, he probably sensed that members of the Ko-hsin movement would perform even less dependably if promoted to the top positions in the government.

The principal reason that Chiang failed to remedy the defects of his regime, however, was that he really did not understand the nature of the problem. This was, perhaps, his chief and even fatal flaw as a national leader. Conceiving of political, behavioral, and even economic problems as essentially moral in nature, he did not comprehend that the political institutions he had created, and the policies he had devised, were the true sources of the regime's frailties. He did not perceive that his bureaucrats were corrupt and inefficient because, in the political system that he had erected, they were largely insulated from external criticism and pressure. Nor did he understand that the soldiers did not fight and the peasants did not cooperate in paying taxes and sending their sons into the army because he had failed to implement policies that might have given them some inducement to fight and to cooperate. True, during 1949 and 1950 he did on occasion reflect that the failure to implement the Principle of People's Livelihood was a cause of the defeat by the Communists.[43] He seems never to have dwelled on the topic, however, and it was manifestly not a factor to which he attributed primary importance. Even in 1956, in his book *Soviet Russia in China,* he continued to speak of the causes of the defeat on the mainland primarily in moralistic and psychological terms. Never once did he ponder the possibility that political institutions which would have provided the people a sense of identification with the government, or social and economic reforms which would have contributed to the people's welfare, might have led to a different conclusion in the struggle with the Communists.

# Conclusion:
## Of Storms and Revolutions

IF A BUILDING collapses in a windstorm, what is the cause of the collapse? A scientific answer would require careful consideration of, first, the structural characteristics of the building and, second, the velocities of the winds. If it were discovered that the building had already deteriorated structurally, one would have to weigh whether, in the absence of a storm, it would have remained erect. But the storm did blow, and the building did collapse. Was, then, the storm the cause of the building's collapse? This question is not without philosophical subtleties. Neither is the question of why the National Government succumbed to the Communist revolution in 1949.

Never did the Nationalists succeed in creating a sound, sturdy political structure. Coming to power in 1927, they were heirs to a political system that had been disintegrating for over a century, and that during the warlord era (1916–27) all but ceased to function. That the Nationalists were able to reverse this process of national disintegration is indisputably to their credit, but nonetheless the authority of the National Government was still limited by the continued existence of warlords in the provinces and by the resistance of local elites in the villages.

The Nationalists' structure was further weakened by the failure to create an effective political administration that would be sensitive to popular needs and capable of carrying out its proclaimed programs of political and economic reform. Shortly after the establishment of the regime, the left wing of the Kuomintang, headed by Wang Ching-wei and Ch'en Kung-po, had proposed instit̃utional and policy alternatives that might have enabled the Nationalists to shore up their political structure. Denouncing Chiang Kai-shek for instituting a one-man dictatorship, the leftists demanded that the Kuomintang revive the policies and spirit that had energized the Nationalist movement during the period of Sun Yat-sen's revolutionary leadership in 1924. They advocated land reforms, punishment of counterrevolutionaries, and greater democracy within the Kuomintang. They also believed that the Kuomintang must strengthen its relations with the common people by promoting autonomous peasant, worker, and other mass organizations. Only with such a mass base, they insisted, could the revolution be prevented from becoming a plaything of bureaucrats and militarists—as indeed it did. Chiang correctly viewed these leftists as a threat to his leadership, and in 1928 he launched an intensive, albeit generally bloodless, suppression of them. Youths, who made up a large part of the rank and file of the left wing, were unequivocally ordered to get out of politics and return to their studies. Other leftists were effectively stripped of power; Wang Ching-wei was reprimanded and Ch'en Kung-po was "expelled forever" from the party. From 1929 on, therefore, Chiang Kai-shek was able to impose his own conception of the revolution upon the party and the government.

During Sun Yat-sen's lifetime, the military had been a relatively disparaged element in the Nationalist movement. Under Chiang, however, Sun's relative ranking—first the party, then the government, and last the army—was turned upside down. During the Nanking Decade the army, led by Chiang Kai-shek, became the dominant branch of the movement, and Chiang himself became the overshadowing presence in the regime.[1] As Franklin Ho, a onetime adviser to Chiang, recalled: "The real authority of the government went wherever the Generalissimo went. In terms of authority, he was the head of everything."[2] Or as Chiang himself told Edgar Snow in 1940, "Wherever I go there is the Government, the Cabinet, and the center of resistance [to the Japanese]."[3]

Because Chiang so dominated the regime, his political outlook was of central importance in determining the character of Nationalist rule. He was, in his view of the political process, profoundly traditional. Like an emperor of the Ch'ing Dynasty, politics for him was a matter of competition among elites. To maximize his power, therefore, he manipulated and combined the support of one group of elites against rival elites. He seemingly never realized that the strong states in the world at the time were those that had successfully mobilized significant segments of the populations, and not just of the elites, in support of their goals. He never comprehended—as Mao Tse-tung did—that it was possible to generate new sources of power by mobilizing support from outside the elite structure. Chiang, of course, talked a great deal about democracy, and he undoubtedly desired popular support. But his concept of democracy and popular support was that the masses should follow their leader unquestioningly, as soldiers obey officers. That concept revealed how poorly he understood the psychology of mass politics, and it prevented him from developing the kind of political participation and economic programs that might have given his regime a firm foundation in society. Thus he never transcended elitist politics and trapped himself in the practice of ruling through the balance of weakness.

Nothing in the preceding paragraphs is meant to imply that if Wang Ching-wei and the left wing of the Kuomintang in 1928–29 had succeeded in the power struggle instead of Chiang, the path to national power and prosperity would assuredly have been smooth. Indeed, there is reason to suspect that they, too, might have been afflicted with the same bureaucratism, corruption, factionalism, and jealousy of power that proved so destructive to the regime under Chiang.[4] What is clear, however, is that Chiang, in silencing the leftists' advocacy of autonomous mass organizations, land reform, democratic procedures within the Kuomintang, and Kuomintang control of the government and army, rejected measures that might possibly have created a sound basis for a popular and efficient government.

Of the winds that assailed the Nationalist structure during its twenty-odd years of rule in China, none was so violent, none imposed such brutal strains, as the war with Japan. The most direct and palpable damage inflicted by the war upon the regime was the weakening of Chiang's army. The wholesale losses sustained by the central forces during the first year of fighting erased, in large measure, the improvements in personnel and equipment, however modest, that had been achieved during the preceding decade. Subsequent combat, diminished sources of supply, and the prolonged stalemate also exacted a heavy toll of Chiang's army. The political effects of the army's enfeeblement were momentous. As Theda Skocpol has observed: "Even after great loss of legitimacy has occurred, a state can remain quite stable—and certainly invulnerable to internal mass-based revolts—especially if its coercive organizations remain coherent and effective."[5] During the war, however, the Nationalists' chief coercive organization, the army, ceased to be "coherent and effective."

The regime had also been weakened by its enforced retreat to West China. On the coast and in the cities of the east, it had possessed secure sources of revenue, an established administrative apparatus that (although never strong at the local level) provided a measure of stability, and ready access to both domestic and foreign sources of supply. In the provinces of West China, by contrast, the Nationalists discovered a strange, almost alien, world. Modernization had barely touched even the major cities there. All of West China, some three-fourths of the nation's territory, had only 4 percent of the nation's electrical capacity and 6 percent of its factories.[6] The economy was overwhelmingly agrarian, and the population felt little identification with the citified officials from "downriver." Local society was dominated by secret societies and rural elites, which were jealous of their longstanding political, military, and economic dominance, and resented the intervention of and competition from the Nationalist regime. The National Government consequently could mobilize resources in West China only with difficulty, and its revenues quickly fell by 63 percent.[7]

The Nationalists committed a serious error in failing to adapt their methods of ruling and fighting to the constraints of the new environment in West China. Prior to the war, the government could ignore the problems of the countryside, because the economic resources of the urban centers were sufficient to sustain it. Its army could also emphasize the orthodox tactics and technologies derived from the West, because it could easily draw weapons and matériel from factories in East China and abroad.

Even though the situation in West China was radically different from that on the coast, the regime made minimal efforts to adjust its political, economic, and military policies to the primitive resource base there. Instead, for example, it attempted to create virtually overnight a modern industrial base in Szechwan and Yunnan. It therefore pumped enormous sums of money into the economy to remove factories from the coast, to import expensive equipment and raw materials from the West, and to construct new highways and railroads. Because it lacked the tax base to support these expenditures, the inflationary spiral began. An alternative would have been for the government to encourage a simpler and cheaper form of industrial production, drawing upon the rich tradition of handicrafts indigenous to West China. The Chinese Industrial Cooperative Association, launched in July 1938, was in fact a privately inspired attempt to provide such an alternative source of industrial goods. The full potential of the industrial cooperatives was never realized, however, because government leaders suspected that this mass-based movement, so different from their own highly bureaucratized system, was manipulated by Communists.[8]

Because the countryside, and not the cities, was the primary wartime source of grain, money, and men, the Nationalists needed to develop a system that would enable them to derive the maximum resources from the rural areas and yet maintain the good will and cooperation of the producing masses. Rather than adjusting their policies to achieve those ends, however, they continued to employ a top-heavy and expensive bureaucracy that ruled in uneasy conjunction with the corrupt and inefficient rural elites. The Nationalists might also have adopted the tactics of guerrilla warfare against the Japanese. But guerrilla warfare requires intimate cooperation between the army and the civilian population, and such cooperation could have been achieved only by improving the discipline of the troops and by revamping the government's social and economic policies so that the people had incentives to contribute to the success of the army.

The Communists in their base areas demonstrated that the primitive and impoverished interior of the nation could indeed sustain a vital political and military movement. Relying on guerrilla tactics, nurturing mass mobilization, and developing small-scale industrial production, the Communists became stronger as the war progressed. The Nationalists, by contrast, retaining their prewar conceptions of ruling and fighting, weakened economically, politically, and militarily.

The most serious result of the failure to adapt to the changed conditions in the interior, and the most pervasively destructive influence of the war upon the Nationalists, was the inflation. By retreating from the eastern seaboard, the Nationalist government largely lost its main sources of revenue, most notably the customs duties, salt taxes, and manufacturing taxes. Because its political controls in the interior—horizontally over the provinces, and vertically down to the rural elites and the urban moneyed classes—remained weak, it never adequately developed alternative sources of revenue, and consequently had to rely inordinately upon deficit financing. Inflation was the result. Initially, prices rose moderately enough, increasing only about 40 percent during the first year of the war. By the latter half of 1941 and through 1944, however, prices were more than doubling each year. Thereafter the rate of increase again spurted sharply upward, prices rising 251 percent in just the seven months from January to August 1945. The results were devastating and enfeebled the entire body politic—the army, the government, the economy, and society generally. The inflation was a major reason why corruption reached unprecedented levels, why the mass of the population suffered grinding poverty, and why the army became dispirited and ineffective.[9]

The war also hurt the Nationalists because it enabled the Communists to grow and become strong. During the decade prior to the war, the Nationalists had hounded the Communists the length and breadth of the country, inflicting substantial losses upon them and preventing them from securing a large, stable base of operations. Nationalist pressure abated after 1937, however, and guerrilla operations in the nominally Japanese-occupied areas permitted the Communists to spread their revolutionary networks to an extent that had been unimaginable prior to the war. During the war, too, the Communists developed organizational skills and acquired military experience that benefited them in the civil war period.[10]

Thus did the war buffet the Nationalist regime. Yet the regime did not collapse in 1944 or 1945, and survived for four years beyond the end of the war with Japan. What were the sources of its staying power? How could it remain standing as long as it did, despite the pervasive infirmities that have been documented in the preceding chapters? Some of the answers may lie in the low political consciousness of most Chinese, and in the regime's extensive reliance upon political repression to silence those few who did have the temerity to engage in antigovernment actions within the areas controlled by the Nationalists. Both these subjects deserve further study. Systemic features that actually made the regime weak may also have contributed, paradoxically, to its durability. For example, the lack of a social base and institutionalized means of incorporating the population into the political process left the regime not directly accountable for its sins of omission and commission. If it had been a parliamentary democracy, its term in office would have been short indeed; but because it was a regime supported by the army, public opinion had little direct effect on its political longevity. Military force at this time was the primary source of political power, and if the regime were to fall, it would probably be the result of armed opposition. That might have happened when the provincial militarists formed an alliance against Chungking in 1944. Chiang was, however, a master at manipulating his rivals, and as he had done innumerable times in the 1920's and 1930's, he successfully prevented his rivals during the war from forming a firm alliance against him. As we saw in Chapter 1, for instance, he several times mollified Lung Yün and the Yunnanese by granting them financial compensation for provincial concessions. During the

Ichigo campaign, too, he supplied them with weapons in return for their abandoning the planned revolt.

The regime also survived because it generally accommodated, rather than challenged, the status quo. If the Nationalists had attempted to carry out their proclaimed programs of land reform, or if they had tried during the war to take control of the tax-in-kind and conscription systems out of the hands of the local elites, or again if they had ordered the provincial militarists to demobilize their armies, they would surely have faced large-scale revolts. Because the regime tolerated the elites of the old society, however, those elites tolerated the regime. This was not a formula that produced progressive reforms or strong government, but in the short run, at least, it helped keep the Nationalists in power.

The Nationalist government might have remained in power longer than it did, however, had it not been for the Russian intervention in Manchuria following the war with Japan. On the basis of the Yalta Agreement of February 1945, the Soviet Union declared war against Japan on August 8—two days after the first atomic bomb burst over Hiroshima—and quickly occupied the whole of Manchuria. Once in control there, the Russians facilitated the Chinese Communists' entry into the northeastern provinces and turned over to them large stores of surrendered Japanese war matériel. They also delayed Nationalist efforts to reestablish a military and administrative presence there and carried away much of Manchuria's industrial plant. Much has been written about these events—many of which blatantly violated Chinese sovereignty and which the United States opposed—but their effect upon the fate of the Nationalist regime has seldom been brought into sharp focus.[11]

If, for example, the Russians had not entered Manchuria, thereby providing the Chinese Communists with a springboard for the conquest of China proper, the Nationalists could arguably have devoted their attention and resources to postwar reconstruction, rather than being forced to conduct a full-scale civil war. The Chinese Communists would still have posed a threat within China proper, of course, but the scale of the hostilities would presumably have been smaller, and the insurgent forces would not have been strengthened by the supply of Japanese arms and equipment.

The consequences for the Nationalist regime of such a scenario might have been profound. Economically, the rich resources of Manchuria could have been reintegrated into the economy of China proper. Rather than having to send large stores of food and grain to the Nationalist troops in the Northeast, thereby contributing to the impoverishment and anger of farmers in China proper, the Nationalists could have used the large food surpluses of Manchuria to relieve the chronic shortages of North China. The sizable industrial base created by the Japanese could have provided the products of heavy industry to facilitate the industrial recovery of China proper, and of light industry to ease the enormous postwar need for consumer goods. Manchuria's potential to contribute to the nation's economic recovery is suggested by the fact that, for example, during 1944–45 it produced 8.5 times more pig iron than had ever been produced in a single year in China proper, 2.5 times more electric power, and 8.5 times more cement. Manchuria in 1944 also harvested 3,549,000 tons of soybeans; if that amount had been available to Nationalist China in the postwar period, it would have generated annually through exports some U.S. $60 million to $90 million in foreign exchange. And Manchuria's 144 lumber mills would largely have eliminated the need for imports of foreign lumber.[12]

Moreover, because the industrial sector of China proper was plagued after the war by a multitude of problems, including shortages of raw materials and fuel (much of which might have been obtained from Manchuria), it could not produce the consumer goods so desperately needed after eight years of war. To ease this demand and thereby to lessen the inflationary pressures, the National Government felt constrained to encourage imports from abroad, which then flooded into the country. As a direct consequence of this policy, the country's reserves of foreign currency had by February 1947 been virtually depleted. Im-

ports also injured China's native industries, and foreign shipments of cotton, rice, and other agricultural products pushed
down farm prices, hurting the farmers and delaying recovery of
the rural areas.[13]

The most damaging effect of the events in Manchuria, however, was the increased inflation they brought about. During the
period 1945–49, fully 65–70 percent of government spending
was devoted to the military, and much of it was used to fight the
war in Manchuria. To finance the civil war, the government re-
sorted, as it had done during the war against Japan, to printing
paper money. Significantly, the amount of deficit spending during the post-1945 period—65 percent—was approximately equal
to the figure for military expenditures. Without the large military budget, therefore, the National Government could nearly
have covered its total expenditures by means of taxation and
other noninflationary measures, and would then have avoided
the hyperinflation that proved to be so costly to the regime and
to the people.[14]

These are only some suggestions of how the course of events
in China might have been altered if the Nationalists had been
able to reassert sovereign control over Manchuria after the war.
The National Government's passage through the shoals of the
postwar period would still have been fraught with difficulties,
yet it is at least arguable that the difficulties would have been of
lesser magnitude, and that the National Government would
have been able to cope with them, had it not been for the train of
events set in motion by the Russian occupation of Manchuria.

Yet the Russian occupation of Manchuria was at most one of
the immediate causes of the regime's collapse. The basic causes
lay deeper, in the inherent structural infirmities of a military-
authoritarian regime lacking a base in society and in the ener-
vating effects of the war with Japan. As a result of these two factors, the Nationalist movement was by 1945 utterly debilitated, its
weaknesses evidenced in the limited reach of its political sway,
the corruption and ineffectiveness of its administration, the self-
destructive fighting of its several factions, and the pervasive incompetence and demoralization of its army. In view of this thor-

oughgoing disintegration, it appears highly unlikely that the Nationalist regime would have been able to consolidate effective rule over the nation even with full control of the Northeast. The Russian intervention, therefore, was but a gust of wind that helped topple the rotting structure. Without that wind, the building might have stood a little longer, but that it would come down—and sooner rather than later—seems certain, because no government exists without problems, any more than the building in our original metaphor was likely to exist in a vacuum, untouched by the elements.

*Reference Matter*

# Notes

Complete authors' names, titles, and publishing data for sources cited in the Notes are given in the Bibliography. The following abbreviations are used in the Notes:

CPR  *Chinese Press Review.* Unless specified as the Chungking edition, the Shanghai edition is always meant.

FRUS  *Foreign Relations of the United States.*

TKP  *Ta-kung-pao.* Unless specified as the Chungking edition, the Shanghai edition is always meant.

OSS  Office of Strategic Services (U.S.).

*Introduction*

1. Huntington, p. 196.
2. Sheridan, pp. 14–16.

*Chapter One*

1. Wedemeyer, p. 323.
2. Kapp, *Szechwan and the Chinese Republic,* pp. 121–41.
3. OSS doc. XL24905, Oct. 29, 1945; *Hsin-min pao* (Chungking), Oct. 28, 1945, in *CPR,* Oct. 29, 1945; Service, pp. 57–61; and *The Amerasia Papers,* vol. 1, pp. 767–75.
4. Perkins to State, U.S. State Dept. 893.00 P.R. Yunnan/162, Aug. 31, 1942, p. 8.
5. Boorman, ed., vol. 2, pp. 457–59, vol. 3, pp. 223–25; Hall, pp. 56–61. I am indebted to John Hall for his knowledgeable comments on an early version of this essay.
6. Hall, pp. 119–69.
7. Szechwan was the largest province of China proper until 1924, when it was divided into the two provinces of Szechwan and Sikang. Despite Yunnan's size, the total population of the province in 1934 was only 12 million. See Chang Hsiao-mei, p. A29.
8. Political Report for December 1937, U.S. State Dept. 893.00 P.R. Yunnan/111, p. 4. See also Perkins to State, U.S. State Dept. 893.00 P.R. Yunnan/162, Aug. 31, 1942, p. 22; and Hall, pp. 179–80.

9. Political Report for September 1935, U.S. State Dept. 893.00 P.R. Yunnan/84, p. 5; Political Report for August 1935, U.S. State Dept. 893.00 P.R. Yunnan/83, p. 3. On the development of roads and railways, see Chang Hsiao-mei, Chaps. 7–9. Hall, pp. 170–80, provides a more detailed picture of Yunnan's relations with the central government after the Long March and prior to the Sino-Japanese War.

10. Political Report for April 1936, U.S. State Dept. 893.00 P.R. Yunnan/91, p. 7.

11. Perkins to State, U.S. State Dept. 893.00 P.R. Yunnan/162, Aug. 31, 1942, p. 23.

12. Chin Tien-jung, pp. 24–25; Ch'iao Chia-ts'ai, pp. 112–15; Te-kong Tong and Li Tsung-jen, pp. 321–22; Chang Wen-shih, p. 62.

13. Political Report for January 1938, U.S. State Dept. 893.00 P.R. Yunnan/112, p. 5; Meyer to State, U.S. State Dept. 893.00/14218, Jan. 29, 1938, encl. 1, p. 1, and encl. 2, p. 1.

14. Perkins to State, U.S. State Dept. 893.00 P.R. Yunnan/162, Aug. 31, 1942, p. 17. Population figures on Kunming are in Chang Hsiao-mei, p. E12. See also Chen Ta, *Population in Modern China*, p. 51.

15. Perkins to State, U.S. State Dept. 893.00 P.R. Yunnan/162, Aug. 31, 1942, pp. 4–5; Chang Hsiao-mei, Chap. 15; "Shō Kai-seki no Unnan chūōka kōsaku," pp. 35–36.

16. Political Report for December 1937, U.S. State Dept. 893.00 P.R. Yunnan/111, p. 6.

17. Meyer to Johnson, U.S. State Dept. 893.00/14218, Jan. 29, 1938, p. 2; Political Report for May 1939, U.S. State Dept. 893.00 P.R. Yunnan/126, p. 4.

18. Perkins to State, U.S. State Dept. 893.00 P.R. Yunnan/162, Aug. 31, 1942, p. 9. In some outlying areas of Yunnan, however, provincial currency was still commonly used in 1944. See *FRUS, 1944*, vol. 6, p. 375.

19. Southard to State, U.S. State Dept. 893.00/14300, Jan. 12, 1939, p. 1. See also Perkins to State, U.S. State Dept. 893.00 P.R. Yunnan/162, Aug. 31, 1942, p. 8.

20. Perkins to State, U.S. State Dept. 893.00 P.R. Yunnan/162, Aug. 31, 1942, pp. 7–8.

21. *Ibid.*, pp. 11–14. A similar but even sharper controversy was waged over Yunnan's totally illegal (in the eyes of the central government) Special Consumption Tax, which was simply a euphemism for the *likin* tax that had been proscribed by Nanking in 1931. This dispute was resolved in an identical way—albeit not until 1942—when the Chungking government agreed to send a subsidy to Yunnan

in an amount approximately equal to the previous revenues from that tax.

22. On the defection of Wang, see Boyle, *China and Japan at War,* and Bunker, *The Peace Conspiracy.*

23. Liu Chien-ch'ün, p. 127.

24. Political Report for February 1939, U.S. State Dept. 893.00 P.R. Yunnan/123, pp. 6–7; Boyle, p. 225.

25. Political Report for February 1939, U.S. State Dept. 893.00 P.R. Yunnan/123, p. 7; Political Report for May 1939, U.S. State Dept. 893.00 P.R. Yunnan/126, p. 4.

26. Chang Hsiao-mei, pp. U32–33, U48–49; Perkins to State, U.S. State Dept. 893.51/7060, Feb. 12, 1940. p. 3. See note 21 above.

27. Perkins to State, U.S. State Dept. 893.00 P.R. Yunnan/162, Aug. 31, 1942, p. 10.

28. *Ibid.*

29. Peck to State, U.S. State Dept. 893.00/14381, June 3, 1939, pp. 1–2.

30. Meyer to Johnson, U.S. State Dept. 893.00/14457, Oct. 19, 1939, p. 5; Perkins to State, U.S. State Dept. 893.00 P.R. Yunnan/162, Aug. 31, 1942, p. 10.

31. Perkins to State, U.S. State Dept. 893.00 P.R. Yunnan/162, Aug. 31, 1942, pp. 1–5, 9–11.

32. Political Report for October 1939, U.S. State Dept. 893.00 P.R. Yunnan/131, pp. 4–5.

33. Meyer to Johnson, U.S. State Dept. 893.00/14457, Oct. 19, 1939, p. 4.

34. "Shō Kai-seki no Unnan chūōka kōsaku," pp. 36–37.

35. *Ibid.,* pp. 32–41; "Unnanshō no seiji keizaiteki chi'i," pp. 27–30; Perkins to State, U.S. State Dept. 893.00 P.R. Yunnan/162, Aug. 31, 1942, p. 20; *Tōa nisshi,* Jan.–June 1940, vol. 1, pt. 5, p. 84.

36. Political Report for August 1940, U.S. State Dept. 893.00 P.R. Yunnan/141, p. 4; Perkins to State, U.S. State Dept. 893.00 P.R. Yunnan/162, Aug. 31, 1942, pp. 20–21.

37. Perkins to State, U.S. State Dept. 893.00 P.R. Yunnan/162, Aug. 31, 1942, pp. 20–21; Ludden to Gauss, Mar. 5, 1943, p. 2, in OSS doc. 34044; Jung Chai, pp. 121–22.

38. Memorandum by Sprouse, U.S. State Dept. 893.00/2-2745, Feb. 27, 1945, p. 2.

39. Shyu, "The People's Political Council and China's Wartime Problems," p. 149; Chang Wen-shih, pp. 16, 42.

40. Political Report for September 1939, U.S. State Dept. 893.00 P.R. Yunnan/130, p. 4.

41. *Tōa nisshi*, Jan.–June 1940, vol. 1, pt. 5, p. 85.

42. Langdon to State, U.S. State Dept. 893.00/7-1444, July 14, 1944, p. 2; OSS doc. L50379, Dec. 12, 1944, p. 1; OSS doc. 355.2/AX1231S/c. 2, p. 3; memorandum by Graham Peck, U.S. State Dept. 893.00/15319, encl. 1, pp. 4–5.

43. Memorandum by Sprouse, U.S. State Dept. 893.00/2-2745, Feb. 27, 1945, pp. 1–3.

44. Li Tsung-huang, *Li Tsung-huang hui-i-lu*, vol. 4, p. 215.

45. Gauss to State, U.S. State Dept. 893.00/15214, Dec. 10, 1943, sect. 2, p. 2. See also *FRUS, 1944*, vol. 6, p. 493.

46. The ascendancy of the CC Clique became particularly apparent in May 1944 when its members completely dominated the proceedings of the 12th Plenum of the Central Executive Committee of the Kuomintang. See Gauss to State, U.S. State Dept. 893.00/6-844, June 8, 1944.

47. Drumright to Vincent, U.S. State Dept. 893.105/93, Apr. 26, 1943, p. 2.

48. Hattori Takushirō, pp. 617–29; Romanus and Sunderland, *Stilwell's Command Problems*, pp. 316–20; Romanus and Sunderland, *Time Runs Out*, pp. 169–76.

49. *FRUS, 1944*, p. 492. See also Langdon to State, U.S. State Dept. 893.00/7-1444, July 14, 1944, pp. 3, 5.

50. Ringwalt to Gauss, U.S. State Dept. 893.00/7-644, July 6, 1944, encl., p. 2.

51. For biographical information on Li Chi-shen, see Boorman, ed., vol. 2, pp. 292–95; *Gendai Chūgoku jimmei jiten*, p. 1029; and Ringwalt to Gauss, U.S. State Dept. 893.00/8-2844, Aug. 28, 1944, pp. 2–4.

52. Lindsey to Hearn, July 21, 1944, Rad #CCA 71, Stilwell Papers, Box 4, File #2703. Lung Yün in early 1944 was also negotiating with the Japanese, who hoped to persuade him to revolt against Chungking. Lung maintained contact with the Japanese through his messengers and by wireless radio. Nothing came of these contacts. "Statements of Japanese Officers, World War II," Statement No. 516, p. 2.

53. Richard M. Service to Atcheson, U.S. State Dept. 893.00/4-545, Mar. 23, 1945, encl.; Ringwalt to Gauss, U.S. State Dept. 893.00/7-644, July 6, 1944; Ringwalt to Gauss, U.S. State Dept. 893.00/8-2844, Aug. 28, 1944, p. 8.

54. Not all members of the Federation supported this movement. See Ringwalt to Gauss, U.S. State Dept. 893.00/8-2844, Aug. 28, 1944, p. 5; Langdon to State, U.S. State Dept. 893.00/7-1444, July 14, 1944, p. 5. Leaders of the Federation who were reportedly privy to the movement,

and presumably involved, were Carsun Chang, Tso Shun-sheng, Shen Chün-ju, and Chang Po-chün. See Gauss to State, Oct. 30, 1944, encl. 1, pp. 1–2, OSS doc. 102284.

55. Gauss to State, Oct. 30, 1944, encl. 1, p. 1, OSS doc. 102284. See also Sprouse to State, U.S. State Dept. 893.00/7-1444, July 14, 1944, p. 3; Sprouse to Gauss, U.S. State Dept. 893.00/8-2344, Aug. 14, 1944, encl. 1, p. 1.

56. Ringwalt to Gauss, U.S. State Dept. 893.00/15420, May 8, 1944, p. 3.

57. Sprouse to Gauss, U.S. State Dept. 893.00/8-2344, Aug. 14, 1944, encl. 1, p. 3.

58. *Ibid.*; Sprouse to State, U.S. State Dept. 893.00/7-1444, July 14, 1944, p. 4; Richard M. Service to Hurley, U.S. State Dept. 893.00/1-345, Jan. 23, 1945, p. 2.

59. Ringwalt to Gauss, U.S. State Dept. 893.00/15420, May 8, 1944, p. 2; Langdon to State, U.S. State Dept. 893.00/7-1444, July 14, 1944, p. 4; Sprouse to Gauss, U.S. State Dept. 893.00/8-2344, Aug. 14, 1944, encl. 1, p. 2.

60. Ringwalt to Gauss, U.S. State Dept. 893.00/8-2844, Aug. 28, 1944, p. 8.

61. Memorandum by Sprouse, U.S. State Dept. 893.00/2-2745, Feb. 27, 1945, p. 1; OSS doc. 108069, Nov. 25, 1944.

62. Memorandum by Sprouse, U.S. State Dept. 893.00/2-2745, Feb. 27, 1945, pp. 1–2.

63. *Ibid.*; *FRUS, 1944*, vol. 6, pp. 175–76.

64. Richard M. Service to Hurley, U.S. State Dept. 740.0011 P.W./1-2045, Jan. 20, 1945, p. 2.

65. *Ibid.*, pp. 2–3.

66. Liu Chien-ch'ün, pp. 125–26, 128.

67. Memorandum by Sprouse, U.S. State Dept. 893.00/2-2745, Feb. 27, 1945.

68. Li Tsung-huang, *Hui-i-lu*, vol. 4, p. 210.

69. The complicity of the United States in the eventual coup against Lung is mentioned in both Chinese and Western sources, but I have found no conclusive evidence of it. Frank Dorn speaks of "American planning and support . . . to overthrow the scoundrel warlord governor of the province, Lung Yun" (p. 163). See also Jung Chai, pp. 122–23.

70. Jung Chai, pp. 93–95.

71. Li Tsung-huang, *Hui-i-lu*, vol. 4, pp. 204–8; Sprouse to State,

U.S. State Dept. 893.00/10-2945, Oct. 29, 1945; Jung Chai, pp. 95, 105–6. Li Tsung-huang was actually awarded the post of acting chairman; Lu Han subsequently took over the post of provincial chairman.

72. Sprouse to State, U.S. State Dept. 893.00/10-2045, Oct. 20, 1945, p. 8.

73. Boorman, ed., vol. 2, p. 446. On the militia, see Li Tsung-huang, *Hui-i-lu*, vol. 4, p. 211; and Jung Chai, p. 108.

74. Li Tsung-huang, *Hui-i-lu*, vol. 4, p. 210; Sprouse to State, U.S. State Dept. 893.00/10-2045, Oct. 20, 1945, p. 3. On this entire incident, see also Ssu-t'u Ni-ying, pp. 4–6.

75. Sprouse to State, U.S. State Dept. 893.00/10-2045, Oct. 20, 1945; Office of War Information, Box 378, C: China 0.1-C (Oct. 11, 1945).

76. Chin Tien-jung, part 9, p. 8.

77. Li Tsung-huang, *Hui-i-lu*, vol. 4, p. 209.

78. Jung Chai, pp. 93–95, 115–16. See also Li Tsung-huang, *Hui-i-lu*, vol. 4, pp. 207–8.

79. Office of War Information, Box 378, C: China 0.1-C (Oct. 11, 1945), pp. 1–11. This report (p. 2) estimated that total casualties in the coup were about 600. See also Payne, pp. 183–92. An official Nationalist source, however, stated that casualties were less than rumors indicated, and that the total of dead *and wounded* in the three days of fighting was only 236. See Li Tsung-huang, *Chu Tien*, pp. 4–7.

80. Jung Chai, p. 109; Li Tsung-huang, *Hui-i-lu*, vol. 4, pp. 211, 217.

81. Jung Chai, p. 108; Payne, p. 188.

82. Li Tsung-huang, *Hui-i-lu*, vol. 4, pp. 216–17; Sprouse to State, U.S. State Dept. 893.00/10-2045, Oct. 20, 1945, p. 4.

83. *Shih-chieh jih-pao* (Chungking), in *CPR* (Chungking), Oct. 5, 1945, p. 1.

84. Chin Tien-jung, part 9, p. 9.

85. Sprouse to State, U.S. State Dept. 893.00/11-1745, Nov. 17, 1945, pp. 1–5; Sprouse to State, U.S. State Dept. 893.00/12-2045, Dec. 20, 1945, pp. 1–18.

86. There exist numerous descriptions of the December First Incident in both Chinese and English. See, for example, *I-erh-i ts'an-an t'e-chi*; and Pepper, pp. 44–52. On the assassinations of Li and Wen, see Kai-yu Hsü, *Wen I-to*, pp. 169–75; and Pepper, pp. 143–45.

87. Chang Wen-shih, p. 25.

88. *Ibid.*, p. 58.

89. *Ibid.*, pp. 22–25, 56–63.

90. *Ibid.*, pp. 64–67; Boorman, ed., vol. 2, pp. 458–59; Feng Yu-ta, p. 11.

91. Boorman, ed., vol. 2, pp. 446–47.

92. Wu Ch'i-yüan, pp. 17–18; Romanus and Sunderland, *Time Runs Out*, p. 10.

93. Wang Yu-chuan, p. 88.

94. See, for example, Kapp, "The Kuomintang and Rural China," pp. 165–73.

95. Eastman, "Facets of an Ambivalent Relationship," pp. 298–300.

96. On the People's Political Council, see Shyu, "China's 'Wartime Parliament,'" pp. 273–313.

97. Tong Te-kong and Li Tsung-jen, pp. 435–38, 470; Liang Sheng-chün, p. 22; Chang Kan-p'ing, pp. 183–84.

*Chapter 2*

1. Contemporary reports about the condition of the farmers during the early part of the war vary and are often contradictory. Freyn (p. 131) spoke of a "rural depression" until late 1940, after which the peasants' standard of living improved. A U.S. State Department official, by contrast, reporting on a tour through western Szechwan in mid-1941, wrote: "The average farmer never seemed more prosperous. It seems indubitable that the inflated value of the national currency has redounded very much to his benefit. The greatly increased prices he has received for his products have enabled him to liquidate his perennial burden of debt; and his taxes, owing to inflation and the failure of the government tax organs to raise taxes to a level commensurate with the incidence of inflation, are not more than one-tenth of the burden of preconflict days. . . . Truly, one of the most significant developments of the Sino-Japanese conflict appears to be the emancipation of the average Chinese farmer, the lifting of the shackles of debt and the constant burden of penury." (Everett F. Drumright, "Report Concerning Some Observations of a Six-Weeks' Trip to Western Szechwan and Eastern Sikang," Sept. 16, 1941, pp. 15–16, in U.S. State Dept. 893.00/14800, Gauss to State, Sept. 18, 1941.) Compare also Tung Shih-chin, "K'ang-chan i-lai Ssu-ch'uan chih nung-yeh," p. 48; and Ch'en Ta, *Lang-chi shih-nien*, p. 288. Those observers who concluded that the living standard of farmers had declined early in the war apparently did so on the basis of the relatively low prices of farm products rather than direct observations of village conditions.

2. Wu Hsiang-hsiang, *Ti-erh-tz'u Chung-Jih chan-cheng shih*, vol. 2, p. 631; Chang Kia-ngau, p. 34; Chang P'ei-kang, p. 13.

3. Shen Tsung-han, "Food Production and Distribution," pp. 182, 187; Ch'en Yu-san and Ch'en Ssu-te, p. 11; Hsü K'an, "K'ang-chan

shih-ch'i liang-cheng chi-yao," p. 10; Hsü K'an, *Hsü K'o-t'ing hsien-sheng wen-ts'un*, pp. 110–11.

4. Roth, p. 365.

5. Wu Hsiang-hsiang, *Ti-erh-tz'u Chung-Jih chan-cheng shih*, vol. 2, p. 631; Chang Kia-ngau, pp. 344–45; Liang-hsiung, vol. 1, pp. 252–53.

6. Roth, p. 364. See also *TKP* (Chungking), Oct. 31, 1943, p. 2; and Chang Hsi-ch'ao. Peasants might sell some of their miscellaneous crops —potatoes, beans, etc.—but these sales did not significantly ameliorate their straitened circumstances.

7. In P'eng-hsien, Szechwan, for example, farmers customarily sold 90 percent of their marketed produce within two months of harvest. Pan, p. 295.

8. Chen Kuang, p. 10; *Ssu-ch'uan-sheng ching-chi tiao-ch'a pao-kao*, p. 143; Chang Hsi-ch'ang et al., pp. 110–11. Existing data provide no clear indication of how much rents increased. See also *Kuo-min jih-pao* (Citizens' daily), Apr. 25, 1942, in "Nung-yeh tiao-ch'a" (Agricultural surveys), book 2, in the collections of the Chinese Research Institute of Land Economics; and Ch'en Hung-chin, pp. 254–55. Ch'en Po-ta also stresses the increases of farm rents during the war in *Land Rent in Pre-Liberation China*, but his work is not reliable.

9. Chang Hsi-ch'ang, p. 111; Ching Sheng, p. 132; *Ta-hou-fang nung-ts'un ching-chi p'o-huai te ts'an-hsiang*, pp. 1–5; Ch'en Hung-chin, p. 254; *TKP* (Chungking), Oct. 31, 1943, p. 2.

10. *TKP* (Chungking), Oct. 19, 1942, p. 2; *Ta-hou-fang nung-ts'un ching-chi p'o-huai te ts'an-hsiang*, pp. 1, 5.

11. Chang Hsi-ch'ao; Ch'en Han-sheng, p. 3; *TKP* (Chungking), Apr. 10, 1944, p. 3; Ch'en Hung-chin, pp. 254–55. Rents and tenantry were less of a problem in northern provinces such as Shansi and Kansu, yet life for the peasants there, too, had become more difficult. See Chen Kuang, pp. 11–12.

12. Hsü Tao-fu, p. 13; Chang Hsi-ch'ang, p. 112; Chen Kuang, p. 11; Hu Feng, p. 13.

13. Wang Yin-yuen, "Changes in Farm Wages in Szechwan," pp. 63–66; Wang Yin-yüan, "Ssu-ch'uan chan-shih nung-kung wen-t'i," p. 106.

14. *Kuo-min jih-pao*, Apr. 25, 1942 (cited in n. 8 above); Ch'en Hung-chin, p. 254.

15. Ch'en Yu-san and Ch'en Ssu-te, p. 3; Sung T'ung-fu, pp. 167–70.

16. Ch'en Yu-san and Ch'en Ssu-te, p. 3.

17. Chang Kia-ngau, pp. 15–16. These data are for 1939.

18. Ch'en Yu-san and Ch'en Ssu-te, pp. 11–14; Ma Hua, "Ssu-ch'uan t'ien-fu," p. 141.

19. Ch'en Yu-san and Ch'en Ssu-te, pp. 16–30. Several provinces, such as Szechwan, Yunnan, Kwangsi, and Kweichow, had not completed this organizational change by the end of 1943. See also *Hu-pei-sheng-cheng-fu pao-kao, 1942/4–10*, p. 33.

20. Ch'en Yu-san and Ch'en Ssu-te, p. 14; Ma Hua, "Ssu-ch'uan t'ien-fu," p. 144.

21. Ch'en Yu-san and Ch'en Ssu-te, p. 41.

22. *Ibid.*, pp. 34, 36–43. In the cotton districts of Hupeh, however, apparently at the province's own initiative, the tax-in-kind was collected in cotton at least as early as 1942. See *Hu-pei-sheng-cheng-fu pao-kao, 1942/4–10*, p. 30.

23. Ch'en Yu-san and Ch'en Ssu-te, p. 31.

24. *Ts'ai-cheng nien-chien, san-pien*, sec. 5, p. 15; Ch'en Yu-san and Ch'en Ssu-te, table 2 (following p. 33); Hsü K'an, "K'ang-chan shih-ch'i," p. 16; Hsü K'an, *Hsü K'o-t'ing*, p. 128.

25. Chu Tzu-shuang, *Chung-kuo kuo-min-tang liang-shih cheng-ts'e*, pp. 97–98; *Hu-pei-sheng-cheng-fu shih-cheng pao-kao (t'ien-liang pu-fen) 1942/ 11–1943/9*, pp. 11–13; *Hu-pei-sheng-cheng-fu shih-cheng pao-kao, 1943/ 10–1944/9*, p. 101. In Hupeh, the assessment was set in 1942 and 1943 at four shih-sheng (standard pints) for each yüan of assessed land tax. This levy may have been a loan, because in Hunan after the war the central government began repaying this levy with interest. The repayments were not allocated to the farmers, however, but were used by local authorities to create an agricultural reconstruction corporation. See "Hu-nan 'Nung-chien kung-ssu' chiu-fen nei-mu," p. 354.

26. Ma Hua, "Ssu-ch'uan t'ien-fu," pp. 143–44.

27. In a few provinces, such as Szechwan, Hupeh, and Sikang, the poorest taxpayers were exempt from the compulsory purchase or borrowing of grain. In Hupeh, moreover, large tenants (farming 30 or more mou)—as well as the larger landowners (with 20 or more mou)—were subject to this exaction. See Ch'en Yu-san and Ch'en Ssu-te, table 2 (following p. 33); and *Hu-pei-sheng-cheng-fu pao-kao, 1942/4–10*, pp. 79–80.

28. Freyn, p. 110. In Hupeh, 40 percent of the price of rice, but 30 percent of the price of wheat, was to be paid in cash. See *Hu-pei-sheng-cheng-fu pao-kao, 1942/4–10*, p. 80. The promissory notes were to pay 5 percent annual interest, and were to be fully redeemed in five years. See Hsü K'an, "Chung-kuo chan-shih te liang-cheng," p. 7.

29. Chang Kia-ngau, p. 141; *Wartime China as Seen by Westerners*, p. 50;

"Chung-yang cheng-wu chi-kuan san-shih-nien-tu kung-tso ch'eng-chi k'ao-ch'a pao-kao," vol. 1, p. 110a.

30. *China Handbook, 1937–1945*, p. 196.

31. *TKP*, June 18, 1947, p. 7; *TKP*, Oct. 20, 1948, p. 3; *Sin Wen Pao*, June 6, 1946, in *CPR*, June 13, 1946, pp. 10–11.

32. Ch'en Yu-san and Ch'en Ssu-te, p. 28; Li T'i-ch'ien, p. 7.

33. *Hsin-min-pao*, in *CPR* (Chungking), Feb. 5, 1946, p. 7. See also Hsü K'an, *Hsü K'o-t'ing*, p. 130.

34. "Ch'üan-kuo t'ien-liang hui-i chi-yao," p. 82. A similar estimate of the cost of delivering the tax is given in Li T'i-ch'ien, p. 7.

35. Chang Kia-ngau, p. 142; Li T'i-ch'ien, p. 7; Ch'ien Chiang-ch'ao, p. 6.

36. Young, *China's Wartime Finance and Inflation*, p. 36; Ho Yüeh-seng, "Kan-k'uai chiu-cheng she-hui te p'ien-hsiang," p. 9.

37. Ch'en Yu-san and Ch'en Ssu-te, pp. 58–65; *China Handbook, 1937–1945*, p. 202. From available data, it appears that much less than these percentages was actually allocated to the local governments. See Young, *China's Wartime Finance and Inflation*, pp. 16, 29. These allocations, until at least mid-1944, were made in cash rather than in grain, and consequently contributed to the inflationary pressures.

38. Kuan Chi-yü, pp. 222–25; Hsu Dau-lin, Chap. 3, pp. 60–61. In Hupeh, for example, the slaughter tax in 1943 was set at 6 percent of the price of meat and was the provincial government's most important single source of revenue. See *Hu-pei-sheng-cheng-fu shih-cheng pao-kao, 1943/10–1944/9*, p. 43. On the situation in Kweichow, see Wu Ting-ch'ang, pp. 47a, 48a. According to Hsu Dau-lin, Chap. 3, p. 61, the slaughter tax accounted for 44 percent of all provincial government revenues in 1942.

39. Wu Tan-ko, p. 176.

40. The survey actually counted a total of 616 t'an-p'ai, but many of these were simply the same type of t'an-p'ai under different names.

41. Wu Tan-ko, pp. 176, 177.

42. Wu Ting-ch'ang, pp. 6a–b.

43. Army authorities sometimes paid for the requisitioned goods—in which case they were still termed t'an-p'ai—but the prices paid were invariably only a small fraction of the market value. See *Tung-nan jih-pao* (Southeastern daily), June 25, 1944, in "Nung-ts'un ching-chi," book 5, in the collections of the Chinese Research Institute of Land Economics.

44. Hsü K'an, "K'ang-chan shih-ch'i," p. 13; *Shun Pao*, Nov. 23, 1946,

in *CPR*, Feb. 25, 1947, p. 9; *Tung-nan jih-pao*, June 25, 1944 (cited in n. 43 above).

45. Hsü K'an, "K'ang-chan shih-ch'i," p. 13.

46. Hsiao-chuang, p. 15.

47. *Hu-pei-sheng-cheng-fu pao-kao, 1942/4–10*, p. 80.

48. *Hu shang-chiang Tsung-nan nien-p'u*, p. 233.

49. *China Handbook, 1937–1945*, p. 220.

50. P'an Kuang-sheng, p. 11.

51. Chiang Shang-ch'ing, *Cheng-hai mi-wen*, p. 157; State Dept. doc. #893.00/15251, encl. 1, Jan. 18, 1944, p. 1.

52. *Hu-pei-sheng-cheng-fu pao-kao, 1942/4–10*, p. 82.

53. Li P'in-hsien, pp. 195–96.

54. P'an Kuang-sheng, pp. 11–12.

55. *Wartime China as Seen by Westerners*, p. 44.

56. Ch'en Ying-lung, p. 34.

57. Hsü K'an, "K'ang-chan shih-ch'i," p. 18.

58. Interview with Col. Sung Kuang-jen, Taipei, Aug. 27, 1981.

59. Yü Ch'ang-ho, pp. 39–41.

60. *Ibid.*

61. *Hu-pei-sheng-cheng-fu pao-kao, 1942/4–10*, p. 18.

62. I discovered that this continues to be an intensely emotional issue when I presented a preliminary version of this chapter to the Conference on the History of the Republic of China, Taipei, Aug. 26, 1981.

63. The figure of five times is derived as follows: (a) the tax-in-kind was fixed in 1941 at a rate equal to the prewar land tax and related surtaxes; (b) that rate was doubled in 1942; (c) the system of compulsory purchase in 1942 approximately doubled the tax-in-kind exaction of that year; and (d) the hsien-level public grain levy (30 percent of the tax-in-kind exaction) and the grain-for-storage assessment (13 percent of that exaction) together amounted to 86 percent of the prewar tax.

64. Ch'en Yu-san and Ch'en Ssu-te, table 2 (following p. 33).

65. *Ibid.*, p. 31.

66. Ma Hua, "Ssu-ch'uan t'ien-fu," pp. 148–49; *Ts'ai-cheng nien-chien, san-pien*, sec. 5, pp. 72, 78; Chang Kia-ngau, p. 142.

67. *Ts'ai-cheng nien-chien, san-pien*, tables following p. 71. See also *Hu-pei-sheng-cheng-fu shih-cheng pao-kao (t'ien-liang pu-fen), 1942/11–1943/9*, pp. 3–4; Ma Hua, "Ssu-ch'uan t'ien-fu," p. 144; Young, *China's Wartime Finance*, p. 22; *China Handbook, 1937–1945*, p. 197. The land surveys did not, however, assure that the taxes were collected equitably. See *TKP* (Chungking), Aug. 21, 1947, p. 2; *TKP* (Chungking), Feb. 26, 1945, p. 3.

68. Ma Hua, "Ssu-ch'uan t'ien-fu," p. 147; "T'ien-fu kai-cheng shih-wu te ching-yen ho hsin-te" (Experience and achievements of converting the land tax to in-kind collections), by Ch'ang-hua (Chekiang) hsien government (ditto), Nov. 25, 1941, in "Ch'üan-kuo t'ien-fu," in the collections of the Chinese Research Institute of Land Economics.

69. Ch'en Yu-san and Ch'en Ssu-te, table 2 (following p. 33); Ma Hua, "Ssu-ch'uan t'ien-fu," p. 147; Ku Pao, p. 283.

70. Chang Kia-ngau, p. 142; Ch'ien Chiang-ch'ao, p. 6; "T'ien-fu kai-cheng shih-wu te ching-yen ho hsin-te" (cited in n. 68 above); "Ch'üan-kuo t'ien-fu k'ai-shih cheng-shih," p. 2. This last reference contains a list of the defects in the tax-in-kind that needed correction, issued Aug. 3, 1946, by the Ministry of Food.

71. Lou Li-chai, p. 13; *TKP* (Chungking), Oct. 16, 1943, p. 3.

72. Ch'en Cheng-mo, "T'ien-fu cheng-shih," pp. 320–21.

73. Wu Hsiang-hsiang, *Ti-erh-tz'u Chung-Jih chan-cheng shih*, vol. 2, p. 625; Chao Hsiao-i, p. 17.

74. *TKP* (Chungking), Sept. 7, 1944, p. 2.

75. *TKP* (Chungking), Sept. 11, 1944, p. 3.

76. Ch'en Cheng-mo, "T'ien-fu cheng-shih," p. 320. Chang Kia-ngau, p. 142, estimates that corruption resulted in a loss of only 5 percent, but that figure appears entirely too low.

77. This was demonstrated by the problems created after the government nationalized the land tax in 1941 and again in 1945–46 when the land tax was remitted in provinces that had been occupied by the Japanese. See Hsü K'an, *Hsü K'o-t'ing*, pp. 128, 218.

78. Wu Tan-ko, p. 175; *Tung-nan jih-pao*, June 25, 1944 (cited in n. 43 above); *TKP*, Aug. 21, 1947, p. 2; Ch'ien Chiang-ch'ao, p. 6; Ho Yüeh-seng, "Kan-k'uai chiu-cheng she-hui te p'ien-hsiang," p. 9.

79. Wu Tan-ko, pp. 191–92.

80. *Ibid.*, pp. 189–90. The official *Ts'ai-cheng nien-chien, san-pien*, sec. 5, p. 3, stated that large landlords (*ta-hu*) often paid their taxes in a dilatory fashion, whereas small and middle ones paid their taxes on time.

81. Chiang's 1942 remarks are in Chiang Kai-shek, *Chiang tsung-t'ung ssu-hsiang yen-lun chi*, vol. 17, p. 137; his 1947 remarks are in "Ch'üan-kuo t'ien-liang hui-i chi-yao," p. 82.

82. Fei Hsiao-t'ung, *China's Gentry*, p. 27.

83. *Ibid.*, pp. 196–97.

84. Wu Tan-ko, p. 196.

85. Ch'ien Chiang-ch'ao, p. 6.

86. *Ts'ai-cheng nien-chien, san-pien*, sec. 5, p. 34.

87. *TKP* (Chungking), Feb. 3, 1945, p. 2 (editorial).

88. *Tung-nan jih-pao*, June 25, 1944 (cited in n. 43 above); Service, p. 13; Ringwalt to Atcheson, Aug. 24, 1943, State Dept. doc. #893.00/1544, Sept. 18, 1943, encl. 1, p. 4; *Sin Wen Pao*, June 6, 1946, in *CPR*, June 13, 1946, p. 10; *Chung-kuo ching-chi nien-chien, 1947*, sec. 2, pp. 61–62.

89. Scott, pp. 29–34.

90. Ma Hua, "San-shih-san-nien Ssu-ch'uan," p. 116.

91. *China Handbook, 1937–1945*, p. 55.

92. Chou K'ai-ch'ing, pp. 274–75; *TKP* (Chungking), Apr. 26, 1945, p. 2; Hsü K'an, *Hsü K'o-t'ing*, p. 153. A similar system, called "progressive borrowing" (*lei-chin cheng-chieh*), was established in 1944 in several provinces. See *Ts'ai-cheng nien-chien, san-pien*, sec. 5, pp. 2, 11–13.

93. *Hsin-hua jih-pao*, Apr. 24, 1944, in "Nung-ts'un ching-chi," book 5, in the collections of the Chinese Research Institute of Land Economics; Ch'en Po-ta, p. 65.

94. *Chung-yang jih-pao* (Chungking), Aug. 1–2, 1942, and Feb. 27, 1944; *TKP* (Chungking), Oct. 16, 1942, p. 3. See also Wang Yin-yüan, "Hsien-chia yü t'ien-ti hsien-tsu," pp. 165–67; Ch'en Hung-chin, p. 257; and Liu Ch'iu-[?], pp. 153–54.

95. Meng Hsien-chang, p. 228.

96. John Lossing Buck and Chong-chan Yien reported that changes of land ownership in P'eng-hsien—near Chengtu, where land concentration was supposedly increasing rapidly—between 1937 and 1942 affected only 0.4 percent of the land. In one village, they reported, 0.7 percent of the land changed hands, "largely from small holders to large holders, and mostly to landlords." See "Economic Effects of War upon Farmers in Peng-hsien, Szechwan," p. 112. On the other hand, a set of data compiled by the National Government's Ministry of Agriculture and Forestry shows that "self-tilling farmers" in Szechwan and Yunnan increased 8 percentage points from 1937 to 1946. Self-tilling farmers were not necessarily landlords, and consequently these data do not definitively show that land concentration had increased significantly. See Yang Chia-lo, ed., vol. 4, pp. 1240–41.

97. Chang Kia-ngau, p. 60.

98. Buck and Yien, p. 111.

99. Chow, p. 17. See also *Yün-nan jih-pao* (Yunnan daily news), Apr. 13, 1945, in "Nung-ts'un ching-chi," book 5, in the collections of the

Chinese Research Institute of Land Economics. This issue stated that farmers in Yunnan had fallen into an "unimaginable condition" by 1945. Only half of them had enough rice to feed their families for six months after the autumn harvest. Thereafter, they subsisted on beans, potatoes, corn, and pumpkins.

100. Wu Ting-ch'ang, p. 42b. See also Hu Feng, pp. 12–13.

101. *TKP* (Chungking), Feb. 1, 1943, p. 2; Service, pp. 9–19; *Tung-nan jih-pao*, June 25, 1944 (cited in n. 43 above); State Dept. doc. 893.00/15251, encl. 1, Jan. 18, 1944, p. 1; White and Jacoby, pp. 166–78; White, pp. 144–53.

102. Interview with Col. Sung Kuang-jen, Taipei, Aug. 27, 1981.

103. White, p. 152.

104. *Hu shang-chiang Tsung-nan nien-p'u*, pp. 118–21.

105. *Hu-pei-sheng-cheng-fu shih-cheng pao-kao, 1943/10–1944/9*, p. 132.

106. *Ibid.*

107. *Yü-shang-wu jih-pao* (Szechwan commercial daily), Nov. 30, 1945, in "Nung-yeh tiao-ch'a," book 3, in the collections of the Chinese Research Institute of Land Economics; "Uprisings in Kansu Province," State Dept. doc. 893.00/15033, May 19, 1943, p. 1; "Conditions in Kweichow Province: Unrest in Free China," State Dept. doc. 893.00/15095, July 27, 1943, pp. 1–2; conversation with Eugene Wu.

108. Gauss to State, Nov. 30, 1943, in *FRUS, 1943: China*, p. 169.

109. Wu Ting-ch'ang, pp. 194b–95a.

110. John C. Caldwell, "General Report on Fukien Province," p. 2, encl. to State Dept. doc. 893.00/15300.

111. Drumright to Vincent, May 31, 1943, encl. to State Dept. doc. 893.00/15037.

*Chapter 3*

1. Woodbridge, vol. 2, p. 406.

2. "Opening Address of Director-General Tingfu F. Tsiang at the National Conference of CNRRA Regional and Field Directors" (Nanking, Sept. 5, 1946), in the National Resources Commission archives; Li Tsung-ying, p. 19; *Chung-kuo ching-chi nien-chien, 1947*, part 1, p. 107.

3. Data on wartime destruction are notoriously unreliable. (See Wu Ching-ch'ao, p. 19.) The following tabulation provides impressionistic evidence of the wartime losses in Hunan and Kwangsi, two provinces that had lain in the path of the Ichigo Offensive. It is based on "UNRRA Regional Office, Hunan—History," UNRRA Archives, China 122, Box 2781, p. 7; Lei Ch'in, p. 28. The figure for the dead in Kwangsi includes

those reported as missing, and that for houses destroyed in Hunan includes houses damaged.

| Category | Hunan | Kwangsi |
|---|---|---|
| Persons dead | 577,500 | 115,159 |
| Persons wounded | 1,676,000 | 163,446 |
| Refugees | — | 2,443,964 |
| Houses destroyed | 945,000 | 391,963 |
| Water buffalo killed | — | 200,000 |
| Grain destroyed (shih-tan) | — | 14,000,000 |

4. The best description of the famine areas, including farm conditions, is in Wu Ching-ch'ao. See also *TKP*, May 10, 1946, p. 2; *Chiang Kuan-ch'ü chen-ch'ing shih-lu*, p. 2.

5. "UNRRA Regional Office, Hunan—History," UNRRA Archives, China 122, Box 2781, pp. 8, 70; Cottrell, p. 12. Food production in Honan was also reported to be one quarter of the prewar level. See "Honan Regional Office: History as of 31 March 1947," UNRRA Archives, "Honan—China—No. 119," Attachment II, p. 2.

6. "Welfare Survey: Ling-ling area, Hunan Province," UNRRA Archives, "Famine Areas—Surveys," Box 80,008, pp. 2–3. For a similar description, see "Welfare Survey, Hengyang Area, Hunan Province, China," UNRRA Archives, "Famine Areas—Surveys," Box 80,008, p. 6.

7. Wu Ching-ch'ao, pp. 20–31; "Nutrition Survey, Hengyang-Ling-ling Region," UNRRA Archives, "Famine Areas—Surveys," Box 80,008, part II, pp. 1–3; "UNRRA Regional Office, Hunan—History," p. 8; "Welfare Survey: Ling-ling Area, Hunan Province," p. 3.

8. "Nutrition Survey of Kwangsi Province, Chuan Hsien," UNRRA Archives, "Famine Areas—Surveys," Box 80,008, p. 2.

9. "Nutrition Survey of Kwangsi Province: Chuan Hsien," UNRRA Archives, "Famine Areas—Surveys," Box 80,008, p. 1; "Honan Regional Office: History," Attachment III, p. 1; *ibid.*, Health Section, p. 3; *ibid.*, Attachment IV, p. 7; "Welfare Survey: Ling-ling Area," p. 5.

10. "Honan Regional Office: History," Attachment III, p. 1; *ibid.*, Attachment IV, p. 7; *ibid.*, Health Section, p. 3.

11. *Ibid.*, Attachment IV, p. 7; *ibid.*, Attachment III, p. 2.

12. *Ts'ai-cheng nien-chien*, sec. 5, pp. 57–58; Lou Li-chai, p. 13.

13. Hsü K'an, *Hsü K'o-t'ing*, pp. 217–18.

14. *Chiang-su-sheng-cheng-fu 34/35 nien cheng-ch'ing shu-yao*, Ts'ai-cheng (Section on financial administration).

15. *Ibid.*, p. 8.

16. *Ibid.*, pp. 8, 10. In Shantung, borrowing also burdened the people. See *China Weekly Review*, 105, no. 13 (May 24, 1947), p. 350.

17. *Chiang-su-sheng-cheng-fu 34/35 nien*, Ts'ai-cheng, pp. 8, 16. To eliminate the need of local governments to levy t'an-p'ai, the central government in 1946 stipulated that a portion of the land tax revenues should be allotted to the local governments. Thus, 50 percent of the land tax would be allocated to the hsien governments and 20 percent to the provincial governments; only 30 percent would be reserved by the central government for itself. See Lou Li-chai, p. 13; Chu, "Liang-shih cheng-chieh yü liang-chia," p. 3.

18. *Wen-hui-pao*, in *CPR*, May 14, 1946, p. 1.

19. Hsü K'an, "K'ang-chan shih-ch'i liang-cheng chi-yao," p. 14.

20. *TKP*, Mar. 30, 1946, p. 3; *Chung-yang jih-pao* (Shanghai), May 13, 1946, p. 2 (editorial).

21. *China Handbook, 1937–1945*, p. 779.

22. *Chiang-su-sheng-cheng-fu 34/35 nien*, section on land tax, p. 7.

23. "Honan Regional Office: History," Attachment III, p. 1 (cited in n. 5 above). UNRRA's definition of desperate, or "critical," is in Woodbridge, p. 406.

24. *TKP*, Mar. 19, 1946, p. 2; *Wen-hui-pao*, in *CPR*, May 14, 1946, p. 1; "Honan Regional Office: History," Attachment 3, p. 9 (cited in n. 5 above).

25. Woodbridge, p. 408.

26. Wu Ching-ch'ao, p. 111; *Chiang kuan-ch'ü chen-ch'ing shih-lu*, pp. 2–3.

27. *TKP* (Chungking), Mar. 27, 1946, p. 2. Even members of the Kuomintang's Central Executive Committee complained bitterly about military grain exactions. Seven committeemen from Honan stated in a resolution to the Second Plenum in March 1946 that "the people cannot bear its bitterness." See *Ti-liu-chieh chung-yang chih-hsing wei-yüan-hui ti-erh-tz'u ch'üan-t'i hui-i t'i-an yüan-wen*, vol. 1, pp. 85, 102–3.

28. *Chung-kuo ching-chi nien-chien, 1947*, section 1, p. 32.

29. For detailed figures on farm production, by provinces, and the amount of shortages, see (for 1946) *Ch'üan-kuo liang-shih kai-k'uang*, pp. 11–15; and (for 1947) Chang Ch'i-ying, "San-shih-liu-nien Chung-kuo ching-chi kai-k'uang," pp. 10–12 (p. 12 gives figures on grain imports).

30. Chang Ch'i-ying, "San-shih-liu-nien Chung-kuo ching-chi kai-k'uang," p. 13.

31. Chang Kia-ngau, p. 231; *China Handbook, 1950*, pp. 442–43; *Chung-kuo ching-chi nien-chien, 1947*, section 1, p. 21.

32. Chang Ch'i-ying, "Mi-ch'ao te fen-hsi," p. 15; Wang Chung-wu, "Hsien-chieh-tuan chih wu-chia wen-t'i," p. 8 (table 8).

33. *Chung-kuo ching-chi nien-chien,* 1947, section 1, p. 21.

34. Yen Lin, p. 19; *TKP,* June 6, 1947, p. 2; *Chung-kuo ching-chi nien-chien,* 1947, section 1, pp. 5, 107.

35. *Chung-kuo ching-chi nien-chien,* 1947, section 1, pp. 21–22; *China Weekly Review,* 102, no. 10 (Aug. 3, 1946), p. 234.

36. Chang Ch'i-ying, "San-shih-wu-nien-tu te Chung-kuo ching-chi," p. 49; Wang Chung-wu, "Wan-chiu tang-ch'ien ching-chi wei-chi chih tui-ts'e," p. 5.

37. Chang Ch'i-ying, "San-shih-liu-nien Chung-kuo ching-chi kai-k'uang," p. 12; *TKP,* July 30, 1947, p. 6; Chang Kia-ngau, pp. 230–34.

38. *TKP,* Apr. 24, 1947, p. 2.

39. "Ch'üan-kuo t'ien-liang hui-i chi-yao," p. 82.

40. *Ibid.,* p. 83.

41. *Chung-yang jih-pao* (Shanghai), Aug. 1, 1947, p. 2 (editorial).

42. "Ch'üan-kuo t'ien-liang hui-i chi-yao," p. 82.

43. *Ibid.* See also Li T'i-ch'ien, p. 7.

44. "Ch'üan-kuo t'ien-liang hui-i chi-yao," p. 82.

45. Chang Ch'ün estimated that the government needed as much as 40.5 to 45 million *tan* of grain. Yet in January 1948, less than half that amount had been procured during 1947 through the combined land taxes. Approximately another 13 million *tan* had been purchased from local governments. This suggests the seriousness of the grain shortages. See "Ch'üan-kuo t'ien-liang hui-i chi-yao," p. 82; *China Weekly Review* (Jan. 10, 1948), p. 177. On the even more serious grain shortages in 1948, see *North China Daily News,* Nov. 3, 1948, p. 1:2; *TKP,* Oct. 13, 1948, p. 2 (editorial); *New York Times,* Nov. 3, 1948, p. 24:5.

46. *TKP,* Oct. 13, 1948, p. 2 (editorial).

47. *TKP,* May 12, 1948, p. 7; *TKP,* May 18, 1948, p. 6; *Shen-pao,* in *CPR,* June 15, 1948, p. 5.

48. *TKP,* May 14, 1946, p. 5; *TKP,* Jan. 31, 1948, p. 7; Hu Fa-p'eng, p. 355.

49. *TKP,* Sept. 13, 1948, p. 2; *TKP,* Sept. 30, 1948, p. 2.

50. In 1948, A. Doak Barnett wrote: "this system [of substitutes] gives some clue to the type of raw material that is often provided for the Chinese Nationalist Army" (*China on the Eve of Communist Takeover,* p. 122).

51. *TKP,* Feb. 18, 1948, p. 7; *TKP,* Aug. 31, 1948, p. 6.

52. *Ching-chi chou-pao,* 5, no. 6 (Aug. 7, 1947), pp. 6, 18; *TKP,* Apr. 16, 1948, p. 3.

53. *TKP,* Sept. 30, 1948, p. 2; *Ching-chi chou-pao,* 5, no. 6 (Aug. 7, 1947), p. 18.

54. *TKP*, Sept. 30, 1948, p. 2.

55. Wang Chung-wu, "Wan-chiu tang-ch'ien ching-chi wei-chi chih tui-ts'e," p. 5. The Ministry of Social Affairs reported that, as of June 1948, 55 million people were homeless as a result of civil war and floods. See *North China Daily News*, Sept. 14, 1948, p. 1:4.

56. *TKP*, May 3, 1946, p. 5; "Ch'üan-kuo t'ien-fu k'ai-shih cheng-shih," p. 2.

57. *TKP*, Sept. 30, 1947, p. 2.

58. One was Hsiao Cheng; see his memoirs, *T'u-ti kai-ko wu-shih-nien.*

59. Chang I-fan, pp. 9–10.

60. *TKP*, Apr. 23, 1948, p. 6; *TKP*, May 6, 1948, p. 2; *TKP*, Aug. 1, 1948, p. 2.

61. *TKP*, Sept. 22, 1948, p. 2. See also *TKP*, Oct. 4, 1948, p. 2 (editorial); *China Handbook, 1950*, pp. 589–90.

62. Wang Fei, p. 7; *Shun Pao*, in *CPR*, Oct. 21, 1948, p. 7.

63. *Ho-p'ing jih-pao*, in *CPR*, Oct. 1, 1948, p. 9.

64. *Sin-wen-pao*, Jan. 1, 1949, in *CPR*, Jan. 4, 1949, p. 9; *TKP*, June 19, 1948, pp. 2, 6; *TKP*, July 26, 1948, p. 6; Hsiao Cheng, pp. 305–6.

65. Hsiao Cheng, pp. 304–6; *TKP*, Sept. 22, 1948, p. 2; *TKP*, Sept. 29, 1948, p. 2.

66. Tung Shih-chin, "T'u-ti fen-p'ei wen-t'i," pp. 3–7. See also Fei Hsiao-t'ung, "P'ing Yen Yang-ch'u 'K'ai-fa min-li chien-she hsiang-ts'un,'" pp. 4–7.

67. *TKP*, Sept. 22, 1948, p. 2; *TKP*, Sept. 29, 1948, p. 2; Hsiao Cheng, pp. 304–5.

68. Shen Tsung-han, *The Sino-American Joint Commission on Rural Reconstruction.*

69. See, for example, Lefebvre's *The Great Fear of 1789* and Gill's *Peasants and Government in the Russian Revolution.* In this section, I distinguish the revolutionary roles of the peasants in the French and Russian revolutions on the one hand, and the Chinese revolution on the other. I originally presented this analysis to the China Colloquium of the University of Illinois' Center for Asian Studies in Nov. 1979. Subsequently, I read Theda Skocpol's *States and Social Revolutions*, published in 1979, in which she makes essentially the same analysis. She went farther than I, however, by explaining the different roles of the peasants in the three revolutions in terms of differing social structures.

70. *Chung-kuo ching-chi nien-chien, 1947*, section 1, pp. 81, 109; *TKP*, Aug. 21, 1947, p. 2; Yen Ling, p. 20.

71. Eckstein, p. 18.

72. Premier Wong Wen-hao in 1948 admitted that the villagers' tax

burdens far exceeded those of the urban residents. See Ta I-chin, "Ch'i-ko-yüeh-lai te Chung-kuo ching-chi ch'ing-shih," p. 11.

73. Chang Kia-ngau, p. 158.

74. *TKP*, Sept. 16, 1947, p. 1.

75. *Chien-sien jih-pao*, in *CPR*, Oct. 22, 1948, p. 3.

76. Chang Chia-mo et al.

77. *Tung-nan jih-pao*, in *CPR*, Sept. 22, 1948, p. 1.

78. On the close links at the local level between landlords and official representatives, see *TKP*, May 25, 1948, p. 2 (editorial); *TKP*, Sept. 30, 1948, p. 2.

*Chapter 4*

1. Chang Ch'i-yün, vol. 3, pp. 1236–37.

2. Ch'en Pu-lei, p. 101; Chang Ch'i-yün, vol. 3, pp. 1236–37.

3. On the People's Political Council, see Shyu, "China's 'Wartime Parliament,'" pp. 273–313; and Shyu, "The People's Political Council and China's Wartime Problems."

4. Chu Tzu-shuang, *Chung-kuo kuo-min-tang li-tz'u ch'üan-kuo tai-piao ta-hui yao-lan*, p. 70.

5. *Ibid.*, p. 71.

6. *Ibid.*, p. 74.

7. Chang Ch'i-yün, vol. 3, pp. 1224–25. This quotation is Chang Ch'i-yün's paraphrase, but it is doubtless close to the original. Compare Chu Tzu-shuang, *Chung-kuo kuo-min-tang . . . ta-hui yao-lan*, pp. 71–72.

8. *Ko-ming wen-hsien*, vol. 62, p. 25.

9. Chang Ch'i-yün, vol. 3, p. 1229. See also Chiang Kai-shek, *Chiang tsung-t'ung*, vol. 14, p. 199.

10. *Ko-ming wen-hsien*, vol. 62, pp. 1–4; *San-min-chu-i ch'ing-nien-t'uan t'uan-shih tzu-liao ti-i-chi ch'u-kao*, pp. 1–77; Chü-wai-jen, part 7, p. 11; Ch'en Shao-hsiao, *Hei-wang-lu*, p. 68.

11. *Ko-ming wen-hsien*, vol. 62, p. 3.

12. Interview with Hsiao Cheng, Taipei, Aug. 14, 1981; *San-min-chu-i ch'ing-nien-t'uan t'uan-shih tzu-liao*, p. 20.

13. *Ko-ming wen-hsien*, vol. 62, pp. 16–17.

14. *Ibid.*, pp. 17, 19.

15. *Tang yü t'uan te kuan-hsi*, p. 15.

16. *Ko-ming wen-hsien*, vol. 62, p. 22 (emphasis added). See also *ibid.*, pp. 33, 39. Only later did the documents of the corps begin referring to corps members as the "new corpuscles" of the party, a phrase that clearly implied the perpetuation of the Kuomintang. See *ibid.*, p. 50.

17. *Ibid.*, p. 5.

18. *Tang yü t'uan te kuan-hsi*, p. 17.

19. *Ibid.*, p. 16.

20. *Ibid.*, p. 18. This indication of the party's dominance over the corps is a dissonant note in Ch'en Ch'eng's speech, and possibly it was added to the original speech by the editor of this source.

21. *Ko-ming wen-hsien*, vol. 62, p. 2; *San-min-chu-i ch'ing-nien-t'uan t'uan-shih tzu-liao*, p. 1; Gillin, p. 843.

22. *Ko-ming wen-hsien*, vol. 62, p. 2. See also *San-min-chu-i ch'ing-nien-t'uan t'uan-shih tzu-liao*, p. 1.

23. *San-min-chu-i ch'ing-nien-t'uan t'uan-shih tzu-liao*, p. 175.

24. *Tang yü t'uan te kuan-hsi*, p. 8. The age limits were changed again to 16–30 *sui* when the corps' bylaws were revised at the First National Congress in 1943. See Chang Ch'i-yün, vol. 4, p. 1734.

25. *Ko-ming wen-hsien*, vol. 62, pp. 23–25, 39–40, 49, 62.

26. *Ibid.*, p. 49; Chiang Kai-shek, *Chiang tsung-t'ung*, vol. 25, p. 161; *Tang yü t'uan te kuan-hsi*, p. 28.

27. *Tang yü t'uan te kuan-hsi*, pp. 3–4.

28. *San-min-chu-i ch'ing-nien-t'uan t'uan-shih tzu-liao*, p. 56.

29. "Kuo-min-tang tang-t'uan ho-ping ch'ien-hou," p. 17; *The Personalities and Political Machinery of Formosa*, p. 9; Chü-wai-jen, part 6, p. 24.

30. Wang Cheng, p. 42.

31. Chü-wai-jen, part 6, p. 24; *The Personalities and Political Machinery of Formosa*, p. 89. K'ang Tse was initially acting head of the Organization Department, but he assumed the formal headship in about 1939.

32. Interviews with Jen Cho-hsüan, Taipei, July 6, 1978, and with Huang Chi-lu, Taipei, June 14, 1978.

33. *San-min-chu-i ch'ing-nien-t'uan t'uan-shih tzu-liao*, pp. 20, 56.

34. *Ko-ming wen-hsien*, vol. 62, pp. 60–110, vol. 63, pp. 1–286; Teng Wen-i, pp. 131–34; *China Handbook, 1937–1945*, p. 65.

35. *Ko-ming wen-hsien*, vol. 63, pp. 35–36.

36. *China Handbook, 1937–1945*, p. 65.

37. Chang Ch'i-yün, vol. 4, p. 1757; Vincent to State, "Meeting of Szechuan Delegates of San Min Chu I Youth Corps," U.S. State Dept. doc. 893.408/1, Mar. 17, 1943, p. 1; Perkins to State, "The Nationalization of Yunnan," U.S. State Dept. doc. 893.00 P.R. Yunnan/162, Aug. 31, 1942, p. 25.

38. *China Handbook, 1937–1945*, p. 65; OSS doc. XL33752, Nov. 5, 1945, p. 1; Wang Cheng, p. 76; Vincent to State, U.S. State Dept. doc. 893.00/15019, encl. by Sprouse, "Conditions in Peiping Area," May 3, 1943, p. 1; *Ko-ming wen-hsien*, vol. 62, pp. 127–28, vol. 63, p. 43; "San-min shugi seinendan no seikaku to ninmu," p. 29.

39. "T'ai-yüeh san-ch'ing-t'uan hsiu-cheng fan-kung kung-tso shou-ts'e," p. 28; *Fang-tieh ch'u-chien hsü-chih*, p. 22; *San-ch'ing-t'uan te ch'an-sheng yü mu-ti ho hsing-chih.*

40. *Fang-tieh ch'u-chien hsü-chih*, p. 22.

41. *Kuo-min-tang te t'e-wu cheng-ts'e*, preface, pp. 1–3; Sprouse, "Conditions in Peiping Area" (cited in n. 38), p. 1.

42. *San-ch'ing-t'uan te ch'an-sheng yü mu-ti ho hsing-chih*, p. 8; *China Handbook, 1937–1945*, p. 65; Wu Hsiang-hsiang, *Ti-erh-tz'u Chung-Jih chan-cheng shih*, vol. 2, p. 694. Analysis of the composition of the corps is based on K'ang Tse, p. 9. A similar analysis of the 1946 membership reveals closely comparable percentages. See Wu Hsiang-hsiang, *Ti-erh-tz'u Chung-Jih chan-cheng shih*, vol. 2, p. 694.

43. *San-min-chu-i ch'ing-nien-t'uan ti-i-tz'u ch'üan-kuo tai-piao ta-hui t'i-an hui-lu*, vol. 5, pp. 2, 95.

44. *Ko-ming wen-hsien*, vol. 62, p. 127; Chang Ch'i-yün, vol. 4, pp. 1760, 1764; Chin Ta-k'ai, p. 16.

45. Yang Li-k'uei, p. 2.

46. *Ko-ming wen-hsien*, vol. 62, p. 129.

47. *Ibid.*, pp. 128–219.

48. Gauss to State, "Dr. Sun Fo's Speech Criticizing the Present Objectives and Methods of the San Min Chu I Youth Corps," U.S. State Dept. doc. 893.00/15366, Apr. 25, 1944, encl. p. 2.

49. *Tang yü t'uan te kuan-hsi*, pp. 41–42; *T'uan-wu huo-tung shou-ts'e*, p. 18.

50. *Tang yü t'uan te kuan-hsi*, p. 5.

51. Chiang Kai-shek, *Chiang tsung-t'ung*, vol. 16, p. 245; Li P'in-hsien, pp. 181–83.

52. *San-min chu-i ch'ing-nien-t'uan ti-i-tz'u ch'üan-kuo tai-piao ta-hui t'i-an hui-lu*, vol. 2, p. 5.

53. Ch'en Tun-cheng, p. 82.

54. *Ibid.*

55. Chiang Shang-ch'ing, *Wang-shih chin-t'an*, p. 97.

56. *Ibid.*, pp. 101–2. See also *Hsin kuan-ch'ang hsien-hsing chi*. These sources are unofficial, and perhaps not accurate in every detail. The general picture they present was corroborated, however, in discussion with Li Yün-han, Taipei, June 16, 1978. See also Wu T'ieh-ch'eng, pp. 226–27.

57. An exception to the mutual criticism of Kuomintang and Youth Corps members is noted in Chapter 5 on the Ko-hsin Movement.

58. Chang Hsiang-p'u, p. 49; "Kuo-min-tang tang-t'uan ho-ping ch'ien-hou," pp. 17–18; Mo Hsüan-yüan, "Tang cheng ko-hsin te t'u-

ching," p. 6; *Lih Pao*, Oct. 7, 1947, in *CPR*, Oct. 13, 1947, pp. 9–10. Wang Cheng, p. 25, wrote: "it was commonly assumed by those who joined it that the new Corps would in time replace the aging Kuomintang."

59. *TKP*, Sept. 5, 1946, p. 2.
60. Chang Hsiang-p'u, p. 49. Huang's statement is not enclosed in quotation marks in the source.
61. *Ibid.* See also *TKP*, Sept. 7, 1946, p. 2.
62. Wu Hsiang-hsiang, *Ti-erh-tz'u Chung-Jih chan-cheng shih*, vol. 2, p. 694; *TKP*, June 5, 1946, p. 2.
63. Liu Chien-ch'ün, pp. 136–37. See also Lin Chen, p. 34.
64. Wu Shan, p. 174; "Kuo-min-tang tang-t'uan ho-ping ch'ien-hou," p. 18.
65. *Tang-t'uan t'ung-i tsu-chih chung-yao wen-hsien*, p. 26; Hsiao Cheng, p. 296.
66. *Tang-t'uan t'ung-i tsu-chih chung-yao wen-hsien*, p. 25.
67. *Ibid.*, pp. 25–27. See also Hsiao Cheng, p. 296.
68. Hsiao Cheng, p. 296; *Chung-yang jih-pao* (Shanghai), July 1, 1947, p. 2. Chiang Kai-shek's speech to the Standing Committee is in *TKP*, Sept. 11, 1947, p. 2.
69. Hsiao Cheng, p. 296.
70. Lin Chen, p. 35; *Chung-yang jih-pao* (Shanghai), Sept. 6, 1947, p. 2.
71. *FRUS, 1947*, vol. 7, p. 282.
72. Ts'ai Chen-yün, pp. 16–17.
73. *Chung-yang jih-pao* (Shanghai), Sept. 9, 1947, p. 2; Sept. 10, 1947, p. 2.
74. *TKP*, Sept. 11, 1947, p. 2.
75. *TKP*, Sept. 10, 1947, p. 2. See also *FRUS, 1947*, vol. 7, pp. 284–85.
76. *TKP*, Sept. 13, 1947, p. 2.
77. *Ibid.*
78. "Tang-t'uan t'ung-i i-hou," p. 3. This article states that the struggles had been resolved, but it in fact reveals the intensity of the continuing conflicts.
79. *China Weekly Review*, Aug. 7, 1948, p. 278.
80. *New Hope Weekly*, Mar. 21, 1949, in *CPR*, Mar. 25, 1949, p. 14.
81. Shieh, p. 210.

Chapter 5
1. *United States Relations with China*, p. 688.
2. Han Ssu, p. 43.

3. Hsiao Cheng, p. 252.

4. *Ibid.*, pp. 252–53.

5. *Ibid.*, p. 253.

6. *Ibid.*, p. 254.

7. *Ibid.*

8. *TKP* (Chungking), Jan. 10, 1945, p. 2. The *Ta-kung-pao* published numerous other editorials during the first three months of 1945 urging governmental reform.

9. Hsiao Cheng, p. 254.

10. *Ibid.*, p. 253.

11. Han Ssu, pp. 12, 15; Chiang Shang-ch'ing, *Wang-shih chin-t'an,* pp. 98–100.

12. Ch'en Yü, p. 8; Huang Chien-ch'ing, p. 7; Juan Hua-kuo, p. 6.

13. Hsiao Cheng, p. 270; Levine, "Comments on Chin-tung Liang," p. 400.

14. Hsiao Cheng, p. 271.

15. *Ibid.*, pp. 271–72.

16. Ch'ien Tuan-sheng, p. 376; Tsou, p. 296; *China Handbook, 1950,* p. 267.

17. *China Handbook, 1950,* pp. 267–69; Lo Lung-chi, "China's Political Situation After the PCC," *Wen Hui Pao,* May 11 and 12, 1946, in *CPR,* May 31, 1946, pp. 12–16, and June 1, 1946, pp. 8–9.

18. Yao Cheng-min, p. 6 (emphasis added). Descriptions of the Chiao-ch'ang-k'ou Incident are in *Chung-kuo lao-kung yün-tung shih,* vol. 4, pp. 1585–87; and *TKP,* Feb. 11, 1946, p. 2.

19. *Tang-cheng ko-hsin yün-tung,* p. 10; Ju Hsin, "Before and After the 2nd Plenary Session of the 6th KMT C.E.C.," *Wen Hui Pao,* Mar. 23, 1946, in *CPR,* Apr. 3, 1946, p. 8; *Chung-yang jih-pao* (Shanghai), Mar. 4, 1946, p. 2, and Mar. 5, 1946, p. 2.

20. "Wo-men te hu-sheng," pp. 1–9.

21. *P'ing erh-chung-ch'üan-hui,* pp. 19–21; Ju Hsin, in *CPR,* Apr. 3, 1946, pp. 8–10; *TKP,* Mar. 7, 1946, p. 3.

22. See *FRUS, 1946,* vol. 9, pp. 154, 158, 161.

23. Fan Hui, p. 5; *Wen Hui Pao,* Mar. 17, 1946, in *CPR,* Mar. 23, 1946, p. 8.

24. *Wen Hui Pao,* Mar. 17, 1946, in *CPR,* Mar. 23, 1946, p. 8.

25. Fan Hui, p. 5.

26. Interview, Taipei. The source of this information, who was one of the eleven Ko-hsin members in that meeting, was adamant that his identity be kept secret.

27. Ju Hsin, in *CPR*, Apr. 3, 1946, p. 10; *China Handbook, 1950*, p. 269.

28. *China Handbook, 1950*, p. 269.

29. *United States Relations with China*, p. 144; Chou En-lai, "P'ing kuo-min-tang erh-chung-ch'üan-hui chüeh-i" (Criticizing the decisions of the Kuomintang's second plenum), in *Hsin ch'ou-an-hui*, pp. 1–5; *P'ing erh-chung-ch'üan-hui*, p. 7; Fan Hui, pp. 4–5. Among the controversial decisions of the plenum, it was decided that a Central Political Council should now be recreated, with the evident intent that it would be superior to the State Council—thus rendering illusory the claim that the government would be a multiparty coalition prior to the promulgation of a constitution. The plenum also rejected the concept of a cabinet system of government; rejected the federalist principle for the provinces; and reaffirmed its old stand regarding the powers of the National Assembly. It also ignored the PCC's principle of military disbandment and called for the creation of a reserve army of over one million men. See *China Handbook, 1950*, pp. 762–63; *Chung-yang jih-pao* (Shanghai), Mar. 19, 1946, p. 2; Fan Hui, p. 4.

30. *United States Relations with China*, p. 144; Tsou, pp. 409–10.

31. Jen Chang, p. 6; "Chung-kuo kuo-min-tang tang-yüan tang-cheng ko-hsin yün-tung ch'u-ch'i kung-tso fang-an," pp. 21–23. See also *Tang-cheng ko-hsin yün-tung*, p. 4.

32. *Ko-hsin yüeh-k'an*, 1 (Aug. 1, 1946), pp. 14–16, 19; 2 (Sept. 1, 1946), pp. 18, 20.

33. *Ko-hsin yüeh-k'an*, 1 (Aug. 1, 1946), p. 15; 2 (Sept. 1, 1946), p. 18. Of the various publications of the movement, the only three I have located are: *Ko-hsin chou-k'an* (Nanking), *Ko-hsin yüeh-k'an* (Changsha), and *Tang-cheng ko-hsin yün-tung* (Yunnan).

34. *Tang-cheng ko-hsin yün-tung*, p. 26.

35. Ch'eng Yüan-ch'en, p. 4.

36. Liang Han-ts'ao, p. 1.

37. Ho Yüeh-seng, "Tang te ping-pai yüan-yin chih fen-hsi," p. 8.

38. Li Ta, p. 5.

39. Kao Shu-k'ang, p. 2; Ch'en Cheng-mo, "Cheng-chih ko-hsin yü hsing-cheng hsiao-lü," p. 10; *Ko-hsin yüeh-k'an*, 5 (Dec. 10, 1946), p. 4.

40. Liang Han-ts'ao, p. 2.

41. See, e.g., Ch'en Chien-fu, p. 6; Yeh Feng-ch'un, pp. 2–4; Ch'eng Yüan-ch'en, pp. 3–5.

42. Ho Yüeh-seng, "Tang te fu-pai yüan-yin chih fen-hsi," pp. 8–9; Ho Yüeh-seng, "Ju-ho t'ui-chin tang te ko-hsin yün-tung," p. 6; Yeh Ch'ing, "Shih-hsing tang-nei min-chu," pp. 1–3; [Ch'in] Shou-chang, "Shih-hsing tang-nei min-chu," p. 3.

43. Liu Pu-t'ung, p. 2; [Ch'in] Shou-chang, "Shih-hsing tang-nei min-chu," p. 3.

44. Yen Cheng-wu, p. 3. See also *Tang-cheng ko-hsin yün-tung*, p. 2.

45. Ch'eng Yüan-ch'en, p. 5.

46. Liu Pu-t'ung, p. 1. See also Jen Chang, p. 3; Mo Hsüan-yüan, "Tang-cheng ko-hsin yün-tung chih yao-i," pp. 9–10.

47. "Wo-men te hu-sheng," p. 2. On bureaucratism, see for example Yeh Ch'ing, "Su-ch'ing kuan-liao chu-i," pp. 1–4; Ch'in Shou-chang, "Kuan-liao cheng-chih te p'o-shih," pp. 17–19.

48. Yeh Ch'ing, "Ko-hsin yün-tung ti-i-ko chi-pen yüan-tse," p. 1.

49. Yang Yu-chiung, p. 7; Mo Hsüan-yüan, "Tang-cheng ko-hsin yün-tung chih yao-i," p. 8.

50. [Ch'in] Shou-chang, "Shih-hsing tang-nei min-chu," p. 3.

51. "Wo-men te hu-sheng," p. 2.

52. Yeh Ch'ing, "Ta-tao kuan-liao tzu-pen," pp. 124–35; "Tang-cheng ko-hsin yün-tung te ching-kuo ho yao-i" (The experience and basic meaning of the party-government renovation movement), in *Tang-cheng ko-hsin yün-tung*, p. 12.

53. Wei Min, p. 3.

54. "Hsin chü-mien ch'ien-hsi te p'ai-hsi cheng-tou chi jen-shih pu-chih," p. 17. The attitude of the Ko-hsin participants toward Soong may have been complex. One former leader of the movement asserted that they did *not* oppose Soong, because he was a "new" bureaucratic cap-italist—meaning that he was concerned for the economic livelihood of the common people. H. H. Kung, by contrast, was an "old" bureau-cratic capitalist and had no such concern. Interview, Taipei.

55. "Tang-cheng ko-hsin yün-tung chan-hsing kang-ling" (The pro-visional program of the party-government renovation movement), in *Tang-cheng ko-hsin yün-tung*, p. 8.

56. Yeh Ch'ing, "Tang-yüan tsung-ch'ing-ch'a yü ko-hsin yün-tung," p. 5.

57. Juan Hua-kuo, p. 6.

58. *Ibid.*

59. *Sin Min Wan Pao*, Feb. 21, 1947, in *CPR*, Mar. 4, 1947, pp. 10–13; *Chung Hwa Shih Pao*, in *CPR*, Mar. 4, 1947, p. 2; *CC hao-men tzu-pen nei-mu*, pp. 41–42.

60. *Hsin-wen t'ien-ti*, May 1, 1947, pp. 13–15; P'u Hsi-hsiu, p. 16.

61. *TKP*, Mar. 24, 1947, p. 2; *Ching-chi chou-pao*, 4, no. 13 (Mar. 1947), pp. 2–3.

62. "Ts'ung li-fa-yüan te p'ai-hsi shuo-tao kuo-min-tang te kai-tsao," p. 11.

63. Interview, Taipei.
64. *TKP*, Nov. 10, 1948, p. 2; Chü-wai-jen, part 6, p. 23. This club still exists in the Legislative Yüan.
65. *Li Pao*, Dec. 27, 1948, in *CPR*, Dec. 28, 1948, p. 13.
66. Yeh Ch'ing, "Ko-hsin yün-tung ti-i-ko chi-pen yüan-tse," pp. 2-3. See also Ch'en Chien-fu, p. 6.
67. *Ibid.*
68. Juan Hua-kuo, p. 6.
69. Ch'en Li-fu, pp. 5-7. Ch'en objected, among other things, to the attacks on H. H. Kung and Wong Wen-hao, with whom he maintained fairly cordial relations. Ch'en's general tendency, an informant remarked, was to be harmonious in personal relations (*t'iao-ho*). Interview, Taipei.
70. P'u Hsi-hsiu, p. 16.
71. Wei Min, p. 3.
72. Interview, Taipei.

*Chapter 6*

1. Chiang Kai-shek recognized this dependence of the regime upon the army, as will be discussed below. The "militarization of politics and administration" (as Hung-mao Tien terms it) that was so evident in the Nanking decade greatly increased during the post-1937 period. See Tien, pp. 39-44; Eastman, *China Under Nationalist Rule*, pp. 12, 98-100.
2. The Chinese Communists as well as the Nationalists participated in the resistance to the Japanese, and the relative contribution of the two has been the subject of controversy. See, for example, Ho Ying-ch'in, p. 26; Li I-yeh, p. 66.
3. Dorn, p. 7.
4. F. F. Liu, p. 112. The strength of the Nationalist's standing army at the beginning of the war was 1,700,000 men. See Ch'en Ch'eng, pp. 2-3.
5. F. F. Liu, pp. 99-101; Carlson, p. 30; Kirby, pp. 385-88.
6. Kalyagin, p. 45. I am extremely grateful to Professor Steven I. Levine for making his translation of this valuable work available to me.
7. Wu Hsiang-hsiang, "Total Strategy Used by China," p. 48. Chiang had actually suggested establishing the national capital in Szechwan in the event of war with Japan as early as about 1932. See Chang Ch'i-yün, vol. 2, pp. 913-14.
8. Wu Hsiang-hsiang, "Total Strategy," pp. 37-72, provides a representative statement of Nationalist strategic thinking throughout the war. See also Chiang Kai-shek's speeches in his *Resistance and Recon-*

*struction.* The reasons why the Nationalist high command decided to stage a firm resistance at Shanghai are discussed in Eastman, *China Under Nationalist Rule*, pp. 86–87, and in Ch'i Hsi-sheng, pp. 43–49.

9. H. K. Tong, p. 72.

10. Chiang Kai-shek, *Resistance and Reconstruction*, p. 108.

11. Kataoka, p. 152.

12. Wu Hsiang-hsiang, *Ti-erh-tz'u Chung-Jih chan-cheng shih*, vol. 2, pp. 587–88.

13. Butow, p. 153; Fujiwara, p. 191; Boyle, p. 300.

14. Chennault, p. 263; Romanus and Sunderland, *Time Runs Out*, p. 168.

15. Young, *China and the Helping Hand*, pp. 125–53; Young, *China's Wartime Finance*, pp. 97–122; Eastman, *China Under Nationalist Rule*, pp. 150–68.

16. Young, *China's Wartime Finance*, p. 16, table 3. The figures in this table should be corrected for inflation. See *ibid.*, p. 351, table 51.

17. In an interview in Taipei, June 23, 1978, Ch'in Hsiao-i, director of the Kuomintang Commission on Party History, strongly emphasized that the Nationalists faced two enemies during most of the war. A document of the Central Bureau of Investigation and Statistics stated explicitly in 1941 that the Kuomintang's policy had shifted since the New Fourth Army Incident in January of that year from "passive precautions" (*hsiao-chi fang-fan*) to "active restraint" (*chi-chi chih chih-ts'ai*). In accordance with the latter policy, Anhwei, Kiangsu, Shantung, Honan, and some cities were classified as "extermination areas" (*ch'ing-chiao ch'ü*). (See "Ch'üan-kuo ko-tan-wei t'e-ch'ing kai-k'uang.") See also Kataoka, pp. 143–82; Johnson, pp. 115–40.

18. "Ping-i chih-tu chih san-p'ing yüan-tse," p. 34.

19. Chiang Kai-shek, *Chiang tsung-t'ung*, vol. 25, pp. 254, 272–80, 291, 330–32.

20. Ch'i Hsi-sheng, p. 63.

21. Ch'i Hsi-sheng, pp. 91–92, contends that the disastrous winter offensive of 1939–40 convinced Chiang Kai-shek once and for all that the Nationalist army was incapable of offensive operations. Talking to his officers following that offensive, however, Chiang repeatedly stated that their current defensive posture was temporary, and that they would resume the offensive later. See Chiang Kai-shek, *Chiang tsung-t'ung*, vol. 15, pp. 319, 323, 325. Chiang's true intentions are impossible to discern—at least on the basis of the information now available.

22. Hsu Long-hsuen and Chang Ming-kai, comps., vol. 2, p. 694;

Gauss to State, "Observations by a Chinese Newspaper Correspondent on Conditions in the Lake District of Western Hupeh after the Hupeh Battle in May 1943," U.S. State Dept. doc. 740.0011 Pacific War/3559, Nov. 5, 1943, p. 1; Epstein, p. 311.

23. *Hu-pei-sheng-cheng-fu pao-kao, 1942/4–10*, p. 111.

24. *Ibid.*, p. 110; *Hu-pei-sheng-cheng-fu shih-cheng pao-kao, 1942/11–1943/9*, pp. 70–71; *Hu-pei-sheng-cheng-fu shih-cheng pao-kao, 1943/10–1944/9*, pp. 131–32.

25. Chiang Kai-shek, *Chiang tsung-t'ung*, vol. 18, pp. 159–69.

26. Romanus and Sunderland, *Stilwell's Command Problems*, p. 308.

27. *Ibid.*

28. Bōei Kenshūjo Senshishitsu, pp. 23–27; Romanus and Sunderland, *Stilwell's Command Problems*, pp. 316–28, 399–422; Romanus and Sunderland, *Time Runs Out*, pp. 142–79; Wedemeyer, pp. 290, 328; White and Jacoby, pp. 177–98.

29. Romanus and Sunderland, *Stilwell's Command Problems*, pp. 319–27; White and Jacoby, p. 178.

30. *T'ang En-po hsien-sheng chi-nien chi*, p. *ping* 101. The following material is drawn from T'ang's lectures in *ibid.*, pp. *ping* 88–102. Except where quotation marks are used, the material paraphrases, rather than translates, T'ang's remarks.

31. Hal to Donovan, "Recent Events and Trends in China," OSS doc. XL2032 (Sept. 4, 1944), pp. 1–2; Rice to Atcheson, "The Conscription, Treatment, Training, and Behaviour of Chinese Central Government Troops in the Shantung-Kiangsu-Honan-Anhwei Border Area," OSS doc. 116311, p. 2; White and Jacoby, p. 178; Chiang Kai-shek, *Chiang tsung-t'ung*, vol. 18, pp. 161–62.

32. *T'ang En-po hsien-sheng chi-nien chi*, pp. *ping* 97–100.

33. Gillespie, pp. 37–53, 102–24, 313–14; F. F. Liu, p. 151.

34. Gillin, pp. 844–47; Wedemeyer, p. 325; Romanus and Sunderland, *Time Runs Out*, p. 167; Romanus and Sunderland, *Stilwell's Command Problems*, pp. 411, 437; Snow, *The Battle for Asia*, pp. 184–85.

35. Ch'i Hsi-sheng, pp. 86–87; Kirby, pp. 388–89.

36. Romanus and Sunderland, *Stilwell's Mission*, p. 35; F. F. Liu, p. 112.

37. Kalyagin, pp. 3, 337; Atcheson to State, "General Conditions in China," U.S. State Dept. doc. 893.00/15144, Sept. 18, 1943, encl. p. 5.

38. Romanus and Sunderland, *Stilwell's Command Problems*, p. 372.

39. Kalyagin, pp. 88, 337; Ch'i Hsi-sheng, pp. 89–93.

40. Ch'i Hsi-sheng, p. 87. Kalyagin, p. 92, also commented that the

fractious character of the Nationalist army was of paramount importance: "Most of all, we had to come to grips with the tactics of the Chinese militarists, which were based on the principle of 'my army,' 'my province.'"

41. F. F. Liu, p. 147.

42. *Ibid.*, p. 149.

43. Romanus and Sunderland, *Time Runs Out*, p. 233. Ellipsis in source. See also Wedemeyer, p. 325.

44. Romanus and Sunderland, *Time Runs Out*, p. 52.

45. *Ibid.*, pp. 72, 154; Kalyagin, p. 234.

46. Kalyagin, p. 352. See also Chiang Kai-shek, *Chiang tsung-t'ung*, vol. 15, pp. 274, 277; Romanus and Sunderland, *Time Runs Out*, p. 267.

47. Romanus and Sunderland, *Stilwell's Command Problems*, pp. 346, 348. See also F. F. Liu, pp. 143–45.

48. F. F. Liu, p. 145.

49. Romanus and Sunderland, *Stilwell's Command Problems*, p. 351; Kalyagin, p. 191.

50. Kalyagin, p. 194.

51. *Ibid.*, p. 318.

52. Liu Chih, p. 147; Romanus and Sunderland, *Stilwell's Mission*, pp. 434–35; Tong and Li Tsung-jen, p. 428.

53. Stilwell, p. 117. See also Romanus and Sunderland, *Stilwell's Mission*, pp. 156–57; Chennault, p. 77. Chiang continued to interfere in military operations in the postwar period. See F. F. Liu, p. 258; Wu Kuo-chen, p. 70; Tong and Li Tsung-jen, pp. 473–77; Lei Chen, p. 16.

54. OSS doc. 104822, Oct. 26, 1944, pp. 1–2; Romanus and Sunderland, *Time Runs Out*, pp. 165, 289.

55. F. F. Liu, p. 179. See also Kalyagin, p. 266.

56. The draft law was promulgated in 1933, but not implemented until 1936. A new draft law was issued in 1942, but not immediately implemented. The system was also revised several times. See *K'ang-chan pa-nien-lai ping-i hsing-cheng kung-tso tsung-pao-kao*; Lin Chen-yung, pp. 81–82; Ch'eng Tse-jun, pp. 5–8; Weng Kuo-kuei, pp. 18–19; Tai Kao-hsiang, pp. 21–24.

57. Ch'en Wei-hua, p. 21.

58. Chiang Kai-shek, *Chiang tsung-t'ung*, vol. 18, p. 165.

59. Cheng Chao-ch'iu, pp. 9–10; Shou-chung, pp. 6–7; *TKP* (Chungking), Oct. 19, 1942, p. 2.

60. Tai Kao-hsiang, p. 24; *Hu-pei-sheng-cheng-fu pao-kao, 1942/4-10*, p. 118.

61. Lin Chen-yung, pp. 236–40; Wang Tsu-hua, "Chien-ch'üan ping-i te chi-ko hsien-chüeh wen-t'i," pp. 28–29.

62. Li I-wei, pp. 20–21. See also Tai Kao-hsiang, p. 24.

63. Li I-wei, p. 21; Hu Ch'i-ju, p. 15.

64. Ch'in Te-ch'un, p. 193; Lin Chen-yung, pp. 240–44; interview with Col. Sung Kuang-jen, Taipei, Aug. 27, 1981.

65. Tai Kao-hsiang, p. 24. Hupeh could fill less than half its quota of conscripts in 1943. *Hu-pei-sheng-cheng-fu shih-cheng pao-kao, 1942/11–1943/9,* pp. 77–78. See also Li I-wei, pp. 20, 23.

66. Romanus and Sunderland, *Time Runs Out,* p. 369.

67. Miles, p. 348.

68. Chou Hsing, p. 24.

69. Lei Chao-yüan, p. 24; Li Tsung-huang, *Chu Tien hui-i-lu,* p. 53; Wang Tsu-hua, "Kai-shan i-cheng-fa te chi-ko ch'ieh-yao wen-t'i," p. 17.

70. "Ju-ho kai-chin chin-hou te ping-i," p. 14.

71. Powell, pp. 204–6.

72. Cheng Chao-ch'iu, pp. 5, 7–8.

73. Ch'en Wei-hua, p. 22; Ch'in Te-ch'un, p. 193; Lin Chen-yung, p. 245.

74. Ch'en Wei-hua, p. 22; Feng Yü-hsiang, p. 111; Service, pp. 33–37; Ringwalt to Atcheson, "The Chinese Soldier," U.S. State Dept. doc. 893.22/50, Aug. 14, 1943, encl. p. 2.

75. Chiang Kai-shek, *Chiang tsung-t'ung,* vol. 18, p. 165.

76. Romanus and Sunderland, *Time Runs Out,* p. 370. See also Powell, pp. 206–7.

77. Chiang Meng-lin, p. 90; Langdon to State, "Conscription Campaign at Kunming: Malpractices Connected with Conscription and Treatment of Soldiers," U.S. State Dept. doc. 893.2222/7-144, July 1, 1944, pp. 2–3; Ch'en Wei-hua, p. 22.

78. Ch'eng Tse-jun, p. 7. Chiang Kai-shek remarked in 1944 that he had for five years been ordering reforms in conscription, but without any improvement. Chiang Kai-shek, *Chiang tsung-t'ung,* vol. 18, p. 165.

79. *Ta-kung wan-pao,* July 10, 1945, in *CPR* (Chungking), July 11, 1945, p. 5; Shih-hsin, p. 3.

80. Chiang Kai-shek, *Chiang tsung-t'ung,* vol. 18, p. 165.

81. Chiang Meng-lin, p. 90.

82. F. F. Liu, p. 137.

83. The precise number of mortalities among the conscripts will never be known. One official source acknowledges that 1,867,283 conscripts were lost during the war. (Information provided me in July 1978 by the director of the Ministry of Defense's Bureau of Military History,

based on *K'ang-chan shih-liao ts'ung-pien ch'u-chi* [Collectanea of historical materials regarding the war of resistance, first collection], p. 295.)
Unfortunately, an analysis of this figure in terms of deaths and desertions is not given. Chiang Meng-lin, who was a strong supporter of the
National Government and a confidant of Chiang Kai-shek, estimated
on the basis of secret documents that at least 14 million recruits died
before they had reached their units. This figure is too large to be credible, and it is probably meant to be 1.4 million. (See Chiang Meng-lin,
p. 91.) That the mortalities among conscripts were of this order of magnitude is also suggested in Hsü Fu-kuan, pp. 6–7.

84. Romanus and Sunderland, *Time Runs Out*, pp. 242–44; *Hu-pei-
sheng-cheng-fu pao-kao, 1942/4–10*, p. 113; Wang Tzu-liang, pp. 77–78;
Ch'en Ta, *Lang-chi shih-nien*, p. 198. Chiang Kai-shek in 1944 complained that it had become an accepted practice for officers to squeeze
rations, on the grounds that this was necessary to sustain their livelihood and to pay other expenses. (Chiang Kai-shek, *Chiang tsung-t'ung*,
vol. 18, p. 164.)

85. Chiang Kai-shek expressed deep concern about troops' relations
with civilians. See Chiang Kai-shek, *Chiang tsung-t'ung*, vol. 14, p. 267;
vol. 17, p. 8; vol. 18, p. 162. Chennault, p. 208, said that the worst of the
Chinese troops degenerated into "predatory mobs."

86. Wang Tzu-liang, pp. 77–78; Romanus and Sunderland, *Time Runs
Out*, pp. 64–65. See also Gauss to State, "The Conditions of Health of
Chinese Troops," U.S. State Dept. doc. 893.22/47, Sept. 14, 1942, encl.,
p. 2; and Gauss to State, "Observations by a Chinese Newspaper Correspondent on Conditions in the Lake District of Western Hupeh after the
Hupeh Battle in May 1943," U.S. State Dept. doc. 740.0011 Pacific War/
3559, Nov. 5, 1943, encl., pp. 4–5.

87. Romanus and Sunderland, *Time Runs Out*, p. 242; White and Jacoby, pp. 136–38; Gauss to State, "The Conditions of Health of Chinese
Troops" (cited in n. 86 above), encl., p. 2.

88. Gauss to State, "The Conditions of Health of Chinese Troops"
(cited in n. 86 above), encl., p. 2; Ringwalt to Atcheson, "The Chinese
Soldier" (cited in n. 74 above), encl., p. 3; Rice to Gauss, "The Health of
Chinese Troops Observed at Lanchow," U.S. State Dept. doc. 893.22/52,
Dec. 4, 1943; White and Jacoby, pp. 135–37.

89. Romanus and Sunderland, *Time Runs Out*, p. 245.

90. Barrett, p. 60.

91. Romanus and Sunderland, *Time Runs Out*, p. 242.

92. Gauss to State, "Observations by a Chinese Newspaper Correspondent" (cited in n. 86 above), encl., p. 5.

93. Gauss to State, "The Conditions of Health of Chinese Troops" (cited in n. 86 above), encl., p. 2.

94. Romanus and Sunderland, *Time Runs Out*, p. 371.

95. Sze, p. 44; Hanson, p. 326. Dr. Robert Lim estimated in 1942 that there were only 1,000 army doctors of "various degrees of competence." See Gauss to State, "The Conditions of Health of Chinese Troops" (cited in n. 86 above), encl., p. 2.

96. Hanson, p. 326; Powell, pp. 56–57.

97. Powell, p. 56.

98. Powell, p. 94. See also Chang Shao-tseng, p. 15; Utley, pp. 125–26.

99. *TKP* (Chungking), May 18, 1945, p. 2 (editorial); Hanson, p. 236; Atcheson to State, "General Conditions in China," U.S. State Dept. doc. 893.00/15144, encl., p. 5.

100. Utley, pp. 122–23; Powell, p. 57; Chang Shao-tseng, p. 15.

101. Chang Shao-tseng, p. 15.

102. Ch'ing Lin, p. 2; Wang Chung-wen, p. 1.

103. Kalyagin, p. 227. See also Chiang Kai-shek, *Chiang tsung-t'ung*, vol. 14, pp. 271–72.

104. Powell, p. 57; Utley, pp. 123–24.

105. Farmer, p. 137.

106. This conclusion is based on the fact that insignificant numbers of soldiers were released from the army during the war, and that, in addition to the nearly 1.7 million in the army in July 1937, 14,053,988 men were conscripted in 1937–45. Yet the Nationalist army in August 1945 numbered (by Chinese count) only about 3.5 million, or (by United States count) 2.7 million. Total casualties (including 1,761,335 wounded, some of whom doubtless returned to duty) were 3,211,419. An additional 500,000 or so defected to the Japanese. I have seen no figures on the number of prisoners taken by the Japanese, but the figure surely did not exceed another 500,000. Simple arithmetic suggests that at least 8 million, and perhaps as many as 9 million, men were unaccounted for. (This figure includes the 1,867,283 recruits that the government acknowledges were unaccounted for. See n. 83 above.) For the sources of these figures, see *China Handbook, 1950*, pp. 182, 185. Figures on the size of the army are in Ch'en Ch'eng, table 9; and Romanus and Sunderland, *Time Runs Out*, p. 382. The above conclusion is drawn from the Nationalists' own data, but it is incompatible with their published figures for wartime desertions (598,107) and deaths owing to illness (422,479). See Ch'en Ch'eng, table 10. This contradiction in the official

data demonstrates the unreliability of Nationalist figures pertaining to the military. In fact, a former Nationalist general in Taiwan responded to my inquiries by asserting that the Chinese army had placed no value on mathematical exactness regarding casualties.

107. Gauss to State, "Observations by a Chinese Newspaper Correspondent" (cited in n. 86 above), p. 3, and encl., p. 5. See also Chiang Kai-shek, *Chiang tsung-t'ung*, vol. 14, p. 272.

108. Ho Ying-ch'in, pp. 29–30.

109. Romanus and Sunderland, *Time Runs Out*, pp. 285–86, 368, 372–73.

## Chapter 7

1. Chassin, p. 177.

2. *United States Relations with China*, p. 238.

3. *United States Relations with China*, pp. 354–57; Anthony Kubek, pp. 394–96.

4. *Chiao-fei chung-yao chan-i chih chui-shu yü chien-t'ao*. Hereafter abbreviated as *Chiao-fei . . . chui-shu*.

5. Kuo-fang-pu, *Chung-yang . . . pao-kao*, p. 29.

6. *Chiao-fei . . . chui-shu*, vol. 6, pp. 104, 123. See also Kuo-fang-pu shih-cheng-chü, *K'an-luan chien-shih*, vol. 4, pp. 407–8, which lists what it regards as the main reasons for the military defeat, but does not mention the lack of weapons.

7. Chassin, p. 208. See also Chang Kan-p'ing, p. 222. The American military attaché in China reported in December 1948 that 75 percent of the equipment sent to the Nationalists by the United States had been captured by the Communists. (*United States Relations with China*, p. 357.) Cf. Kubek, p. 397.

8. Kuo-fang-pu tsung-cheng-chih-pu, *Kuo-chün cheng-chih kung-tso chih-tao yao-tien*, p. 6. General Kuan Lin-cheng also asserted that the Nationalists lost no battle or city as a result of shortages of equipment, and that the plenitude of American aid was revealed in the large quantities of U.S. equipment that were captured and used by the Communist forces. (Chang Kan-p'ing, p. 222.)

9. *Chiao-fei . . . chui-shu*, vol. 4, p. 128.

10. Liu Chih, p. 173.

11. *Chiao-fei . . . chui-shu*, vol. 4, p. 77.

12. *Ibid.*, p. 133.

13. *Ibid.*, p. 78. See also *ibid.*, vol. 6, pp. 71–72.

14. Ch'en Ch'eng especially favored Tu Yü-ming, Wang Yao-wu, Fan

Han-chüeh, and Hu Tsung-nan, of whom only Hu Tsung-nan had considerable combat experience. (Chang Kan-p'ing, p. 202.)

15. Chang Kan-p'ing, p. 200. The *North China Daily News* also remarked that the government persistently gave top field commands to old-fashioned and untested officers, whereas the young generals who had distinguished themselves in the Burma campaign were largely relegated to administrative and training assignments. (*North China Daily News*, Sept. 7, 1948, p. 2:2.)

16. Chang Kan-p'ing, p. 224; Tong and Li Tsung-jen, pp. 471–72. Ch'en Ming-jen subsequently, in May 1949, revolted and defected to the Communists. Sun Chen, p. 8.

17. Chang Kan-p'ing, pp. 209–11.

18. Feng I-lu, pp. 65–67; Clubb, pp. 392–93. Tong and Li Tsung-jen, pp. 476–77, give a different version of Ch'iu's motives in this incident.

19. *Chiao-fei . . . chui-shu*, vol. 6, pp. 94–95. See also *ibid.*, vol. 4, pp. 79, 132; vol. 6, p. 72.

20. Teng Wen-i, vol. 2, p. 230. See also Liu Chih, p. 171.

21. Chu Yüeh-shan, ed., p. 7; Tong and Li Tsung-jen, pp. 444–45; Belden, pp. 325–29. Smaller units than Kao's had defected on October 12 and 25. See Chu Yüeh-shan, ed., p. 7; and "Kuo-min-tang chün-tui shen-ming ta-i kuang-jung chuang-chü."

22. Chassin, p. 208; Liu Chih, p. 172.

23. *Chiao-fei . . . chui-shu*, vol. 4, pp. 124–25. On the relative sizes of the Nationalist and Communist armies during the civil war, estimates of which vary greatly, see Jerome Ch'en, p. 374, appendix E.

24. Tong and Li Tsung-jen, pp. 472, 477; "Ti-hsia tou-cheng lu-hsien kang-ling," p. 3. A good example of antiwar sentiment in the provincial forces is the statement by the commander of the Yunnanese 184th Division after his defection. See Chang Wen-shih, pp. 23–24.

25. *Chiao-fei . . . chui-shu*, vol. 4, pp. 122–23; vol. 6, p. 77.

26. *Hu shang-chiang Tsung-nan nien-p'u*, p. 233.

27. *China Weekly Review*, June 5, 1948, p. 26. The Ministry of National Defense in 1962 remarked upon the debilitating effects of poor morale (Kuo-fang-pu shih-cheng-chü, *K'an-luan chien-shih*, vol. 4, pp. 407–8).

28. "Shan-pao liu-t'uan ch'üan-t'i kuan-ping k'ai tso-t'an-hui" and "Kuo-min-tang chün-kuan-ping-men ch'i-lai!"

29. *Chiao-fei . . . chui-shu*, vol. 4, pp. 122–23.

30. *Ibid.*, p. 122; vol. 6, pp. 71, 95.

31. Teng Wen-i, vol. 2, p. 230. See also *Chiao-fei . . . chui-shu*, vol. 4, p. 122.

32. *Kuan-ch'a*, 5, no. 9 (Oct. 23, 1948), p. 8; *China Weekly Review*, 111, no. 1 (Sept. 4, 1948), p. 11; *China Weekly Review*, 111, no. 5 (Oct. 2, 1948), p. 116.

33. Sha Hsüeh-chün, pp. 48–49; Ling Yün, p. 44; Ch'in Te-ch'un, pp. 198–99.

34. Liu Chih, p. 171.

35. Ling Yün, p. 44; Lo Tun-wei, p. 181. Joseph W. Stilwell inscribed an unforgettable portrait of this man who became a Communist spy (Stilwell, pp. 144–46):

*"September 9/1942* . . . Liu Fei in to educate me: 2½ hours of pure crap. I'd like to push him off a dock. Exhausted with the effort. . . .

"Gems of thought by Liu Fei, No. 2 in the Board of Military Operations, a cadaverous bird who needs a haircut. Takes himself seriously, very seriously. Never out of character, always the brilliant staff adviser, always in deep thought, every idea profound and thoroughly thought out. Knows everything. Nobody else knows anything. . . .

"New and valuable conception of Liu Fei: The Jap occupation of Canton is a *point*. They have control of the sea, so we can't attack them. The Jap occupation of the Yangtze is a *line*. They have ships and planes, so we can't cut it. The Jap occupation of the north is an *area*. It is all spread out, so we can't attack that, either."

36. Lo Tun-wei, p. 181; Sha Hsüeh-chün, p. 48.

37. *Chuan-chi wen-hsüeh*, no. 253 (June 1983), p. 148. I am indebted to Liu Shao-t'ang for bringing this reference to my attention.

38. *Chiao-fei . . . chui-shu*, vol. 6, pp. 93–94.

39. Lo Tun-wei, pp. 191–92; Tong and Li Tsung-jen, pp. 511–14; Yün An, p. 43; Ch'en Shao-hsiao, *Chin-ling ts'an-chao chi*, pp. 147–52.

40. Tsou, p. 495.

41. *Chiao-fei . . . chui-shu*, vol. 4, p. 124.

42. *Ibid.*, p. 125.

43. *Ibid.*, p. 78.

44. *Ibid.*; vol. 6, p. 71.

45. *Ibid.*, vol. 6, pp. 71–72.

46. *Ibid.*, vol. 4, pp. 124–25. The reader may have noted that the relative autonomy of commanders on the battlefield, which the *Recollections* asserted was a virtue in the Communist forces, was described by Kalyagin as a liability in the Nationalist army (see above, p. 145). The explanation for this seeming contradiction, I believe, lies in the motivations of the commanders: Communist commanders retreated in order to fight again elsewhere, more effectively, whereas provincial commanders in

the Nationalist army retreated in order to avoid combat altogether, thereby preserving their military and political power.

47. *Ibid.*, p. 77. See also *ibid.*, p. 124; vol. 6, p. 72.
48. *Ibid.*, vol. 4, p. 123.
49. *Ibid.*, p. 122.
50. *Ibid.*, vol. 6, pp. 126–27.
51. Chi T'ien, p. 13.

## Chapter 8

1. Chao Shih-hsün, p. 46. For a contrasting view, that the causes of the defeat on the mainland lay much deeper than just the gold yüan reform, see Chu Wen-chang, p. 51.
2. Shen Yün-lung, "Wang Yün-lao yü chin-yüan-ch'üan-an chih-i," p. 42.
3. Wu Hsiang-hsiang, "Wang Yün-wu yü chin-yüan-ch'üan te fa-hsing," pp. 44–50; Shen Yün-lung, "Tui chin-yüan-ch'üan-an ying chin-i-pu chui-tsung yen-chiu," pp. 40–42.
4. A detailed description and analysis of the postwar economy is much needed. For economic conditions in 1947–48, see *TKP*, Apr. 13, 1948, p. 2, and Apr. 16, 1948, p. 3; Chi-mei, pp. 12–15; Ta I-chin, "Ch'i-ko-yüeh-lai te Chung-kuo ching-chi ch'ing-shih," pp. 10–12; and Chang Ch'i-ying, "San-shih-liu-nien," pp. 1–21.
5. Cheng, *Foreign Trade*, p. 160; Chou Shun-hsin, p. 301; *FRUS, 1948*, vol. 8, p. 397.
6. Chang Ch'i-ying, "San-shih-liu-nien," p. 7.
7. Cheng, *Foreign Trade*, p. 160. See also Chang Kia-ngau, p. 270.
8. *TKP*, June 17, 1948, p. 6; *TKP*, July 1, 1948, p. 6; *TKP*, July 13, 1948, p. 6; *China Weekly Review*, July 24, 1948, p. 235; *New York Times*, July 11, 1948, p. 28:1.
9. *FRUS, 1948*, vol. 8, p. 377. See also *China Weekly Review*, July 10, 1948, p. 173.
10. *New York Times*, Aug. 14, 1948, p. 5:2; Yao Sung-ling, p. 67; *China Weekly Review*, July 24, 1948, p. 238; *Lih Pao*, July 19, 1948, in *CPR*, July 17–19, 1948, p. 3.
11. *TKP*, Aug. 5, 1948, p. 2 (editorial).
12. *Shun Pao*, in *CPR*, Aug. 4, 1948, p. 1; *Cheng Yien Pao*, Aug. 29, 1948, in *CPR*, Aug. 27–30, 1948, pp. 3–4; *China Weekly Review*, Aug. 7, 1948, p. 285; *FRUS, 1948*, vol. 8, p. 370.
13. *FRUS, 1948*, vol. 8, pp. 368, 373.
14. *Ibid.*, p. 373.

15. *Ibid.*, p. 380.
16. Ta I-chin, "Cheng-i-chung te pi-chih wen-t'i," p. 6; Yen Jen-keng, pp. 9–12; Young, *China and the Helping Hand*, pp. 386–87.
17. *FRUS, 1948*, vol. 8, pp. 373–74.
18. *Ibid.*, pp. 374–75.
19. Hsiao Cheng, p. 304.
20. *FRUS, 1948*, vol. 8, pp. 384, 387.
21. *Ibid.*, p. 390. Cyril Rogers reportedly authored Plan "B." See *ibid.*, p. 386.
22. *Ibid.*, p. 386; Hsiao Cheng, p. 304.
23. Major stipulations in the Financial and Economic Emergency Measures were as follows, according to *Chung-yang jih-pao*, Aug. 20, 1948, p. 2. First, a new currency, called the gold yüan, would replace the old fa-pi at the rate of 3,000,000 fa-pi for one gold yüan. The gold yüan, although not convertible, was to be backed by a 100 percent reserve—40 percent in gold, silver, and foreign currencies, and 60 percent in marketable securities and shares in government enterprises. The deadline for redemption of fa-pi was November 20, 1948. Second, to build public confidence in the gold yüan, the total issue of the new money was limited to GY2 billion. Third, commodity prices in each locality were to be frozen at the levels of August 19. Wages were not to exceed the levels of the first half of August. Fourth, foreign currencies, together with gold and silver coins and bullion, would be nationalized. All citizens were required to turn in their holdings of foreign currencies and precious metals by September 30, in exchange for the new gold yüan at the rate of GY4 for each U.S. dollar; GY200 for each ounce of gold (this was for a standard Chinese ounce, which weighed 31.25 grams); and GY3 for each ounce of silver. The possession and transfer of ornamental gold and silver would still be permissible, although sales of such jewelry must not exceed the official prices and the jewelry itself not weigh more than two ounces. (The deadline for turning in foreign exchange and gold was subsequently changed to October 31, and for turning in silver to November 30. See *FRUS, 1948*, vol. 8, p. 416.) Fifth, Chinese nationals were required to register all wealth and property abroad in excess of U.S. $3,000 by September 30.
24. *TKP*, Aug. 20, 1948, p. 2; *FRUS, 1948*, vol. 8, p. 380; "Tsung-chieh che ch'i-shih-t'ien," p. 360.
25. *New York Times*, Aug. 20, 1948, p. 1:6; Chang Kia-ngau, pp. 80, 154.
26. *TKP*, Aug. 20, 1948, p. 2; *FRUS, 1948*, vol. 8, p. 386.
27. *FRUS, 1948*, vol. 8, pp. 387–88, 390, 396, 398–99; *New York Times*,

266    Notes to Pages 180–82

Aug. 21, 1948, p. 3:8. Nanking, however, never formally requested the loan from Washington. The Chinese had been encouraged to think that a Republican administration would more actively assist the National Government by William C. Bullitt, among other people. Bullitt, former U.S. ambassador to Russia, told Chinese officials during a visit to China that George C. Marshall was anti-Chinese, that Truman would be defeated in the forthcoming presidential elections, and that Republicans would give unstinting aid in the fight against Communism. See *FRUS, 1948*, vol. 8, pp. 237–39.

28. *FRUS, 1948*, vol. 8, p. 390. See also *North China Daily News*, Aug. 25, 1948, p. 1:7–8. Foreign Minister Wang Shih-chieh also informed Secretary of State George C. Marshall that "The signing of the Sino-American bilateral agreement regarding American aid [concluded on July 3, 1946, providing for implementation of the China Aid Act and stressing that China should "undertake a vigorous program of self-help"] was one of the chief factors which pushed through these measures" (*FRUS, 1948*, vol. 8, p. 394). The text of this agreement is in *China Weekly Review*, July 17, 1948, pp. 207–9. Earlier Chinese interest in a stabilization loan had come to nothing, the Chinese being given to understand that the current session of Congress would probably not approve such a request. (*United States Relations with China*, pp. 367–69.)

29. *TKP*, Aug. 22, 1948, p. 2.

30. *TKP*, Sept. 24, 1948, p. 2 (editorial); *TKP*, Oct. 2, 1948, p. 5 (on situation in Kwangtung); *FRUS, 1948*, vol. 8, p. 414. Chang Li-sheng's concept of enforcement, notably different from that of Chiang Ching-kuo, was reported in *TKP*, Sept. 11, 1948, p. 2.

31. Wu Hsiang-hsiang, *Min-kuo pai-jen chuan*, vol. 4, pp. 367–75; Fessler; Boorman, ed., vol. 1, pp. 306–12.

32. Wu Kuo-chen, p. 89.

33. *TKP*, Aug. 27, 1948, p. 4; *North China Daily News*, Aug. 27, 1948, p. 3:7.

34. Chiang made these remarks in a major public address on Sept. 12, entitled "Shang-hai wang ho-ch'u ch'ü?" (Where is Shanghai going?). The text used here is in Ts'ai Chen-yün, pp. 45–62. A translation of the speech, "Whither Shanghai," is in *CPR*, Sept. 16, 1948, pp. i–vii.

35. Chiang Ching-kuo, "Hu-pin jih-chi," p. 95.

36. *Ibid.*, p. 100.

37. Ts'ai Chen-yün, pp. 39–40.

38. *Ibid.*, p. 54.

39. *Ibid.*, p. 45.

40. *Ibid.*, p. 49.

41. "Hu-pin jih-chi," p. 90. Actually the text of the diary used for this translation is in Chiang Ching-kuo, *Tien-ti tsai hsin-t'ou*, p. 81. This latter text is an edited version of the 1955 text, and I have used it for this one quote because it is less allusive than the 1955 text.

42. "Hu-pin jih-chi," p. 96.

43. *Ibid.*, pp. 98, 117, 121; Tung Chia-mu, p. 3.

44. *CPR*, Oct. 1, 1948, pp. 6–7.

45. *Sin Wen Pao*, Oct. 25, 1948, in *CPR*, Oct. 23–25, 1948, p. 10; *Fei Pao*, in *CPR*, Oct. 26, 1948, p. 8. The estimate of 30,000 men is based on a press report that two Ta-tui together contained more than 10,000 men.

46. *TKP*, Aug. 28, 1948, p. 4; *TKP*, Aug. 30, 1948, p. 4; *TKP*, Sept. 1, 1948, p. 4; *I-shih-pao*, in *CPR*, Sept. 25–27, 1948, p. 8.

47. *Chien-Sien Jih-Pao*, in *CPR*, Sept. 10, 1948, p. 5; *TKP*, Sept. 26, p. 4.

48. Ts'ai Chen-yün, pp. 41–42. See also *Chien-Sien Jih-Pao*, in *CPR*, Sept. 23, 1948, pp. 6–7.

49. *TKP*, Sept. 26, 1948, p. 4. See also Ts'ai Chen-yün, pp. 39–44.

50. *North China Daily News*, Aug. 22, 1948, p. 1; Aug. 23, 1948, p. 1.

51. *FRUS, 1948*, vol. 8, pp. 401, 412; *TKP*, Sept. 17, 1948, p. 2; *Shang Pao*, Sept. 27, 1948, in *CPR*, Sept. 25–27, 1948, p. 10; "T'ou-chi-chia te hsin lo-yüan," p. 12.

52. Carey, p. 280; *TKP*, Aug. 28, 1948, p. 4.

53. *TKP*, Sept. 18, 1948, p. 4.

54. Aw Haw, however, fled to Hong Kong just in time to evade arrest. See *TKP*, Sept. 27, 1948, p. 4; Sept. 28, p. 4; Sept. 29, p. 4. Chiang Ching-kuo was deeply embarrassed by Aw's escape. See "Hu-pin jih-chi," p. 111.

55. This percentage is found in a speech by Chiang Ching-kuo. See *TKP*, Oct. 7, 1948, p. 2. Figures published by the *Ta-kung-pao*, however, suggest that the percentage for the period Aug. 23–Sept. 30 was actually over 71 percent. See *TKP*, Oct. 2, 1948, p. 5.

56. *FRUS, 1948*, vol. 8, pp. 392–93, 404.

57. *Tung-Nan Jih-Pao*, in *CPR*, Oct. 6, 1948, p. 3.

58. Wang Yün-wu was the source of this information. See *FRUS, 1948*, vol. 8, p. 412. The U.S. ambassador, John Leighton Stuart, wrote that the really wealthy conspicuously avoided complying with the regulations (*Fifty Years in China*, p. 194).

59. Pepper, p. 123, states—without citing a source—that over 3,000 speculators and profiteers were arrested. I have discovered no official

figures on the number of arrests, but a perusal of the *Ta-kung-pao*, which may not have reported all arrests, leads to an estimate of only about 200 persons arrested. Two of the largest arrests were reported in *TKP*, Aug. 26, 1948, p. 4 (20 merchants), and *TKP*, Sept. 24, 1948, p. 4 (over 40 stall vendors). See also *TKP*, Aug. 28, p. 4; *TKP*, Aug. 29, p. 4. On the other hand, *FRUS, 1948*, vol. 8, pp. 394–95 reported over 100 arrests on just Aug. 23–24, but I have seen no press reports that corroborate this figure. The *New York Times*, Sept. 13, p. 2:3, reported that "more than a hundred bankers and business men [have been] arrested." Two military officers were also executed in Shanghai during the reform for extortion. The punishments were ordered by Nanking, not by Chiang Ching-kuo's offices. See *TKP*, Sept. 6, p. 4; *TKP*, Sept. 22, p. 4.

60. *TKP*, Aug. 26, 1948, p. 4; *TKP*, Aug. 29, 1948, p. 4.

61. "Hu-pin jih-chi," p. 96.

62. *TKP*, Sept. 4, 1948, p. 4; Ts'ai Chen-yün, pp. 28–30.

63. *TKP*, Sept. 4, 1948, p. 4. Wang was executed on Sept. 24. See *TKP*, Sept. 25, p. 4.

64. "Hu-pin jih-chi," p. 97. One alleged "Big Tiger" escaped Chiang Ching-kuo's net. That was K'ung Ling-k'an (David Kung), son of H. H. Kung and nephew of President and Mme. Chiang. K'ung was general manager of the Yangtze Development Corporation, a search of whose premises on Sept. 29 uncovered a huge store of goods suspected of being hoarded. K'ung claimed that the goods had been legally registered with the government, and therefore had not been hoarded. Not until late December did the Control Yüan return a bill of indictment against K'ung. By that time, however, young K'ung had flown to the United States. Chiang Ching-kuo in his journal stated his conviction that K'ung had a strong legal claim to innocence, and therefore he, Ching-kuo, could take no action against him. The public, however, generally believed that K'ung was being protected by his political connections, and the incident became a cause célèbre that damaged the prestige of Ching-kuo as well as the National Government. See *TKP*, Oct. 3, p. 4; Dec. 22, p. 1. "Hu-pin jih-chi," pp. 116, 119–20, 123. *CPR*, Nov. 5, pp. 9–10; Nov. 9, pp. 10–12. It has been suggested that the gold yüan reform ultimately failed because of the political opposition of the "Big Tigers" to Chiang Ching-kuo's vigorous enforcement of the regulations. For this view see Panikkar, pp. 32–33. I have seen no evidence to support this contention.

65. *TKP*, Sept. 7, 1948, p. 4; *North China Daily News*, Sept. 10, p. 2:5, and Sept. 11, p. 5:1; *China Weekly Review*, Sept. 18, p. 66.

66. Panikkar, p. 32. Nor, apparently, was this an exaggeration. See *Shih-Shih Hsin-Pao,* in *CPR,* Sept. 22, 1948, p. 2: "During the past month everybody has been living under great nervous strain, fearing that what he or she did might be contrary to the law. The merchants have not dared to do business, so that a state of depression has prevailed in the markets and economic activities have partly come to a standstill." See also *China Weekly Review,* Sept. 18, 1948, p. 5.

67. *TKP,* Oct. 4, 1948, p. 5.

68. "Hu-pin jih-chi," p. 107.

69. The regulations designed to proscribe hoarding and speculation are in *TKP,* Sept. 11, 1948, p. 2. Information on the proscription of exports is in *TKP,* Sept. 10, p. 5, and Sept. 30, p. 4. The proscription was eased later. See *TKP,* Oct. 9, p. 4. On the procurement agency, see *TKP,* Sept. 15, p. 5, and Sept. 16, p. 5.

70. *TKP,* Oct. 1, 1948, p. 2. The jurisdictions of the other two Economic Supervisors' Offices were likewise enlarged, and a fourth such office was created for Central China, with headquarters in Hankow.

71. See *TKP,* Oct. 3, 1948, p. 4; Oct. 4, p. 4; and Oct. 7, p. 2 (editorial). See also *North China Daily News,* Oct. 4, p. 3:7. The tax increases ranged from 76 percent on cigarettes to over eleven times on rolled tobacco.

72. *TKP,* Oct. 4, 1948, p. 4; Oct. 7, p. 2 (editorial); and the following, all in *North China Daily News:* Oct. 29, 1948, p. 3:4; Oct. 30, p. 1:4; Oct. 31, p. 3:4.

73. *New York Times,* Oct. 23, 1948, p. 5:3; *North China Daily News,* Oct. 22, p. 3:2. See also the following issues of *TKP:* Oct. 9, p. 4; Oct. 13, p. 4; Oct. 28, p. 2 (editorial).

74. *North China Daily News,* Oct. 16, p. 3:4; *Tung-Nan Jih-Pao,* in *CPR,* Oct. 28, 1948, p. 10; Shih Fu-liang, p. 2; *I-shih-pao,* in *CPR,* Oct. 5, 1948, p. 5; *TKP,* Oct. 6, 1948, p. 4.

75. *TKP,* Oct. 16, 1948, p. 4; *North China Daily News,* Oct. 16, p. 3:1.

76. *TKP,* Sept. 4, 1948, p. 4.

77. *TKP,* Oct. 7, 1948, p. 4; "Hu-pin jih-chi," p. 114.

78. *TKP,* Oct. 14, 1948, p. 4; "Hu-pin jih-chi," pp. 124–25.

79. *TKP,* Oct. 13, p. 4; and *North China Daily News:* Oct. 18, p. 3:5 and Oct. 31, p. 3:1. According to a U.S. State Department official, the plans for a system of barter "were never . . . fully developed even on paper." See *FRUS, 1948,* vol. 8, p. 427.

80. *TKP,* Oct. 14, 1948, p. 4.

81. Press statements at the time indicated a very serious crisis of industry. The *North China Daily News* (Nov. 1, 1948, p. 1:3) reported that

"Shanghai business [is in] a perilous state of near-collapse"; and *China Weekly Review* (Oct. 30, p. 235) announced that "industrial production almost came to a standstill." The subsequent assessment of the semi-official *China Handbook, 1950* (pp. 471–72) was similar: ". . . the demand for finished goods and raw materials far exceeded the supply. It soon turned out that both the wholesale and retail commodity prices were even below the actual cost of production. Manufacturers stopped producing goods. It became impossible for shops and stores to replenish their stock. . . . Most businesses were at a standstill." If the above assessments are correct, it is curious that, in October, industrial use of electricity (which is usually a good indicator of industrial production) in Shanghai was only 18 percent below the July 1948 level. See *TKP*, Dec. 18, 1948, p. 3.

82. Chiang Ching-kuo, "Hu-pin jih-chi," p. 125; *Chien-Sien Jih-Pao*, in *CPR*, Oct. 29, 1948, pp. 5 and 12.

83. *TKP*, Nov. 2, 1948, p. 2; *Shang Pao*, Nov. 1, 1948, in *CPR*, Oct. 30–Nov. 1, 1948, p. 9.

84. *TKP*, Nov. 2, 1948, p. 4; Chiang Ching-kuo, "Hu-pin jih-chi," p. 128.

85. *TKP*, Nov. 5, 1948, p. 4; *TKP*, Nov. 12, p. 2.

86. *Ho-Ping Jih-Pao*, in *CPR*, Nov. 9, 1948, p. 2. On the overall military situation, see Chassin, pp. 183–99.

87. *TKP*, Nov. 11, 1948, p. 4. I express some doubts in the text here about the explanation offered for the slow sales, because the Chinese demonstrated that they possessed considerable money a few weeks later, when the government began selling gold. See below.

88. *TKP*, Nov. 10, 1948, p. 2 (editorial).

89. See the following, all in *TKP*: Nov. 5, 1948, p. 2 (editorial); Nov. 12, pp. 4, 5; Nov. 13, p. 4; Nov. 17, p. 2 (editorial). Also see *CPR*, Nov. 6–8, pp. 12–13.

90. *TKP*, Dec. 18, 1948, p. 3; *FRUS, 1948*, vol. 8, pp. 432, 439; *North China Daily News*, Nov. 10, p. 1:2.

91. *FRUS, 1948*, vol. 8, p. 436; *TKP*, Nov. 24, 1948, p. 5.

92. *TKP*, Dec. 24, 1948, p. 4, reporting a disturbance of December 23.

93. Wu Yuan-li, p. 55. See also Chang Kia-ngau, p. 373.

94. *TKP*, Dec. 2, 1948, p. 1; *TKP*, Dec. 10, p. 5 (advertisement). *CPR*, Nov. 20–22, p. 12; Nov. 25–26, p. 9; Nov. 30–Dec. 1, p. 10; Dec. 2, p. 6. *FRUS, 1948*, vol. 8, p. 439.

95. Wu Kuo-chen, pp. 88–89.

96. *I-shih-pao*, in *CPR*, Dec. 15, 1948, p. 2. See also *Sin Wen Pao*, Nov.

27, 1948, in *CPR*, Nov. 27–29, p. 4; *North China Daily News*, Oct. 24, 1948, p. 1:4.

97. Cyril Rogers in mid-July, for instance, gave the government only an even chance of lasting 3–6 months. *FRUS, 1948*, vol. 8, p. 373.

98. *North China Daily News*, Aug. 21, 1948, p. 1:3.

99. *Sin Min Wan Pao*, Oct. 26, 1948, in *CPR*, Oct. 27, 1948, p. 10.

100. *TKP*, Oct. 7, 1948, p. 5; Hsien, pp. 1–2. *North China Daily News*, Aug. 24, p. 1:3, gives a notably larger figure for anticipated sales. Of the enterprises whose shares were being sold, the China Textile Development Corporation was the most attractive, selling GY2,860,000 in shares; Taiwan Sugar was second with GY1,035,200. Tientsin Paper, by contrast, sold only GY4,000.

101. *FRUS, 1948*, vol. 8, p. 415; *China Weekly Review*, Aug. 21, 1948, p. 333.

102. Chang Kia-ngau, p. 81.

103. The government had announced that it was committing U.S. $200 million of its foreign reserve to back the new currency. (*North China Daily News*, Aug. 24, 1948, p. 1:3.) Scholarly sources suggest, however, that the foreign reserve at the outset of the reforms fell far short of that figure. Chang Kia-ngau, p. 81, put the value of the reserve at about U.S. $130 million; Chou Shun-hsin, pp. 170–71, put the value at only U.S. $36.6 million. I am unable to account for the disparity between these figures. On the gold crisis of February 1947, see Ch'ien Chia-chü, pp. 51–71.

104. Chiang Ching-kuo, "Hu-pin jih-chi," p. 90.

105. *Ibid.*, p. 97.

106. *Ibid.*, pp. 99, 117, 118, 121.

107. *Ibid.*, p. 98; *TKP*, Sept. 22, 1948, p. 4.

108. "Hu-pin jih-chi," pp. 120, 122.

109. *Ibid.*, p. 124.

110. *Ibid.*, p. 126.

## Chapter 9

1. Chiang Kai-shek, *Chiang tsung-t'ung*, vol. 19, p. 291.

2. *Ibid.*, pp. 241, 261.        3. *Ibid.*, pp. 304–5.

4. *Ibid.*, p. 305.              5. *Ibid.*, p. 243; see also p. 254.

6. *Ibid.*, p. 305.              7. *Ibid.*, p. 253.

8. *Ibid.*, p. 243.              9. *Ibid.*, p. 305.

10. *Ibid.*, p. 243 (emphasis added).

11. *Ibid.*, pp. 240, 242.       12. *Ibid.*, p. 264.

13. *Ibid.*, p. 240.

14. *Ibid.*, p. 252.

15. *Ibid.*, pp. 258, 306.

16. *Ibid.*, p. 262.

17. *Ibid.*, p. 258.

18. *Ibid.*, p. 253.

19. *Tang-t'uan t'ung-i tsu-chih chung-yao wen-hsien*, pp. 17–18.

20. Chiang Kai-shek, *Chiang tsung-t'ung*, vol. 19, p. 281.

21. *Ibid.*, pp. 290–91.

22. *Ibid.*, pp. 292, 303. See also *ibid.*, pp. 253–54; *Tang-t'uan t'ung-i tsu-chih chung-yao wen-hsien*, p. 20.

23. Chiang Kai-shek, *Chiang tsung-t'ung*, vol. 19, pp. 283, 302–3.

24. *Ibid.*, p. 283.

25. Ts'ao Sheng-fen, pp. 9–10; Chiang Ching-kuo, *Calm in the Eye of a Storm*, pp. 154–208.

26. Ts'ao Sheng-fen, p. 10.

27. *Ibid.*

28. Li Shou-k'ung, pp. 282–83.

29. Chiang Kai-shek, *Chiang tsung-t'ung*, vol. 19, pp. 379, 397; vol. 20, p. 102.

30. *Ibid.*, vol. 19, p. 378. On the poor organization of the army, see also *ibid.*, p. 397.

31. *Ibid.*, p. 379.

32. *Ibid.*, vol. 20, p. 7. See also *ibid.*, vol. 19, pp. 282, 380–81; vol. 26, p. 35.

33. *Ibid.*, vol. 19, p. 398.

34. *United States Relations with China*, p. 131; Tsou, pp. 341–42. The U.S. government did, however, acquiesce in the face of Chiang's eagerness to reassert Nationalist sovereignty in Manchuria and agreed to transport Chinese troops to Manchurian ports. See *United States Relations with China*, p. 607; and Feis, pp. 420–21.

35. Chiang Kai-shek, *Chiang tsung-t'ung*, vol. 19, p. 388.

36. *Ibid.*, p. 400.

37. Eastman, *Abortive Revolution*, pp. 4–5.

38. *United States Relations with China*, p. 358.

39. Chiang Kai-shek, *Soviet Russia in China*, p. 256 (emphasis added). In the "Reform Program of the Kuomintang," prepared by Chiang and adopted by the Central Standing Committee of the Kuomintang in July 1950, Chiang placed what was for him a unique stress on the economic causes of defeat: "the failure of the anti-Communist war in the past four years was due to the fact that we have not put into effect the Principle of the People's Livelihood." See Shieh, p. 215.

40. Chennault, p. 77 (emphasis added).

41. Wu T'ieh-ch'eng, p. 200.
42. Ch'en Pu-lei, p. 99.
43. Shieh, p. 215; Chiang Ching-kuo, *Calm in the Eye of a Storm*, p. 155.

*Conclusion*

1. On the Nationalists during the Nanking Decade, and for more detailed references, see Eastman, *Abortive Revolution*; and Eastman, *China Under Nationalist Rule*, pp. 1–82.
2. Franklin L. Ho, p. 160.
3. Snow, "The Generalissimo," p. 646.
4. Eastman, *Abortive Revolution*, p. 306.
5. Skocpol, p. 32.
6. Li Tzu-hsiang, p. 23; Wu Hsiang-hsiang, *Ti-erh-tz'u Chung-Jih chancheng shih*, vol. 2, p. 659.
7. Kapp, *Szechwan and the Chinese Republic*, pp. 156–57; Chang Kia-ngau, pp. 15–16.
8. On the industrial-cooperative movement, see Reynolds.
9. Eastman, *China Under Nationalist Rule*, pp. 136–50.
10. This is a major theme in Kataoka's *Resistance and Revolution in China*.
11. See, for example, Tsou, pp. 237–87, 324–40.
12. Chang Kia-ngau, pp. 222, 225; Yu-kwei Cheng, p. 193.
13. Chang Kia-ngau, pp. 223–24.
14. Yu-kwei Cheng, p. 158.

# Bibliography

The locations and file numbers of hard-to-find items are indicated within parentheses in the Bibliography. Archives and libraries in Taiwan thus referred to are the Bureau of Investigation (under the Ministry of Justice, Hsin-tien); the archives of the National Resources Commission (in the Academia Historica, or Kuo-shih-kuan, Ta-ch'i-chiao); the Institute of Modern History, Academia Sinica (Nan-kang); the Tang-shih-hui (Kuomintang Party History Commission, Taipei); the Sun Yat-sen Library (in the Sun Yat-sen Memorial Hall, Taipei); and the Taiwan Branch of the National Central Library (Taipei).

Archival materials were obtained also from the following repositories in the United States: the National Archives in Washington, D.C. (records of the Department of State, Office of Strategic Services, and Office of War Information); the Office of the Chief of Military History in Washington, D.C.; and the Archives of the United Nations in New York City (records of the United Nations Relief and Rehabilitation Administration).

I also used the collections of the Chinese Research Institute of Land Economics (Chung-kuo ti-cheng yen-chiu-so) in Taipei. This collection has now been microfilmed and is available from the Chinese Materials Center (Taipei) under the title "Materials on Chinese Problems in Economy, Agriculture, Lands, and Water Utilization in the 1930's and 1940's."

*The Amerasia Papers: A Clue to the Catastrophe of China.* 2 vols. Washington, D.C., 1970.

Barnett, A. Doak. *China on the Eve of Communist Takeover.* New York, 1963.

Barrett, David D. *Dixie Mission: The United States Army Observer Group in Yenan, 1944.* Berkeley, Calif., 1970.

Belden, Jack. *China Shakes the World*, New York, 1949.

Bōei Kenshūjo Senshishitsu. *Kanan no Kaisen* (The Honan campaign). Tokyo, 1967.

Boorman, Howard L., ed. *Biographical Dictionary of Republican China.* 4 vols. New York, 1967–70.

Boyle, John Hunter. *China and Japan at War, 1937–1945: The Politics of Collaboration.* Stanford, Calif., 1972.

Buck, John Lossing. *An Agricultural Survey of Szechwan Province, China.* Chungking, 1943.

————, and Chong-chan Yien. "Economic Effects of War upon Farmers in Peng-hsien, Szechwan," *Economic Facts,* 19 (Apr. 1943).

Bunker, Gerald E. *The Peace Conspiracy: Wang Ching-wei and the China War, 1937–1941.* Cambridge, Mass., 1972.

Butow, Robert J. C. *Tojo and the Coming of the War.* Princeton, N.J., 1961.

Carey, Arch. *The War Years at Shanghai, 1941–45–48.* New York, 1963.

Carlson, Evans Fordyce. *The Chinese Army: Its Organization and Military Efficiency.* New York, 1940.

*CC hao-men tzu-pen nei-mu* (The inside story of the CC Clique's wealth). N.p. [Hong Kong?], 1947.

*Chan-shih i-cheng* (Wartime medical administration). 1938. (Tang-shih-hui #6355/6477.)

Chang Ch'i-ying. "Mi-ch'ao te fen-hsi" (Analysis of the rice riots), *Ching-chi p'ing-lun,* 1, no. 9 (May 30, 1947).

————. "San-shih-liu-nien Chung-kuo ching-chi kai-k'uang" (China's economic situation in 1947), *Tung-fang tsa-chih,* 44, no. 7 (July 1948).

————. "San-shih-wu-nien-tu te Chung-kuo ching-chi" (The Chinese economy in 1946, part 2), *Tung-fang tsa-chih,* 43, no. 11 (June 15, 1947).

Chang Ch'i-yün. *Tang-shih kai-yao* (Survey of party history), 5 vols. Taipei, 1951.

Chang Chia-mo et al. *P'an-pien fu-fei fen-tzu miu-lun* (The lies of those who rebelled and defected to the Communists). N.p., n.d. (Bureau of Investigation #213.52/369.)

Chang Hsi-ch'ang et al. *Chan-shih te Chung-kuo ching-chi* (China's wartime economy). Kweilin, 1943.

Chang Hsi-ch'ao. "K'ang-chan wu-nien yü nung-ts'un ching-chi" (Five years of war and the village economy), *Chung-kuo nung-ts'un,* 8, no. 5/6 (1942).

Chang Hsiang-p'u. "Chin-shan i-chiu" (Memories at Chin-shan), *Chung-wai tsa-chih,* 12, no. 5 (Nov. 1972).

Chang Hsiao-mei. *Yün-nan ching-chi* (The economy of Yunnan). Chungking, 1941.

Chang I-fan. "'Ching-chi kai-ko fang-an' chih p'i-p'ing yü Kuo-min-tang ching-chi cheng-ts'e chih 'chuan-pien'" (A critique of the 'Economic reform proposal' and the 'reversal' of the Kuomintang's economic policy), *Ching-chi chou-pao*, 4, no. 19 (May 8, 1947).

Chang Kan-p'ing. *K'ang-Jih ming-chiang Kuan Lin-cheng* (Kuan Lin-cheng, famous general during the war against Japan). Hong Kong, 1969.

Chang Kia-ngau. *The Inflationary Spiral: The Experience in China, 1939–1950*. Cambridge, Mass., 1958.

Chang P'ei-kang. "T'ung-huo-p'eng-chang-hsia te nung-yeh ho nung-min" (Agriculture and peasants during inflation), *Ching-chi p'ing-lun*, 1, no. 2 (Apr. 12, 1947).

Chang Shao-tseng. "Ju-ho chieh-chüeh shih-ping t'ao-wang wen-t'i" (How to resolve the problem of troop desertions), *Cheng-kung chou-pao*, 3, no. 4 (Aug. 8, 1941).

Chang Wen-shih. *Yün-nan nei-mu* (Inside story of Yunnan). Hong Kong, 1949.

Chao Hsiao-i. "Fa-yang Ch'ung-ch'ing ching-shen" (Glorify the spirit of Chungking), *Chung-wai tsa-chih*, 10, no. 6 (Dec. 1, 1971).

Chao Shih-hsün. "'Wang Yün-lao yü chin-yüan-ch'üan-an chih-i' chih pu-ch'ung" (Addenda to 'Doubts about Wang Yün-wu and the case of the gold yüan'), *Chuan-chi wen-hsüeh*, no. 211 (Dec. 1979).

Chassin, Lionel Max. *The Communist Conquest of China: A History of the Civil War, 1945–1949*. Cambridge, Mass., 1965.

Chen Kuang. "Ch'uan-Shan-Kan nung-ts'un ching-chi niao-k'an" (An overview of the village economy of Szechwan, Shensi, and Kansu), *Ching-chi chou-pao*, 2, no. 3 (Jan. 17, 1946).

Chen, Ta. *See* Ch'en Ta.

Ch'en Cheng-mo. "Cheng-chih ko-hsin yü hsing-cheng hsiao-lü" (Political renovation and administrative efficiency), *Ko-hsin chou-k'an*, 1, no. 5 (Aug. 24, 1946).

———. "T'ien-fu cheng-shih yü liang-shih cheng-chieh chih chien-t'ao" (An evaluation of the tax-in-kind and compulsory grain borrowing), *Ssu-ch'uan ching-chi chi-k'an*, 1, no. 2 (Mar. 15, 1944).

Ch'en Ch'eng. *Pa-nien k'ang-chan ching-kuo kai-yao* (A summary of experiences in the eight-year war of resistance). N.p., n.d. Published by the Ministry of Defense.

Ch'en Chien-fu. "Ko-hsin te chi-pen yüan-wang" (The fundamental hope of renovation), *Ko-hsin chou-k'an*, 1, no. 1 (July 27, 1946).

Ch'en Han-sheng. "Wu-chia yü Chung-ts'un" (Prices and China's villages), *Chung-kuo nung-ts'un*, 8, no. 5/6 (1942).

Ch'en Hsiao-wei. *Wei-she-ma shih-ch'ü ta-lu* (Why we lost the mainland). Taipei, 1964.

Ch'en Hung-chin. "San-shih-erh-nien chih Ssu-ch'uan nung-yeh" (Sze-chwan's economy in 1943), *Ssu-ch'uan ching-chi chi-k'an*, 1, no. 2 (Mar. 15, 1944).

Ch'en, Jerome. *Mao and the Chinese Revolution*. London, 1965.

Ch'en Li-fu. "Chien-kuo chih tao" (The way to national reconstruction), *Ko-hsin yüeh-k'an*, 1 (Aug. 1, 1946).

Ch'en Po-ta. *Land Rent in Pre-Liberation China*. Peking, 1958.

Ch'en Pu-lei. *Ch'en Pu-lei hui-i-lu* (Memoirs of Ch'en Pu-lei). Hong Kong, 1962.

Ch'en Shao-hsiao. *Chin-ling ts'an-chao chi* (Sunset at Nanking). Hong Kong, 1963.

————. *Hei-wang-lu* (Records of the black net). Hong Kong, 1966.

Ch'en Ta. *Lang-chi shih-nien* (Ten years' wandering). Shanghai, 1946.

———— (Chen Ta). *Population in Modern China*. Chicago, 1946.

Ch'en Tun-cheng. *Tung-luan te hui-i* (Memoirs of upheaval). Taipei, 1979.

Ch'en Wei-hua. "Pan-li i-cheng te chi-ko chung-yao chieh-tuan" (Several important phases of managing conscription), *Cheng-hsün yüeh-k'an*, 1, no. 2/3 (Mar. 23, 1941).

Ch'en Ying-lung. "K'ang-chan ch'i-chien wo-te sheng-huo p'ien-tuan" (A slice of my life during the war against Japan), *I-wen-chih*, 148 (Jan. 1978).

Ch'en Yu-san, and Ch'en Ssu-te. *T'ien-fu cheng-shih chih-tu* (The system of collecting the land tax in kind). Chungking, 1945.

Ch'en Yü. "Wei ko-hsin yün-tung chin i-chiao" (Some thoughts on the ko-hsin movement), *Ko-hsin chou-k'an*, 1, no. 7 (Sept. 7, 1946).

Cheng Chao-ch'iu. "Ping-i hsün-shih so-chi" (Observations during a tour of inspection of conscription), *Cheng-hsün yüeh-k'an*, 1, no. 2/3 (Mar. 23, 1941).

*Cheng-hsün yüeh-k'an* (Conscription and training monthly). 1940–41. Published by Headquarters, Hunan Provincial Army-Control Area. (Tang-shih-hui #2824/0277.)

*Cheng-kung chou-pao* (Political work weekly). 1941. Published by the Political Bureau of the Military Affairs Commission. (Tang-shih-hui #1814/1037.)

Cheng, Yu-kwei. *Foreign Trade and Industrial Development of China*. Washington, D.C., 1956.

*Ch'eng-ku ch'ing-nien* (Ch'eng-ku youth). Shensi. 1941. (Bureau of Investigation #4315/6050.)

Ch'eng Tse-jun. *Hsien-chieh-tuan-te ping-i wen-t'i* (Problems of conscription at the present stage). N.p., 1942. (Bureau of Investigation #590.1107/440.)

Ch'eng Yüan-ch'en. "Ko-hsin yün-tung chih hsü ch'eng-kung pu hsü shih-pai" (The renovation movement can only succeed, it must not fail), *Ko-hsin chou-k'an*, 1, no. 5 (Aug. 24, 1946).

Chennault, Claire Lee. *Way of a Fighter*. New York, 1949.

Chi-mei. "Tang-ch'ien fang-chih-yeh te wei-chi" (The current textile crisis), *Ching-chi chou-pao*, no. 13 (Sept. 25, 1948).

Chi T'ien. *Cheng-chih chiang-hua* (Political talks). Taipei, 1950. Published by the Ministry of Defense.

Ch'i, Hsi-sheng. *Nationalist China at War: Military Defeats and Political Collapse, 1937–1945*. Ann Arbor, Mich., 1982.

Chiang Ching-kuo. *Calm in the Eye of a Storm*. Taipei, 1978.

———. "Hu-pin jih-chi" (Shanghai diary), in *T'ung-ting ssu-t'ung*.

———. *Tien-ti tsai hsin-t'ou* (Drops in the heart). Taipei, 1978.

———. *T'ung-ting ssu-t'ung* (Contemplating pains of the past). N.p., 1955.

Chiang Kai-shek. *Chiang tsung-t'ung ssu-hsiang yen-lun chi* (A collection of President Chiang's thoughts and speeches). 30 vols. Taipei, 1966.

———. *Resistance and Reconstruction: Messages During China's Six Years of War, 1937–1943*. New York, 1943.

———. *Soviet Russia in China: A Summing Up at Seventy*. Taipei, 1969. Original edition 1956.

*Chiang kuan-ch'ü chen-ch'ing shih-lu* (A true record of conditions in the areas controlled by Chiang Kai-shek). N.p., n.d. [1946?]. (Bureau of Investigation #281/811.)

Chiang Meng-lin. "Hsin-ch'ao" (New tide), *Chuan-chi wen-hsüeh*, 11, no. 2 (Aug. 1967).

Chiang Shang-ch'ing. *Cheng-hai mi-wen* (Inside stories of the political world). Hong Kong, 1966.

———. *Wang-shih chin-t'an* (Reminiscences of times past). 3d ed. Hong Kong, 1972.

*Chiang-su-sheng-cheng-fu 34/35 nien cheng-ch'ing shu-yao* (Essentials of the administrative situation of the Kiangsu government in 1945 and 1946). N.p., preface dated Dec. 1946. (Institute of Modern History #927.214/089.)

*Chiao-fei chung-yao chan-i chih chui-shu yü chien-t'ao* (Recollections and evaluations of important Communist-suppression campaigns). 6 vols. N.p., 1950. (Bureau of Investigation #592.8/741.)

Ch'iao Chia-ts'ai. *T'ieh-hsüeh ching-chung chuan* (A biography of resolve and loyalty). Taipei, 1978.

Ch'ien Chia-chü. *Chung-kuo ching-chi hsien-shih chiang-hua* (Talks on the current condition of the Chinese economy). Hong Kong, 1947.

Ch'ien Chiang-ch'ao. "Tang-ch'ien nung-min te hsü-yao" (The peasants' current needs), *Nung-kung yüeh-k'an*, 4 (July 15, 1947).

Ch'ien Tuan-sheng. *The Government and Politics of China*. Cambridge, Mass., 1961.

Chin Ta-k'ai. "Chung-kuo ch'ing-nien te chüeh-hsing" (The awakening of China's youth), *Min-chu p'ing-lun*, 2, no. 4 (Aug. 20, 1950).

Chin Tien-jung. "Hsi-nan lao-chiang Liu Chen-huan chuan-chi" (Biography of the old general from the southwest, Liu Chen-huan, parts 8 and 9), *Ch'un-ch'iu*, 173 (Sept. 16, 1964), 174 (Oct. 1, 1964).

Ch'in Shou-chang. "Kuan-liao cheng-chih te p'o-shih" (A dissection of bureaucratic government), *Ko-hsin yüeh-k'an*, 6 (Jan. 10, 1947).

————. "Shih-hsing tang-nei min-chu" (Implement democracy within the party), *Ko-hsin yüeh-k'an*, 1 (Aug. 1, 1946).

Ch'in Te-ch'un. *Ch'in Te-ch'un hui-i-lu* (Ch'in Te-ch'un's memoirs). Taipei, 1967.

*China Handbook, 1937–1945*. New York, 1947.

*China Handbook, 1950*. New York, 1950.

*China Weekly Review*. Shanghai. 1945–49.

*Chinese Press Review*. Prepared by the U.S. Consulates General in Chungking and Shanghai. (Microfilm.)

*Ching-chi chou-pao* (Economics weekly). Shanghai. 1945–48.

*Ching-chi p'ing-lun* (Economics review). Shanghai. 1947–48.

Ching Sheng. *Chan-shih Chung-kuo ching-chi lun-k'uo* (Survey of China's wartime economy). N.p., 1944.

Ch'ing Lin. "Shu-sung shang-ping chuan-yüan te kan-hsiang" (Thoughts about transferring wounded to the hospitals), *Chan-shih i-cheng*, 9 (May 21, 1938).

*Ch'ing-nien t'ung-hsün* (Youth report). 1943. Published by Central Headquarters, Three People's Principles Youth Corps. (Tang-shih-hui #5022/8037.)

Chou Hsing. "Kuo-ch'ü pan-li cheng-ping chih i-pan cheng-chieh" (General problems of managing conscription in the past), *Cheng-hsün yüeh-k'an*, 1, no. 2/3 (Mar. 23, 1941).

Chou K'ai-ch'ing. *Ssu-ch'uan yü tui-Jih k'ang-chan* (Szechwan and the anti-Japanese war). Taipei, 1971.

*Chou-pao* (Weekly report). Shanghai. 1945–46.

Chou Shun-hsin. *The Chinese Inflation, 1937–1949*. New York, 1963.

Chow, Yung-teh. *Social Mobility in China: Status Careers Among Gentry in a Chinese Community*. New York, 1966.

Chu. "Liang-shih cheng-chieh yü liang-chia" (The tax-in-kind and grain prices), *Ching-chi p'ing-lun*, 1, no. 19 (Aug. 9, 1947).

Chu Tzu-shuang. *Chung-kuo kuo-min-tang li-tz'u ch'üan-kuo tai-piao ta-hui yao-lan* (Successive national party congresses of the Chinese Kuomintang, an anthology). Chungking, 1945.

————. *Chung-kuo kuo-min-tang liang-shih cheng-ts'e* (The Chinese Kuomintang's grain policy). Chungking, 1944.

Chu Wen-ch'ang. "Wo tui 'Wang Yün-lao yü chin-yüan-ch'üan' te k'anfa" (My view of 'Wang Yün-wu and the gold yüan'), *Chuan-chi wenhsüeh*, 213 (Feb. 1980), pp. 51–52.

Chu Yüeh-shan, ed. *Hsiang-mo chi* (Record of quelling demons). N.p., 1946. (Bureau of Investigation #281/940.)

Chü-wai-jen. "Chi tang-nien ch'uan-shuo-chung te 'shih-san t'ai-pao'" (Reminiscences of the legendary thirteen princes, parts 1–24), *Ch'unch'iu*, 95–118 (June 16, 1961–June 1, 1962).

*Chuan-chi wen-hsüeh* (Biographical literature). Taipei. 1962–82.

"Ch'üan-kuo ko-tan-wei t'e-ch'ing kai-k'uang" (The situation of the secret services in the various units throughout the country). Prepared by Chung-yang tiao-ch'a t'ung-chi chü (Central party bureau of investigation and statistics). Handwritten document, ca. 1941. (Bureau of Investigation #276/815.)

*Ch'üan-kuo liang-shih kai-k'uang* (The national grain situation). Ed. Hsing-cheng-yüan hsin-wen-chü (News office of the Executive Yüan). N.p., 1947. (Bureau of Investigation #554.6/716.)

"Ch'üan-kuo t'ien-fu k'ai-shih cheng-shih" (The whole nation begins collecting the tax-in-kind), *Ching-chi chou-pao*, 3, no. 6 (Aug. 8, 1946).

"Ch'üan-kuo t'ien-liang hui-i chi-yao" (Essentials of the national grain conference), *Ts'ai-cheng p'ing-lun*, 17, no. 2 (Aug. 1947).

*Ch'un-ch'iu* ("The Observation Post"). Hong Kong. 1957–82.

*Chung-kuo ching-chi nien-chien, 1947* (Chinese Economic Year-Book, 1947). Comp. T'i Ch'ao-pai. Hong Kong, 1947.

"Chung-kuo kuo-min-tang tang-yüan tang-cheng ko-hsin yün-tung ch'u-ch'i kung-tso fang-an" (Work program for the first stage of the Kuomintang's party-government renovation movement), *Ko-hsin yüeh-k'an*, 2 (Sept. 1, 1946).

*Chung-kuo lao-kung yün-tung shih* (History of the Chinese labor movement), 5 vols. Taipei, 1959.

*Chung-kuo nung-ts'un* (Village China). Kweilin. 1942.

*Chung-wai tsa-chih* ("Kaleidoscope Monthly"). Taipei. 1967–82.

"Chung-yang cheng-wu chi-kuan san-shih-nien-tu kung-tso ch'eng-chi k'ao-ch'a pao-kao" (A report of an investigation of the achievements of central administrative agencies in 1941). Comp. Hsing-cheng-yüan mi-shu-ch'u (Secretariat of the Executive Yüan). Handwritten, dittoed. (Bureau of Investigation #573/806.)

*Chung-yang jih-pao* (Central daily). Shanghai. 1945–49.

Clubb, Edmund. "Chiang Kai-shek's Waterloo: The Battle of Hwai-Hai," *Pacific Historical Review*, 25, no. 4 (Nov. 1956).

Cottrell, A. "Hu-nan chi-huang te ts'an-hsiang" (The tragedy of the Hunan famine), *Ching-chi chou-pao*, 3, no. 6 (Aug. 8, 1946).

Dorn, Frank. *The Sino-Japanese War, 1937–41: From Marco Polo Bridge to Pearl Harbor*. New York, 1974.

Eastman, Lloyd E. *The Abortive Revolution: China Under Nationalist Rule, 1927–1937*. Cambridge, Mass., 1974.

———. *China Under Nationalist Rule: Two Essays*. Urbana, Ill., 1981.

———. "Facets of am Ambivalent Relationship: Smuggling, Puppets, and Atrocities During the War, 1937–1945," in Akira Iriye, ed., *The Chinese and the Japanese: Essays in Political and Cultural Interactions*. Princeton, N.J., 1980.

Eckstein, Harry. "On the Etiology of Internal Wars," in Ivo K. Feierabend et al., eds., *Anger, Violence, and Politics: Theories and Research*. Englewood Cliffs, N.J., 1972.

*Economic Facts*. Published by Department of Agricultural Economics, University of Nanking, Chengtu, 1943–46.

Epstein, Israel. *The Unfinished Revolution in China*. Boston, 1947.

Fan Hui. "K'an che yen-chung te liang-ko yüeh" (Consider these two critical months), *Chou-pao*, 30 (Mar. 30, 1946).

*Fang-tieh ch'u-chien hsü-chih* (Essentials for rooting out enemy agents). N.p., n.d. [1943]. (Bureau of Investigation #276.2/804.)

Farmer, Rhodes. *Shanghai Harvest: A Diary of Three Years in the China War*. London, 1945.

Fei Hsiao-t'ung. *China's Gentry: Essays in Rural-Urban Relations*. Chicago, 1953.

———. "P'ing Yen Yang-ch'u 'K'ai-fa min-li chien-she hsiang-ts'ung'" (A critique of Jimmy Yen's 'Develop the people's strength and reconstruct the villages'), *Kuan-ch'a*, 5, no. 1 (Aug. 28, 1948).

Feis, Herbert. *The China Tangle: The American Effort in China from Pearl Harbor to the Marshall Mission*. Princeton, N.J., 1953.

Feng I-lu. *Hsü-P'ang chan-i chien-wen lu* (A record of what I saw and heard of the battle of Hsü-P'ang). Hong Kong, 1964.

Feng Yü-hsiang. *Wo so-jen-shih-te Chiang Chieh-shih* (The Chiang Kai-shek I know). Hong Kong, 1949.

Feng Yu-ta. "Lung Yün t'ao-tiao-le!" (Lung Yün has escaped!), *Hsin-wen t'ien-ti*, 54 (Dec. 16, 1948).

Fessler, Loren. "Who is CCK? What is Taiwan?" *American Universities Field Staff: Reports*, no. 28 (part 2) and no. 29 (part 3) (1978).

*Foreign Relations of the United States*. Washington, D.C., 1937–1949.

Freyn, Hubert. *Free China's New Deal*. New York, 1943.

Fujiwara Akira. "The Role of the Japanese Army," in Dorothy Borg and Shumpei Okamoto, eds., *Pearl Harbor as History: Japanese-American Relations, 1931–1941*. New York, 1973.

*Gendai Chūgoku jimmei jiten* (Biographical dictionary of Republican China). Tokyo, 1966.

Gill, Graeme J. *Peasants and Government in the Russian Revolution*. New York, 1979.

Gillespie, Richard Eugene. "Whampoa and the Nanking Decade (1924–1936)." Ph.D. diss., The American University, 1971.

Gillin, Donald G. "Problems of Centralization in Republican China: The Case of Ch'en Ch'eng and the Kuomintang," *Journal of Asian Studies*, 29, no. 4 (Aug. 1970).

Hall, J. C. S. *The Yunnan Provincial Faction, 1927–1937*. Canberra, 1976.

Han Ssu. *K'an! Cheng-hsüeh-hsi* (Look! The Political Study Clique). Hong Kong, 1947.

Hanson, Haldore. *Humane Endeavor: The Story of the China War*. New York, 1939.

Hattori Takushirō. *Dai Tōa sensō zenshi* (The Great East Asian War). Tokyo, 1965.

Ho, Franklin L. "The Reminiscences of Ho Lien (Franklin L. Ho)," as told to Crystal Lorch, postscript dated July 1966. Unpub. ms. in Special Collections Library, Butler Library, Columbia University.

Ho Ying-ch'in. "Chi-nien ch'i-ch'i k'ang-chan tsai po chung-kung te hsü-wei hsüan-ch'uan" (Commemorating the Sino-Japanese war and again refuting the Communists' false propaganda), *Tzu-yu chung*, 3, no. 3 (Sept. 20, 1972).

Ho Yüeh-seng. "Ju-ho t'ui-chin tang te ko-hsin yün-tung" (How to advance the party's renovation movement), *Ko-hsin chou-k'an*, 1, no. 5 (Aug. 24, 1946).

———. "Kan-k'uai chiu-cheng she-hui te p'ien-hsiang" (Quickly correct society's tendencies), *She-hui p'ing-lun*, 3 (Sept. 16, 1945).

———. "Tang te fu-pai yüan-yin chih fen-hsi" (An analysis of the party's decadence), *Ko-hsin chou-k'an*, 1, no. 4 (Aug. 17, 1946).

———. "Tang te ping-pai yüan-yin chih fen-hsi" (An analysis of the causes of the party's sickness), *Ko-hsin chou-k'an*, 1, no. 3 (Aug. 10, 1946).

Hsiao Cheng. *T'u-ti kai-ko wu-shih-nien: Hsiao Cheng hui-i-lu* (Fifty years of land reform: memoirs of Hsiao Cheng). Taipei, 1980.

Hsiao-chuang. "T'ou-shih Ch'uan-hsi te nung-ti yü nung-ts'un" (Western Szechwan's farmland and villages in perspective), *Kuan-ch'a*, 5, no. 4 (Sept. 18, 1948).

Hsien. "Kuo-ying shih-yeh ku-p'iao k'ai-shih ch'u-shou" (Sales of shares in state-run enterprises begin), *Ching-chi p'ing-lun*, 3, no. 23 (Sept. 18, 1948).

*Hsin-ching-chi pan-yüeh-k'an* (New economics semi-monthly). 1939–45.

*Hsin ch'ou-an-hui* (The new peace-planning conference). N.p., 1946.

*Hsin-Chung-hua, fu-k'an* (New China, supplement). 1944–49.

"Hsin chü-mien ch'ien-hsi te p'ai-hsi cheng-tou chi jen-shih pu-chih" (Factional conflicts and personnel arrangements on the eve of the new situation), *Kuan-ch'a*, 2, no. 8 (Apr. 19, 1947).

*Hsin kuan-ch'ang hsien-hsing chi* (A new "current situation in officialdom"). N.p., 1946.

*Hsin-wen t'ien-ti* (News world). Chungking. 1945.

*Hsing-tsung chou-k'an* (CNRRA weekly). 1946–47. Published by the Compilation and Translation Department, Chinese National Relief and Rehabilitation Administration. (Tang-shih-hui #2122/2693.)

Hsu Dau-lin. "Chinese Local Administration Under the National Government: Democracy and Self-Government Versus Traditional Centralism." Unpub. manuscript.

Hsu Long-hsuen and Chang Ming-kai, comps. *History of the Sino-Japanese War (1937–1945)*. Taipei, 1971.

Hsü Fu-kuan. "Shih shei chi-k'uei-le Chung-kuo she-hui fan-kung te li-liang?" (Who is it that destroys the anti-Communist force of Chinese society?), *Min-chu p'ing-lun*, 1, no. 7 (Sept. 16, 1949).

Hsü, K'ai-yü. *Wen I-to*. Boston, 1979.

Hsü K'an. "Chung-kuo chan-shih te liang-cheng" (China's wartime grain administration), *Liang-cheng yüeh-k'an*, 1, no. 1 (Apr. 16, 1943).

———. *Hsü K'o-t'ing hsien-sheng wen-ts'un* (Collected papers of Hsü K'an). Taipei, 1970.

———. "K'ang-chan shih-ch'i liang-cheng chi-yao" (A record of grain administration during the war against Japan), *Ssu-ch'uan wen-hsien yüeh-k'an*, 11/12 (July 1, 1963).

Hsü Tao-fu. "Chiang-hsi liang-chia k'uang-chang yüan-yin chih yen-chiu" (A study of the reasons for the wild increases of grain prices in Kiangsi), *Liang-cheng yüeh-k'an*, 1, no. 4 (Apr. 1941).

Hu Ch'i-ju. "Ch'u-hsün Ting-fan tui ch'ü-pao-chia chang chi ko-chieh chiang-tz'u" (Lecture to heads of ch'ü, pao, and chia and to all circles during an inspection of Ting-fan hsien), *Ping-i hsün-k'an*, 2 (Nov. 25, 1939).

Hu Fa-p'eng. "Chiang-hsi nung-ts'un tsai k'u-nan-chung" (Kiangsi's villages in distress), *Ching-chi chou-pao*, 7, no. 18 (Nov. 4, 1948).

Hu Feng. "Chan-shih Che-chiang nung-ts'un ching-chi te hui-ku" (A look back at Chekiang's wartime rural economy), *Ching-chi chou-pao*, 2, no. 12 (Mar. 28, 1946).

"Hu-nan 'Nung-chien kung-ssu' chiu-fen nei-mu" (Inside story of the dispute over the Hunan Agricultural Reconstruction Corporation), *Ching-chi chou-pao*, 7, no. 8 (Nov. 4, 1948).

*Hu-pei-sheng-cheng-fu pao-kao, 1942/4–10* (Report of the Hupeh provincial government, Apr.–Oct. 1942). N.p., n.d.

*Hu-pei-sheng-cheng-fu shih-cheng pao-kao, 1942/11–1943/9* (Administrative report of the Hupeh provincial government, Nov. 1942–Sept. 1943). N.p., n.d.

*Hu-pei-sheng-cheng-fu shih-cheng pao-kao (t'ien-liang pu-fen), 1942/11–1943/9* (Administrative report of the Hupeh provincial government [section on grain], Nov. 1942–Sept. 1943). N.p., n.d.

*Hu-pei-sheng-cheng-fu shih-cheng pao-kao, 1943/10–1944/9* (Administrative report of the Hupeh provincial government, Oct. 1943–Sept. 1944). N.p., n.d.

*Hu shang-chiang Tsung-nan nien-p'u* (Chronological biography of General Hu Tsung-nan). Taipei, n.d.

Huang Chien-ch'ing. "Chih yu i-t'iao-lu: ch'ing-tang" (There is only one way: party purge), *Ko-hsin chou-k'an*, 1, no. 10 (Sept. 28, 1946).

Huntington, Samuel P. *Political Order in Changing Societies*. New Haven, Conn., 1968.

*I-cheng yüeh-k'an* (Conscription monthly). 1945. Published by Ministry of Conscription. (Tang-shih-hui #615/2724/1877.)

*I-erh-i ts'an-an t'e-chi* (Special collection on the December 1 Massacre). N.p., n.d.

*I-wen-chih* ("The Art and Literature Journal"). Taipei. 1972.

Jen Chang. "Wei ko-hsin yün-tung ta-pien" (Retorting for the renovation movement), *Ko-hsin chou-k'an*, 1, no. 2 (Aug. 3, 1946).

Johnson, Chalmers A. *Peasant Nationalism and Communist Power: The Emergence of Revolutionary China, 1937–1945*. Stanford, Calif., 1962.

"Ju-ho kai-chin chin-hou te ping-i" (How to improve conscription in the future), *Ping-i hsün-k'an*, 7 (Jan. 15, 1940).

Juan Hua-kuo. "Ko-hsin sheng-chung ti-i-p'ao: tang-yüan tsung-ch'ing-ch'a" (The first shot of renovation: the general review of party members), *Ko-hsin chou-k'an*, 1, no. 13.

Jung Chai. *Chin-ling chiu-meng* (Old dreams of Nanking). Hong Kong, 1968.

Kalyagin, Aleksandr Ya. *Along Alien Roads.* Unpublished translation by Steven I. Levine of *Po Neznakomym dorogam* (Moscow, 1969).

*K'ang-chan pa-nien-lai ping-i hsing-cheng kung-tso tsung-pao-kao* (General report of administration of military conscription during the eight-year war of resistance). N.p., 1945.

K'ang Tse. "Pen-t'uan tsu-chih kung-tso kai-k'uang yü san-shih-i-nien-tu chi-chien chung-yao kung-tso" (The organizational work of this corps and several important tasks in 1942), *Ch'ing-nien t'ung-hsün*, 3, no. 1 (Jan. 31, 1943).

Kao Shu-k'ang. "Ko-hsin yün-tung te t'ung-chih-men hsing-tung ch'i-lai!" (Comrades of the renovation movement, become active!), *Ko-hsin chou-k'an*, 1, no. 5 (Aug. 24, 1946).

Kapp, Robert A. "The Kuomintang and Rural China in the War of Resistance, 1937–1945," in F. Gilbert Chan, ed., *China at the Crossroads: Nationalists and Communists, 1927–1949.* Boulder, Col., 1980.

―――. *Szechwan and the Chinese Republic: Provincial Militarism and Central Power, 1911–1938.* New Haven, Conn., 1973.

Kataoka, Tetsuya. *Resistance and Revolution in China: The Communists and the Second United Front.* Berkeley, Calif., 1974.

Kirby, William Corbin. "Foreign Models and Chinese Modernization: Germany and Republican China, 1921–1941." Ph.D. diss., Harvard University, 1981.

*Ko-hsin chou-k'an* (Renovation weekly). Nanking. 1946. (Tang-shih-hui #4450/0292.)

*Ko-hsin yüeh-k'an* (Renovation monthly). Changsha. 1946. (Taiwan Branch, National Central Library #S/005.05/4072/1.)

*Ko-ming wen-hsien* (Documents of the revolution), vols. 62–63. Taipei, 1973.

Ku Pao. "Yün-nan t'ien-fu cheng-shih yü nung-min fu-tan" (Yunnan's tax-in-kind and the farmers' burden), *Hsin-ching-chi*, 6, no. 11 (Mar. 1, 1942).

*Kuan-ch'a* (The observer). Shanghai. 1946–48.

Kuan Chi-yü. *Chung-kuo shui-chih* (China's tax system). N.p., 1945.

Kuo-fang-pu (Ministry of National Defense). *Chung-yang chih-hsing wei-yüan-hui ti-liu-chieh ti-ssu-tz'u ch'üan-t'i hui-i chün-shih pao-kao* (Military report to the 4th plenum of the 6th CEC). N.p., 1947. (Bureau of Investigation #166.517/741.)

Kuo-fang-pu shih-cheng-chü (Office of Military History, Ministry of National Defense). *K'an-luan chien-shih* (Brief history of rebellion-suppression). 4 vols. N.p., 1962.

Kuo-fang-pu tsung-cheng-chih-pu (General Political Bureau, Ministry of National Defense). *Kuo-chün cheng-chih kung-tso chih-tao yao-tien* (Important points to guide political work in the national army). N.p., 1950. (Bureau of Investigation #596.72/741.)

Kuo Jung-chao. *Mei-kuo Ya-erh-ta mi-yüeh yü Chung-kuo* (A Critical Study of the Yalta Agreement and Sino-American Relations). Taipei, 1967.

"Kuo-min-tang chün-kuan-ping-men ch'i-lai!" (Officers and men in the Kuomintang army, arise!), in Chang Chia-mo et al., *P'an-pien fu-fei fen-tzu miu-lun.*

"Kuo-min-tang chün-tui shen-ming ta-i kuang-jung chuang-chü" (Daring and glorious achievements of the Kuomintang's armed forces), in Chang Chia-mo et al., *P'an-pien fu-fei fen-tzu miu-lun.*

"Kuo-min-tang tang-t'uan ho-ping ch'ien-hou" (The full story of the merger of the Kuomintang's party and corps), *Kuan-ch'a*, 3, no. 5 (Sept. 27, 1947).

Lefebvre, Georges. *The Great Fear of 1789: Rural Panic in Revolutionary France.* New York, 1973.

Lei Chao-yüan. "Ling i-nien-lai i-cheng chih chien-t'ao" (Discussion of administering conscription in Ling-hsien during the past year), *Cheng-hsün yüeh-k'an*, 1, no. 2/3 (Mar. 23, 1941).

Lei Chen. *Lei Chen hui-i-lu* (Lei Chen's memoirs). Hong Kong, 1978.

Lei Ch'in. "Kuang-hsi shan-hou chiu-chi wen-t'i ch'u-i" (My views on the question of relief and rehabilitation in Kwangsi), *Ling-piao lun-t'an*, 1, no. 1 (Dec. 15, 1945).

Levine, Steven I. "Comments on Chin-tung Liang, 'The Sino-Soviet Treaty of Friendship and Alliance of 1945: The Inside Story,'" in Paul K. T. Sih, ed., *Nationalist China During the Sino-Japanese War.*

———. "Mobilizing for War: Rural Revolution in Manchuria as an Instrument of War." Paper presented to the Conference on Chinese Communist Rural Bases, Cambridge, Mass., Aug. 14–21, 1978.

Li I-wei. "Pan-li Li-ling i-cheng chih kai-shu" (General observations on managing conscription in Li-ling hsien), *Cheng-hsün yüeh-k'an*, 1, no. 4 (Apr. 30, 1941).

Li I-yeh. *Chung-kuo jen-min tse-yang ta-pai Jih-pen ti-kuo-chu-i* (How the Chinese people defeated Japanese imperialism). Peking, 1951.

Li P'in-hsien. *Li P'in-hsien hui-i-lu* (Memoirs of Li P'in-hsien). Taipei, 1975.

Li Shou-k'ung. *Chung-kuo hsien-tai shih* (Chinese contemporary history). 4th ed. Taipei, 1967.

Li Ta. "Ko-hsin yün-tung te san ta ching-shen" (The renovation movement's three great sources of vitality), *Ko-hsin chou-k'an*, 1, no. 6 (Aug. 31, 1946).

Li T'i-ch'ien. "T'ien-fu ying che-cheng fa-pi" (The land tax should be collected in fa-pi), *She-hui p'ing-lun*, 24 (Aug. 16, 1946).

Li Tsung-huang. *Chu Tien hui-i-lu* (Memoirs of my chairmanship of Yunnan). Nanking, 1947.

————. *Li Tsung-huang hui-i-lu* (Memoirs of Li Tsung-huang). Taipei, 1972.

Li Tsung-ying. "Shan-hou kung-tso chien-t'ao" (Discussion of rehabilitation work), *Hsing-tsung chou-k'an*, 22 (Sept. 14, 1946).

Li Tzu-hsiang. "K'ang-chan i-lai Ssu-ch'uan chih kung-yeh" (Szechwan's industry during the war), *Ssu-ch'uan ching-chi chi-k'an*, 1, no. 1 (Dec. 15, 1943).

*Liang-cheng yüeh-k'an* (Grain administration monthly). 1941. Published by the Grain-Control Department, Ninth War Zone. (Tang-shih-hui #9393/1877.)

Liang Han-ts'ao. "Fa-k'an tz'u" (Inaugural statement), *Ko-hsin chou-k'an*, 1, no. 1 (July 27, 1946).

Liang-hsiung. *Tai Li chuan* (Biography of Tai Li). Taipei, 1980.

Liang Sheng-chün. *Chiang Li tou-cheng nei-mu* (The inside story of the struggle between Chiang Kai-shek and Li Tsung-jen). Hong Kong, 1954.

Lin Chen. *Chung-kuo nei-mu* (Chinese inside story). Shanghai, 1948.

Lin Chen-yung. *Ping-i-chih kai-lun* (Survey of the military conscription system). N.p., 1940.

*Ling-piao lun-t'an* (Ling-piao forum). Kweilin. 1945–46. (Tang-shih-hui #2238/5008.)

Ling Yün. "Shang-hsin wang-shih hua ho-t'an" (Sadly recounting the peace talks), *I-wen-chih*, 87 (Dec. 1972).

Liu Chien-ch'ün. *Yin-ho i-wang* (Memories at Yin-ho). Taipei, 1966.

Liu Chih. *Wo-te hui-i* (My reminiscences). Taipei, 1966.

Liu Ch'iu-[?]. "Chan-shih Ssu-ch'uan liang-shih sheng-ch'an" (Wartime Szechwan's grain production), *Ssu-ch'uan ching-chi chi-k'an*, 2, no. 4 (Oct. 1, 1945).

Liu, F. F. *A Military History of Modern China, 1924–1949*. Princeton, N.J., 1956.

Liu Pu-t'ung. "Lun kuo-min-tang chih fu-hsing" (On revival of the Kuomintang), *Ko-hsin chou-k'an*, 1, no. 6 (Aug. 31, 1946).

Lo Tun-wei. *Wu-shih-nien hui-i-lu* (Memoirs of fifty years). Taipei, 1952.

Lou Li-chai. "Kuan-yü t'ien-fu cheng-shih" (Regarding the tax-in-kind), *Ching-chi chou-pao*, 2, no. 23 (Mar. 13, 1946).

Ma Hua. "San-shih-san-nien Ssu-ch'uan chih t'ien-fu cheng-shih yü cheng-chieh" (Szechwan's tax-in-kind and compulsory borrowing in 1944), *Ssu-ch'uan ching-chi chi-k'an*, 2, no. 2 (Apr. 1, 1945).

————. "Ssu-ch'uan t'ien-fu cheng-shih yü liang-shih cheng-kou [-chieh] wen-t'i" (The problem of the tax-in-kind and compulsory grain purchases [borrowing] in Szechwan), *Ssu-ch'uan ching-chi chi-k'an*, 1, no. 2 (Mar. 15, 1944).

Meng Hsien-chang. *Chung-kuo chin-tai ching-chi-shih chiao-ch'eng* (Lectures on China's modern economic history). Shanghai, 1951.

Miles, Milton E. *A Different Kind of War*. Garden City, N.Y., 1967.

*Min-chu p'ing-lun* ("The Democratic Review"). Hong Kong. 1949–50.

Mo Hsüan-yüan. "Tang-cheng ko-hsin te t'u-ching" (The path of party and government renovation), *Ko-hsin yüeh-k'an*, 2 (Sept. 1, 1946).

————. "Tang-cheng ko-hsin yün-tung chih yao-i" (The basic meaning of the party-government renovation movement), *Ko-hsin yüeh-k'an*, 1 (Aug. 1, 1946).

*New York Times*. 1937–49.

*North China Daily News*. Shanghai. 1948.

*Nung-kung yüeh-k'an* (Ministry of agriculture and industry monthly). (Tang-shih-hui #5523/1077.)

Oliver, Frank. *Special Undeclared War*. London, 1939.

Pan, Hong-shen. "Marketing of Agricultural Products in Penghsien, Szechwan," *Economic Facts*, 26 (Nov. 1943).

P'an Kuang-sheng. "K'ang-chan shih-ch'i Ssu-ch'uan t'e-chung kung-ch'eng chi-shih" (A record of special building projects in Szechwan during the war), *Ssu-ch'uan wen-hsien*, 81 (May 1, 1969).

Panikkar, K. M. *In Two Chinas: Memoirs of a Diplomat*. London, 1955.

Payne, Robert. *China Awake*. New York, 1947.

Pepper, Suzanne. *Civil War in China: The Political Struggle, 1945–1949*. Berkeley, Calif., 1978.

*The Personalities and Political Machinery of Formosa: From Personal Recollections*. Cambridge, Mass., 1954.

"Ping-i chih-tu chih san-p'ing yüan-tse" (The conscription system's three-equals principle), *Ping-i hsün-k'an*, 2 (Nov. 25, 1939).

*Ping-i hsün-k'an* (Conscription). 1939–40. Published by Headquarters, Kuei-Hsing Division-Control Area. (Tang-shih-hui #2727/7280.)

*P'ing erh-chung-ch'üan-hui* (Criticizing the second plenum). N.p., n.d. [1946].

Powell, Lyle Stephenson. *A Surgeon in Wartime China*. Lawrence, Kans., 1946.

P'u Hsi-hsiu. "Kuo-min-tang san-chung-ch'üan-hui chi" (A record of the Kuomintang's third plenum), *Kuan-ch'a*, 2, no. 6 (Apr. 5, 1947).

Reynolds, Douglas Robertson. "The Chinese Industrial Cooperative Movement and the Political Polarization of Wartime China, 1938–1945." Ph.D. diss., Columbia University, 1975.

Romanus, Charles F., and Riley Sunderland. *Stilwell's Command Problems*. Washington, D.C., 1956.

————. *Stilwell's Mission to China*. Washington, D.C., 1953.

————. *Time Runs Out in CBI*. Washington, D.C., 1959.

Roth, Andrew. "Szechwan: The Key to China's Resistance," *Amerasia*, 5, no. 8 (Oct. 1941).

*San-ch'ing-t'uan te ch'an-sheng yü mu-ti ho hsing-chih* (The origins, purpose, and nature of the Three People's Principles Youth Corps). N.p., n.d. Handwritten, dittoed. (Bureau of Investigation #282/804.)

*San-min-chu-i ch'ing-nien-t'uan ti-i-tz'u ch'üan-kuo tai-piao ta-hui t'i-an hui-lu* (Resolutions of the Youth Corps' first national congress). N.p., 1943. (Sun Yat-sen Library #038.16/1:04.)

*San-min-chu-i ch'ing-nien-t'uan t'uan-shih tzu-liao ti-i-chi ch'u-kao* (Historical materials on the Three People's Principles Youth Corps, first collection, first draft). N.p., 1946. (Sun Yat-sen Library #038.19/01/1.)

"Sanmin shugi seinendan no seikaku to ninmu" (The nature and tasks of the Three People's Principles Youth Corps), *Tōa*, 14, no. 5 (May 1, 1941).

Scott, James C. *The Moral Economy of the Peasant: Rebellion and Subsistence in Southeast Asia*. New Haven, Conn., 1976.

Service, John S. *Lost Chance in China*, ed. Joseph W. Esherick. New York, 1974.

Sha Hsüeh-chün. "Chung-kung ts'an-t'ou kuo-fang-pu tao-chih ta-lu pien-se" (Communists infiltrate the Ministry of Defense, leading to the mainland's changing colors), *Tung-fang tsa-chih*, 7, no. 8 (Feb. 1, 1974).

"Shan-pao liu-t'uan ch'üan-t'i kuan-ping k'ai tso-t'an-hui" (All officers and men of the 6th regiment of the Shansi militia hold a meeting), in Chang Chia-mo et al., *P'an-pien fu-fei fen-tzu miu-lun*.

*She-hui p'ing-lun* (Society review). 1945–48. (Tang-shih-hui #3421/8001.)

Shen Tsung-han. "Food Production and Distribution for Civilian and Military Needs in Wartime China, 1937–1945," in Paul K. T. Sih, ed., *Nationalist China During the Sino-Japanese War*.

————. *The Sino-American Joint Commission on Rural Reconstruction:*

*Twenty Years of Cooperation for Agricultural Development.* Ithaca, N.Y., 1970.

Shen Yün-lung. "Tui chin-yüan-ch'üan-an ying chin-i-pu chui-tsung yen-chiu" (We ought further to pursue and research the case of the gold yüan), *Chuan-chi wen-hsüeh*, 214 (Mar. 1980).

———. "Wang Yün-lao yü chin-yüan-ch'üan-an chih-i" (Doubts about Wang Yün-wu and the case of the gold yüan), *Chuan-chi wen-hsüeh*, 209 (Oct. 1979).

Sheridan, James E. *Chinese Warlord: The Career of Feng Yü-hsiang.* Stanford, Calif., 1966.

Shieh, Milton J. T. *The Kuomintang: Selected Historical Documents, 1894–1969.* New York, 1972.

*Shih-chi p'ing-lun* ("The Century Critic"). Nanking. 1947–48.

Shih Fu-liang. "Lun tang-ch'ien te ching-kuan ch'ing-hsing" (On the current state of economic controls), *Kuan-ch'a*, 5, no. 10 (Oct. 30, 1948).

Shih-hsin. "Wei-yüan-chang shih-ts'ung-shih fu-wu chi-wang" (Reminiscences of serving in the generalissimo's office of attendants), *Ch'un-ch'iu*, 125 (Sept. 16, 1962).

*Shih yü wen* ("Time and Culture"). Shanghai. 1947–48.

"Shō Kai-seki no Unnan chūōka kōsaku" (Chiang Kai-shek's centralization of Yunnan), *Tōa*, 13, no. 3 (Mar. 1, 1940).

Shou-chung. "T'ui-hsing ping-i chih ch'u-lun" (On promoting military service), *Ping-i hsün-k'an*, 34 (Nov. 30, 1940).

Shyu, Lawrence Nae-lih. "China's 'Wartime Parliament': The People's Political Council, 1938–1945," in Paul K. T. Sih, ed., *Nationalist China During the Sino-Japanese War.*

———. "The People's Political Council and China's Wartime Problems, 1937–1945." Ph.D. diss., Columbia University, 1972.

Sih, Paul K. T., ed. *Nationalist China During the Sino-Japanese War, 1937–1945.* Hicksville, N.Y., 1977.

Skocpol, Theda. *States and Social Revolutions: A Comparative Analysis of France, Russia, and China.* Cambridge, Eng., 1979.

Smith, Robert Gillen. "History of the Attempt of the United States Medical Department to Improve the Effectiveness of the Chinese Army Medical Service, 1941–1945." Ph.D. diss., Columbia University, 1950.

Snow, Edgar. *The Battle for Asia.* New York, 1941.

———. "The Generalissimo," *Asia*, Dec. 1940, pp. 646–48.

*Ssu-ch'uan ching-chi chi-k'an* (Szechwan economics quarterly). Chungking. 1943–46.

*Ssu-ch'uan-sheng ching-chi tiao-ch'a pao-kao* (Report on an investigation of the Szechwan economy). Comp. Chung-kuo nung-min yin-hang. In

*Chung-hua-min-kuo shih-liao ts'ung-pien* (Miscellany of historical materials on the Chinese Republic), vol. A32. Taipei, 1976.

*Ssu-ch'uan wen-hsien yüeh-k'an* (Szechwan documents monthly). Taipei. 1963–72.

Ssu-t'u Ni-ying. "Lung Yün li-k'ai Yün-nan" (Lung Yün's departure from Yunnan), *Hsin-wen t'ien-ti*, 21 (Mar. 1, 1947).

"Statements of Japanese Officers, World War II." Office of the Chief of Military History, Washington, D.C.

Stilwell, Joseph W. *The Stilwell Papers*. Arr. and ed. by Theodore H. White. New York, 1972.

Stilwell Papers. National Archives, Washington, D.C.

Stuart, John Leighton. *Fifty Years in China*. New York, 1954.

Sun Chen. "K'an-luan chung-ch'i ta-lu lun-hsien chih ching-kuo" (The middle phase of rebellion-suppression: experiences during the fall of the mainland), *Ssu-ch'uan wen-hsien yüeh-k'an*, 58 (June 1, 1967).

Sung T'ung-fu. "T'ien-fu cheng-shih yü chün-hsü min-shih" (The tax-in-kind and military and civilian rations), in Wu Hsiang-hsiang et al., eds., *Chung-kuo chin-tai-shih lun-ts'ung* (Anthology on modern Chinese history), series 1, vol. 9. Taipei, 1956.

Sze, Szeming. *China's Health Problems*. Washington, D.C., 1944.

*Ta-hou-fang nung-ts'un ching-chi p'o-huai te ts'an-hsiang* (The tragic situation of the economic bankruptcy of the villages in the wartime rear areas). N.p., n.d. [1944]. (Bureau of Investigation #289/843.)

Ta I-chin. "Cheng-i-chung te pi-chih wen-t'i" (The monetary question in debate), *Ching-chi chou-pao*, 5, no. 7 (Aug. 14, 1947).

————. "Ch'i-ko-yüeh-lai te Chung-kuo ching-chi ch'ing-shih" (China's economic situation in the past seven months), *Kuan-ch'a*, 4, no. 23/24 (Aug. 7, 1948).

*Ta-kung-pao* ("L'Impartial"). Chungking and Shanghai. 1937–49.

Tai Kao-hsiang. "K'ang-chan shih-ch'i chih Ssu-ch'uan i-cheng" (Conscription in Szechwan during the war of resistance), *Ssu-ch'uan wen-hsien yüeh-k'an*, 11/12 (July 1, 1963).

"T'ai-yüeh san-ch'ing-t'uan hsiu-cheng fan-kung kung-tso shou-ts'e" (Anti-Communist work-manual, revised by the Three People's Principles Youth Corps of T'ai-yüeh), in *Kuo-min-tang te t'e-wu cheng-ts'e* (The Kuomintang's special-services policy). Printed by Shan-tung-chün-ch'ü cheng-chih-pu (Political Bureau of the Shangtung military zone). N.p., 1944. (Bureau of Investigation #276/803.)

*Tang-cheng ko-hsin yün-tung* (The party-government renovation movement). Ed. Chung-kuo kuo-min-tang yün-nan-sheng chih-hsing wei-yüan-hui (Yunnan provincial executive committee of the Kuomintang). N.p., n.d. (Taiwan Branch, National Central Library #005.28/ 1490.)

"Tang-t'uan t'ung-i i-hou" (After unification of the party and the corps), *Ko-hsin yüeh-k'an*, 16 (Dec. 15, 1947).

*Tang-t'uan t'ung-i tsu-chih chung-yao wen-hsien* (Important documents pertaining to organizational unification of the party and the corps). N.p., n.d.

*Tang yü t'uan te kuan-hsi* (The relationship between the party and the corps). Ed. San-min-chu-i ch'ing-nien-t'uan chung-yang t'uan-pu (Central Headquarters, Three People's Principles Youth Corps). N.p., 1940.

*T'ang En-po hsien-sheng chi-nien chi* (T'ang En-po festschrift). N.p., 1964.

Teng Wen-i. *Mao-hsien fan-nan chi* (A record of braving dangers and withstanding difficulties). 2 vols. Taipei, 1973.

"Ti-hsia tou-cheng lu-hsien kang-ling" (Essentials of the policy of underground struggle), *Kung-fei yü min-meng chih chien* (Between the Communist bandits and the Democratic League). N.p., 1947. (Bureau of Investigation #263.31/817.)

*Ti-liu-chieh chung-yang chih-hsing wei-yüan-hui ti-erh-tz'u ch'üan-t'i hui-i t'i-an yüan-wen* (Resolutions presented to the 2d plenum of the 6th central executive committee). 2 vols. (Sun Yat-sen Library #036.1/ 6:24/1.)

Tien, Hung-mao. *Government and Politics in Kuomintang China, 1927– 1937.* Stanford, Calif., 1972.

*Tōa* (East Asia). Tokyo, 1928–45.

*Tōa nisshi* (East Asian chronological record). Tokyo. 1940.

Tong, Hollington K. *China and the World Press.* Nanking, Preface dated Feb. 1948.

Tong, Te-kong, and Li Tsung-jen. *The Memoirs of Li Tsung-jen.* Boulder, Col. 1979.

"T'ou-chi-chia te hsin lo-yüan" (Opportunist's new playground), *Shih-chi p'ing-lun*, 4, no. 14 (Oct. 2, 1948).

Ts'ai Chen-yün. *Chiang Ching-kuo tsai Shang-hai* (Chiang Ching-kuo in Shanghai). Nanking, 1948.

*Ts'ai-cheng nien-chien, san-pien* (Financial administration yearbook, part 3). Comp. Ts'ai-cheng-pu ts'ai-cheng nien-chien pien-tsuan ch'u. Nanking, 1948.

*Ts'ai-cheng p'ing-lun* (Financial review). Hong Kong. 1939–47.

Ts'ao Sheng-fen. "Ts'ung Hsi-k'ou tao Ch'eng-tu" (From Hsi-k'ou to Chengtu), *Chung-wai tsa-chih*, 2, no. 5 (Nov. 1967).

Tsou, Tang. *America's Failure in China, 1941–1950.* Chicago, 1963.

"Tsung-chieh che ch'i-shih-t'ien" (General assessment of these seventy days), *Ching-chi p'ing-lun*, 7, no. 19 (Nov. 11, 1948).

"Ts'ung li-fa-yüan te p'ai-hsi shuo-tao kuo-min-tang te kai-tsao" (Factions in the Legislative Yüan and Kuomintang reform), *Kuan-ch'a*, 4, no. 22 (July 31, 1948).

*T'uan-wu huo-tung shou-ts'e* (Manual for corps activities). N.p., 1944. (Bureau of Investigation #167.43/811.)

Tung Chia-mu. "Chiang Ching-kuo chi-mo fan-nao" (Chiang Ching-kuo: lonely and troubled), *Hsin-wen t'ien-ti*, 50 (Oct. 16, 1948).

*Tung-fang tsa-chih* ("Eastern Miscellany"). Shanghai, 1947–48; Taiwan, 1974.

Tung Shih-chin. "K'ang-chan i-lai Ssu-ch'uan chih nung-yeh" (Szechwan's agriculture since the beginning of the war against Japan), *Ssu-ch'uan ching-chi chi-k'an*, 1, no. 1 (Dec. 15, 1943).

———. "T'u-ti fen-p'ei wen-t'i" (The question of land distribution), *Ching-chi p'ing-lun*, 3, no. 10 (June 12, 1948).

*Tzu-yu chung* (Freedom bell). Hong Kong. 1972.

*United States Relations with China: With Special Reference to the Period 1944–1949.* Washington, D.C., 1949.

"Unnanshō no seiji keizaiteki chi'i" (The political and economic position of Yunnan), *Tōa*, 15, no. 7 (July 1, 1942).

Utley, Freda. *China at War.* New York, 1939.

Wang Cheng. "The Kuomintang: A Sociological Study of Demoralization." Ph.D. diss., Stanford University, 1953.

Wang Chung-wen. "Wei fu-shang chiang-shih hu-yü ping kung-hsien chi-tien chiu-shang kung-tso-shang te i-chien" (Appealing on behalf of officers and men, and presenting some suggestions regarding first-aid work), *Chan-shih i-cheng*, 16 (Aug. 1, 1938).

Wang Chung-wu. "Hsien-chieh-tuan chih wu-chia wen-t'i" (The problem of commodity prices at the present time), *Tung-fang tsa-chih*, 43, no. 16 (Oct. 1947).

———. "Wan-chiu tang-ch'ien ching-chi wei-chi chih tui-ts'e" (The means of resolving the current economic crisis), *Tung-fang tsa-chih*, 44, no. 8 (Aug. 1948).

Wang Fei. "Lun sui-ch'ing-ch'ü t'u-ti chai-ch'üan te fa-hsing chün-pei" (On preparations for the issuance of land loans in the pacification areas), *Ching-chi p'ing-lun*, 3, no. 10 (June 12, 1948).

Wang Tsu-hua. "Chien-ch'üan ping-i te chi-ko hsien-chüeh wen-t'i" (Several priority questions regarding military conscription), *I-cheng yüeh-k'an*, 1, no. 1 (Apr. 1945).

———. "Kai-shan i-cheng-fa te chi-ko ch'ieh-yao wen-t'i" (Several critical questions regarding improving the conscription law), *I-cheng yüeh-k'an*, 1, no. 2 (May 1945).

Wang Tzu-liang. *Che-hsi k'ang-chan chi-lüeh* (A record of the war of resistance in western Chekiang). Taipei, 1966.

Wang, Yin-yuen. "Changes in Farm Wages in Szechwan," *Economic Facts*, 43 (Apr. 1945).

Wang Yin-yüan. "Hsien-chia yü t'ien-ti hsien-tsu" (Price control and rent control on land), *Hsin-ching-chi*, 8, no. 9 (Mar. 1, 1943).

———. "Ssu-ch'uan chan-shih nung-kung wen-t'i" (The problem of farm wages in wartime Szechwan), *Ssu-ch'uan ching-chi chi-k'an*, 2, no. 3 (July 1, 1945).

———. "Ssu-ch'uan chan-shih wu-chia yü ko-chi jen-min chih kou-mai-li" (Commodity prices in Szechwan during the war and the people's standard of living), *Ssu-ch'uan ching-chi chi-k'an*, 1, no. 3 (June 15, 1944).

Wang Yu-chuan. "The Organization of a Typical Guerrilla Area in South Shantung," in Evans Fordyce Carlson, *The Chinese Army: Its Organization and Military Efficiency.*

*Wartime China as Seen by Westerners.* Chungking, preface dated 1942.

Wedemeyer, Albert C. *Wedemeyer Reports!* New York, 1958.

Wei Min. "Ko-hsin te chung-tien" (The crux of renovation), *Ko-hsin yüeh-k'an*, 2 (Sept. 1, 1946).

Weng Kuo-kuei. "San-shih-ssu nien-tu i-cheng chih chan-wang" (The outlook for conscription in 1945), *I-cheng yüeh-k'an*, 1, no. 1 (Apr. 1945).

White, Theodore H. *In Search of History: A Personal Adventure.* New York, 1978.

———, and Annalee Jacoby. *Thunder Out of China.* New York, 1946.

"Wo-men te hu-sheng" (Our cry), *Tang-cheng ko-hsin yün-tung*, pp. 1–9.

Woodbridge, George. *UNRRA: The History of the United Nations Relief and Rehabilitation Administration.* New York, 1950.

Wu Ch'i-yüan. *Yu chan-shih ching-chi tao p'ing-shih ching-chi* (From a wartime economy to a peacetime economy). Shanghai, 1946.

Wu Ching-ch'ao. *Chieh-hou tsai-li* (Calamity after pillage). Shanghai, 1947.

Wu Hsiang-hsiang. *Min-kuo pai-jen chuan* (One-hundred biographies of the republican period). Taipei, 1971.

———. *Ti-erh-tz'u Chung-Jih chan-cheng shih* (History of the second Sino-Japanese war). 2 vols. Taipei, 1973.

———. "Total Strategy Used by China and Some Major Engagements in the Sino-Japanese War of 1937–1945," in Paul K. T. Sih, ed., *Nationalist China During the Sino-Japanese War.*

————. "Wang Yün-wu yü chin-yüan-ch'üan te fa-hsing" (Wang Yün-wu and the issuance of the gold yüan), *Chuan-chi wen-hsüeh*, 213 (Feb. 1980).

Wu Kuo-chen. "Reminiscences of Dr. Wu Kuo-cheng (October 21, 1953–   ) for the years 1946–1953 as told to Prof. Nathaniel Peffer, Nov. 1960." Unpub. ms. in Special Collections Library, Butler Library, Columbia University.

Wu Shan. "Hu-nan te tang-t'uan hu-tou" (Conflict between the party and the corps in Hunan), *Shih yü wen*, 2, no. 7 (Oct. 24, 1947).

Wu Tan-ko. "Ssu-ch'uan-sheng ti-fang t'an-pai" (Szechwan's local t'an-pai), *Ssu-ch'uan ching-chi chi-k'an*, 1, no. 2 (Mar. 15, 1944).

Wu T'ieh-ch'eng. *Wu T'ieh-ch'eng hui-i-lu* (Memoirs of Wu T'ieh-ch'eng). Taipei, 1969.

Wu Ting-ch'ang. *Hua-ch'i hsien-pi hsü-chi* (Random notes in Hua-chi, supplement). Kweiyang, 1943.

Wu Yuan-li. *An Economic Survey of Communist China*. New York, 1956.

Yang Chia-lo, ed., *Ta-lu lun-hsien-ch'ien chih Chung-hua min-kuo* (The Chinese Republic before the loss of the mainland). 5 vols. Taipei, 1974.

Yang Li-k'uei. "Ch'ing-nien hsün-lien yü t'ung-chih" (The training and control of youth), *Ch'eng-ku ch'ing-nien*, 1 (Apr. 1941).

Yang Yu-chiung. "Wo-men yao-ch'iu kai-pien cheng-chih feng-ch'i" (We demand a change in governmental style), *Ko-hsin chou-k'an*, 1, no. 1 (July 27, 1946).

Yao Cheng-min. "P'ei-tu hsüeh-sheng yün-tung chih hui-ku" (Recollections of the student movement at Chungking), *Ssu-ch'uan wen-hsien yüeh-k'an*, 124 (Dec. 1, 1972).

Yao Sung-ling. "Ching-tao Chang Kung-ch'üan hsien-sheng" (In memory of Chang Kia-ngau), *Chuan-chi wen-hsüeh*, 211 (Dec. 1979).

Yeh Ch'ing. "Ko-hsin yün-tung ti-i-ko chi-pen yüan-tse" (The first principle of the renovation movement), *Ko-hsin chou-k'an*, 1, no. 4 (Aug. 17, 1946).

————. "Shih-hsing tang-nei min-chu" (Implement democracy within the party), *Ko-hsin chou-k'an*, 1, no. 7 (Sept. 7, 1946).

————. "Su-ch'ing kuan-liao-chu-i" (Eliminate bureaucratism), *Ko-hsin chou-k'an*, 1, no. 12.

————. "Ta-tao kuan-liao tzu-pen" (Down with bureaucratic capitalism), *Ko-hsin chou-k'an*, 1, no. 15 (Nov. 2, 1946). Reprinted in Ch'en Chung-min, *Kuan-liao tzu-pen p'i-p'an* (A critique of bureaucratic capitalism). Nanking, 1948.

————. "Tang-yüan tsung-ch'ing-ch'a yü ko-hsin yün-tung" (The general review of party members and the renovation movement), *Ko-hsin chou-k'an*, 1, no. 13.

Yeh Feng-ch'un. "Wo-men yao-ch'iu chan-k'ai ko-hsin yün-tung" (We demand the expanding of the renovation movement), *Ko-hsin chou-k'an*, 1, no. 2 (Aug. 3, 1946).

Yen Cheng-wu. "Tse-yang t'uan-chieh ko-ming t'ung-chih" (How to unite revolutionary comrades), *Ko-hsin chou-k'an*, 1, no. 4 (Aug. 17, 1946).

Yen Jen-keng. "Ching-chi hu? Cheng-chih hu?" (Economics? Politics?), *Ching-chi p'ing-lun*, 1, no. 12 (June 21, 1947).

Yen Lin. "Nung-ts'un p'o-ch'an yü tang-ch'ien ching-chi wei-chi" (Rural collapse and the current economic crisis), *Ching-chi chou-pao*, 3, no. 24 (Dec. 12, 1946).

Yen Ling. "Ching-chi 'tsung-tung-yüan' i-hou" (After the general mobilization of the economy), *Ching-chi chou-pao*, 5, no. 3 (July 17, 1947).

Young, Arthur N. *China and the Helping Hand, 1937–1945*. Cambridge, Mass., 1963.

———. *China's Wartime Finance and Inflation, 1937–1945*. Cambridge, Mass., 1965.

Yü Ch'ang-ho. "Wo-kuo chan-shih lao-tung cheng-ts'e" (China's wartime labor policy), *Hsin-Chung-hua, fu-k'an*, 2, no. 9 (Sept. 1944).

Yün An. *Chiang-nan mi-shih* (Secret history of southern Kiangsu). Hong Kong, 1952.

# Character List

Chan P'ei-lin 詹沛霖

Chang, Carsun (Chang Chün-mai) 張君勱

Chang, Ch'i-yün 張其昀

Chang Chih-chung 張治中

Chang Ch'ün 張群

Chang Fa-k'uei 張發奎

Chang Kia-ngau 張嘉璈

Chang Li-sheng 張厲生

Chang Po-chün 章伯鈞

Chang Tao-fan 張道藩

chao-chi-jen 召集人

Ch'en I 陳儀

Ch'en Ming-jen 陳明仁

Ch'en Pu-lei 陳布雷

cheng 徵

cheng-chieh 徵借

cheng-feng 整風

cheng-kou 徵購

Ch'eng T'ien-fang 程天放

chi-chi chih chih-ts'ai 積極之制裁

chi-ku 積谷

ch'i-hsi 奇襲

Chiang Ting-wen 蔣鼎文

Chiang-yin 江陰

ch'iang-kung 強攻

Chiao-ch'ang-k'ou 較場口

chieh-ping-tui 接兵隊

chien 件

chih-hui 指揮

chih-tao 指導

chin-yüan ch'üan 金圓券

ch'ing-chiao ch'ü 清劋區

Ch'ing-pai-she 青白社

Ch'iu Ch'ing-ch'üan 邱清泉

Chu Chia-hua 朱家驊

Ch'üan Hsien 金縣

chün-liang 軍糧

Chün-shih-wei-yüan-hui-chang
  Tien-Ch'ien hsing-ying
軍事委員會長滇黔行營

chung-ssu-le 臕死了

chung-tseng chieh-chi
中層階級

chung-yang chün 中央軍

fa-pi 法幣

fang-ch'ü 防區

Fei Hsiao-t'ung 費孝通

Fu-hsing-she 復興社

Fu Ssu-nien 傅斯年

fu-tsa 複雜

Hao-hsüeh 郝穴

Hirota Kōki 廣田弘毅

Ho Chung-han 賀衷寒

Ho Lien 何廉

hsiang 鄉

hsiang-hu te tso-yung
相互的作用
Hsiao Cheng 蕭錚

hsiao-chi fang-fan 消極防範    Huang Chi-lu 黃季陸

Hsiao Chi-shan 蕭吉珊    Huang I-ts'ung 黃冰聰

Hsiao Tsan-yü 蕭贊育    Huang Po-t'ao 黃百韜

hsien-chi kung-liang 縣級公糧    Huang Yü-jen 黃宇人

Hsin-cheng chü-lo-pu (Club) 新政俱樂部    Hung-ch'iang-hui 紅槍會

Hsiung Shih-hui 熊式輝    i-tang t'ung-cheng 以黨統政

hsiung-wan chiao-hua 兇頑狡猾    Ichigo 一号

Hsü En-tseng 徐恩曾    Jen Cho-hsüan 任卓宣

Hsü K'an 徐堪    Jung Hung-yüan 榮鴻元

hsü-li 胥吏    kan-shih-hui 幹事會

Hsüeh Yüeh 薛岳    K'an-luan chien-kuo ta-tui 戡亂建國大隊

Hu Hao 胡好    K'ang Tse 康澤

Hu Kuei 胡軌    Kao Shu-hsün 高樹勳

Hu Wen-hu 胡文虎    Ko-hsin 革新

huai-t'ou 壞頭    Ko-jen te ling-tao chih-tu 個人的領導制度

Kogo  ゴ号

Konoe Fumimaro  近衛文麿

Ku Cheng-kang  谷正綱

Ku Cheng-ting  谷正鼎

Kuan Lin-cheng  關麟徵

Kuang-chi  廣濟

K'ung Ling-k'an  孔令侃

Kuo-fang cheng-fu  國防政府

Kuo Ju-kuei  郭汝瑰

Kuo-min-tang chung-shih t'ung-chih-hui  國民黨忠實同志會

Kuo Mo-jo  郭沫若

la-ping  拉兵

Lai Lien  賴璉

lao-pai-hsing  老百姓

lei-chin cheng-chieh  累進徵借

Li Chi-shen  李濟琛

Li Han-hun  李漢魂

Li Kung-p'u  李公樸

Li-ling hsien  醴陵縣

Li P'in-hsien  李品仙

Li Shih-tseng  李石曾

Li Tsung-huang  李宗黃

Liang Han-ts'ao  梁寒操

Lin K'o-sheng  林可勝

Liu Chien-ch'ün  劉健群

Liu Fei  劉斐

Liu Hsiang  劉湘

liu-mang  流氓

Liu Wen-hui  劉文輝

Lo Lung-chi  羅隆基

Lu Han 盧漢

Lu-kou-ch'iao 盧溝橋

Lu Tso-fu 盧作孚

Lung-men 龍門

Lung Yün 龍雲

Ma Ch'ao-chün 馬超俊

Min-chu ko-ming t'ung-chih hui 民主革命同志會

mou 畝

nan-man-tzu 南蠻子

pa-pao-fan 八寶飯

P'an Kuang-tan 潘光旦

P'an Kung-chan 潘公展

P'an Ta-kuei 潘大逵

P'an Wen-hua 潘文華

pao-chia 保甲

pao erh pu-pan 包而不辦

p'i-pei chih yü 疲憊之餘

p'ing-fan 平凡

pu-chi pu-li 不即不離

Sa K'ung-liao 薩空了

san-p'ing yüan-tzu 三平原則

shan-liang 善良

Shao Li-tzu 邵力子

Shen Chün-ju 沈鈞儒

Shen Hung-lieh 沈鴻烈

Shen Yün-lung 沈雲龍

sheng 升

sheng-kuan fa-ts'ai 升官發財

shih 市

Shih 石

shih-li 實力

shih-sheng 市升

shih-tan 市石

shih-tou 市斗

shou 收

Shou-tu tso-t'an-hui
首都座談會

Ssu-shui 泗水

sui 歲

Sui-Tsao 隨〔縣〕棗〔陽〕

Sun Li-jen 孫立人

Sun Wei-ju 孫蔚如

Sung Hsi-lien 宋希濂

ta-hu 大戶

ta hu-t'u chang 打糊塗仗

ta-lao-hu 大老虎

ta-p'ao 大砲

ta-ping 大餅

Ta-Shang-hai ch'ing-nien
  fu-wu tsung-tui
大上海青年服務總隊

Ta-tui 大隊

Tai Jung-kuang 戴戎光

Tai Li 戴笠

Tan¹ 擡

Tan² 担

tan 石

t'an-p'ai 攤派

T'an P'ing-shan 譚平山

t'an-wu wu-neng 貪污無能

tang-fang 黨方

T'ang Chi-yao 唐繼堯

T'ang En-po 湯恩伯

T'ao Hsi-sheng 陶希聖

Teng Hsi-hou 鄧錫侯

Teng Wen-i 鄧文儀

t'iao-ho 調和

tien-fan-ling 典範令

Tien-pi 滇幣

to-lo le 墮落了

tou 斗

Ts'ai-cheng ching-chi chin-chi ch'u-fen ming-ling 財政經濟緊急處分命令

Tseng Tse-sheng 曾澤生

Tso Shun-sheng 左舜生

tsui-chin chiang-lai 最近將來

tsung ch'ing-ch'a 總清查

Tu Wei-ping 杜維屏

Tu Yü-ming 杜聿明

Tu Yüeh-sheng 杜月笙

t'u-hao lieh-shen 土豪烈紳

t'uan-fang 團方

t'ui-t'ang ho fu-pai 頹唐和腐敗

Tung Shih-chin 董時進

Wang Ch'un-che 王春哲

Wang Ping-chün 王秉鈞

Wang Sheng 王昇

Wang Shih-chieh 王世杰

Wang Tsuan-hsü 王鑽緒

Wang Yao-wu 王耀武

Wang Yün-wu 王雲五

wei-i te tsu-chih 唯一的組織

Wong Wen-hao 翁文灝

wu-k'ung pu-ju 無孔不入

Wu Kuo-chen    吳國楨

Wu Li-ch'ing    吳禮卿

wu-neng    無能

Wu T'ieh-ch'eng    吳鐵城

Wu Ting-ch'ang    吳鼎昌

ya-chin    押金

Yang Hu-ch'eng    楊虎城

Yang Yu-chiung    楊幼炯

Yeh Ch'ing    葉青

yen-hsien chan-tien    延續佔點

yu-tzu    游資

Yü Ching-t'ang    余井塘

Yü Han-mou    余漢謀

Yü Hsia-ch'ing    虞洽卿

Yü-hsien    禹縣

Yü Hung-chün    俞鴻鈞

yüan    圓

# Index